Chechnya: From Past to Future

Chechnya:
From Past to Future

Edited by
RICHARD SAKWA

Anthem Press

Anthem Press
An imprint of Wimbledon Publishing Company
75-76 Blackfriars Road, London SE1 8HA
or
PO Box 9779, London SW19 7ZG
www.anthempress.com

This edition first published by Anthem Press 2005

British Library Cataloguing in Publication Data
A catalogue record for this book is available from the British Library.

Library of Congress Cataloging in Publication Data
A catalog record for this book has been requested.

1 3 5 7 9 10 8 6 4 2

ISBN 1 84331 164 X (Hbk)
ISBN 1 84331 165 8 (Pbk)

Cover Photograph: *Getty Images*

Typeset by Footprint Labs Ltd, London
www.footprintlabs.com

Printed in India

To
Dzhabrail Gakaev and His People

Contents

Acknowledgements

The debts incurred in writing this book are numerous. I would like in particular to thank all the authors, many of whom endured much exhortation and cajolement to complete and revise their chapters on time. I would like to thank in particular the translators, Natalia Chernysheva of Kings College, London, who translated the chapter by Valentin Mikhailov, David Fairhurst of the University of Bradford, who translated the chapters by Emil Pain and Valeri Tishkov, and Roza Sakwa, who translated the chapter by Alexander Cherkasov and Dmitry Grushkin, and the chapter by Dzhabrail Gakaev. I am most grateful for the help offered by Dr Mara Ustinova of the Fund for Humanitarian Assistance to the Chechen Republic at the Institute of Ethnography and Anthropology of the Russian Academy of Sciences. The staff of Memorial in Moscow have been unfailingly helpful, and I am delighted that we have a chapter by two of their leading activists. It is my great pleasure to thank the Nuffield Foundation (Grant No. SGS/00730/G) for their assistance in the preparation of this book. Last and far from least, conversations with professor Gakaev in Moscow, unfailingly accompanied by warm hospitality, have thrown enormous light on the Chechen conflict for me; and his courage and humanity have acted as a beacon of hope in these difficult times. It is for this reason that this book is dedicated to him and to all those like him.

Notes on the Contributors

Pavel Baev
Dr. Pavel K. Baev is a Senior Researcher at the International Peace Research Institute, Oslo (PRIO). He also leads a working group on international dimensions of civil wars at the Centre for the Study of Civil War at PRIO. After graduating from Moscow State University (MA in Political Geography, 1979) he worked in a research institute in the USSR Defence Ministry and the Russian Academy of Science's Institute of Europe, Moscow. In 1995–2001 he was the editor of PRIO's quarterly *Security Dialogue*. His research interests include the transformation of the Russian military, Russian-European relations, and the post-Soviet conflicts in the Caucasus and the greater Caspian area.

Mike Bowker
Dr Mike Bowker is a Lecturer in Politics at the University of East Anglia, Norwich. He has written extensively on Russian foreign policy and the Cold War. His books include *Superpower Detente: A Reaapraisal* with Phil Williams (Sage, 1988); *Russian Foreign Policy and the End of the Cold War* (Ashgate, 1997), and the co-edited volumes: *From Cold War to Collapse: Theory and World Politics in the 1980s* with Robin Brown (Cambridge, 1993), and *Russia After the Cold War* with Cameron Ross (Longman, 2000).

Alexander Cherkasov
Alexander Cherkasov is a physical engineer, working from 1983 at the Institute of Atomic Energy and the Institute of Molecular Genetics. Since the late 1980s he has participated in the work of the Human Rights Centre 'Memorial' in Moscow, and since 1990 has been to many of the 'hot spots' in the former Soviet Union including Abkhazia, Nagorno-Karabakh and Transdniestria. For the last decade he has focused primarily on the North Caucasus, and in particular Chechnya. He has published numerous works on the topic, including a contribution to Memorial's book *Russia-Chechnya: Chain of Mistakes and Crimes* (1998), and frequently contributes to newspapers and the electronic media. He is a member of the Expert Council for the Human Rights Ombudsman.

Thomas de Waal

Thomas de Waal is a writer and journalist specializing in Russia and the Caucasus. He studied Russian and Modern Greek at Balliol College, Oxford, before joining the BBC World Service. From 1993 to 1997 he worked in Moscow for the *Moscow Times*, *The Times* and the *Economist*. *Chechnya: A Small Victorious War* (1997), co-authored with Carlotta Gall, won a James Cameron Award for Outstanding Reporting. In 2003 he published *Black Garden: Armenia and Azerbaijan Through Peace and War*, the first full-length study in English of the Nagorny Karabakh conflict. He is currently Caucasus Editor with the Institute for War and Peace Reporting in London.

Dzhabrail Gakaev

Dzhabrail Jokolaevich Gakaev is a professor and doctor of historical studies, and has been decorated as a distinguished scholar of the Russian Federation. A historian by training, he wrote his doctorate on the Russian army in three revolutions. He was the president of the Chechen-Ingush Social Science Association, Vice President of the Chechen-Ingush Academy of Sciences and chair of the History Faculty at the Chechen-Ingush State University in Grozny until 1994, when he moved to Moscow. He is currently a senior academic researcher at the Institute of Ethnography and Anthropology of the Russian Academy of Sciences and head of the Chechen Society of Cultural Organisations in Russia. He is the author of numerous works, including *Ocherki politicheskoi istorii Chechni (XX vek)* (Moscow, Chechen Cultural Centre, 1997).

Dmitry Grushkin

Dmitry Grushkin is a lecturer in the History Department of Moscow State University, and since 1996 has been a fellow of the 'Memorial' Human Rights Centre in Moscow. He has written numerous reports and articles on ethnic aspects of the human rights in Russia, and in particular focused on legal aspects of Russian laws on ethnic minority rights. He has conducted fieldwork in many of Russia's ethno-federal republics, and has co-written monographs on Bashkortostan, on problems of Russian federalism, and on the human aspect of the Chechen wars.

James Hughes

Dr James Hughes is a Reader in Comparative Politics at the London School of Economics. He has written extensively on the problems of post-Soviet Russian federalism, and nationalism and ethnic conflict. He co-edited, with Gwendolyn Sasse, *Ethnicity and Territory in the Former Soviet Union: Regions in Conflict* (London, Frank Cass, 2002). He is currently writing a book on the conflict in Chechnya.

Lord Frank Judd

From 1999 to 2003 Lord Judd was Rapporteur of the Political Affairs Committee of the Council of Europe on the conflict in the Chechen Republic.

Valentin Mikhailov

Valentin Mikhailov is currently a postgraduate student at the Moscow State Civil Service University, preparing a doctoral dissertation on a historical review of transformations in Russian republics. During 1994–96 he was a member of State Duma of the Russian Federation, a member of the Committee for Federal Affairs and Regional Policy, and during 1990–94 he was a member of Supreme Soviet of the Republic of Tatarstan, a member of the Legislative Committee. His recent publications include *Republic of Tatarstan: Democracy or Sovereignty?* (Moscow, 2004), pp. 466; 'Democratizatization in Russia and Regional Authoritarianism: Tatarstan and Bashkortostan', in Gerald Hinteregger and Hans-Georg Heinrich (eds), *Russia: Continuity and Change* (Vienna and New York, Springer, 2004), pp. 511-26; 'Regional Elections and Democratization in Russia', in Cameron Ross (ed.), *Russian Politics under Putin* (Manchester University Press, 2004); 'Tatarstan: Eight Years of Sovereignty – An Evaluation' (in German), *Osteuropa*, No. 4, 1999, pp. 366-86. He is co-editor (with Valentin Bazhanov and Midkhat Farukshin), *Osobaya zona: vybory v Tatarstane* (Ul'yanovsk, Kompa, 2000), pp. 318.; (with Midkhat Farukshin), *Chto khotel by znat' izbiratel' Tatarstana o vyborakh* (Kazan, Grandan – KOMPA-IRIS, 2002), pp. 162. His current research interests include studies of the state of democracy in different regions of Russia.

Emil Pain

Dr Emil Pain is Director of the Centre for the Study of Xenophobia and Extremism of the Institute of Sociology, Russian Academy of Sciences, and at the same time Director of the Centre for Ethno-Political and Regional Studies. He is a consultant for the Russian State Duma. He was Galina Starovoitova Fellow on Human Rights and Conflict Resolution at the Kennan Institute in 2000–01, an adviser to the Russian president in 1996–99, and Deputy Director of the Analytical Department of the presidential administration in 1993–96. He has published 13 books and over 200 articles, focusing on nationality politics in the USSR and Russia. His latest book is *The Ethno-Political Pendulum: The Dynamics and Mechanisms of Ethno-Political Processes in Post-Soviet Russia* (Moscow, Institute of Sociology, 2004).

John Russell

Dr John Russell is Senior Lecturer in both Peace Studies and Russian Studies at the University of Bradford. He is author of a number of articles on the Russo-Chechen conflict and the war on terrorism and has led seminars on the topic for the Foreign & Commonwealth Office, the Royal Institute of International Affairs and (in Russia) the International Institute for Strategic Studies. In 2003, he appeared as an expert witness on behalf of the defence at the extradition trial in London of Akhmed Zakaev. He is currently planning a monograph on this trial as well as another on the Russo-Chechen wars.

Richard Sakwa

Richard Sakwa is Professor of Russian and European Politics at the University of Kent. He has published widely on Soviet, Russian and post-communist affairs. Recent books include *Soviet Politics in Perspective* (Routledge, 1998), *Postcommunism* (Open University Press, 1999), *The Rise and Fall of the Soviet Union, 1917–1991* (Routledge, 1999), co-edited (with Bruno Coppieters of the Vrije Universiteit Brussel) *Contextualising Secession: Normative Aspects of Secession Struggles* (Oxford University Press, 2003), and *Putin: Russia's Choice* (Routledge, 2004) His current research interests focus on problems of democratic development and the state in Russia, the nature of post-communism, and the global challenges facing the former communist countries.

Peter Shearman

Peter Shearman is Associate Professor of International Relations and Security Studies, University of Melbourne. His books include, *The Soviet Union and Cuba* (London, Routledge & Kegan Paul, 1987); edited with Phil Williams, *The Superpowers, Central America and the Middle East* (London, Brasseys Defence Publishers, 1988); edited, *Russian Foreign Policy Since 1990* (Boulder, CO, Westview, 1995); edited with Matthew Sussex, *European Security after 9/11* (Aldershot, Ashgate, 2004). He has published in leading journals, including, *Review of International Studies*, *International Affairs*, *Millennium*, *Journal of Communist* Studies, *Third World Quarterly*, *APS*: *Proceedings of the (US) Academy of Political Science*. He is currently editing (with Derek McDougall) a book on *New and Old Security Agenda: Australian Perspectives*; and working on a book examining the war in Chechnya from the perspectives of modern and postmodern wars. He is also conducting research on the Anglo alliance (US, UK, Australia) and the war in Iraq.

Matthew Sussex

Matthew Sussex is Lecturer in Government at the University of Tasmania. He received his doctorate on Russian foreign policy at the University of Melbourne in 2001. Matthew's research interests include Russian and European security issues, great power foreign policies, and international relations theory. He is co-editor (with Peter Shearman) of *European Security After 9/11* (Cheltenahm, Ashgate, 2004).

V. A. Tishkov

Valery Tishkov is Professor of History and Anthropology and Director of the Institute of Ethnography and Anthropology of the Russian Academy of Sciences. He has published many books in Russian and is also the author of *Ethnicity, Nationalism, and Conflict in and after the Soviet Union: The Mind Aflame* (London, Sage, 1997) and *Chechnya: Life in a War-Torn Society* (University of California Press, 2004). He served as a Minister for Nationalities in Yeltsin's government in 1992.

Robert Bruce Ware

Robert Ware completed his doctorate at Oxford University in 1995 and now serves as an associate professor at Southern Illinois University Edwardsville. He is the author of *Hegel: The Logic of Self-consciousness and the Legacy of Subjective Freedom* (Edinburgh University Press, 1999). Since 1995 he has conducted extensive field research in the North Caucasus and has published extensively on the politics, ethnography, and religion of the region in scholarly journals and in the popular media. He is working on a collection of oral histories titled *The Fight of Our Lives: Reflections of the Generation that Built the Soviet Union*.

MAP 1: CHECHNYA

MAP 2: THE CAUCASUS REGION

1

Introduction: Why Chechnya?

Richard Sakwa

Chechnya is just one of Russia's 21 ethnically defined republics, yet it is
here that one of the most terrible conflicts in modern times has raged in various ways since 1991. There has been considerable debate over what provokes one area to seek secession, while another in apparently similar
circumstances remains within the existing constitutional order. Why has it
been Chechnya, and not one of the other republics or regions of Russia, that
has taken this tragic path? Here, I will place the conflict in its broader historical and theoretical context; the details of the background to the independence struggle will be examined in more detail in other chapters.

Comparative Debates

Michael Hechter has observed that it is typically the poorest regions that are
most disposed to secede.[1] Certainly, there is a socio-economic dynamic at
work in the case of Chechnya, which was close to the bottom in most indicators of modernization in comparison with other regions of the Union of
Soviet Socialist Republics (USSR) and Russia. Levels of educational and general socio-economic attainment were poor, while a high birth rate fuelled
exceptionally high levels of unemployment. Reserves of oil had declined and
by the early 1980s constituted no more than three per cent of Russian oil production.[2] In most aspects of socio-economic development, Chechnya was in
last place in Russia, with over half the population under 30 years of age and
with unemployment among ethnic Chechens reaching 30 per cent, forcing
some 40 per cent of Chechens of working age to become migrant workers

---

[1] Michael Hechter, *Internal Colonialism: The Celtic Fringe in British National Development,
1536–1966* (Berkeley, University of California Press, 1975); *Acta Sociologica*, Vol. 35, 1992,
pp. 267–83.
[2] Anatol Lieven, *Chechnya: Tombstone of Russian Power* (New Haven, CT, Yale University
Press, 1998), p. 57.

(*otkhodniki*), with at least 25,000 men leaving each spring to work in Russia to work on building sites as itinerant workers (*shabashniki*).

The argument that relative poverty provokes secessionist struggles has however been challenged by several authors.[3] In a comparative study of some 45 cases in the former USSR, Henry E Hale examined the question of why some ethnic regions sought to secede while others tried to save the multinational state. He arrived at a different conclusion to Hechter, finding that separatism was strongest in the wealthiest regions, those containing the least assimilated ethnic groups and those already enjoying the highest levels of autonomy.[4] The cases of the Basque country, Flanders, 'Padania' in Northern Italy, Catalonia and Scotland seem to confirm his findings. Other factors examined include the history of previous persecution or memories of historical independence, but ultimately the study argued that 'it is the richest, rather than the poorest, ethnic regions that are the most eager to secede since they have the most to lose should they be exploited by other groups that control the state'.[5] In that context, concessions and attempts to buy off regional elites are unlikely to succeed, and would in all probability only whet their appetites for greater freedom. The case of Dagestan certainly confirms Hale's argument that the poorest regions, rather than the richest, are the most dependent on subsidies and infrastructural resources, thus becoming the greatest supporters of the supranational state.[6]

From the perspective of a regional bargaining model, Daniel Treisman has argued that regions will use the institutional resources at their disposal to bargain with the centre to achieve yet greater advantages, with separatist claims themselves one of the most effective tools in the armoury of regional elites in the bargaining process.[7] Thus ethnic and historical factors are considered secondary, and instead bargaining processes come to the fore. This is not the case in Chechnya, where ethnicity and a burning sense of historical grievance were at the very core of the insurgency against Russian power.

Another factor much discussed in the literature is whether blocked upward social mobility of ethnic groups promotes or inhibits separatist movements. While it would appear logical that blocked career opportunities would provoke alienation, David Laitin has argued that it is in fact the most

---

[3] Such as Donald Horowitz, *Ethnic Groups in Conflict* (Berkeley, University of California Press, 1985).

[4] Henry E Hale, 'The Parade of Sovereignties: Testing Theories of Secession in the Soviet Setting', *British Journal of Political Science*, Vol. 30, 2000, pp. 31–56.

[5] Hale, 'The Parade of Sovereignties', p. 32.

[6] See Robert Bruce Ware and Enver Kisriev, 'Political Stability in Dagestan: Ethnic Stability and Religious Polarization', *Problems of Post-Communism*, Vol. 47, No. 2, March/April 2000, pp. 23–33.

[7] Daniel S Treisman, 'Russia's "Ethnic Revival": The Separatist Activism of Regional Leaders in a Postcommunist Order', *World Politics*, Vol. 41, 1997, pp. 212–49. See also his *After the Deluge: Regional Crises and Political Consolidation in Russia* (Ann Arbor, MI, The University of Michigan Press, 1999).

upwardly mobile (what he calls 'most favoured lords') who adopt the most radical separatist stances when a regime begins to liberalize in an attempt to defend their positions against more youthful (and usually more radical) insurgents from below.[8] In the Chechen case, the local Communist leadership was largely 'Chechenized' only in the very last years of Soviet power. This was too late to develop a substantial ethnic Chechen communist elite in the republic, and by the time this elite came to power the Soviet leadership was already disintegrating. It was not clear to whom they were to be loyal: to the official reforming president of the USSR, Mikhail Gorbachev, who was willing to devolve considerable responsibility to the fifteen Union Republics that made up the USSR, but who from late 1990 sought to mobilize the leaders of some of the autonomous republics *within* Russia in his struggle against the nascent sovereign Russian state; the so-called hardliners who sought to defend much of the old Communist system and the territorial integrity of the country, who launched a coup against Gorbachev between 18 and 21 August 1991; or the Russian leadership headed by Boris Yeltsin, who had been elected Russia's first president on 12 June 1991.

The attempts of Doku Zavgaev, the head of the Chechen Communist Party organization from June 1989, to place himself at the head of the national movement misfired spectacularly as outsider groups ousted the newly empowered Chechen communist elite. Zavgaev had sought to deflect the challenge by co-opting the movements that in the summer of 1990 came together to form an Acting Committee of the All-National Congress of the Chechen People (the Chechen National Congress), an informal body made up of clan elders and excluding much of the urban population. This organization, with Yeltsin's support, had been intended to put pressure on the Soviet leadership and on Gorbachev personally. The Chechen National Congress, however, soon moved into opposition to Zavgaev. In March 1991 Major-General Dzhokhar Dudaev (1944–96) was elected leader of the Congress, and the Chechen revolution soon far outran attempts to liberalize and 'nationalize' the regime. Dudaev had been the first Chechen to attain the rank of general in the Soviet air force, having served in Afghanistan and then appointed to the command of a flight of strategic bombers stationed in Tartu in the late 1980s. One of Dudaev's main criticisms of Zavgaev was the latter's irresolution during the August coup at a time when, paradoxically in the light of later events, Dudaev supported Yeltsin and the official Soviet authorities against those who had launched the ill-fated coup. Following the coup Dudaev condemned the Chechen communist elite for having supported the hardliners in Moscow, and they were soon swept away. This was the only republic in Russia where the fall of communism was accompanied by such a radical rupture in elite continuity.

[8] David D. Laitin, 'The National Uprisings in the Soviet Union', *World Politics*, Vol. 44, 1991, pp. 139–77, p. 157.

In one of the most rigorous studies of secessionism in the Soviet context, Emizet and Hesli examined the point at which a region declared itself sovereign in the USSR, and used this as a measure of separatism: the study assumed that the earlier the sovereignty declaration, the stronger the separatism.[9] This does not fit the Chechen case either, whose sovereignty and independence declarations were effectively one and the same, provoked by the events surrounding the failed coup in Moscow in August 1991 and Zavgaev's subsequent removal from power by the armed insurgency led by Dudaev.

In Chechnya it was yet another variable that was primary, and called by Hale 'historical symbolical resources'. Chechnya was indeed rich in these 'resources', factors that turned out to be a liability in any attempt to create an ordered post-communist system. These resources were not 'system integrative', as pertains when there is a shared memory of former statehood (for example, the cases of the Baltic republics and, more tenuously, Ukraine), but instead Chechnya focused overwhelmingly on shared memories of armed resistance, oppression and deportation. Hale's study found no evidence to support the theory that dramatic histories of national independence or ethnic victimization provoked separatism,[10] a somewhat surprising finding in the light of the Chechen case. It appears that not only is Chechnya an uncomfortable participant in the Russian community, it is also an anomalous case when it comes to comparative political science.

History and State Building

There are two key elements that help explain the Chechen syndrome of militant secessionism: a distinctive appropriation of historical memory and constricted state building. Neither of these was absolutely determining, although undoubtedly important, and the various leaderships and their strategies retained scope for autonomous action in response to changing circumstances.

Monochronic Historicism

The core of Chechen identity is more historical than ethnic in nature.[11] Chechnya's claim to independence rests on a distinctive 'historicist' reading of its relationship with imperial Russia, the Soviet Union and post-communist

---

[9] Kisangani N Emizet and Vicki L Hesli, 'The Disposition to Secede: An Analysis of the Soviet Case', *Comparative Political Studies*, Vol. 27, 1995, pp. 492–536.

[10] Hale, 'The Parade of Sovereignties', pp. 52–3.

[11] Of course, this is not confined to the Chechens alone. Fred Halliday has identified a 'carnival of mendacity' (p. 167) in the generation of nationalist movements: 'History, and legal claims, are there to be defined by the goals of the community' (p. 166), 'The Perils of Community: Reason and Unreason in Nationalist Ideology', *Nations and Nationalism*, Vol. 6, No. 2, 2000, pp. 153–71.

Russia.[12] This relationship is interpreted in black-and-white, or 'monochronic', terms of exploitation and subjugation of the Chechen nation, accompanied by heroic narratives of resistance. This is what Ralph Premdas in his study of Asian secessionism calls 'primordial' factors, compared to 'secondary' factors like exploitation and discrimination.[13] We call this approach to the past 'monochronic' for two reasons: it leaves out of account subtle shadings and instead sees everything in stark black-and-white terms; and it has a single narrative line that remains unbroken and insulated from other histories and the fate of other peoples. A good example of such an approach is the book *Chechnya through the Eyes of a Chechen* by the Western-educated Umalat Umalatov, whose moving account of his family's tribulations – including exile to Turkey at the end of the great Caucasian war in the 1860s – and the course of Chechen history becomes ever more monochronic.[14] By the time we get to 1991, there appears to be no choice: history demands Chechen independence, even though international law and much of the rest of modern world history proclaims the principle of the territorial integrity of states. Despite declarations in favour of the self-determination of peoples in the 1948 Universal Declaration of Human Rights and later documents, successful secession is the exception rather than the rule. The exception is times of state breakdown, as in the disintegration of the USSR and Yugolsavia in the early 1990s, but even in these two cases independence was granted only to those units that already enjoyed the equivalent of the constitutional right to secede in the old system. A sub-national region cannot simply proclaim independence, and only in exceptional circumstances are new states formed.[15] We label the monochronic view 'historicist' because of its teleological approach to the historical process: not only is the meaning and purpose of history knowable, but a clear, ineluctable and single plan of action inevitably emerges – in our case Chechen independence. Anyone who challenges this view is clearly mistaken, or worse, a traitor. All means thus become legitimate in the pursuit of this historically ordained goal. The room for compromise and negotiation is limited.

---

[12] There are plenty of good discussions of this relationship. In addition to the literature cited elsewhere in this volume, the following book, drawing on Russian literature, memoirs, travel reports and official documents, is particularly useful: A. Blinskii (ed.), *Rossiya i Chechnya: 200-letnaya voina* (St Petersburg, Satis, 2000). Another useful book in English is Ben Fowkes (ed.), *Russia and Chechnia: The Permanent Crisis* (Basingstoke, Macmillan, 1998).

[13] Ralph Premdas, 'Secessionist Movements in Comparative Perspective', in Ralph Premdas et al. (eds), *Secessionist Movements in Comparative Perspective* (London, Pinter Press, 1990), pp. 12–31.

[14] Umalat Umalatov, *Chechnya glazami chechentsa* (Moscow, Edinstvo, 2001).

[15] For a discussion of these conditions, see Allen Buchanan, *Secession: The Morality of Political Divorce From Fort Sumter to Lithuania and Quebec* (Boulder, CO, Westview Press, 1991); and Margaret Moore (ed.), *National Self-Determination and Secession* (Oxford, Oxford University Press, 1998).

There is plenty of evidence to substantiate a monochronic historicist account of Chechnya's past, but it leaves out any more complex diachronic contextualization of the relationship between 'empire' and constituent peoples. The Russian empire was a complex organization that adopted a variety of strategies towards the elements that constituted it.[16] It was far from a single story of endless repression, and following the end of Imam Shamil's struggle in the 1860s Chechnya entered a period of relative development and prosperity. Similarly, although the Soviet experience brought untold suffering to the Chechen people, above all the deportation of the whole nation in February 1944, the period between 1957 (the reconstitution of the Chechen republic, with Ingushetia) and 1991 is seen by many as a relatively benign period of peace when the republic developed culturally and economically – although, as we have noted above, it remained relatively backward and the Chechens were not trusted to rule themselves until the very final period.

Following the fall of communism in 1991 a distinctive reading of Chechen history was appropriated by insurgent groups to seize and maintain power. Nevertheless, as Moshe Gammer notes, the Chechen argument with Moscow was still conducted to a large extent within the Soviet paradigm: 'Thus, while striving to de-sovietize, the new Chechen historical narrative is still strongly linked to Soviet narratives, ways of arguing and moulds of thinking'.[17] While the Chechen struggle for independence raises global normative issues, above all the conditions and circumstances in which a state can secede, the Chechen leadership appeared parochial in its single-minded focus on its relationship with Russia while being unable to consider that struggle in its international setting. There were alternative voices, but these were soon marginalized. A monochronic historicist account of a nation's past can be considered, like many nationality questions, as pre-political: there can be no political process, since there is nothing to discuss – independence is non-negotiable. Perhaps the most important political consequence is the displacement of sovereignty from the actual, existing people living in the present to a mythical historicized people represented by the political struggle, whose views become ascriptive and authoritative rather than representative and contentious. This was the background to Chechnya's distinctive brand of monochronic ideological politics.

Chechnya's monochronic historicism is not simply an abstract characteristic of the political culture of a people, but is rooted in specific social conditions. In particular, much is made of the Chechen system of values in

---

[16] See, for example, Geoffrey Hosking, *Russia: People and Empire 1552–1917* (London, Harper Collins, 1997).

[17] Moshe Gammer, 'Nationalism and History: Rewriting the Chechen National Past', in Bruno Coppieters and Michel Huysseune (eds), *Secession, History and the Social Sciences* (Brussels, VUB University Press, 2002), pp. 117–40, at p. 118.

which freedom and equality are prominent.[18] Paradoxically, the repression of the early Soviet years that culminated in the 1944 deportation destroyed 'modernized' groups like the intelligentsia and Party bureaucracy, and thus served to accentuate the traditional social order and values. Even after the reconstitution of the Chechen-Ingush republic in 1957, mosque-building was not permitted, and thus no loyal Islamic hierarchy came into being to undermine the independent Sufi brotherhoods. The Communist Party bureaucracy remained overwhelmingly Russian, as did the leader of the republic until 1989. The gulf between the communist *nomenklatura* (the office holding class) and the people in Chechnya was reinforced by ethnic divisions, with few Chechens implicated in the regime. The tiny intelligentsia-bureaucratic layer that did emerge was swept away by the Chechen national revolution of 1991.[19] Chechnya under Soviet power remained an overwhelmingly agrarian society where the majority of the urban population consisted of Russians brought in to service the oil industry.

　　The social structures supporting monochronic historicism were predominant at the moment of breakdown in 1991. The Chechen revolution of late 1991 represented not only the replacement of a Sovietized elite by insurgent outsiders, but also the replacement of relatively Sovietized lowlanders by more traditionalist Southern highlander groups. This shift was reinforced by the actions of the Russian leadership in the fateful months following the August coup.[20] However, although the monochromic historicist perspective was undoubtedly important, it was not the only significant current of thinking. Although the social basis for liberalism in Chechnya was weak, it was not entirely absent and there were alternative narratives of the way that Chechnya's future could be shaped. Dzhabrail Gakaev, a contributor to this volume, is a notable example of the liberal approach.[21] Even Dudaev's approach was relatively nuanced, however fanciful some of his suggestions may have been. Dudaev's official position was for Chechnya to become a full republic outside Russia but within the Soviet Union. Up to his death in April 1996 he remained a consistent 'Soviet loyalist', even though the USSR that he had long served in the airforce no longer existed.[22] At the same time,

---

[18] See Zalpa Bersanova, 'Sistema tsennostei sovremennykh chechentsev (po materialam oprosov)', in Dmitrii Furman (ed.), *Chechnya i Rossiya: obshchestva i gosudarstva*, Vol. 3 of *Mir, progress, prava cheloveka*, publications of the Andrei Sakharov Museum and Public Centre (Moscow, 1999), pp. 223–49.

[19] The argument is made by Dmitrii Furman, 'Samyi trudnyi narod dlya Rossii', in *Chechnya i Rossiya*, pp. 12–13.

[20] The Russian leadership at this time, it should be noted, included the Chechen Ruslan Khasbulatov at the head of the Russian parliament, the Congress of People's Deputies and its smaller operative Supreme Soviet. The interaction of Khasbulatov with the insurgent Chechen leadership was far from helpful to a peaceful outcome.

[21] See also Dzhabrail Gakaev, 'Put' k chechenskoi revolyutsii', in Furman (ed.), *Chechnya i Rossiya*, pp. 150–76.

[22] Lieven, *Chechnya*, p. 58.

the contemporary appreciation of even the greatest of Chechnya's heroes, Imam Shamil, who had led the long war (1834–59) against Russian domination in the mid-nineteenth century, is mixed. As Umar Avturkhanov, the leader in 1994 of one of the groups opposed to Dudaev's 'crazed tyranny', had put it to Anatol Lieven:

> They talk about the tradition of Shamil, but what did Shamil do for Chechnya in fact? He brought us only decades of unnecessary war, the ruin of the country and the death of half its people. And he wasn't even a Chechen. He came here from Daghestan, preaching his crazy religious fanaticism, hatred of the Russians and holy war, and we Chechens behaved like fools as usual, and followed him, to our destruction.[23]

Chechens may well have a predominantly mythopoeic view of history (a characteristic shared by the part of the Serbian nation's willingness to follow Slobodan Milosevic in the 1990s), but this does not enter unmediated into policy. Shamil was at the cornerstone of the Chechen myth about unrelenting and dogged resistance to Russian power at any cost. During the quarter century of Shamil's war, before surrendering in 1859, he behaved with exemplary brutality towards the Chechens themselves, executing potential rivals and all those who questioned the wisdom of fighting a hopeless war. Shamil's ruthless imposition of discipline on Chechnya accustomed them to government, something that made the job of the Russians in ruling the area later somewhat easier. The last years of Russian imperial rule over Chechnya (from the 1870s into the early twentieth century), like the last years of Soviet power, were two interludes of relative peace and prosperity.[24] Even today, after a generation has grown up used to war, the social basis for some sort of accommodation with Russia has not disappeared.

Constricted State Building: The Lure of Supra-state Universalism

The relative role of the national and the religious in Chechnya's wars remains a matter of controversy. If the long resistance, albeit sporadic, between 1785 and 1921 was largely religious in origin, thereafter the national took primacy, and the war of 1994–6 was overwhelmingly a war of national sovereignty. It was this evolution from the 'universalistic' religious to the specifically national that was so sharply and dramatically reversed during Chechnya's brief independence after 1996, and in part provoked the failure of that independence to take root in the institutions of statehood. Dudaev's Sovietism, noted above, was also beyond the national. After 1996 the national was again subordinated to alternative universalistic models, in

---

[23] Lieven, *Chechnya*, p. 304.

particular those of Islam and regionalism (in this case greater Caucasianism), a mix that prompted the invasions of Dagestan in 1999.

The political closure discussed above reflected the second problem – the under-development of the Chechen state. This issue raises fundamental questions about the relationship of state and society and the development of a differentiated political society. Chechen society is divided into clan-like *teip* structures, and although in some respects Chechnya is thoroughly modernized, it is simultaneously pre-modern. A *teip* is an extended kinship community (there are about 130 in Chechnya) consisting of family groups who can trace their origins to a single individual. Chechens have conventionally known the history of their clan up to seven generations back. The wars have eroded the traditional role of the *teip* and, although their 'elders' (*starosty*) still have a role to play, they have been overshadowed by field commanders. Like many of the 'quasi-states' examined by Robert Jackson,[25] Chechen society (even without Russian intervention) appears unable to sustain the weight of a modern state. The anarchic egalitarianism of a people unused to state authority refuses to subordinate itself even to its own legitimate authorities (except in time of war, and even then only partially and reluctantly). This was already strongly in evidence under Dudaev, compounded by his inability to decide what sort of state Chechnya should become: democratic market-oriented or Asiatic-statist (bureaucratic), retaining property in its grasp. He inclined at first to the former, but by the end his residual Sovietism shifted towards the latter. The Khasavyurt agreement of 31 August 1996 (see Appendix 1) effectively granted Chechnya independence, but the opportunity was wasted. As Anatol Lieven puts it:

> The Chechens can be called a 'primordial ethnic nation', and their nationalism was not created or even significantly shaped by processes of state formation, economic development or mass literacy. Their victory was part of an intermittent historical pattern whereby apparently 'primitive' forces, through superior morale, tactical skill and the right circumstances, have defeated modern imperial armies in the course of this century, and as such it is a warning against not just Russian racism but Western technological arrogance too. However, while Chechen society has previously been able to generate a rather effective form of 'ordered anarchy', it seems unable to bear the weight of any modern state – even a Chechen one.[26]

[24] Igor' Rotar' reports that even battle-hardened Chechen insurgents regretted the break-up of the USSR and remembered the Soviet period as 'the best days of my life', *Pod zelënym znamenem islama: islamskie radikaly v Rossii i SNG* (Moscow, AIRO-XX, 2001), p. 21.
[25] Robert Jackson, *Quasi-States: Sovereignty, International Relations, and the Third World* (Cambridge, Cambridge University Press, 1990).
[26] Lieven, *Chechnya*, p. ix.

A pre-modern society, in Lieven's view, was able to exploit the cracks in modern capitalist economies to establish a criminalized clan-type social order that simply could not be fitted into the constraints of a modern law-governed political order. Like many other anti-colonial movements in the twentieth century, victory over the imperial power was the relatively easy part: establishing an effective (let alone democratic) state afterwards proved more difficult. In Chechnya, militarized and ethnicized traditions made the task even more daunting. This was a society based on clan-like egalitarian principles, lacking a feudal nobility, lords, or even a military or merchant class. What there was of a native Chechen intelligentsia was by definition Soviet-educated (like Ruslan Khasbulatov, the Speaker of the Russian parliament between 1991 and 1993) and was generally held in contempt, above all its liberal element.[27] This archaic egalitarianism proved an unstable foundation on which to build an inclusive democratic state, and prompted many to argue that the only stable political order possible in Chechnya would be one imposed on the restless and fragmented society from outside.[28]

These contradictions came into full play during the leadership of Aslan Maskhadov between 1996 and 1999. One of Dudaev's most able generals, following the Khasavyurt peace accord with Russia he sought to turn himself from leader of an insurgency into a statesman. Winning the presidency of Chechnya on 27 January 1997 in what is generally reckoned to have been a fair election (although see Gakaev's comments in Chapter 2), he was recognized by Russia as the legitimate leader of what had effectively become an independent state – although it was not recognized as such by the rest of the world or Russia. The Khasavyurt agreement postponed a decision on Chechnya's final status for five years, while the 'Peace Treaty and Principles of Interrelations between the Russian Federation and Chechen Republic of Ichkeria' of 12 May 1997 resolved 'To reject forever the use of force or threat of force in resolving all matters of dispute' (Appendix 2). Tragically, this was not to be, and the three years of Chechen quasi-independence saw the republic plunge into an orgy of lawlessness that threatened not only its own citizens, but also its neighbouring regions and ultimately Russia itself. The pre-political concept of a historicized victim people, which sustained aspirations for *national* self-determination, came into contradiction with the political process of *state*-building, which would entail compromises and civic inclusion. The Chechen leadership was unable to disaggregate the two.

It was in this period of effective independence that radical forms of Islam took a hold on Chechen society, and in particular a section of the leading

[27] Lieven, *Chechnya*, p. 317.
[28] An argument that is increasingly heard in some of the 'failed states' of Africa, e.g. Sierra Leone, and in response a new 'neo-imperial' literature has emerged. See, for example, Andrew J. Bacevich, *The Imperial Tense: Prospects and Problems of American Empire* (Lanham, MD, Rowman & Littlefield, 2003); Robert Cooper, *The Breaking of Nations: Order and Chaos in the Twenty-first Century* (London, Atlantic Books, 2003); David Harvey, *The New Imperialism* (Oxford, Oxford University Press, 2003).

fighters in the first war.[29] Maskahdov was not able, and ultimately was unwilling, to challenge the increasingly Islamicized and jihadist rhetoric of the warlords, notably Shamil Basaev, despite Russia's offers of support. The restless energy in society could find no structured integrative form. Instead, it turned in on itself in numerous social pathologies, above all kidnapping, ransoming, slavery and banditry, and external aggression, raids into neighbouring regions and ultimately in August and September 1999, two invasions of Dagestan. There was little attempt to mediate domestic conflict through structured politics. It proved impossible to find a modern democratic political form for a traditional free tribal society.

Anna Matveeva describes developments in the whole Caucasian region as a struggle for political order, where historical and demographic factors are extremely important but, notwithstanding, 'the challenges facing the region are basically modern'.[30] While the challenges may well be modern, the responses (as in Iran in 1978–9) are traditional, and it is this combination that makes politics in Chechnya so unstable. The Chechen experience did not inspire secessionist movements in other North Caucasian republics, and provided a salutary warning to republics like Tatarstan (see Chapter 3). Developments in Chechnya were not replicated elsewhere, although poverty, unemployment, sectarian and exclusive patterns of elite consolidation threatened to shatter the precarious stability. Whatever demonstration effect Chechnya may have had, it was largely a negative one. Chechnya had a very specific and powerful *national* project; it did not have a commensurate political project, and therein lies the core of the Chechen tragedy.

The Question of Chechen Independence

The year 1991 was for the Soviet Union what Robert Jackson calls 'the Grotian moment', the reshuffling of the title to sovereignty.[31] Viva Ona Bartkus has theorized these liminal periods in the constitution of states as the 'opportune moment' when the weakening of central government (or foreign intervention) raises the prospects for success of a bid for independence.[32] In both the former USSR and Yugoslavia, however, the Grotian moment was limited to existing constituent republics and, despite repeated wars (Slovenia, Croatia, Bosnia, Serbia (Kosovo), Moldova (Transdniester),

---

[29] The Islamic factor is analysed in Dmitri Trenin and Aleksei Malashenko, with Anatol Lieven, *Russia's Restless Frontier: The Chechnya Factor in Post-Soviet Russia* (Washington DC, Carnegie Endowment for International Peace, 2004), Chapter 4, pp. 71–102.

[30] Anna Matveeva, *The North Caucasus: Russia's Fragile Borderland* (London, Royal Institute for International Affairs, 1999), Summary.

[31] Robert Jackson, 'Sovereignty in World Politics: a Glance at the Conceptual and Historical Landscape', *Political Studies*, Vol. XLVII, Special Issue 1999, *Sovereignty at the Millennium*, p. 434.

[32] Viva Ona Bartkus, *The Dynamics of Secession* (Cambridge, Cambridge University Press, 1999), '"Opportune Moments": a reduction in the costs of secession', pp. 145–66.

Georgia (Abkhazia, South Ossetia), Azerbaijan (Nagorno-Karabakh), and Russia), the new borders have been upheld.

The Chechen secession bid was an attempt to expand the Grotian consensus without a basis in 'just cause', that is, an immediate threat to the existence of the people. Russia in 1991 was beginning the arduous attempt to establish some sort of democratic state, and the prevailing liberal consensus at that time could not have been further from contemplating any kind of repression against Chechens. It is this that distinguishes Chechnya from Kosovo, whose putative secession is clearly grounded in the remedial right to put an end to the persistent violation of human rights.[33] International law and practice does not recognize the unilateral right to secession under whatever conditions and through any procedure, however democratic (like a referendum). In addition, just as the 'opportune moment' of 1917–18, when the collapse of Tsarism prompted independence bids by at least fifteen communities, came to an end with the restoration of state power under the Bolsheviks so, too, this window of opportunity in postcommunist Russia was closed with the onset of the new millennium.

Strobe Talbott has argued that secessionist movements in places like Chechnya, Kosovo, East Timor, Aceh and West Papua (Irian Jaya) could be contained and constrained by the rise of interdependence, a phenomenon that in his view 'offers a remedy for intrastate conflicts that is better than secession: that is, to combine the promotion of democracy on the part of central government with efforts to help would-be breakaway areas benefit from cross-border economic development and political cooperation'.[34] This is the voice of classic liberal reasonableness. It is, however, a sentiment shared by many. A recent book edited by Metta Spencer demonstrates the high costs of separatism and partition through wars of secession.[35] The argument is reinforced by Schaeffer's arguments against those who try to resolve ethnic conflicts by partitioning states.[36] The problem, of course, is one of definition. Is Russia in the position of imperial states who have to accept the loss of their colonial possessions once the costs of attempting to hold on them become unacceptably high? Or is Russia faced with a situation where its very national existence and democratic achievements are under threat from an armed insurgency and, like the Union forces in the American Civil War, cannot but fight the war to a victorious conclusion?

---

[33] UN Resolution 1244 recognized the 'sovereignty and territorial integrity of the Federal Republic of Yugoslavia', but by Autumn 2000 the USA began to envisage an independent Kosovo and this probably will be the outcome in due course.

[34] Strobe Talbottt, 'Self-Determination in an Interdependent World', *Foreign Policy*, Spring 2000, abstracted in http://www.foreign policy.com/articles/Spring 2000/Talbottt.htm

[35] Metta Spencer (ed.), *Separatism: Democracy and Disintegration* (Lanham, MD, Rowman & Littlefield, 1998).

[36] Robert K Schaeffer, *Severed States: Dilemmas of Democracy in a Divided World* (Lanham, MD, Rowman & Littlefield, 1999).

Henry E Hale argues that 'Chechnya is a localized issue focused around the perceived threat of terrorism, not a symptom of naked Russian aggression'.[37] Both wars were relatively insulated from the mainstream of Russian political life and exerted remarkably little influence on it. There were popular protests in the first war and some elite mobilization to oppose it, the financial and budgetary implications of both wars were considerable, and the wars accentuated the callousness of social relations within the armed forces and in society at large.[38] For most of the population, however, the Chechen wars were perceived as being somehow 'foreign', even though they were fought precisely to ensure that Chechnya remained 'domestic'. Rather than acting as a force for fragmentation, the sense of duty to complete a necessary but unpleasant task appeared to unite the Russian people in the wake of some of the more egregious atrocities, such as the seizure of the Dubrovka theatre (showing the popular Nord-Ost musical) in Moscow in October 2002 and the Beslan school siege in North Ossetia of 1–3 September 2004. However, the way that the authorities handled both crises, and the persistent sense that the public was far from being given the whole truth, intensified the prevalent sense of unease that the regime was irresponsible, if not downright incompetent, and unaccountable to its own people.

The comparison is often drawn between the wars in Chechnya and Algeria's bloody struggle for independence from 1954. As far as France was concerned, Algeria was part of the metropolis, and it was only in 1962, after the war rocked the very foundations of the French state, that independence was granted. Russia does not have the luxury of a sea between it and its rebellious province. In *normative* terms, the Chechen case can be assessed as follows:[39]

• The *universal* right of nations to self-determination. While this abstract principle is certainly conceded by a number of international normative acts, it is usually hedged in by limitations. The international community has tended to endorse independence (typically after the fact) during the break-up of empires, the voluntary dissolution of a political entity (such as the Soviet Union or Czechoslovakia), the involuntary disintegration of a community (Yugoslavia), or as a result of obviously illegal occupation (Kuwait, with Tibet falling into a grey zone). The international community hesitated to recognize the independence of the former Yugoslav republics, but accepted the result of internationally monitored referendums to recognize the new states. It is far from universally accepted that Russia

---

[37] Henry E Hale, 'Is Russian Nationalism on the Rise?', Program on New Approaches to Russian Security, Davis Center for Russian Studies, Harvard University, *Policy Memo Series*, No. 110, February 2000, p. 1.

[38] See Anna Politkovskaya, *Putin's Russia* (London, Harvill, 2004).

[39] For a full discussion see Bruno Coppieters and Richard Sakwa (eds), *Contextualizing Secession: Normative Studies in Comparative Perspective* (Oxford, Oxford University Press, 2003), and in particular Richard Sakwa, 'Chechnya: A Just War Fought Unjustly?', pp. 156–86.

was an empire in the classical sense, although the Russian and Soviet relationship with the North Caucasus approximated most closely the classical model. Nevertheless, while the independence of the former Union Republics was swiftly recognized in 1991, that of the autonomous republics contained within Russia and some other Union Republics was not: the imperial or illegal occupation models were thus implicitly judged not to be appropriate in this context. There are limits to the universal right of nations to self-determination, and the Chechen case fell within those limits. Instead, dissatisfied political communities are urged to find solutions that fall short of full independence. These usually take the form of federal or consociational arrangements. The Dudaev regime did not effectively explore these possibilities, insisting on defending the indivisible concept of sovereignty announced in the 1992 Chechen constitution. Equally, Maskhadov's willingness to accept an indeterminate status for Chechnya in the Khasavyurt accords, and to sign the May 1997 agreement renouncing the use of force in Russo-Chechen relations, signalled the beginning of a process of political negotiation that was destroyed by the failure of the Chechen state to sustain itself as an interlocutor in that process. Despite the onset of the second war in September 1999, Maskhadov declared himself ready to.enter a negotiation process right up to his death at the hands of Russian forces on 8 March 2005.

- The *remedial* right to secession. This is considered justified if a nation has suffered a history of exploitation or discrimination. Few nations have suffered as much as Chechnya has at the hands of the Russian empire and its Soviet successor, culminating in the 1944 deportation. Nevertheless, the remedial right to secession is only considered appropriate if all other alternatives have been exhausted. A further tragic edge to the conflicts of the 1990s is that from 1990 Russia itself had for the first time had taken a liberal approach to national issues, guaranteeing the rights and privileges of minority groups and beginning to transform the pseudo-federalism of the Soviet Union into genuine federalism – although under president Vladimir Putin this has taken a more centralizing turn. The Chechen side, however, failed to engage with the democratization and federalizing processes in Russia itself, an omission that weakened the ethical thrust of the Chechen bid for independence. Indeed, the unilateral Chechen bid for independence weakened the ability of Russia proper to sustain its own democratization project.

- *Procedural* issues are no less important. Both the above principles are predicated on the assumption that independence would be supported by a demonstrable majority of the population in the seceding region, and that the population in the country from which secession is taking place harboured no overwhelming objection to the process. There is no doubt that Chechen elites were bitterly divided over Dudaev's maximalist approach to independence, while the majority of Russians in the republic evidently desired to stay within Russia. During the first war, Russian public opinion was ready to accept Chechen independence, and this view gained force during Chechnya's period of proto-independence between 1996 and 1999, only to evaporate during the second war. While all national communities may aspire to autonomy, unless these aspirations are subordinated to a negotiated process they threaten to reduce world politics to a state of permanent war. For much of the Chechen leadership after 1991 independence was non-negotiable, although both Dudaev (sporadically) and Maskhadov (more consistently) were willing to negotiate the terms on which disengagement with Russia would take place. Russia's own internal divisions, above all the struggle between Yeltsin and Khasbulatov, made negotiations more difficult, but Russia's attempts to find a mechanism to integrate the divergent demands of its republics – ranging from the Federal Treaties of 1992 to the bilateral treaty signed with Tatarstan in 1994 – were rebuffed by the Chechen leadership.[40]

- The *outcome* of independence inevitably colours normative principles. As in so many post-colonial countries, independence led to the establishment of a regime that diminished democracy and pluralism. Minority groups, above all Russians, found themselves the target of criminal groups and political harassment, provoking a mass exodus of over a quarter of a million in 1992–3. In addition, it was clear that an independent Chechnya under Dudaev and his successors would pose a permanent security threat to Russia's southern marches and for all of its neighbouring states.

- The *processual* factor in prosecuting what may well be a justified war is crucial. Anatol Lieven argues that 'Russia's legal right to prosecute this [the second Chechen] war is incontestable': Chechnya is an internationally recognized part of Russian territory; and when given the chance of self-rule from 1996 'the government there proved incapable of controlling its own territory'.[41] But there is a difference between the right to make war (*jus ad bellum*) and the manner of its conduct (*jus in bello*), a tension that in the contemporary world is particularly acute, and when the latter is taken to extremes, can vitiate the right to the former. Basic military competence, as well as concern for military and civilian casualties, suggest that war should only be pursued if there is a reasonable expectation of being able to achieve the goals without excessive losses or cost, the principle of proportionality in just war theory. This applies to both sides in the conflict.

[40] There remains considerable controversy whether a bilateral treaty with Chechnya in 1994 could have averted war. It appears that only personal factors prevented such a treaty being signed. See Tracey C German, *Russia's Chechen War* (London, Routledge, 2003), Chapter 6, pp. 94–111. Matthew Evangelista provides a vivid account of the 'missed opportunities' to come to an agreement with Dudaev's regime, Matthew Evangelista, Matthew, *The Chechen Wars: Will Russia go the Way of the Soviet Union?* (Washington, DC, Brookings institution Press, 2003), pp. 27–33.

The costs to the secessionist region are clear, but there are also important implications for the state from which the region is attempting to secede. Protracted warfare in Chechnya clearly degrades the quality of Russian political and social life, especially since there has been a tendency to dehumanize the Chechen insurgents, the Chechens as a people and Russian servicemen.

Peace and War

The collapse of the Soviet Union opened up a power vacuum throughout the Caucasus and Central Asia, while Russia struggled to find an effective way of asserting its interests. The militant warlords in Chechnya sought to take advantage of Russian weakness to separate more territory from Russia and to create 'an Islamic republic from the Black to the Caspian Seas'.[42] In response, Russia argued that it was obliged to act within the terms of the 'Code of Conduct on Politico-Military Aspects of Security' that was signed at the OSCE summit in Budapest in December 1994. Paragraph 6 states that 'participating states will take appropriate measures to prevent and combat terrorism in all its forms', while paragraph 25 states that 'the participating states will not tolerate or support forces that are not accountable to or controlled by their constitutionally established authorities'.[43] The applicability of both these provisions to Chechnya are clear. By 1999, as William Church puts it, 'Russia was faced with an autonomous state within its political control that had disintegrated into warlord factions, and which invaded a neighbouring state'.[44]

Although Russia's intervention in Chechnya in September 1999 violated the terms of the 1996 Khasavyurt agreement and the treaty of May 1997, the maintenance of some order in the region was, many argued, not only Russia's right but its duty. Following soon after the invasions of Dagestan, a succession of apartment bombings in Buinaksk (Dagestan) (4 September 1999, 62 dead), Moscow, Guryanov Street (9 September, 100 dead); Moscow, Kashirskoe Highway (13 September, 124 dead) and Volgodonsk (15 September, 19 dead) created a climate of fear and anger against Chechens – although Chechen involvement in them remains a controversial question, especially in the light of the Ryazan incident at the time, in which a primed bomb was found in the basement of an apartment block, which the Federal Security Service (FSB) claimed to be part of a training exercise.

The second North Caucasian military operation began on 2 August 1999 when federal forces supported Dagestani units to repel the first Chechen

[41] Anatol Lieven, 'Morality and Reality in Approaches to War Crimes: The Case of Chechnya', *East European Constitutional Review*, Vol. 10, Nos 2/3, Spring/Summer 2001, p. 72.
[42] S Shermatova, 'Tak nazyvaemye vakhkhabity', in *Chechnya i Rossiya: obshchestva i gosudarstva* (Moscow, 1999), p. 419.
[43] Quoted in William Church, 'Moscow's Actions: Rationale Deserve Reappraisal', *Defense News*, 20 March 2000.
[44] Church, 'Moscow's Actions'.

invasion of the republic, and federal forces then entered Chechnya on 1 October 1999. Already by February 2000 Russian losses were officially stated to be 1,458 servicemen killed and 4,495 wounded,[45] a figure that according to Putin had risen to 2,600 deaths by November 2000.[46] By the time the full-scale military phase of the war ended in 2000, reports from the human rights organization Memorial (covering only one-third of the territory) state that nearly 3,000 people had been abducted; Memorial also has records on 1,254 taken between 1 January 2002 to August 2004, 148 of whom are known to be dead and 757 of whom are still missing.[47] Russian mop-up operations (*zachistki*) continued. Maskhadov, moreover, decreed that all those who tried to restore the civil infrastructure and civic administration were to be killed, a position that he later modified when he stated that the insurgents would 'no longer commit terrorist acts against civilians', although he made little attempt to enforce this.[48]

The mission statement of the Russian armed forces in the first war was that their task was to 'restore constitutional order', while the second war was described more as a 'counter-terrorist operation'. This was reflected in the high degree of public support for the second war.[49] However, this was an internal war 'where its own citizens were mixed in with the Chechen warlords'.[50] While the ambition may have been accurate, the methods employed were far from commensurate with these aims. The problem, in the words of Lord David Russell-Johnston, president of the Parliamentary Assembly of the Council of Europe (PACE), is the way in which the civilian population suffered from 'the disproportionate and indiscriminate' use of force by Russian troops. As he noted, the Council of Europe 'was set up to defend human rights, democracy and the rule of law. This is a mandate that leaves very little room for *realpolitik*'.[51] Russia's voting rights in the Parliamentary

---

[45] *Nezavisimaya gazeta*, 12 February 2000.

[46] RFE/RL *Newsline*, 21 November 2000.

[47] Nick Paton Walsh, 'The Road to Beslan', *The Guardian: G2*, 30 September 2004, p. 6.

[48] *Moskovskie novosti*, No. 46, November 2000.

[49] Emil' Pain suggests that part of the reason for strong support for the war was the manipulation of mass consciousness, 'Vtoraya Chechenskaya voina i ee posledstviya', in Nikolai Petrov (ed.), *Regiony Rossii v 1999g.: Ezhegodnoe prilozhenie k "Politicheskomu al'manakhu Rossii"*, Moscow Carnegie Center (Moscow, Gendal'f, 2001), pp. 280–94. Although the overwhelming majority of the Russian population supported the second Chechen war, with opinion polls showing a steady 70-odd per cent in favour, there are certain ambiguities. In February 2000, for example, 48 per cent supported the ending of hostilities and the resolution of the Chechen problem by negotiations if Putin proposed such a course of action, while 42 per cent said they would not. A poll in late December 1999 revealed that even among the supporters of the war a large majority, 59 per cent, would accept an independent Chechnya, and another 21 per cent would be 'happy' for this to occur. Poll conducted by VTsIOM, in Henry E Hale, 'Is Russian Nationalism on the Rise?', Program on New Approaches to Russian Security (PONARS), Davis Center for Russian Studies, Harvard University, *Policy Memo Series*, No. 110, February 2000, p. 1.

[50] Church, 'Moscow's Actions'.

[51] David Russell-Johnston, 'Human Rights for the Chechens, Too', *International Herald Tribune*, 14 April 2000.

Assembly were suspended between April 2000 and January 2001. The Council of Europe operated within the framework of two key principles: the territorial integrity of the Russian Federation; and open dialogue with all parties to the conflict. As long as Russia continued to condemn the insurgent Chechen leadership as terrorists it was difficult to see how such a dialogue could be achieved.

Putin distinguished between the first war, which he linked to 'Russia's imperialist ambitions and attempts to rein in the territories it controls', and the second, which he characterised as an 'anti-terrorist operation'.[52] Putin's fear that the Chechen zone of insecurity would move up the Volga and spread to other republics and result in the Yugoslavisation of Russia provoked the second war. An 'enclave of banditry', to use Putin's term, was established in Chechnya; this threatened not only its immediate neighbours but also the trans-Caspian republics of Kyrgyzstan and Uzbekistan.[53] As far as Putin was concerned,

> [T]he essence of the situation in the Caucasus and Chechnya was a continuation of the collapse of the USSR. It was clear that we had to put an end to it at some point... My evaluation of the situation in August [1999] when the bandits attacked Dagestan was that if we don't stop it immediately, Russia as a state in its current form would no longer exist. Then we were talking about stopping the dissolution of the country. I acted assuming it would cost me my political career. This was the minimum price that I was prepared to pay.[54]

If nothing else, Putin has been remarkably consistent in upholding this view. In his emotional speech to the people on 4 September 2004, following the killings at Beslan, he noted that 'Today we are living in conditions that have emerged following the break-up of a vast great state... But today, despite all the difficulties, we have managed to preserve the core of the colossus which was the Soviet Union'.[55] At that time he feared that the very existence of Russia was at stake, and that the country could be engulfed in 'endless and bloody conflicts'. The logic of such a view is that severe measures are justified if they could avert such a catastrophic outcome. However, much of the academic literature suggests that there is not a high

---

[52] RFE/RL *Newsline*, 27 October 2000.

[53] Interview with Vladimir Putin by Mikhail Leont'ev, *Vremya*, ORT, 7 February 2000.

[54] Vladimir Putin, *Ot pervogo litsa: Razgovory s Vladimirom Putinym*, with Nataliya Gevorkyan, Natal'ya Timakova and Andrei Kolesnikov (Moscow, Vagrius, 2000), pp. 133–4; Vladimir Putin, *First Person: An Astonishingly Frank Self-Portrait by Russia's President Vladimir Putin*, with Nataliya Gevorkyan, Natalya Timakova, and Andrei Kolesnikov, translated by Catherine A Fitzpatrick (London, Hutchinson, 2000), pp. 133–4.

[55] *Kommersant*, 6 September 2004, p. 2; http://www.kremlin.ru/text/appears/2004/09/76320.shtml

probability of Russia disintegrating[56] – although things undoubtedly look differently from where Putin is standing.

In his earlier interview Putin insisted that the issue was not secession as such, but security:

> The issue is not secession... Chechnya will not stop with its own independence. It will be used as a staging ground for a further attack on Russia... Why? In order to protect Chechen independence? Of course not. The purpose will be to grab more territory. They would overwhelm Dagestan. Then the whole Caucasus – Dagestan, Ingushetiya, and then up along the Volga – Bashkortostan, Tatarstan, following this direction into the depths of the country... When I started to compare the scale of the possible tragedy with what we have there now, I had no doubt that we should act as we are acting, maybe even more firmly.[57]

From this it is clear that Putin viewed the Chechen issue in stark terms. However, a policy that in late 1999 served to consolidate the Russian people later increasingly looked like a stubborn attempt to achieve a military victory at all costs. Putin's thinking remained torn between two concerns: security and sovereignty. Even before 9/11, security had tended to predominate over sovereignty issues, but the defence of the territorial integrity of the Russian Federation was never far from the surface. Putin did not consider Chechen independence a realistic option for both these reasons.[58]

As the war ground on, many in Chechnya, including the Mufti of Chechnya, Akhmed-hadji Kadyrov, argued that there could not be any order in Chechnya without the direct participation of the federal authorities.[59] Kadyrov had been a military commander with the insurgents in the first war, but had been appalled by Maskhadov's toleration of the emergence of Islamic fundamentalists (the so-called Wahhabis) in Chechnya, and had thus gone over to the federal side. On 20 June 2000 Kadyrov was appointed to head the interim administration as part of Putin's 'Chechenization' plan, and as we shall see in more detail in later chapters, was elected president on 5 October 2003 and served in that post until assassinated in a bomb blast in Grozny stadium on 9 May 2004. In the context of direct rule from Russia, many argued that a key element of any future settlement would be the

---

[56] For example, Henry E Hale and Rein Taagepera, 'Russia: Consolidation or Collapse?, *Europe-Asia Studies*, Vol. 54, No. 7, 2002, pp. 1101–25.

[57] Putin, *Ot pervogo litsa*, p. 135; *First Person*, pp. 141–2.

[58] Speech of 20 November 2000, RFE/RL *Newsline*, 21 November 2000. He was supported in his view by the Russian elite: a poll conducted by ROMIR-Gallup International in December 2000 found that the overwhelming majority, 92.1%, insisted that Chechnya should remain part of the Russian Federation, reported in *Johnson's Russia List*, No. 4675/6.

[59] Igor Zadvornov and Aleksandr Khalmukhamedov, 'Posle pobedy: o perekhodnom periode v politicheskoi istorii Chechenskoi Respubliki', *Osobaya papka NG*, No. 2 (5), 29 February 2000, p. 14.

development of Chechnya's rich tradition of local self-government. Khasbulatov, the former Speaker of the dissolved Russian Supreme Soviet, also found himself a role. In April 2000 he was named chairman of the newly created Public Council for the North Caucasus, a body established to build consensus for a peaceful resolution of the Chechen and broader North Caucasian problems.[60] His appointment suggested that some of the divisions of the Yeltsin era were being healed.[61] With the election of Aslanbek Aslakhanov, the head of Chechnya's Association of Law Enforcement Workers and someone who had never advocated Chechen independence, as a parliamentary deputy to the Russian State Duma on 20 August 2000, it appeared that Chechnya was gradually being reintegrated into the Russian political community. In the Duma, Aslakhanov lost no opportunity to condemn the arbitrary detention, beating and torture of Chechen civilians.[62] Aslakhanov later became Putin's advisor on Chechnya.

Others, however, like former presidential advisor Emil Pain, characterize Russia's entire policy as 'colonial wars' (see Chapter 4). Despite military successes, the lack of a clear Kremlin strategy to win over the Chechen people in the second war led one commentator to adopt the term 'victorious defeat' to describe the stalemate.[63] Another report noted that 'political regulation of the Chechen problem is impossible': 'Russia has won. The war continues'.[64] The Russian presidential spokesman, Sergei Yastrzhembsky, argued in May 2001 that the conflict in Chechnya was likely to last for years, noting that there were some thirty low-intensity conflicts in the world, and that Chechnya would probably join their number.[65] Few commentators thought that Russia could win the war, which poisoned Russian politics and threatened to inhibit Russia's further development as a democracy. As Dmitrii Furman, a senior scholar at the Russian Academy of Sciences Institute of Europe, put it, Moscow's approach to both Chechnya and the Chechens left him unable to 'imagine a peaceful integration of Chechens into Russian society'. His conclusion was that Russian democracy was impossible without Chechen independence.[66] Fighting settled down for the long haul in a war that Russia could neither win nor lose, given adequate resources and commitment. The only way out is some sort of negotiated settlement accompanied possibly by the internationalization of the peace process.

---

[60] *Nezavisimaya gazeta*, 18 April 2000.
[61] Khasbulatov is a prolific commentator on Chechen affairs. See in particular *Kreml'i Rossiisko-Chechenskaya voina: razmyshleniya o voine i mire* (Moscow, Graal', 2002), and in the same series *Kreml' i Rossiisko-Chechenskaya voina: Chuzhie (istoriko-politicheskii ocherk o chechentsakh i ikh gosudarstvennosti)* (Moscow, Graal', 2003).
[62] E.g. on 19 October, RFE/RL *Newsline* 20 October 2000.
[63] Otto Latsis, 'Ups and Downs of Political Will', *The Russia Journal*, 7–13 October 2000.
[64] Zakhar Vinogradov, 'Vtoraya chechenskaya kampaniya: pobednyi god', *Nezavisimaya gazeta*, 6 October 2000, p. 4.
[65] RFE/RL, *Chechnya Weekly*, 30 May 2001.
[66] Cited by Paul Goble, 'On Equal Terms', RFE/RL, *Newsline*, 14 March 2000.

2

Chechnya in Russia and Russia in Chechnya

Dzhabrail Gakaev

The Chechen crisis is a complex phenomenon, and there are many aspects of it that cannot be understood to this day. The conflict does not have a simple explanation, and each side has its own truth. However, a scholarly analysis of events makes it possible to draw a number of general conclusions.

Major Factors of the Crisis

The August 1991 events in Moscow, when a conservative group led by the State Committee for the State of Emergency (SCSE) tried to seize power and force Mikhail Gorbachev to moderate his programme of reforms, was followed soon after by the dissolution of the USSR. This gave the multinational people of the Chechen-Ingush Republic a unique chance to replace the communist bureaucracy with a democratic system of power by peaceful constitutional means, and to define the status of the republic by means of a national referendum. It also made possible an acceptable form of relations with the Russian Federation, through which Chechnya might gradually acquire real economic and political independence in the framework of a renewed federal union of equal nations and republics of the new democratic Russia.

However, this way of resolving the aggravated problem of power and sovereignty proposed by the democratic community of Chechnya did not suit certain political structures in Moscow or in the republic itself. As a result, the Chechen-Ingush Republic and its political elites found themselves at the epicentre of the Russian leadership's struggle with the union centre (representing the Soviet Union) over the division of power and property. The Chechen-Ingush Supreme Soviet led by Doku Zavgaev supported Gorbachev in the attempt to stay in power. Gorbachev in turn sought to play the Russian autonomy card (promising to raise the status of Russia's and other autonomous republics to that of the union republics in the reformed union) against the separatist tendencies of the Russian leadership. The USSR at that time consisted of 15 union republics and within Russia there were 16 autonomous republics, one of which was Chechnya-Ingushetia. The Chechen national-radicals, led by Dzhokhar Dudaev, came out against the attempted coup by the SCSE and, having supported Yeltsin and Khasbulatov during the August events, received carte blanche to take over power in Grozny. Gambling on the support of the shadow economy and radicalizing the idea of sovereignty – thereby gaining the support of outsider groups and the poorer marginalised sections of the population – Dudaev and the forces supporting him gained power in the republic. However, if Yeltsin had not introduced the state of emergency in the Chechen Republic in early November 1991, the chances of the Dudaev group holding on to power were practically nil. Faced by the Russian threat, the population rallied to the Chechen leadership, however much they may have despised the individuals concerned. In the ensuing struggle for the redistribution of power and property, Chechnya's new quasi-elite used aggressive separatism to consolidate its power and privileges. As a result, an irrational and distorted version of radical sovereignty was foisted on the people of Chechnya.

Even then, it was clear to many people in Chechnya that this policy of independence was being pursued without the necessary conditions for a fair plebiscite, with the stress on the seizure of power, and with a revolutionary sense of justice dominating society and the low level of political culture of the ruling elites both in Russia and Chechnya. Given these conditions, as well as the criminal nature of the regime in Grozny, the split in Chechen society over the question of how to achieve independence and the irreconcilable actions of anti-Chechen forces, conflict and massive loss of human life seemed – and was – an inevitable consequence.

The proposition in favour of an independent Chechnya is a fiction and a myth calculated to play on the beliefs of ignorant people. In the modern, interconnected, interdependent and integrated world the existence of totally independent states is impossible. More than that, in order to safeguard their vital interests, Chechens themselves are acutely aware of the need to preserve a unified political, legal, economic and cultural space with Russia. The reality is that Russia is in Chechnya and Chechnya is in Russia, and they are destined to remain together. Policies that do not take this situation into account risk finding themselves groundless. Contrary to established opinion, Dudaev understood perfectly well that Chechnya was inconceivable without Russia. His seeming intransigence on the question of Chechnya's sovereignty served as cover under which he pursued his chief aim: the legitimization of his own power. In the run-up to the first war, which began in December 1994, he tried hard to gain an audience with the Russian president. However, Yeltsin's milieu stubbornly avoided direct contact with Dudaev, and convinced Yeltsin not to receive the leader of Ichkeria (the Chechen name for the republic, and the term used to describe the effectively independent region between

1996 and 1999) but to support the armed opposition. If Yeltsin and Dudaev had met, the conflict could well have been avoided since the two men had much in common, including a shared Soviet past. At the same time Yeltsin and his team used Dudaev and his regime in the struggle against the Russian Supreme Soviet headed by Ruslan Khasbulatov – the 'Khasbulatov factor'. The fear that Khasbulatov would gain political credibility by brokering some sort of deal in Chechnya meant that Yeltsin's team resolutely sought to exclude Khasbulatov from any involvement in negotiations. As an ethnic Chechen with close links to his home republic and at the same time a leading Russian politician, Khasbulatov was in a unique position to act as an intermediary. The policy of radical sovereignty in Chechnya used violence as an instrument of power, but this did not necessarily have to turn into armed conflict with Russia.

Contradictory socio-economic and political processes were reflected in events in Chechnya itself. On the one hand, the historical aspirations of the Chechen people to self-determination; on the other, the struggle of deprived groups for equality and social justice. The tragedy in Chechnya was that outsider groups forced their way to power on the back of the democratic and national movement. As a result, another division of power and property in the corporate interests of various groups took place under cover of the idea of national revival and sovereignty. As often happens in an immature society, having overthrown the much detested communist *nomenklatura*, the rebellious lower classes fell victim to a new power – the dictatorship of a post-soviet quasi-elite, national in form but mafia-like in essence.

The Chechen crisis emerged as the result of a split within Chechnya over ways of dealing with the problem of power and property. Leaders of certain clans and political elites in Chechnya, who refused to act in unison for the greater interest of the nation, provoked this split in society, thereby losing the opportunity to create a multiethnic legal and civil society. These divisions were exploited by certain groups to provoke armed conflict. From the moment Dudaev and his associates assumed power and the intra-Chechen confrontation started, external and internal factors influenced the character of the conflict. The first of these relates to the problem of the self-determination of the Chechen people and the search for an adequate new status for the Chechen-Ingush Republic. The second concerns the struggle between the various political forces and clans for power and property in Chechnya, and this, after the beginning of the second Chechen campaign, defines the correlation of political forces in the republic. The repeated assaults against the Chechen people during tsarist and Soviet times undermined the emergence of a national intelligentsia and an organic ruling class. The nation's immune system was weakened and created the conditions for the establishment of a kleptocracy.

The Chechen crisis came about, above all, as a result of the sporadic and incomplete modernization process in Chechnya. The Chechens lagged considerably behind many other Russian peoples in their quality of life.

This was manifested in a high birth rate, leading to a large proportion of young people not of working age; the predominance of the rural population; a comparatively low level of education; a distorted social-professional structure, including a disproportionate share of workers in the agricultural and service sector; the absence of a national vanguard of industrial workers and technical intelligentsia; a high infant-mortality rate; widespread infection with tuberculosis; a high unemployment rate (which among Chechens of working age reached almost 40 per cent) and an extraordinarily high number of *otkhodniki* (migrant workers), with about 100,000 leaving the republic annually. In Chechnya the harshest social and political experiments have been carried out, including 16 partial and 1 full deportation. The full deportation took place in February 1944, with the Chechens accused of collaborating with the German forces occupying the North Caucasus.[1]

The political distrust of the Soviet leadership towards Chechens was reflected in the low representation of this titular people (the people after whom the republic was named) in the communist *nomenklatura*. In contrast to other national republics, the Chechen *nomenklatura* was small in numbers and was relatively newly-formed and had thus not taken root in Chechen society. The policy of Russification, the incompleteness of the nation-forming process, the lack of a genuine national spiritual and political elite (destroyed in the 1920s through to the 1940s and only just beginning to develop by the early 1990s) all adds to a picture of incomplete Soviet modernization in Chechnya.

The most dangerous consequence of the new spirit, born out of the Chechen revolution accompanying the seizure of power by Dudaev and his outsider groups, was the development of a dismissive attitude to work, to accumulating personal and public wealth through honest labour. Easy criminal ways of making money through financial manipulations, robbery of Russians and others in the towns and other forms of banditry, fabulously enriched thousands of people without kith or kin or any occupation very quickly, creating a 'new elite' out of yesterday's poorly-educated outsiders. They became the social basis of the new regime. The emergence of an enormously rich elite destroyed the foundations of the traditional way of life and the culture of Chechen society. It should be stressed that the criminalization of Chechnya has nothing to do with the national peculiarities of the Chechen people. This phenomenon can be seen throughout the post-Soviet space.

The extremist national-radical propagandists such as Zelimkhan Yandarbiev (who rose to prominence following Dudaev's death) and

---

[1] Some 387,000 Chechens and 91,000 Ingush were deported to Central Asia (primarily to Kazakhstan), of whom at least a quarter died on the way. In 1991 a third of Chechens living at that time were returnees with memories of those bitter days. For his own description of the exile, see Ruslan Khasbulatov, *The Struggle for Russia: Power and Change in the Democratic Revolution*, edited and introduced by Richard Sakwa (London and New York, Routledge, 1993), pp. 3–4, 11–12.

Movladi Udugov, peddling myths about the absolute and irreconcilable priority of Chechen independence and cultural war against Russia based on Islam and native traditionalism, inflicted terrible damage on traditional Chechen culture. The cult of force and national exclusivity, the scornful attitude to other nations that is uncharacteristic of Chechens, the stirring up of ethnic hatred towards Russians, the encouraging of the baser instincts of the people, became the basis of the official ideology. To sum up, the Dudaev period of Chechen history once again demonstrated the old truth: the level of democracy cannot surpass the level of the culture.

At the root of the Chechen conflict are the conflicting interests of criminal mafia groupings and the political elites of the federal centre and the Chechen Republic supporting them, and these interests focused above all on oil. By 1991 in Chechnya-Ingushetia up to 4.2 million tons of oil per year were being extracted. During the Soviet period, the Chechen-Ingush Republic refined up to 18 million tons of oil a year, providing 6 per cent of the USSR's joint gross national product. After the dissolution of the USSR, Chechnya continued to play a major role in the economic life of the country. Major oil and gas pipelines passed through Chechnya's territory to ports on the Black Sea. These included the branches coming from the Caspian and the Tengiz oil deposits in Kazakhstan. Such a huge oil resource, which in 1991 had essentially been left without a clear owner, added fuel to the struggle among the new quasi-elites of Moscow and Grozny; indeed, oil was being transferred from other regions of Russia along the pipelines to Grozny for refining and transportation right up to Autumn 1994. The profits from the oil operations and from associated oil products in the Chechen enclave came to tens of millions of dollars, the majority of which disappeared into the pockets of Russian officials and the accounts of intermediary firms and banks for laundering. The struggle over Chechnya became even more intense after the signing of 'the contract of the century' concerning the exploitation and transportation of Caspian oil to Novorossiisk on the Black Sea. Here and in debates over the export of Azerbaijani oil a clash of interests occurred between Russia, the USA, Turkey, Iran, the Caucasian republics and international petroleum companies over pipeline routes. Recent events in Dagestan and in Chechnya are thus connected with the struggle of trans-national petroleum companies for the oil of the Caspian basin.[2]

In the early 1990s, Chechen shadow capital rapidly legalized itself and became firmly established in Moscow, St. Petersburg, Kiev and other major cities of the former USSR. It became a serious competitor to the Jewish, Russian and Ukrainian financial mafia, above all in the sphere of the speculative banking business, financial pyramids and the 'grabitization' of Chubais-style privatization. Anatoly Chubais was the Russian minister

---

[2] Hooshang Amirahmadi, *The Caspian Region at a Crossroad: Challenges of a New Frontier of Energy and Development* (Basingstoke, Macmillan, 2000).

responsible for masterminding the rapid disbursement of Russian economic wealth.[3] The task that emerged in Russia was to eliminate dangerous and aggressive Chechen rivals by any means, by pushing them out of the spheres of the legal banking, gambling and commercial businesses in Russia and the countries of the Commonwealth of Independent States (CIS).

The Chechen crisis is directly connected with the armaments that were left in Chechnya as Russian forces withdrew in early 1992. At the time, the Soviet Army was exiting many countries in Europe, the Baltic republics and the CIS; however, nowhere did they leave such a quantity of weapons as in Chechnya. Ninety per cent of all the arms available in Chechnya fell into Dudaev's hands. Official estimates of the armaments left in Chechnya were only the tip of the iceberg – but even this quantity is staggering.[4] General Dudaev was left with enough *matériel* to equip an army of one hundred thousand men, including rockets, tanks and aircraft. The idea of the 'impertinent plunder' of the Russian arsenal in Chechnya, the view that Chechen forces raided Russian army stores, does not hold water. There is no doubt that there was an 'amicable' agreement about the transfer of weapons in exchange for appropriate compensation.[5] The Russian political and military leadership of the time condoned the militarization of Chechnya, knowing perfectly well that not only the mercenary interests of the leaders of Ichkeria, the top brass and mafias dealing in armaments were involved, but also that their own far-reaching political aims were being pursued.

Knowing the mentality of Chechens and their traditional love of weapons, the consequences of such a move were clear. The armament business in Chechnya turned out to be very profitable for the military-industrial complex. As with the cases of the false *avizos* (bank instructions sent from Chechnya to Moscow in the early 1990s that released billions of roubles that subsequently disappeared) and Chubais-style 'privatisation', the social base of the power regimes in both Chechnya and Russia was consolidated. This created a stratum of 'new' Russians and Chechens, and in this case the Chechens received a very precious gift from the Russian generals, with the help of which they coped perfectly well with the task of self-destruction.

There are also geopolitical factors, including tensions between the great powers for dominance in the region. Russia's geopolitical rivals sought to

---

[3] Maxim Boycko, Andrei Schleifer and Robert Vishny, *Privatizing Russia* (Cambridge, Mass., MIT Press, 1995); Joseph R. Blasi, Maya Kroumova & Douglas Kruse, *Kremlin Capitalism: Privatizing the Russian Economy* (Ithaca, ILR Press/Cornell University Press, 1997); Rose Brady, *Kapitalizm: Russia's Struggle to Free its Economy* (New Haven, CT, Yale University Press, 1998); Anders Aslund (ed.), *Russia's Economic Transformation in the 1990s* (London, Cassell Academic, 1998).

[4] For a discussion of the issue, see *Rossiya-Chechnya: tsep' oshibok i prestuplenii*, edited by O. P. Orlov and A. V. Cherkasov (Moscow, Memorial/Zven'ya, 1998), pp. 103–8.

[5] One of the best accounts is the chapter by Robert Seely 'Dudayev's Regime: The Handover of Soviet Military Hardware', in his *Russo-Chechen Conflict, 1800–2000: A Deadly Embrace* (London, Frank Cass, 2001), pp. 114–41.

exploit the struggle between the separatist regime and Moscow. There is great potential for the restoration of the union as long as the Russian nucleus is maintained, and for certain geopolitical strategists, this nucleus of empire had to be dismembered.[6] The Chechen crisis has thus become the focus for the struggles of Russia's geopolitical rivals.Thus, the Chechen crisis was born out of a number of heterogeneous phenomena, which came together at the right place at the right time, focused as under a magnifying glass. The saddest thing is that the Chechen national-radicals willingly or unwittingly allowed themselves to be drawn into the conspiracy against their own people.

The First War, 1994–6

Russia's military-political and financial elites nurtured Dudaev's regime for three years, transforming Chechnya into an enclave for laundering money and selling oil products, weapons and narcotics.[7] The idea of independence turned into a mask to cover the criminal speculations of the power elite, robbing the Chechen people and enriching the Chechen and Russian post-Soviet elites. The leaders of Ichkeria proved to be ready to gamble with the very existence of the Chechen nation. Striving to cover up the traces of the crimes committed, civil war was provoked in Chechnya. Russian troops were brought in under the pretext of disarming the opposing sides. The restoration of constitutional order in Chechnya turned into another tragedy for the people and provoked a massacre unprecedented in contemporary history. The actions of the federal troops and Ichkeria's army in Grozny, Argun, Bamut, Samashki, Shatoi, Komsomolsk and so on, bear witness to that. Practically all the battles in Chechnya ended up with the destruction of villages, towns and their inhabitants.[8]

General Yermolov's scorched earth policy, used by Russian generals against Chechnya's civil population in the early nineteenth century, played into the hands of the separatists who provoked mass Chechen resistance. The majority of the Chechen fighters did not support Dudaev and his group but found themselves drawn into the war because of the pogroms carried out in Chechnya by the federal army. The Chechen war can be called a just war only if one looks at it through the eyes of those who became its victims. Between September and November 1994 two socio-political clans were fighting for power, one of which was supported by the Kremlin. After the full-scale Russian intervention of 11 December 1994 the struggle was transformed from

---

[6] Zbigniew Brzezinski, 'The Premature Partnership', *Foreign Affairs*, March–April 1994, pp. 67–82.
[7] Carlotta Gall and Thomas de Waal, *Chechnya: Calamity in the Caucasus* (New York, New York University Press, 1998).
[8] For a description of the war, see Tracey C. German, *Russia's Chechen War* (London, Routledge, 2003).

a civil war into a Russian-Chechen one, and the situation came to be seen in the context of the historical Russian-Chechen conflict. Nevertheless, in spite of all the efforts of Chechen and Russian nationalists, the Chechen war was not primarily fought over ethnicity; rather, it was – and remains – a struggle between mafia-political clans. The conflict ceased to be an internal affair within Chechnya, because practically all the political forces of Russia found themselves drawn into it, trying to mould the situation in Chechnya according for their own opportunist political purposes.[9] Moreover, the conflict is becoming increasingly internationalized, with the separatists being supported, openly or secretly, by certain groups in the Middle East and elsewhere.

The protracted military intervention in Chechnya brought about colossal human and material losses. It turned world public opinion against Russia, and aggravated an existing crisis of power and society in Russia itself. The Russian forces in Chechnya proved unable to disarm the illegal armed formations without harming the local population. In an effort to flush out the fighters, the city of Grozny and its civilians – people who were largely opposed to the criminal regime of Dudaev – were bombed in late 1994 and early 1995. This is what the leaders of Ichkeria, Dudaev and his group, were striving for, engaging the Russian troops in a densely populated city. As a result, the regime destroyed the part of the population with anti-Dudaev inclinations. More than 300,000 inhabitants fled Grozny trying to escape the rocket bombardments by federal forces. The remaining population was used as a human shield by the fighters, and the abandoned property of hundreds of thousands of citizens was easy prey for looting fighters, as well as serving to attract fresh 'volunteers' from the rural regions of the republic. After taking the city, the embittered Ministry of Internal Affairs (MVD) contract soldiers went on looting and killing those citizens of Grozny who had not yet been robbed and finished off by the marauders from the Ichkeria army.

The inappropriate use of force by the federal army resulted in massive losses among the civilian population, thereby overshadowing the crimes of the Dudaev regime in the eyes of the people of Chechnya and provoking a wave of hatred towards the Russian army. Moreover, it brought into the struggle those sections of Chechen society that had kept out of the conflict prior to the bombardments. Before the Russian intervention Dudaev's popularity had fallen dramatically; soon after the Russian military intervention he became a national symbol for a significant proportion of the Chechen people. The opposition that supported union with Russia and opposed Dudaev was discredited. The remainder of Dudaev's army, let out of the city, retreated into the mountains and woods, and later started to attack the federal forces in small mobile groups. Yet by Spring 1995, the Russian army took over Vedeno and Shatoi, the last strongholds of the fighters. The generals were determined to finish off the separatists; it seemed that the war was coming to an end.

---

[9] John Dunlop, *Russia Confronts Chechnya: Roots of a Separatist Conflict* (Cambridge, Cambridge University Press, 1998).

However on 14 June, a detachment of fighters headed by Shamil Basaev, one of the main military commanders on the separatist side, mysteriously turned up in Budennovsk in Stavropol *krai*, the region of Russia to the North of Chechnya. Taking hostage no fewer than two thousand sick women and children, they demanded that the Russian government stop military operations and withdraw troops from the territory of Chechnya. The prime minister, Viktor Chernomyrdin, began negotiations with Basaev and agreed to comply with the terrorists' demands. The terrorists were allowed to return to Chechnya, and negotiations started under the aegis of the Organization for Security and Co-operation in Europe (OSCE) in Grozny. A ceasefire was declared, but negotiations soon reached a deadlock and military operations resumed. It became obvious that as long as the war went on it would be impossible for Yeltsin to secure a second presidential term. Again the Kremlin decided to use Chechnya to achieve a pressing internal political task – in this case, electoral victory for Yeltsin. The attempt to regularize the situation in Chechnya became one of the main issues in the struggle for the Russian presidency. In April 1996 Dudaev was killed by a Russian rocket homing in on his mobile telephone, and in May the temporary acting Chechen president, Yandarbiev, went to Moscow and signed agreements on the cessation of military activities. The peacemaking process with Chechnya secured Yeltsin's re-election for the Russian presidency for a second term. After the end of the presidential campaign, the Chechnya issue faded into the political background. The acute phase of the war appeared to have passed and the conflict became less intense.

On 6 August 1996 600 fighters entered Grozny and, meeting practically no resistance, they took over the city. It still remains a mystery how this could have happened. Having allowed the fighters into Grozny, the Kremlin betrayed the ideals of the anti-Dudaev opposition and breathed new life into the desperate struggle of the separatist leaders. On 31 August 1996 Alexander Lebed and Aslan Maskhadov signed the Khasavyurt agreement (see Appendix 1). The military defeat was not the main factor in achieving peace; Russia had lost the war long before the fighters 'captured' Grozny. It lost the war when the Chechen fighters took on the character of a pervasive force able to pass freely into the most highly-guarded areas. They moved as 'spirits', like the Afghan mujahidin. The war was lost when the authorities in Moscow and other Russian cities started to use illegal acts limiting the rights and freedoms of Russian citizens of Chechen nationality.

Maskhadov's Regime

Aslan Maskhadov, the leader of the Chechen forces in the first war, won the Chechen presidential elections of 27 January 1997. These elections, however, were far from being free and fair. First, half a million refugees, citizens of Chechnya, were unable to take part in them. Second, the elections were essentially uncontested, since the only group that could participate in them were representatives of the victorious 'military party'. The anti-separatist element of Chechnya's population was practically excluded from the electoral process and was unable to nominate its candidates. Nevertheless, the presidential and parliamentary elections in Chechnya gave rise to hope and expectation that the new authorities would adopt a policy of internal Chechen reconciliation and normalization of relations with Russia. An agreement 'On Peace and Cooperation' between the Russian Federation and Chechnya 'Ichkeria', signed by President Yeltsin and the president of Chechnya Maskhadov in Moscow on 12 May 1997, represented a break-through in relations between official Grozny and Moscow (see Appendix 2). This document might have formed the basis for peace and the revival of Chechnya; however, this was not to come to pass.

The three years after the first Chechen war did not bring Chechnya national harmony or civic peace. Indeed, it became obvious for everyone that the Chechen crisis has as much to do with internal factors as external ones, above all the conflict within Chechen society. President Maskhadov failed to consolidate Chechen society, to act as a unifying leader of the nation who might bind together its political and economic elites. The state of Ichkeria failed to achieve international legal recognition (de jure), or to build institutions of public power that were able to protect the basic rights and freedoms of citizens. The quasi-elite of Chechnya that came to power reflected only the interests of the 'victorious' military party and separatist forces. Having sided with the armed minority of the population and having rejected collaboration with centrist political forces and the more developed part of the population, loyal to Russia, Maskhadov aggravated the split in the Chechen society that had existed since 1991. As a result, the regime lost the trust not only of the population in Chechnya itself but also in Russia, where the majority of Chechens (over 500,000) are to be found. Against this background, the political and military confrontation of military groupings for power, control and sources of profits intensified. The struggle above all was between the military commanders of the first war, religious authorities, bandit groupings, and the forces loyal to president Maskhadov.

The power crisis reached a critical juncture in 1998. Its main protagonists were, on the one hand the president, his executive powers and the armed forces under his control, and on the other, the military-political opposition from the former front commanders on the other. The presidential side tried to conduct a political dialogue, whereas the armed opposition, in particular the Wahhabis (fundamentalist Islamicists looking to Saudi Arabia for support), demonstrated contempt towards the authorities, resorting to secret armed actions with the aim of removing Maskhadov and his supporters. In September 1998, the infamous field commanders Salman Raduev, Shamil Basaev and others publicly accused Maskhadov of making a secret deal with Moscow and of betraying Chechen national interests, and demanded his resignation. The Chechen president refused, accusing his opponents of anti-constitutional actions. At the same time, Maskhadov dismissed the government headed by Basaev, taking over the duties of prime minister himself. Maskhadov had hoped that allowing Basaev into the leading position in the government would buy his loyalty, but the latter was unwilling to relinquish the pursuit of his own agenda, above all now the Islamisation of the republic. The majority in parliament, headed by the speaker R. Alikhadzhiev, supported the actions of the Chechen president. However, any measures taken by Maskhadov with the aim of restoring order and disarming the illegal paramilitary formations met with powerful opposition by the leaders of the armed opposition, the former comrades-in-arms of the president. Maskhadov gradually lost control over the former field commanders and over the territory beyond the city of Grozny. Chechnya found itself divided into the fiefdoms of the field commanders, who held sway over the population. Maskhadov fell victim to the forces that he himself had brought to power. Having become hostage to extremist ideas from the very start of a fully independent Chechnya, Maskhadov was left to deal with the national radicals and lost.

During the three-year period of Maskhadov's rule in Chechnya, practically nothing was achieved in terms of restoring the economy and the social sphere, and there was a lack of any constructive effort to do so. There was a real threat of an ecological and epidemiological catastrophe. The cities and destroyed villages were not rebuilt, and thousands inhabited dilapidated housing with no sewerage, no water and often no electricity. There was no medical provision to speak of. People were dying of epidemics and starvation, with the death rate among children particularly high, and practically all the population were in need of some sort of psychotherapy.[10] Apart from a few private colleges, schools and higher educational institutions were not fully functioning. The process of Arabization continued, above all in the form of the Islamisation of the republic and the imposition of Sharia law, and there were clear indications of the disintegration of economic and cultural ties within society. The population was still fleeing the republic. According to the 1989 census the republic had 1,270,000 inhabitants, of whom 30 per cent were Russians and Russian-speakers. Before the second Chechen campaign, the population of Ichkeria did not exceed 400,000 inhabitants, with only about 50,000 Russians left in Chechnya; only those who had nowhere to go remained in the republic.

In Maskhadov's Chechnya the majority of the population endured destitution and degradation accompanied by the continuing enrichment of the leaders of the regime, 'the new Chechens', and the ringleaders of the armed bands who 'grabbed' the national wealth. The situation was aggravated by the fact that underworld groups dominated society, which since 1991 had used the national ideal in their interests. Chechnya became an international criminal cesspit. According to the Russian and Chechen authorities, prior to the beginning of the counter-terrorist operation there were 157 armed

---

[10] Andrew Meier, *Chechnya: To the Heart of a Conflict* (New York, W. W. Norton, 2004).

groups active in the republic, who divided among themselves income and spheres of influence. Owing to its organized criminality, Chechnya became the biggest producer, consumer and dealer in narcotics and weapons in South Russia. Pro-regime groups controlled oil pipelines and the illegal trade in oil products, while other organized groups of criminals specialized in robberies, kidnapping and trade in 'live' goods.

The regions of the North Caucasus contiguous with Chechnya were also drawn into criminal business. In Ingushetia, Dagestan, Stavropol and North Ossetia, a network of staging posts were created, and the importation and sale of oil products out of Chechnya was organized on a large scale. This business was extremely profitable, not only for the regional mafia structures, but also for the government officials and security and law-enforcement organs that were drawn into the process.

In Chechnya there was violation of human rights on a mass scale. Murder, arrests, kidnapping and trade in human beings became commonplace. On average, in Chechnya there were 60–70 crimes a week, including 8 to 10 murders. This is only the tip of the iceberg. The authorities and power structures of the regime were directly involved in the crimes. A slave market openly operated in the centre of Grozny, with hundreds of people (mainly Chechens) held captive as hostages and subjected to violence. Kidnapping people for exchange acquired epidemic proportions, with more than 3,500 Chechens ransomed between 1996 and 1999. Bandits and terrorists killed thousands of Chechens, many of whom had fought against separatists and mercenaries, including hundreds of Chechens who had been decorated with Russian orders and medals for their participation in the anti-terrorist operation. Two of them, Martan Yusup Elmurzaev, head of administration of the city of Urus-Martan, and 15-year-old Mohammed Tashuhadzhiev, were posthumously awarded Heroes of Russia.

Not only did Chechnya become the criminal cesspool of the CIS countries; it also became a base for international terrorism. Terrorists from many different countries became active on its territory, with their activities financed by foreign extremist centres. The group of the infamous Saudi-born terrorist Habib Abd al-Rahman, known as Khattab, who had previously fought in Afghanistan, consisted of a few hundred foreign hirelings; under his leadership Wahhabi training centres helped prepare fighters and were organized and sent for active duty in Chechnya. From Azerbaijan and Georgia, there was a constant flow both of mercenaries, but also of weapons, narcotics and foreign currency. With the internationalizing of the Chechen resistance, Maskhadov and the field commanders sank into the background. Khattab paid the money, and thus 'ordered the music'. Terrorist acts were carried out not only in Chechnya but also in other parts of Russia.

Chechen sovereignty (or as Movladi Udugov put it, 'the Chechen state') turned into an unprecedented free area for ordinary Chechens to be killed, defamed, robbed, kidnapped with impunity, or to die of sickness and starvation. The separatists led a poverty-stricken Chechnya to the brink of national catastrophe, and were pushing it towards a new full-scale war. The unprecedented increase in crime, bloody inter-clan and inter-*teip* struggles, trade in slaves and many other factors, demonstrated Grozny's inability of to fight the bandits, and the inability of the regime to transform itself into a public authority. The situation in the Chechen Republic reached deadlock: the opposing forces in Chechnya found themselves incapable of settling the systemic crisis either by political or coercive methods. There had to be an alternative to armed separatism. This could be served by the modernized part of the Chechen society both in Chechnya and abroad. However, it remained unfulfilled.

The essence of Chechen policy in the Kremlin at this time was formulated by the secretary of the Security Council, Boris Berezovsky, and can be reduced to the elementary postulate: 'that which cannot be bought for money, can be bought for a lot of money' – quite often his own. In diplomatic terms, this effectively meant that the Kremlin not only recognized the separatist regime but also promised the leaders of Ichkeria financial and economic help in exchange for keeping Chechnya within Russia. However, there was insufficient money in the Russian treasury, and the new formula for settling the Chechen conflict failed.[11] The taming of the separatists by granting them political concessions and financial resources was interpreted as an indication of Russia's weakness by the leaders of Ichkeria and only served to whet their appetite.

The refusal of the federal centre to cooperate with other political forces in Chechnya was another failure of Kremlin policy. Having supported Maskhadov's regime, the Kremlin essentially recognized the right of the separatists (the armed minority of the population) to be the only legal exponent of the will of the Chechen people. This revealed the limitations of the post-war political settlement of the Chechen crisis. Having recognised the authority of the national radicals, the Kremlin alienated the majority of Chechen society, loyal to Russia, and the only section of the population that was capable of rejecting the policy of confrontation with Russia and developing an alternative to armed separatism and the attempt to implant Islamic fundamentalism in Chechnya. There was yet another important drawback in the Kremlin's approach. Its Chechen policy was subject to short-term influences and failed to devise a strategic view of the question. Naturally, such short-termism could only lead to the results that we are witnessing today in Chechnya. The saddest thing is that both Maskhadov and the federal centre realised that Chechnya was turning into the base for international terrorism but did not try to prevent it. The process was deliberately allowed to drift,

---

[11] Matthew Evangelista, *The Chechen Wars: Will Russia go the Way of the Soviet Union?* (Washington, DC, Brookings institution Press, 2003), Chapter 3.

with not a single agreed decision on the stabilization of the Chechen situation being fulfilled.

The Second Chechen Campaign

In early August 1999 the situation in the mountain regions of Dagestan bordering Chechnya became strained. Groups of fighters from Chechnya managed to penetrate the Dagestani districts of Tsumadi and Botlikh, occupying over ten villages and proclaiming an Islamic republic in that part of highland Dagestan. The terrorists Basaev and Khattab led the military actions of Dagestani and Chechen 'Wahhabis' to free Dagestan from 'non-believers'. The events assumed the proportions of a large-scale military campaign, with the use of force and regular engagements. However, the Wahhabi gamble on obtaining the support of the population in the struggle against the corrupt Dagestan authorities did not materialize. The actions of the federal army and the leadership of the republic were widely supported by the population of Dagestan, whereas the fighters were perceived as an armed invasion from outside, and this was the decisive factor in turning the local population against them. The authorities managed to play on the national feelings of the Dagestanis, who took the Wahhabi actions as a Chechen invasion (irrespective of the fact that 80 per cent of the bandits who attacked Dagestan were Dagestanis and mercenaries). Maskhadov played unwittingly into the hands of the proponents of a renewed anti-Chechen campaign by failing to adopt a coherent position and not condemning Basaev's and Khattab's actions.[12]

By the end of August, under the pressure of the federal army, the Wahhabis left the villages of Tsumadi and Botlikh districts for Chechnya. However, on 5 September, in the heat of the military action in the villages of Karamakhi and Chabanmakhi, they invaded the Novolaksky district of Dagestan. According to Basaev, the aim of this invasion was to distract the forces assaulting Karamakhi and Chabanmakhi. This time, the Wahhabis counted on the support of the Chechen-Akkins (a local Chechen ethnic group) and the Laks, whose leaders had been persecuted by the republican authorities. However, this gamble did not work out. N. Khachilaev, the leader of the Laks who was in opposition to the authorities, decided not to support the Wahhabis, declaring that he would have nothing to do with them. The leaders of the Akkin community also declared their loyalty to the Dagestan authorities. However, the invasion markedly increased inter-ethnic tension in the region. The Chechen-Akkins found themselves in the crossfire of groundless accusations.

---

[12] Enver Kisriev and Robert Ware, 'Conflict and Catharsis: A Report on Developments in Dagestan Following the Incursions of August and September 1999', *Nationalities Papers*, Vol. 28, No. 3, September 2000, pp. 479–522.

Basaev's raid on Dagestan and the explosions in Moscow achieved their main aim: to prepare the ground for Russian public opinion's acceptance of the use of force to resolve the Chechen problem. The bombing of apartment blocks in Buinaksk, Moscow and Volgodonsk created a climate of fear and, to a degree, retribution against Chechens, although the involvement of Chechens in these atrocities remains uncertain.[13] In a common impulse, both the authorities and civil society supported the new military campaign in Chechnya. It was as if a play was being performed, and all the actors in this political drama played their assigned roles brilliantly. Khattab and Basaev received their money and quietly left Dagestan, the Kremlin strategists secured the electoral victory of the new president of Russia, the Russian soldiers yet again heroically laid down their lives, and the interests of the people of Russia, Chechnya and Dagestan were once again sacrificed to political opportunism.

Rocket and artillery bombardments of Chechnya started on 5 September at the frontier, and spread to Grozny on 23 September. The second Chechen campaign had started. Learning lessons from the first Chechen campaign, Russian generals avoided frontal attacks and contact combat, preferring air raids and artillery assaults. The new tactic was designed to minimize the loss of Russian soldiers and officers, and to inflict maximum casualties on the enemy by using the latest military tactics and equipment. The second Chechen campaign was accompanied by an anti-Chechen campaign in the mass media, unprecedented in its ferocity, in connection with the terrorist acts in Moscow. All Chechens were immediately perceived as suspects. The mass persecution of all Russian citizens of Chechen nationality began, above all through the checking of registration documents.

Unlike in the first Chechen war, the separatists received comparatively little support from the Chechen population. Moreover, people at first welcomed the Russian army, hoping it would defend them from the arbitrary brutalities and exploitation that had characterized the weak rule of the previous years. However, the excessive use of force by the Russian forces soon caused the death of many civilians, as well as mass migration from Russian air raids and artillery bombardments. The number of forced migrants, who found shelter mainly in Ingushetia, reached 200,000. Their sufferings beggar description. Before the eyes of the whole world, a new tragedy unfolded in Chechnya.[14]

In 2001 the Chechen fighters intensified their activities in an attempt to demonstrate not only their capacity to carry out large-scale military actions

---

[13] For a good discussion of the issues, see Andrew Jack, *Inside Putin's Russia* (London, Granta, 2004), 'Prisoner of the Caucasus', pp. 88–130.

[14] See Anna Politkovskaya, *A Dirty War: A Russian Reporter in Chechnya*, Introduction by Thomas de Waal, translated by John Crowfoot (London, The Harvill Press, 2001); and her *A Small Corner of Hell*, translated by Alexander Burry and Tatiana Tulchinsky (Chicago, University of Chicago Press Pounds, 2003).

but also to persuade the federal centre to conduct negotiations. Such a calculation was not implausible, taking into account the pressure from Western countries and the international community, demanding an end to the excessive use of force in dealing with the civilian population of Chechnya and to observe fundamental human rights. However, the terrorist acts of 11 September 2001 blighted all such hopes. The only hope for negotiations was by ending military activities and handing over weapons. Thus, the situation in Chechnya can only be described as a deadlock. The federal centre cannot solve the Chechen problem by using force, and continuing the tactics of robbery and violence risks provoking mass resistance by the population and a negative reaction from the West. The behaviour of the armed forces in Chechnya, the level of their professionalism and choice of methods (including the notorious *zachistki*) are not appropriate to deal with the situation in the republic.[15] The Chechen separatists also have a tough choice: either to continue the armed struggle under extremely unfavourable conditions and to continue to inflict great suffering on the Chechen people, or to seek acceptable conditions for finding a way out of the deadlock.

The Policy of the Federal Centre

On 23 March 2003, for the first time in Chechnya's history, a constitutional referendum was held. The people voted on the draft constitution for the republic and two draft laws on the election of the president and parliament of the Chechen republic. According to official statistics, 89.48 per cent of the electorate took part in the plebiscite, of whom 97 per cent voted in favour. However, it was not possible to win unanimous support everywhere. The highest vote against the constitution was in the mountainous Itum-Kalinsky district. Here the draft constitution was opposed by 11.2 per cent of those who voted, around three times the percentage of the national average throughout the republic. The referendum result in Chechnya is comparable with election results of the Soviet period. It was a big surprise for politicians and observers in Moscow and Grozny. 'They exceeded all our expectations', as Putin commented the day after the referendum at a meeting of the federal government: 'The people of Chechnya have done this directly and in a most democratic manner'. According to Putin, the main outcome of the referendum was that 'we have dealt with the last serious problem connected with the territorial integrity of Russia'. The president stressed that 'the Chechen people have chosen in favour of peace', therefore 'all those who have not yet laid down their arms are from this time onwards fighting not only for their false ideals but also directly against their own people'.[16]

---

[15] See Dmitri Trenin and Aleksei Malashenko, with Anatol Lieven, *Russia's Restless Frontier: The Chechnya Factor in Post-Soviet Russia* (Washington DC, Carnegie Endowment for International Peace, 2004), Chapter 5, 'War and the Military', for details.

[16] *Nezavisimaya gazeta*, 25 March 2003.

The referendum demonstrated that the situation in Chechnya was under federal control, and this time, the fighters did not even try to disrupt the vote. However, not everyone shared the authorities' optimism about the result of the referendum; one newspaper noted that '[t]he real turnout was quite low and workers with the electoral commissions know how to make them higher'.[17] It seems that even before the vote had taken place the opposing sides in Chechnya had decided how they would treat the result. Above all, a significantly higher number of votes were cast than there were voters on the electoral registers. However, both those in favour and those opposed to the referendum must nevertheless recognize the unexpectedly high involvement of Chechen citizens in the vote. This phenomenon, which remains a mystery for many, demonstrates that despite all the horrors of war, the majority of Chechens retain their common sense. They voted in favour of a normal human life for peace and stability, which was promised them by the authorities. The dream of full independence has been discredited by the way that it has been pursued by the radical nationalists, although it was never taken seriously by the majority of Chechens. In voting (or in agreeing that the electoral commissions would vote for them) the citizens of Chechnya did not go too deeply into the content of the – far from perfect – draft constitution, but spoke decisively against the lawlessness and violence of both the federal authorities as well as the fighters.

The referendum greatly strengthened the position of Kadyrov and his Kremlin-appointed administration. Kadyrov had gradually been building up his power based on his extended clan, and his forces now became the most powerful local military grouping in the republic. The referendum put an end to the republic of 'Ichkeria' and its president Maskhadov, and Kadyrov's power gained a degree of legitimacy. With the support of the Kremlin potential challengers were barred from the presidential elections of 5 October 2003, and on a turnout of 87.7 per cent Kadyov easily won the ballot. He began to rule over Chechnya as over a feudal domain. The federal centre itself began to depend on Kadyrov to resolve Chechen problems. Kadyrov became an independent political actor, while his son, Ramzan, developed a powerful independent militia. Kadyrov demanded broad autonomy from Moscow and received Putin's support. The republic gained serious tax and customs benefits and control over domestic energy resources in the republic. Kadyrov established full control over the Chechen MVD, whose head was Alu Alkhanov. Even some of the fighters came over to Kadyrov's side: a group of separatist fighters headed by S Khatiev gave up their arms in March 2003. Kadyrov's strong position was demonstrated by his frequent meetings with the Russian president at a time when many powerful governors were not able to gain an audience with him.

Kadyrov's administration, however, had no real power, and was preoccupied with resolving its own venal problems, and did not enjoy the support

[17] *Vedomosti*, 24 March 2003.

of the population. There is no real trust or close co-operation between the federal and the Chechen power structures, although on a personal level Putin enjoyed good relations with pro-Moscow leaders such as Kadyrov and Alkhanov. The fighters seek to exploit tensions between Moscow and Grozny. Rivalry between groups at the federal and local levels for control over the financial resources allocated for the rebuilding of the economy and the social sphere of Chechnya impede the reconstruction of the republic. The alienation of the population from the authorities, its inability to exert influence on the local administration as well as on the military, badly affects the social atmosphere. In Chechnya, 50 social organizations are registered but they hardly function. There is no guarantee of safety for the work of the independent press, legal and social organisations.

The murder of Kadyrov and five other people, including the chair of the State Council, Khussain Isaev, on 9 May 2004 was intended to destroy the political system that had been constructed so laboriously and to undermine the stabilization process. Having become deeply loyal to Putin personally and enjoying his trust, Kadyrov at the same time sought to limit the arbitrariness of the Russian military in relations with the Chechen population. This led to a positive evaluation of his work among Chechens and at the same time served as an important motivation for his own armed forces, consisting of local people. As a fierce opponent of Maskhadov and Basaev, Kadyrov gave active support to federal forces against the paramilitary forces. At the same time, working independently of Russian forces, he conducted active and reasonably effective negotiations with authoritative figures from the armed opposition. By use of amnesties, Kadyrov was able to gain control over the extraction and processing of Chechnya's oil resources; and this in turn brought him into conflict with the military, which controlled the grey economy of the republic.

Following the terrorist act of 9 May there was a real threat of destabilization of the situation in Chechnya and in the North Caucasus region as a whole. There was also an intensified political struggle for redistribution of power and property and a growth in violence by illegal armed detachments. The Chechen population once again found itself defenceless against the threat of terror and worsening social and economic living conditions. On the other hand, despite the complexity of the situation, there was once again (as in the earlier referendum and presidential election) a historic opportunity to resolve the permanent political crisis in Chechnya through popular, democratic and honest elections and the creation of legal organs of power that enjoy the trust of the population. In the event, candidates for the election of president of 29 August 2004 were once again pre-selected, allowing Alkhanov to win an effectively uncontested election. According to official statistics, major-general of the militia, Alu Alkhanov, on an 85 per cent turnout, received 73 per cent of the vote. The Chechen electoral commission ensured that the selection was an exact copy of the previous elections held on 5 October of the previous year. The only serious competitor to Alkhanov, the entrepreneur Malik Saidullaev, was removed from the list of potential candidates. There were undoubtedly major violations of the electoral procedures, but the election did reflect the overall mood of the republic. For the elections to be valid over 30 per cent of the electorate had to take part, of which half had to be won by the leading candidate. The fact that Alkhanov won this necessary minimum cannot be doubted.

The campaign was conducted against a background of escalating terror. On 22 June 2004 a raid on Nazran, the capital of Ingushetia, led to the deaths of 98 people and 104 injured, 23 of the dead were civilians, 29 were Ingush militiamen, 2 were Chechen MVD workers, 10 FSB workers, 19 soldiers and 7 border guards. Three bodies were unrecognizable. Many of the dead were high officials. The raid in Ingushetia demonstrated a complete lack of coordination between the bodies responsible for security in the North Caucasus, as well as the lack of a single chain of command. On 21 August 2004 a large group of separatists entered the Chechen capital and, dividing into smaller groups, they engaged federal forces for over three hours. Some fighters in vehicles were able to fire on government buildings. At least 78 people died in this raid. How a group of about 300 people were able to enter the capital of Chechnya without impediment is completely incomprehensible. In Ingushetia at least there was an element of surprise, but in Chechnya on the eve of presidential elections the security forces had already been in a state of heightened preparedness. On 24 August, in Tula and Rostov regions, two civilian airliners flying out of Domodedovo airport in Moscow exploded and came down in flames; these explosions were separated by an interval of one minute, The total death toll was 90 people, 73 passengers and 17 crew. On the evening of 31 August, in Moscow, not far from the Riga metro station, according to official statistics, 10 people were killed and 46 injured in a bomb blast.

On 1 September 2004, on the first day of the new academic year, school No.1 in the town of Beslan in North Ossetia was seized and the children and staff kept hostage for three days. The name of this hitherto unknown town entered contemporary world history as the most terrible and inhuman symbol of terror. As a result of the attack by the bandits, 330 people lost their lives, including 172 children. At least 776 others were injured, including 338 children. According to official statistics, the school was seized by 32 fighters, one of whom was taken alive. The raid, we now know, was organized by Shamil Basaev. The seizure of hostages in Beslan was designed to inflame interethnic tensions in the region, in particular between the Ingush and Ossets, to broaden the geographical scope of the Chechen conflict.[18] Tensions remain high in the region.

Towards the Future?

'Russia needs Chechnya without Chechens'; this was the fear expressed by Chechens in the early days of the war and by refugees. As in 1994, faced

---

[18] In autumn 1992, in Prigorodnyi district, the first bloody ethnic conflict took place on Russian territory. 700 people were killed on the borders of North Ossetia and Ingushetia and many thousand Ingush were forced to leave their homes in Ossetia and flee to Ingushetia.

with the Russian threat the armed groups from 1999 were forced to unite and stop the internecine civil strife. On the other hand, the violent confrontation between the Wahhabis and the followers of traditional Islam continued. Many field commanders and leaders of traditional Muslim religious authorities were prepared to make peace with Russia for the sake of eliminating the Wahhabis.[19] The leaders of Ichkeria lacked the support of the population that they had enjoyed during the first Chechen war, with the population losing any remaining illusions by the chaos of the interwar period between 1996 and 1999.

The death of Chechen civilians on a mass scale was the most terrible and severe consequence of the war (for details, see Chapter 7). In Chechnya twenty civilians were killed for each serviceman lost. This correlation is higher than in previous local wars (see Chapter 10 in this volume). Like so many contemporary 'local' wars, brutality is one of the characteristics of the Chechen conflict. The policy of merciless war follows the very nature of the criminal revolution, which took place in Russia and Chechnya. Among the consequences of the war is the moral and psychological trauma inflicted on all the Chechen people. The psychological wounds of this war will heal only slowly, both in Chechen and Russian societies. One should mention the material and economic losses caused as a consequence of the military actions. Out of 428 villages, 380 were bombed, 70 per cent of houses were destroyed, and large parts of the city of Grozny were razed to the ground. More than 60,000 houses and administrative building have been completely or partially destroyed. Industry and agriculture were damaged, and more than 30,000 hectares of agricultural land were contaminated with explosives. In the second Chechen war the oil industry was not spared either. Air and rail communications were disrupted. The republic and the population were looted. Over 90 per cent of the population are now unemployed. The educated, and those with qualifications or able to work left the Chechen Republic, precisely that section of the nation that represents its potential and hope for the future. In the ten years of suffering, Chechnya has returned to becoming a pre-industrial society of artisans. A whole generation of young men (some 150–200,000) have grown up without education. Many of them are involved in the armed conflict and the only skill that they have is to wage war. They may form (if they have not already) a bloc of support for the continuation of war and violence in Chechnya, unless they can be engaged in labour or education.

The cultural losses in this war are simply irreplaceable. In Chechnya, the Academy of Science, the University, the Petroleum and Pedagogical institutes, some twenty branch and research institutes, the same number of technical colleges, most schools, hospitals and libraries have been looted and wrecked; museums, theatres, archives, private libraries and other cultural valuables of

---

[19] See Trenin and Malashenko, *Russia's Restless Frontier*, Chapter 4, 'The Islamic Factor', for details.

the people have been eradicated. Many cultural valuables have been destroyed, burnt down and irrevocably lost. Even more defenceless than Chechens were the ethnic Russians. In the early 1990s over 300,000 left the republic. Thousands were murdered by bandits or killed by bombs in the wars. Today, Russians in Grozny, in Gudermes and in Cossack villages are the most defenceless category of citizens in Chechnya. They are daily victims of criminal forces. Cossacks are regularly kidnapped and killed.

The main forces of the separatists in Chechnya have been defeated. The fighters have neither the power nor the means to carry out large-scale military actions. Instead, they turned to the tactic of diversion and partisan war. Today in Chechnya, children, old people and women die, the civilians live in poverty and suffer at the hands of both the fighters and the federals. The problem of human rights has been exacerbated. From 2002 the desultory character of the war turned into a very profitable business for both the warring sides. The civilian population of the republic is its main victim.

The credit of trust in the national-radicals has been completely exhausted. This deprives the Chechen pseudo-nationalists of any historical potential. However, this process of marginalizing the national radicals will become irreversible only if one condition is satisfied: if Chechens become citizens enjoying full rights in Russia, occupying their proper place (as the third largest ethnic group in the country) in a single multinational federal legal state – the Russian Federation. However, the reality is that while at the beginning of the second Chechen campaign the population welcomed Russian troops in the hope of gaining protection from the bandits; now, after multiple acts of violence and looting by the federal army, the attitude towards them changes for the worse with every passing day. Winning back the trust of the Chechen people is the main condition for settlement of the conflict. The ideology of Wahhabis and the power of kleptocracy are alien to the vast majority of the Chechen people. The opposing powers in Chechnya proved incapable of resolving the crisis either by political or by coercive methods and thus provoked a new war. An alternative to armed separatism is necessary. Only the pro-Russian part of Chechen society can offer this alternative.

However, while there have been some moves towards peaceful reconstruction, the socio-political situation in and around Chechnya continues to be defined by the armed confrontation of the opposing sides. It is obvious for many observers now that there are no objective reasons for the continuation of the Chechen conflict. The Chechen national idea was betrayed and discredited by the separatist leaders, and today it rests at the level of mindless and murderous war. As for Russia, peace and stability in the Caucasus is in its strategic interests. However, in spite of this, conflict is still being fuelled: the war in Chechnya has become a lucrative business for all its participants. The struggle for power and property continues. Instead of effectively fighting the terrorists and bandits directly, the federals recoup their losses by exploiting the civilian population, extorting money at checkpoints and stealing their property. The separatists' leaders and mercenaries move unhindered, and the population suffer not only from the bandits but also from the harsh *zachistki* of the federal troops. The disproportionate use of force against the civilian population has become the main obstacle in the settlement of the conflict. Chechen distrust of the federal centre remains high. Having found themselves between the hammer and anvil, the local population despise the bandits and distrust the federals.

3

Chechnya and Tatarstan: Differences in Search of an Explanation

Valentin Mikhailov

After ten years of intense conflict with the federal centre, Chechnya remains one of the most intractable problems for Russia. Various ideas have been advanced for its solution, some of which draw on comparisons between the rebellious republic and Tatarstan, another republic of the Russian Federation that once proclaimed its desire for independence but has now considerably tempered its demands. Such comparisons are usually based on a number of incidents during 1991–2, when tensions between Tatarstan and the federal centre ran high. During the same period, the media reported that ethnic relations within Tatarstan had also deteriorated considerably. On this basis a number of authors have argued that there are grounds for drawing direct parallels between Tatarstan and events in Chechnya.

Context and Comparisons

Edward W. Walker describes Tatarstan as 'the ethnic republic within Russia that, along with Chechnya, seemed the most likely to secede in late 1991'.[1] This is the mildest perspective on the situation in the republic; others characterized it in much stronger terms. For instance, Radio Liberty reported in 1997 that on the eve of the 21 March 1992 referendum on Tatarstan's status 'it seemed that Tatarstan was on the verge of bloodshed. The situation was no less heated than in Chechnya two years later'.[2] While suggesting that

---

[1] EW Walker, 'The Dog That Didn't Bark: Tatarstan and Asymmetrical Federalism in Russia', *The Harriman Review*, Vol. 9, No. 4, Winter 1996, pp. 1–35.
[2] Radio programme 'Rossiia vchera, segodnia, zavtra', on the fifth anniversary of the referendum in Tatarstan. Hosted by Anatoly Streliany, Radio Liberty, 2 April 1997.

'in the beginning, the nationalist stances of Chechnya and Tatarstan were similar', Ravil Bukharaev poses the following question: 'Why then has Tatarstan avoided war with Moscow, while being so close to it at the second stage of obtaining state sovereignty?'[3] In the Russian electronic version of the same book the author describes the situation in Tatarstan as even more dramatic: 'A tragedy similar to that which befell the unfortunate Chechnya in 1994 could have occurred in Tatarstan as early as 1992. War seemed inevitable'.[4] Bruce Allyn, programme manager of the Conflict Managing Group (CMG), also claimed that in those two regions – Chechnya and Tatarstan – 'the ethnic and political situation was particularly dangerous'.[5]

Signing a treaty with Tatarstan in 1994, the Russian side deemed it possible to turn a blind eye to discrepancies between the clauses of the treaty and the federal constitution. Chairman of the Russian Presidential Commission on the Preparation of Intra-State Treaties Sergei Shakhrai explained that the federal centre was so compliant because the other possible scenario – 'demanding that, as the first step towards normalisation of relations, Tatarstan unconditionally changes its constitutional norms' – 'would have definitely brought the situation to a political and judicial deadlock, *a version of which can be observed today in the Chechen Republic*'.[6]

Jean-Robert Raviot assessed Russian-Tatar relations as peaceful; however, he felt that this 'idyll' was surprising at a time when the central authorities were engaged in bloody war against Chechnya instead of seeking political solutions to the problem there. The reason for Raviot's bewilderment was the fact that 'before the collapse of the USSR, the legal status of Chechnya (an autonomous republic within the Russian Soviet Federal Socialist Republic) had been exactly the same as that of Tatarstan'.[7] The author apparently assumed that if republics initially have the same legal status, this is likely to lead to a similar outcome: military conflict.

Moscow-based political commentator Vladimir Razuvaev also endorsed the theory that 'an outburst of ethnic clashes' was highly probable in Tatarstan in the early 1990s – and he was far from the only analyst in the capital to do so.[8] Two factors have been advanced as reasons for

---

[3] R Bukharaev, *The Model of Tatarstan under President Mintimer Shaimiev* (New York, St. Martin's Press, 1999), p. 116. See also the supplemented Russian version of this book: R. Bukharaev, *Model' Tatarstana pod rukovodstvom Presidenta Mintimera Shaimieva* (St. Petersburg, BLITs, 2000), p. 130.

[4] Bukharaev, *Model' Tatarstana pod rukovodstvom Presidenta Mintimera Shaimieva*, p. 60.

[5] Bruce Allyn, 'Gaagskaia initsiativa', *Panorama Forum*, No. 2, 1995, p. 70.

[6] SM Shakhrai, 'Rol' dogovornykh protsessov v ukreplenii I razvitii rossiiskogo gosudarstvo', in MN Guboglo (ed.), *Federalizm vlasti i vlast' federalizma* (Moscow, State Duma, Russian Academy of Sciences, 1997), p. 152.

[7] Jean-Robert Raviot, 'Tatarstan v tsentre sozdania federalnoi struktury Rossii: inventsia suvereniteta – soiuza', in *Islam v Tatarskom mire* (Kazan, Panorama Forum, 1997). p. 293.

[8] V Razuvaev, 'Shaimiev nuzhen Rossii: Kremlevskaya administratsiya deistvuet zhestko i prosto', *Nezavisimaya gazeta*, November 2000; reprinted in *Vechernyaya Kazan*, 9 November 2000.

'Tatarstan managing to avoid disaster while Chechnya plunged into war'. These are: the wisdom of President Mintimer Shaimiev; and the sensible policy of the federal authorities towards Tatarstan. Trudy Rubin of *The Philadelphia Inquirer* argues that 'Part of the answer lies in the different characters of the leaders of Tatarstan and Chechnya'.[9] The author believes that Tatarstan staved off invasion and bloodshed because, unlike Chechnya, it never called for actual secession from the Russian Federation. Instead, argues Rubin, Shaimiev carried on a dialogue with Russian President Boris Yeltsin for nearly three years, finally concluding a bilateral treaty in 1994. Razuvaev agrees with that. He also believes that the policy pursued by the president of Tatarstan in the early 1990s 'helped to avert the worst'. On the eve of yet another re-election of Shaimiev as president, this was the main argument to convince Razuvaev that 'Russia needs Shaimiev, and that is why he simply has a duty to stay in office for a third term in his republic'.

Bukharaev goes even further, maintaining that it was 'measured actions by the leaders of Tatarstan, whose commitment to national interests has always gone hand in hand with wise political prudence', that helped prevent war at the last minute.[10] Bruce Allyn, on the contrary, gives credit to Moscow, which 'abstained from using military force to keep Tatarstan within the Federation', and believes that this fact allowed the situation to stabilize, benefiting the moderate leader, president Shaimiev.[11] In both analyses the common suggestion is that the conflict between Tatarstan and the federal centre was so strong that at certain points it could have developed into a military one.

An interesting peculiarity is that the elite in Tatarstan itself was interested in maintaining the image of the republic as a place where fierce, even bloody, ethnic conflicts were likely to erupt. Six months before the Russian State Duma elections of December 1999 Shaimiev, the leader of the new and potentially very powerful political bloc of governors All Russia (Vsya Rossiya), said about the events of the early 1990s: 'The treaty gave us time, and that, I should tell you, is priceless. *Because things here could have become worse than in Chechnya, you know.* We responded to people's demands with a sensible policy. Even though some extreme nationalist movements continue to criticise it even today and call it betrayal. [Author's italics]'[12]

A similar version of events was encouraged and developed in neighbouring Bashkortostan. It might seem now as though the period when the threat of ethnic unrest in this republic was an effective argument, as in

---

[9] Trudy Rubin, 'Holding Russians at Bay', *The Philadelphia Inquirer*, 15 February 1995.

[10] Bukharaev. *Model' Tatarstana pod rukovodstvom Prezidenta Mintimera Shaimieva*, p. 60.

[11] Allyn, 'Gaagskaia initsiativa', pp. 70–1.

[12] P Akopov, A Khantsevich, 'Mintimer Shaimiev: I have not once uttered the word "independence": The president of Tatarstan is proud to be trusted by both the Russians and the Tatars equally', *NG Regiony*, No. 11, June 1999, p. 4.

Tatarstan, had already become history. However, this is how a 'source in the Russian presidential administration' explains why the presidential administration unexpectedly favoured the incumbent president Rakhimov on the eve of the second round of presidential elections on 7 December 2003. The source claims that the sharp turn in the Kremlin's tactics resulted from 'an intensive campaign by [Rakhimov's] support group in Moscow', consisting of representatives of power and business structures. They 'lobbied the country's leaders' with the threat, among other things, of 'another Chechnya', and threatened complications for Russia in its relations with Islamic countries if the ethnic Bashkir Rakhimov yielded power [to the Russian Veremeenko].[13]

Leaders of Tatarstan and Bashkortostan have always been fond of comparing their republics to Chechnya. First of all, any demands and declarations by the authorities of these republics seemed moderate or even modest against the background of the Chechen conflict, even if they exceeded anything that governments of any other administrative unit of the federation could afford or dare to do. Another important factor was that the comparison made the leaders of the two republics look like calm, measured and civilized politicians who controlled the situation in a troubled region.

What is the basis for drawing such close parallels between Chechnya and Tatarstan? Did the people of the republic in the Volga region really feel the same burning desire for independence as the people of the self-pronounced state of Ichkeria? Are there enough facts to warrant such a claim? For instance, doubts could arise from discrepancies in the reports about protests taking place in Kazan, the capital of Tatarstan, at the time. Some reports claimed that the protests drew up to 50,000 participants, while others said the number was 25 times smaller. The difference is crucial because a demonstration with two thousand participants in a city of one million residents is not enough to talk about 'a popular movement'.[14]

A possible explanation could be that in the early 1990s, following the events in Yugoslavia and some republics of the former USSR, the world lived in anticipation of ethnic clashes in all regions where it appeared that the societal parameters corresponded with the expectations of scholars. First of all, there was the strong idea that the probability of conflict is greater in a society with a high degree of ethnic, religious and linguistic diversity than in more homogeneous communities. If all major conflicts in the first post-Soviet years were ethnic (Yugoslavia, Nagorno-Karabakh, Chechnya, Abkhazia) then, following this logic, it could be expected

---

[13] A Voronina, A Nikolskii, V Ivanov, 'Rakhimov peresilivaet: Pered vtorym turom ego oblaskala Moskva', *Vedomosti*, 17 December 2003.

[14] V Mikhailov, 'Preobrazovaniya v Tatarstane v postsovetskii period: vzglyady zapadnykh issledovatelei', in A Kulik (ed.), *Professionaly za sotrudnichestvo*, issue 5 (Moscow, Dobrosvet, 2002), pp. 248–9. Witnesses report that in the 1990s there was not a single demonstration involving nationalists with more than 2,000 participants in Kazan.

that other ethnically heterogeneous republics would also become ethnic battlegrounds. Moreover, M. Steven Fish and Robin S. Brooks argue that 'some scholars even use fractionalization as a proxy for the degree of conflict in society, operating on the assumption that higher fractionalization automatically translates into more conflict'.[15]

Tatarstan, whose population is almost neatly divided into two ethnic groups (48.5 per cent are Tatars and 43.3 per cent are Russians), seemed to fit perfectly into such a theory. The mass media routinely reported the declarations of nationalist organizations and the decisions of official authorities demanding the establishment of special relations with Russia. That is why scholars and politicians easily agreed with, and indeed one could say that they expected and accepted, the above interpretation of events in Tatarstan.

Comparative Factors

Let us now examine the two main issues outlined above. First, does the image of Tatarstan as an ethnically troublesome region correspond to reality (as compared to Chechnya)? Second, how appropriate is it to compare the tensions and the possibility of choosing the separatist path in this republic in the early 1990s to Chechnya?[16]

Geography

The geographical location of the two republics could not be more different. Located on a plain near the centre of European Russia, Tatarstan borders four regions (Kirov, Orenburg, Samara and Ulyanovsk) and four republics (Marii-El, Udmurtia, Bashkortostan and Chuvashia). In the Soviet period only those republics with a border that coincided in part with the state border of the USSR could gain the status of a union republic. Proximity to Moscow – only 800km by road or railway from Kazan – made the Federation's consent to the secession of the republic even more unlikely. The River Volga, a historical symbol of the utmost significance for the Tatar people, represents a special, irreplaceable – and as many believe, sacred – symbol for Russia as well. Dividing it into parts that would belong to different states was virtually impossible from the perspective of both an ordinary citizen and a state leader. Everyone in Tatarstan was aware of this factor.

During his famous visit to Tatarstan and Bashkortostan in early August 1990, Boris Yeltsin made a populist promise: 'You will have absolutely all rights – you will take whichever of those rights you wish. Whichever ones

---

[15] MS Fish and RS Brooks, 'Does Diversity Hurt Democracy?', *Journal of Democracy*, Vol. 15, No. 1, 2004, p. 162.

[16] Parts of the analysis and conclusions apply to Bashkortostan as well, but I will not focus on that here.

you will want to delegate to Russia, you will'.[17] However, he also warned at a meeting in Kazan, 'But you are situated in the centre of Russia – and you should think about that'. That is why many, if not everyone, realised that the enclave location of the republic was a serious impediment to the creation of an independent state.

Furthermore, Tatarstan is located at the intersection of two strategically important transport routes – the Volga and the Trans-Siberian Railway. There is a constant and intensive traffic of residents and guests from neighbouring and remote regions, to and from Moscow and cities in Siberia (Omsk is just two days away by train). These human flows presented a major problem for the republic's elite during preparations for the referendum on the republic's status, as the elite's propaganda efforts to convince voters that living conditions in the republic were better than in the neighbouring regions were often negated by people's personal experiences.

Unlike Tatarstan, Chechnya is on Russia's state border. Its extended border with Georgia encourages the separatist tendencies of supporters of independence. Chechen militants have attempted also to exploit part of the neighbouring Georgian territory – the Pankisi Gorge – as a place to regroup and train their units. Proximity to several conflict zones contributed to the military and ideological potential of groups of separatists, nationalists and extreme Islamists. Training for Chechen fighters and commanders was conducted in conditions of real warfare. It is well known that their military leaders, for instance Shamil Basaev and Ruslan Gelaev, acquired military experience while fighting in Abkhazia in 1992, well before the 1994–6 Chechen war.

A strategically important railway runs through Chechnya and links Rostov-on-Don with Baku (and then with Tbilisi and Yerevan). However, this stopped having an inhibiting effect on the conflict after 1992 when the systematic robbing of passing trains began, with the connivance of the Chechen leader, Dzhokhar Dudaev. The traffic became limited and then dried up altogether. All unifying factors gradually fell away as the conflict escalated.

To conclude, there is another comparison. The territory of Tatarstan is a slightly hilly plain covered with less forest than many other parts of Russia. The share of tilled land here is 86 per cent. In contrast, most of Chechnya is 'an endless space of hills dressed in woods, which rise, wave after wave, towards mighty walls and bastions of Jurassic limestone crowned with high tops of the two main ridges'.[18] The opportunity for armed resistance and guerrilla warfare offered by such a landscape have been traditionally exploited by Chechens in all of their resistance campaigns: 'The Caucasus imposes two of the most difficult modes of war on an invading

---

[17] E Chernobrovkina, 'Boris Yeltsin: Vmeste my sil'nee, *Vechernyaya Kazan*, 13 August 1990.
[18] JF Baddeley, *The Rugged Flanks of the Caucasus* (London, 1940), Vol. 1, p. 55.

army: mountain and forest warfare... Both give enormous advantages to the defenders... Before any battle the invaders have to overcome nature.'[19]

The Historical Legacy

Two periods are particularly significant in this context: the nineteenth century and the Soviet period. They include the years that have been most vividly preserved in popular memory. The brutal thirty-year war in the North Caucasus, which Russia waged against local nations from 1830, is well known. From 1834 Imam Shamil led the resistance of Chechnya and Dagestan for most of the war. Many Russian military commanders suffered defeat in that campaign. Both sides estimated their losses at tens of thousands. The war ended only after Shamil was taken prisoner in September 1859. However, eighteen years later Chechens rebelled again.[20]

Another very important historical event for the Chechen nation took place in the mid-twentieth century. That is when Chechens became one of the twelve peoples who were subjected to unlawful forcible expulsion from their homelands.[21] The brutal mass deportation occurred during the days of 23–26 February 1944 when 387,000 Chechens and 91,000 Ingush were deported to Kazakhstan, Kyrgyzstan and Western Siberia. Many thousands were shot and burned during the expulsion operation, and at least a quarter of the displaced people died en route to the place of their relocation.[22] Returning to their native land was made possible only by a decree of the Supreme Soviet of the Soviet Union issued in June 1956. Besides Chechens, the decree also included Karachai and Ingush.

As can be imagined, by 1990 the collective memory of the nation had not yet managed to recover from these major historical traumas when Chechens found themselves facing a new ordeal. Unlike Chechens, Tatars did not offer mass resistance to Russian rulers during the two centuries before the 1917 revolution, and contemporary Tatar historian Indus Tagirov admits: 'The centuries that have passed since the fall of the Tatar Khanates created a *certain "void" in the history of national statehood'*.[23] During the Stalin period the Tatars of the Volga region were not singled out for any special repressive campaign.

[19] M Gammer, *Muslim Resistance to the Tsar: Shamil and the Conquest of Chechnya and Dagestan*, published in Russian as M Gammer, *Shamil. Musul'manskoe soprotivlenie tsarizmu: Zavoevanie Chechni i Dagestana* (Moscow, Kronpress, 1998), p. 33.

[20] Gammer, *Shamil*, pp. 403–10, 392.

[21] Svetlana Alieva (ed.), *Tak eto bylo: Natsional'nye repressii v SSSR v 1919–1952 gg.*, Vols. 1, 2, 3, (Moscow, Insan, 1993).

[22] R Sakwa, 'A Just War Fought Unjustly?', in Bruno Coppieters and Richard Sakwa (eds.), *Contextualizing Secession* (Oxford, Oxford University Press, 2003), p. 161. D. Khozhaev, 'Genotsid', in Alieva (ed.), *Tak eto bylo*, Vol. 2, 1993, pp. 169–73.

[23] IR Tagirov, *Istoriia natsional'noi gosudarstvennosti tatarskogo naroda i Tatarstana. Kazan* (Kazan, Tatknigoizdat, 2000), p. 148.

Population

According to the 1989 census, 57.8 per cent of the population in the Chechen-Ingush Autonomous Soviet Socialist Republic were Chechens, 12.9 per cent were Ingush and 23.1 per cent - Russians. In two districts – Malgobek and Nazran – Ingush were the absolute majority. In another district, Sunzhen, where the three main ethnic groups were represented more equally, Ingush were again the largest group. These three districts later became the Ingush Republic, which was established in 1991 and formally recognised in June 1992. On the territory of the remaining eleven districts and the city of Grozny, which later became the Chechen Republic, almost two thirds (65.7 per cent) of the population were Chechens and a quarter (24.8 per cent) were Russians. Four out of five Russians lived in the capital of the republic.[24] Notably, results of the last Soviet census showed the high concentration of Chechens in most rural districts. Chechens made up over 94 per cent of the population in six out of eleven districts, and 86 per cent in two others. Only in the capital Grozny did Russians constitute a majority: 53 per cent. The city's population also comprised 30.5 per cent Chechens and 5.4 per cent Ingush.

At the same time, in 1989 Tatars made up 48.5 per cent of the population in Tatarstan, while 43.3 per cent of the population were Russians and 3.7 per cent Chuvash. The long-term stability of these ratios is evident from all Soviet censuses from 1926, and reflects the stability of ties and relations between the major ethnic groups in the republic. These groups were distributed more evenly throughout the administrative-territorial units of the republic than in Chechnya. Russians comprised over half of the population in the cities of Kazan, Bugulma, Elabuga, Zelenodolsk and Chistopol as well as in seven of the 43 rural districts. In a number of other districts and cities the percentages of Russians and Tatars were approximately equal, as was the case, for instance, in the second largest city of the republic, Naberezhnye Chelny (40.6 per cent Tatars and 48.7 per cent Russians). Only in four of 39 rural districts did Tatars constitute over 90 per cent, and in another four they comprised over 80 per cent of the population.

First, therefore, there was an approximate parity between the two ethnic groups in Tatarstan, which remained stable for many decades. Second, unlike in Chechnya, there was practically no change in the ratio between the main ethnic groups both in the republic as a whole and in individual cities and regions for many decades before the events in question. Third, the so-called 'titular' nationality, the ethnic group whose name is given to the republic of Tatarstan, was more evenly distributed throughout the territory of the republic than was the case in Chechnya where major ethnic groups populated separate territories. And, finally, the fourth and very important

---

[24] M Yusupov, 'Chechenskaya Respublika', in VA Tishkov (ed.), *Na puti k perepisi* (Moscow, Aviaizdat, 2003), p. 506. Author's calculation for the 11 districts.

conclusion that is partially connected with the previous one: Tatarstan had a high degree (up to one-third) of interethnic marriages (mostly between Tatars and Russians).[25] This suggests relatively relaxed and peaceful relations between these two major ethnic groups in the republic. In Chechnya, and in the Chechen-Ingush autonomous republic before that, two factors prevented inter-ethnic marriages: considerable division of ethnic groups according to place of residence; and memory of the recent (only two generations earlier) deportation of the Chechen and Ingush peoples.

Both Chechens and Tatars are scattered throughout Russia. Two thirds of Tatars live outside Tatarstan in the rest of Russia. Clearly, the influence that the Tatar and Chechen diasporas exert on processes of national consolidation, the strengthening of statehood and support for the political regimes in power in the two republics does not have a uniform orientation. There are a number of Chechen and Tatar public organizations in Russia, and many influential representatives of these two nations live there. Some of them are in mild or even quite definite opposition to the ruling elites of their republics. At the same time, many Tatars who work and live in the Russian capital and regions are quite independent and express their readiness to follow the course of Shaimiev's policy or support nationalist organizations in Tatarstan. That is why comparing the influence of the diasporas on the situations in Chechnya and Tatarstan is a complex and ambiguous question.

There is also a peculiarity related to the ethnic composition of Tatarstan that has no parallel in Chechnya. The unity of the Tatar nation – the factor on which the republic's elite relied to buttress its position in the 1990s – was not subjected to doubts by researchers at the time. But even then a problem existed, as it did many years before, which does not apply to Chechnya. The 2002 census in Russia identified the Orthodox Tatars, an ethnic group that previously was considered part of the single Tatar nation. This census provoked an active political campaign in Tatarstan, with activists of nationalist movements and scholars, supported by government representatives, arguing that defining Orthodox Tatars, as well as Siberian Tatars, as distinct ethnic groups in the list of nationalities was an attempt to divide the Tatar nation into separate groups.[26] The main problem concerned the Orthodox Tatars, who do not practise Islam. David C Lewis wrote: 'About 10 percent of the Tatars did become Russian Orthodox, although Muslim Tatars like to claim that the ancestors of these converts were actually pagans living in the area rather than Muslims. In any case, these Orthodox Tatars have now become almost an ethnic group in themselves, having their own distinctive customs, dress and language'.[27]

[25] David C Lewis, 'Ethnicity and Religion in Tatarstan and the Volga-Ural Region', *Central Asian Survey*, Vol. 16, No. 2, 1997, pp. 215–36.
[26] R Abdrakhmanov, 'Respublika Tatarstan', in Tishkov (ed.), *Na puti k perepisi*, pp. 423–5.
[27] Lewis, 'Ethnicity and Religion in Tatarstan'.

At a time when the republic's elite had spent the last few years trying to gather all the resources of the Tatar nation together in one centre,[28] the 2002 census threatened to set back such efforts. Ethnographer Sergei Sokolovsky believes that 'Political discussion of the "Orthodox Tatar question" in the [2002] census is given urgency by the possibility that the ethnocratic regime can lose its legitimacy by losing the majority'. He argues that discounting Orthodox Tatars would bring the percentage of the Tatars, which make up 52 per cent of the population, down by 5 to 7 per cent, making 'even more conspicuous the existing shift of balance in the power structures in favour of the Tatars, which has attracted the attention of analysts for a long time and which makes one see the defenders of ethnocracy in the supporters of federalism'.[29] Russian television and mass media demonstrated enough examples during the process of the census when the authorities used various excuses to reduce the number of those wishing to register as Orthodox Tatars.

Ildar Gabdrafikov and Guzel Baimukhametova expressed the view that, in terms of registering Tatars and Bashkirs in Bashkortostan, the 2002 census turned from a purely technical procedure of gathering information about people, into 'a political campaign of correcting the number of people in this or that ethnic group'.[30] The same description can justly be applied to the problem of Orthodox Tatars in Tatarstan in 2002. It follows from the above that one tenth of those who are considered to be part of the single Tatar nation can hardly identify their interests with the interests of the Volga region Tatars who belong to another religion, Islam. Besides, the Church of the Orthodox Tatars has much in common with the Russian Orthodox Church, and so the Orthodox Tatars can neither support nor help anyone who would take nationalist anti-Russian stances.

Therefore, even if a rough assessment of the ethnic composition of Chechnya and Tatarstan yields similar results, a more detailed analysis reveals peculiarities that might prove decisive when assessing the likelihood of ethnic conflicts. A number of the abovementioned distinctive features of Tatarstan would considerably impede the development of conflict if anyone tried to stir it up.

---

[28] 'We are standing at a historic turning point when we must take a qualitative leap and create Greater Tatarstan, i.e. to link the state structures of the republic with official organizations of the Tatar nation. The orbit of Greater Tatarstan must include public organisations, mass media, economic and other structures. Joining together of financial, governmental, informational, intellectual and other resources would produce a cumulative effect, and the potential of the Tatars will skyrocket', R Khakimov, 'Kto ty, Tatarin?', in 'Bol'shoi Tatarstan', *Vostochnyi ekspress*, 24–30 May 2002, p. 8.

[29] S Sokolovsky, '"Tatarskaya problema" vo Vserossiiskoi perepisi naselenia', E Filippova, D Arel, K Guseff (eds), *Etnografiia perepisi – 2002* (Moscow, Aviaizdat, 2003), p. 332. The same percentage of Orthodox Tatars is reported by Abdrakhmanov, 'Respublika Tatarstan', in Tishkov (ed.), *Na puti k perepisi*, p. 431.

[30] I Gabdrafikov, G Baimukhametova, 'Respublika Bashkortostan', in Tishkov (ed.), *Na puti k perepisi*, pp. 82–3, 90, 89.

Language and Communication

According to the 1989 census, 99.9 per cent of Chechens and 96.6 per cent of Tatars named their national language as their native one. At that time 73.4 per cent of Chechens and 77.2 per cent of Tatars stated that they were fluent in Russian (this figure was 85.3 per cent among Tatars living in towns). That is where the similarities ended, because only 48.3 per cent of Tatars actually spoke their national language as their native one, while the number of Chechens in the same category was double. Some 94 per cent of them spoke the Chechen language with their families, whereas almost half of the Tatars in Kazan and about 40 per cent of residents in other towns of the republic spoke either Russian with their families or used both languages, Tatar and Russian.

The dynamics during the subsequent years shows that Tatars did not reduce their use of Russian in education and communication. On the contrary, there may well have been a small tendency towards its increase. Thus, the 1997 census showed that 6.8 per cent of Tatars living in Tatarstan considered Russian to be their native language (we saw that this number was 3.4 per cent in 1989) and about the same number of respondents did not speak Tatar at all. At the same time nearly 11 per cent of Tatars said they wanted their children to receive schooling *only in Russian*. In Chechnya only one per cent of Chechens considered Russian to be their native tongue in 1989, and only 2 per cent of Chechen children in primary schools received their schooling only in Russian in 1991.

Thus, two characteristics – recognition of their native language as the national one, and Russian as a second language – were identifiable in both the republics before 1990–5. However, the Tatars' actual *command* of their native language was only half as developed as that of the Chechens, something that can be accounted for by the fact that Tatars in Tatarstan support the idea of speaking both Russian and Tatar at the same time;[31] this indirectly indicates the lack of conflict between the republic's two main ethnic groups.

Culture and Science

Even before the 1917 revolution, Russians in the Kazan province did not live like strangers or missionaries, but were already deeply rooted in the land. If in the nineteenth century the foreign population in Chechnya was colonial in character, in Tatarstan – in Kazan and other towns and villages – Russians, Ukrainians, Jews and others were natural components of the population. Along with prominent figures of the developing Tatar culture,

[31] Yusupov, 'Chechenskaya Respublika', data from tables on pp. 496, 508. F Kh. Mukhametshin and GA Isaev, *Respublika Tatarstan v zerkale obshchestvennogo mneniia* (Kazan, Kabinet ministrov RT, 1998), pp. 66–70. Abdrakhmanov, 'Respublika Tatarstan', pp. 431–3.

many other notables studied, lived and worked here, including famous scientists as Nikolai Lobachevsky, Nikolai Zinin, Aleksandr Butlerov; stars of medicine Vladimir Bekhterev and Aleksandr Vishnevsky; singer Fedor Shaliapin; writers Sergei Aksakov, Leo Tolstoy and Maxim Gorky; poets Gavriil Derzhavin, Evgeny Baratynsky and Velimir Khlebnikov; painter Nikolai Feshin; sculptor Stepan Erzia; and, finally, Vladimir Ulyanov (Lenin) They are well known far beyond the borders of Russia. Kazan's scientific schools of chemistry, various branches of medicine, oriental studies and mathematics were all highly ranked in Russian scholarship.[32] All of this has been woven into the very fabric of history of the republic and Kazan; it is commemorated through a large number of memorials and plaques, recorded in the most popular schoolbooks and has been taught in the numerous universities of the republic throughout the Soviet years: many generations of both Tatars and Russians were brought up on these facts.

Here, it might reasonably be objected that, if fierce ethnic clashes were to flare up, ardent supporters of independence could interpret these very same facts as evidence of 'colonization' and suppression of the Tatar people by the Russians. But it did not happen. No recognized leaders in the republic could exploit the national theme in such a way because the authority of the above-listed Russian figures of culture and science has been too strong. The attempt would be doomed to fail.

Moreover, it was the former activists of the Communist Party of the Soviet Union (CPSU), who before 1990 were first secretaries of district, city and regional committees, who were now the real leaders in the republic's bid for independence. Their shift from international positions to national ones was sudden. But their upbringing and degree of integration into the Russian elite meant they could not, nor did they want to, contribute to actions that would undermine the authority of Russian culture. Yet the role of the political elite in Tatarstan during the years when separatist stances were on the rise was much broader and more significant than simply consolidating Russian cultural authority.

Political Elite

Raviot argued that in Tatarstan 'the political elite not only managed to keep power, but also fully controlled the movement towards independence'.[33] In this respect Tatarstan followed the pattern of all the ex-Soviet Central Asian republics, but not the Baltic republics, the South Caucasian republics and Ukraine, which saw the transfer of power from an old elite to a new one, a transfer in which national movements, created from below, played a significant role.

---

[32] *Istoriya Kazani: Kniga pervaya* (Kazan, Tatknigoizdat, 1988), p. 352. R Bikbulatov, *Kazan: znamenitye liudi* (Kazan, Zaman, 2003), p. 272.

[33] Raviot, 'Tatarstan v tsentre sozdania federalnoi struktury Rossii', p. 301.

Mary McAuley provided a good qualitative assessment of the role played by the old elite in Tatarstan, when she reported that in 1992 seventeen out of thirty ministers, committee chairmen and several other figures of comparable standing (for instance, chairman of the Supreme Court of Tatarstan) in Shaimiev's government had previously held official party posts as first secretaries of city or district party committees or high positions in the regional committee (obkom) of the CPSU.[34] Midkhat Farukshin's analysis confirms this observation using a larger sample. He found that, of 96 members of the Tatarstan elite involved in political and administrative decision-making in 1994, 92 per cent were members of the former *nomenklatura*, 70 per cent of them being former party or Soviet officials.[35] Three years later, Oleg Zaznaev conducted a similar investigation and found that, although some personnel changes had occurred in the ranks of the local elite after 1994, they 'did not affect the qualitative characteristics of this elite'.[36]

In Chechnya, leaders of the Chechen National Congress wrested power from the old elite. During the coup d'état in August 1991, 'the Chechen National Congress under the leadership of Dzhokhar Dudaev gave unconditional support to Russian President Boris Yeltsin, and after the coup failed it vigorously began finishing off the local party and Soviet *nomenklatura*'.[37]

In Tatarstan the leader of the elite since September 1989 has been Mintimer Shaimiev, who graduated from an agricultural institute in 1959 and then began his career in the Communist Party as a regional committee instructor eight years later. Before becoming chairman of the Supreme Soviet of Tatarstan in April 1990, Shaimiev went through all levels of the party and administrative hierarchy: he served as a minister for melioration and water resources, deputy chairman and later chairman of the Council of Ministers of the republic, first secretary of the party regional committee and member of the Central Committee of the CPSU.

His Chechen counterpart Doku Zavgaev had a similar service record up until 1991. Graduate of an agricultural institute, he was a minister for agriculture in the republic, then a secretary, second secretary and, finally in 1989, first secretary of the party regional committee. In March 1990, he

---

[34] Mary McAuley, *Russia's Politics of Uncertainty* (Cambridge, Cambridge University Press 1997), pp. 49–50.

[35] M Farukshin, 'Politicheskaya elita v Tatarstane: vyzovy vremeni i trudnosti adaptatsii', *Polis*, No. 6, 1994, pp. 69–79. *Nomeklatura* denoted groups of people approved by a corresponding Party committee as good workers loyal to the Party line. There were four main levels of *nomenklatura*: central (Moscow), republican, regional, and district.

[36] O Zaznaev, 'Respublika Tatarstan', *Konstitutsionnoe pravo: Vostochnoevropeiskoe obozrenie*, No. 2 (19), 1997, p. 70.

[37] A Malashenko, D Trenin, *Vremya Yuga: Rossiia v Chechne, Chechnya v Rossii* (Moscow, Gendalf, 2002), p. 16. Details of Dudaev's struggle for power in the republic, in which a substantial role was played by the conflicts between Yeltsin and Mikhail Gorbachev (Russia and the Soviet Union) and between Yeltsin and Ruslan Khasbulatov (Russian executive and legislative branches), have been recounted by Richard Sakwa in his 'A Just War', pp. 159–62.

became chairman of the Supreme Soviet of the Chechen-Ingush Autonomous Soviet Socialist Republic. Vigorous actions by the Chechen National Congress and its leader Dudaev pushed Zavgaev out of the leadership position. It can be suggested with a high degree of certainty that had Zavgaev managed to stay in power, events in Chechnya would have followed a very different – peaceful – scenario. 'The relative ease with which Zavgaev was overthrown, however, revealed precisely the weakness of *nomenklatura* rule in Chechnya'.[38]

In Tatarstan, ethnic groups were fairly equally represented in various sectors of administration, but Tatars noticeably dominated the political leadership. As of 1 January 1991 the Tatarstan republican committee of the CPSU had 189 members and candidates, with Tatars accounting for 56 per cent, and 68.6 per cent (35 out of 51) of the first secretaries of the party district and city committees in Tatarstan were Tatars.[39] This fact alone considerably undermined nationalist accusations that Moscow was pursuing an imperialist policy. In Chechnya, 'attempts in the 1980s to achieve the indigenisation *(korenizatsiya)* of Soviet rule were belated... allowing the insurgent part of the Sovietised elite (represented by Dudaev) to come to power by appealing to marginalised groups in society'.[40]

Although formally both the constitution of Chechnya (March 1992) and constitution of Tatarstan (November 1992) contained analogous clauses on the sovereignty of these republics, attitudes towards the two leaders differed. Shaimiev managed to convince Moscow to start negotiations on the future bilateral agreement, which for him was the priority. Relations between Dudaev, the politically inexperienced major-general just out of the Soviet air force, and Russian leaders got off to a bad start. The Kremlin regarded him and his supporters 'extremely negatively'.[41] Dudaev had to carry the heavy burden of being personally disliked in Moscow until the very end. Some believe that had Dudaev and Yeltsin met personally, the first Chechen war that started in late 1994 could have been avoided.

The main reason why this meeting never took place might have been Dudaev's political inexperience, his orientation towards the only acceptable (from his point of view) result. Richard Sakwa believes that his ideological policy was 'fuelled not so much by utopian aspirations but by an uncritical historicism, closing down the scope for discussion of the past and the contestation of different policies for the future'.[42] Shaimiev, having been well connected in Moscow since Soviet times, preferred to continue to adjust his actions to the current circumstances and trying to avoid excessively irritating

---

[38] Sakwa, 'A Just War', p. 167.
[39] V Mikhailov, *Respublika Tatarstan: demokratiya ili suverenitet?* (Moscow, PUBLISHER, 2004), p. 418.
[40] Sakwa, 'A Just War', p. 167.
[41] Malashenko and Trenin, *Vremya Yuga*, p. 17.
[42] Sakwa, 'A Just War', p. 166.

the Russian leaders. His tactics veered from temporising to vigorous action, depending on the political situation in Moscow at a given moment. His rich experience in the Party benefited him immensely, enabling him to predict how the Russian side would react to his actions. But even if he or anyone else in his position decided to take some very radical steps that would lead to the break-up of the republic's ties with the Russian Federation, the remaining party-administrative and Soviet elite of Tatarstan would not have supported him. However, all his actions were governed by the attempt to defend the interests of the republic's elite, so they had no reason to be unhappy.

Public Opinion and Parties

It is hard to assess the extent of public support for the policy pursued by Tatarstan's and Chechnya's regional leaders in their relations with the central authorities in 1990–2, or to know what the general public thought about the future status of their republics. In recent years there has been an acute lack of independent public opinion polls and sociological research in the republics. It became virtually impossible to receive reliable information in Chechnya after the military campaign started. However, the mass exodus of Russians and other nationalities from Chechnya that started in 1990 clearly indicates the views of those who left, and demonstrates a deep polarization of views on the national question among various ethnic groups. This was also the year when the Chechen National Congress and its executive committee started active work. The Congress rapidly became an influential political actor, albeit one unrecognized either by Moscow or Grozny.[43] If in 1990, for every ten Russians moving to Chechnya, there were 26 Russians leaving the republic, in 1991 this ratio was 10 to 72; in 1992 10 to 179; and 10 to 250 in 1993. In the same years more Chechens and Ingush came into the republic than left it.[44]

In Tatarstan the proportions of various ethnic groups did not fluctuate sharply, although the last decade or so showed a tendency towards larger migratory inflows of Tatars than Russians.[45] Demographic data does not allow us to assess Chechen public opinion on key political questions, but judging by the active participation of the population in demonstrations and by support from political leaders, it can be concluded that during his first year Dudaev was strongly supported by the population. Later, in 1992, Chechen society began to split. By this time, Russians no longer played a significant role in Chechnya's internal politics while the opposition, gaining strength, began staging numerous lengthy protests. Thus, in mid-April 1993

---

[43] Malashenko and Trenin, *Vremya Yuga*, p. 15.
[44] Yusupov, 'Chechenskaya Respublika', data from tables on p. 507. The author writes (p. 494) that 'the Russian emigration acquired the character of an avalanche starting from the autumn of 1990'.
[45] Abdrakhmanov, 'Respublika Tatarstan', p. 423.

the opposition announced an 'indefinite rally' (which lasted several days) in central Grozny. By the summer of 1994 the view had become established in Moscow that pro-Russian Chechen public figures had consolidated their position and even controlled most of the republic's territory.[46] The republic was living through a genuine political conflict, which included a conflict between elites and a divided society.

Results of opinion polls conducted in December 1990 and September and October 1991 will help us assess the situation in Tatarstan. The first poll was conducted by the All-Russian Public Opinion Research Centre (VTsIOM); two others were carried out by a sociological group of the Supreme Soviet of Tatarstan. They were conducted with a considerable level of professionalism, and the results of all three coincide to a large degree, producing a clear picture of public opinion at the time.[47] Both in December 1990 and in September 1991, 11 per cent of the respondents, including 3 per cent of Russians and 18 per cent of Tatars, stood for the independent Tatarstan. However, 48 per cent, or more than four times the number, preferred the option of 'Tatarstan as a republic within the Russian Federation'. This was the opinion of approximately two thirds of Russians and about one third of Tatars. Hence, the number of separatists in the republic was slightly less than a quarter of the number of those who wished to preserve the status quo. In addition, another segment of the population (slightly over one third in December 1990) wished to see the status of Tatarstan elevated to the level of a republic within the Soviet Union. In September, when prospects of becoming a union republic faded after the August coup, this figure dropped to one quarter. Further understanding of the consequences of the coup and the actions of the republic authorities, which had challenged Russia again at the October session of the Supreme Soviet of Tatarstan, raised the percentage of those who objected to Tatarstan seceding from Russia to 64 per cent (44 per cent of Tatars and 84 per cent of Russians).

There was therefore little soil in which ethnic tensions could flourish, given that the substantial majority of Chechens had a clear preference for the republic's remaining within the Russian Federation. This was particularly the case as the capital, Kazan, and another major city, Naberezhnye Chelny, always had fewer supporters of independence than the republic as a whole (in September 1991 7.6 per cent and 9.3 per cent, respectively), thereby reducing the chances of the supporters of separatism becoming an effective force. It appears that the share of separatists in the republic did not increase ten years later. Only 10 per cent of experts in a 1999 poll, and 4 per cent in a poll conducted the following year, said that

---

[46] Malashenko and Trenin, *Vremya Yuga*, pp. 18–19.

[47] Mikhailov, *Respublika Tatarstan: demokratiya ili suverenitet?*, pp. 121–31. The results of these surveys were not published in the local press in much detail, and later the practice of conducting such representative studies with clearly formulated questions was either abandoned altogether or concealed from the public.

every nation of the Russian Federation should have independent statehood. The latter figure is lower than results of similar surveys in Stavropol, Astrakhan, Volgodonsk and Mordovia and far lower than results for Kabardino-Balkaria, Ingushetia and Ufa.[48]

The likelihood of a conflict can also be indicated by the factor of readiness of the population to take an active part in the conflict in the interests of their ethnic group. The Institute for Socio-Political Studies of the Russian Academy of Sciences has conducted surveys in various Russian towns for a number of years on this question. The results of a 1998 survey in Kazan revealed that the level of such willingness on the part of both Tatars and Russians here is no higher than in other major Russian cities.[49] Small organizations with a clear and defined nationalist agenda – the Tatar Public Centre (TOTs) and the Ittifak party – had no more than 9 per cent support during the 1990s. For instance, only 2 per cent of the population supported TOTs and 1.3 per cent supported Ittifak in June 1992, three months after the republic's referendum on the status of Tatarstan.[50]

All these findings undermine the presupposition that Shaimiev and his group were forced to act under pressure from the broad national movement. McAuley describes that 'The leadership hesitated, torn between fear of Moscow and of a national movement'; recounting the circumstances of passing the Declaration on State Sovereignty in 1990, she also writes of a 'crowd of about 30,000 people' that surrounded the Supreme Soviet building; elsewhere, she describes Shaimiev's sleepless night following a visit by leaders of the TOTs and Ittifak, after which he put forward a new draft of the declaration without mentioning the RSFSR, which was eventually passed.[51] However, could the representatives of TOTs and Ittifak, supported by fewer than ten per cent of the voters, possibly make the experienced leader nervous and forcing him to alter his position? Besides, as the introduction to this chapter has already stated, witnesses' reports suggest that the author exaggerated by many times the number of demonstrators.

I would suggest that the conclusion reached by Jeff Kahn is broadly correct. He observes that 'Declarations of sovereignty were made under the leadership of the *nomenklatura* elite… nationalists had no opportunity to engage in the process of drafting the document at its final stage'.[52]

---

[48] VN Ivanov and OA Yarovoi, *Rossiiskii federalism: stanovlenie i razvitie*, Second edition (Moscow, Institute of Socio-political Studies of the Russian Academy of Sciences, 2001), pp. 134–202. In 1999 49 experts were questioned, and 50 experts were questioned in 2000.

[49] VN Ivanov (ed.), *Rossiya federativnaya: problemy i perspektivy* (Moscow, ISPS RAS, 2001), pp. 126, 348–9. Unfortunately this large and authoritative study lacks data for Kazan for the earlier years, although there is material for other towns and cities, e.g. Moscow, Ufa and Petrozavodsk.

[50] Mikhailov, 'Preobrazovaniya v Tatarstane v postsovetskii period', p. 251.

[51] McAuley, *Russia's Politics of Uncertainty*, pp. 59, 57.

[52] J Kahn, 'The Parade of Sovereignties: Establishing the Vocabulary of the New Russian Federalism', mimeo, paper presented to the Fifth Annual Convention of the Association for

By running carefully selected articles in the press covering the session of the Tatarstan Supreme Soviet, 'Shaimiev's team wanted to show that the alternative could be much worse from Moscow's point of view. Their message to the Centre was: accept Shaimiev's approach as the most moderate path at this time'.[53]

The popular movements in Chechnya and Tatarstan therefore affected the actions of political leaders differently. The Tatar Public Centre, created with the assistance of the regional committee of the CPSU, openly supported Shaimiev through its members of the Supreme Soviet of Tatarstan. Its analogue in Chechnya – the Chechen National Congress – stood in opposition to Zavgaev, who had initiated its creation, choosing Dudaev as its leader in March 1991. In Tatarstan the protests of a noisy but manageable minority of Tatar nationalists served as an accompaniment to the elite's policy towards Moscow, softening and masking the fact that this policy went against the wishes of the people. Dudaev, on the contrary, did not orchestrate popular support from above (in the beginning he had no way of doing so); rather, he enjoyed spontaneous support. This was his strength, and this was also his weakness. In all the years of his administration and up to the start of the war with Russia, he failed to consolidate his authority and constantly had to respond to attacks from his opponents, including demonstrations organized by them.

Major Enterprises

There were many large enterprises and factories in Kazan, Naberezhnye Chelny, Nizhnekamsk, Almetevsk, Zelenodolsk, Chistopol and other towns. They were mostly enterprises of the military-industrial complex (VPK). Each of them had thousands – some tens of thousands – of engineers and workers, making up a disciplined, responsible and qualified workforce. For those who sought to arouse spontaneous popular support for sovereignty, the existence of such enterprises became a considerable impediment. Citizens working at the large enterprises were in to some extent organized simply by being within the structure of the enterprise, even if they were not involved in any party activity. This quality made them resistant to attempts at agitation or manipulation of public opinion. Besides, they personally felt the danger of major economic hardships that could arise were the declaration of independence to have been followed by the severance of economic ties with Russian enterprises, even if such a break proved only temporary.

Problems with the supply of raw materials and components, caused by the establishment of borders between the former Soviet republics, were

the Studies of Nationalities, New York, April 2000. p. 8. The author's conclusion is based on the analysis of the following documents: minutes of sessions of the republics' parliaments, commissions' reports, nationalist and official newspapers.

[53] Kahn, 'The Parade of Sovereignties', p. 15.

already evident by July 1990 when the draft declaration of independence began to be discussed in public. The administrative hierarchy in the republic was yet to be firmly established at the time, and heads of enterprises, especially those subordinate to the federal authorities, did not bother to conceal their views. Nor did they prevent their workers and colleagues from expressing their opinions. This is why, on the eve of signing the declaration, collectives of enterprises and institutes showered their deputies and the Supreme Soviet of Tatarstan with collectively signed letters. Each letter bore hundreds of signatures, up to one third of which belonged to Tatars. The absolute majority of those letters expressed support for the preservation of Tatarstan's status as a republic within the RSFSR.[54]

Later the situation changed. In the early 1990s, many large enterprises went through restructuring, and their employees suffered considerable job cuts. Their standard of living deteriorated. But even during the subsequent years, many tens of thousands of workers and engineers of the military-industrial complex could not be unconditionally counted on as a support base for the bilateral treaty of equal rights with the Russian Federation. This factor played a much lesser part in Chechnya than in Tatarstan. Chechnya had no enterprises that could be compared to KamAZ, or the two gigantic oil and chemistry enterprises in Nizhnekamsk, or the large factories in Kazan. By 27 October 1991, the day when Dudaev was elected president of the republic, many Russian specialists who formed the basis of the scientific and technical personnel at local enterprises had either left Chechnya already or were intending to do so in the near future.

Oil

The oil deposits under the soil of Tatarstan were frequently referred to by the nationalists at their rallies. They offered calculations of what had been extracted in the past (one slogan ran 'the Tatarstan Republic gave the country 2.5 billion tons of oil, and in return it got…?') and promised to transform the country into another Kuwait. Indeed, the republic can continue extracting 28 million tons of oil per year for many years, just as it did for the last decade. It seems a very strong argument, one sufficient to prompt the government into choosing the option of autonomous industrial development.

However, there exist two more compelling arguments that have a somewhat dampening effect on the desire for independence. First, the quality of oil in Tatarstan (with sulphur and paraffin admixtures) is so poor that it is often sold mixed with oil from Tyumen. Conditions for preparing the mixture for export are subject to negotiations, which makes Tatarstan dependent on the Russian side. Another type of close co-operation (if not dependence) is due to the inevitability of using oil pipelines, which are fully controlled by the Russian authorities.

---

[54] Mikhailov, *Respublika Tatarstan: demokratiya ili suverenitet?*, pp. 108–9.

Oil in Chechnya also played an important role in the secession issue. The volume of extracted petroleum was smaller, but its quality was so good that petrol could be produced using primitive equipment. Besides, insurgents have threatened to siphon off oil products from the Russian pipeline and have acquired resources by means of such blackmail. Later Akhmad Kadyrov, officially the Moscow-supported leader of Chechnya between 2000 and 2004, sought to bring the production and refining of oil under his own control, and took a defiant stand against the federal authorities on this question. At the same time oil continues to be exported by road from Chechnya. . The insurgents allow these trucks to pass freely, suggesting that all sides in Chechnya are interested in allowing this business to proceed unimpeded.

The experience of Tatarstan and Chechnya demonstrates that the presence of oil reserves, the infrastructure for its exploitation, transport and refining is a factor in intensifying separatist tendencies. The example of Bashkortostan, another republic with significant oil reserves, confirms this rule.

Military Aspect

After the Russian troops withdrew from Chechnya in 1991–2, for reasons that have not been adequately explained, a large arsenal of weapons was left behind.[55] These resources were so large that artillery shells seized a decade earlier were still being used by the insurgents to mine highways used by federal forces. This, combined with a significant potential for independence and a reluctance to elect leaders willing to negotiate, made for circumstances that brought about a tragic result: war. In Tatarstan the number of Russian troops was much smaller; besides, they, along with their weapons, withdrew from Tatarstan before the 1992 referendum. Only some of the internal affairs ministry units remained.

Conclusion

We have compared post-Soviet political events in Tatarstan and Chechnya, as well as their geographical and historical contexts. We demonstrated that the situation in Tatarstan had fundamentally different characteristics to those in Chechnya. In the case of Tatarstan, several factors were present, each of which could on its own prevent the escalation of separatist sentiments and considerably weaken people's incentives to support military resistance. These are primarily geographical and historical factors, relations between the main ethnic groups, qualities of the elite and its interaction with the hardcore nationalists.

---

[55] Sakwa, 'A Just War', p. 163.

What we might call the 'geographical' factor breaks down into several important components. In 1995, one of the leaders of a Tatar youth organisation, Azatlyk, made a slip at the end of a long diplomatic and politically correct talk: 'Had we, the Tatars, had mountains and the Chechen character, we would have also shown to Russia!'[56] Yet in addition to the lack of mountains, it was also significant that Tatarstan was an enclave on Russian territory, which had a key position on the Volga and the railway; Russia could not consent to its secession.

The main difference was that the situation in Chechnya was to a large extent determined by the ethnic factor. Dudaev's rise to power was backed by the Chechen nationalists, who still had fresh in their memory the mass deportation of the Chechen people in 1944 and its difficult return in 1956. The proportion of separatists for whom full independence was an ideal was not large, although it was greater than in Tatarstan; however, this group's motivation and level of resolution to take extreme measures to achieve that independence was very considerable. However impractical the approach and however unpredictable the further course of events would be, for them the question of independence was a matter of principle and could not be haggled over. In Tatarstan the question of attaining sovereignty was not the ultimate goal for its initiators – leaders of the political elite whose composition failed to change in 1989–91 – but rather a way for the elite to preserve its positions of power, which it had gained in Soviet times. For this reason alone its ambitions were limited from the start. In this respect, the conclusion reached by James Meek appears accurate: 'Neither Tatarstan nor Russia want the republic to leave the Russian Federation. Rather, the local elite would like to enjoy all the benefits of living in a large, potentially strong country without having to burden themselves with constitutional obligations'.[57]

The question of leaving the Federation was not urgent or important for the Tatar people, who had spent the last three centuries within Russia without any ethnic turbulence, and even less so for the multinational population of the republic who, as we have shown, mostly did not support separatist initiatives. The very idea that the Tatar people had historically aspired to national statehood was put forward and developed either in a more active or calmer mode, depending on the political circumstances of the moment, as an argument to be used in bargaining with Russian authorities. For instance, separatist rhetoric suddenly subsided considerably as soon as the positions of the elite became protected by the 1994 Treaty. On the contrary, in Chechnya, as Sakwa argues, 'the socio-political basis for the development of the Tatarstan variant in Chechnya was largely absent'.[58]

---

[56] Malashenko and Trenin, *Vremya Yuga*, p. 53.
[57] J Meek, 'Ethnicity Comes Between Mother Russia and her Sisters', *The Guardian*, 14 March 1998.
[58] Sakwa, 'A Just War', p. 167.

Let us return to the two questions we posed in the introduction. The potential for escalation of ethnic tensions and separatism existed in both republics; however, in Tatarstan it was considerably less than in Chechnya. A huge majority of the population here had no anti-Russian attitudes, and those who took a pronounced separatist stance found no support among the population. Farukshin, one of the leading experts on Tatarstan, believes that 'Tatarstan experienced no public protests under the banner of independence and secession from Russia; the people of Tatarstan, *including the Tatar nation, would never take up arms* and would not fight the federal troops for the sake of consolidating the rule of the local elite [Author's italics]'.[59] Furthermore, prominent representatives of the republic's political elite Farid Mukhametshin and Georgy Isaev themselves come to the conclusion that their analysis of public opinion polls from the period of 1989–98 'convincingly shows that there is no real basis in the republic for conflictual ethnic interaction to develop.'[60]

It can be seen from the above analysis that there are no grounds for arguing that the levels of tension and possibilities for taking the separatist path were comparable in Tatarstan and Chechnya. I agree with Farukshin that 'the Tatar *nomenklatura* tried to use public protests to heighten political tensions artificially and pressure the federal authorities by threatening them with separatism and other scares'.[61] However, it is also worth observing that, when addressing the public and politicians outside Tatarstan, the republic's elite attempted to spread the myth that the virus of struggle for national sovereignty of the Tatar people was very strong in the republic. Another of Farukshin's observations sums up the situation: 'All comparisons to the situation in Chechnya stem from the lack of knowledge about the people of Tatarstan and elementary misunderstanding of the conditions in the republic in the post-Soviet period and are, to say the least, absurd'.[62] The events in Tatarstan took a peaceful turn because there was much less potential for separatism and extremism here than in Chechnya, and not because the leader of the republic's elite, Shaimiev, or the Kremlin conducted the right policy. On the contrary, we have repeatedly seen that actions by the Tatarstan authorities even contributed to the tensions in the republic.

The above facts lead us to a more general question: do ethnically diverse societies really face additional difficulties in their transition from totalitarian regimes to political transparency and democracy? We know, for instance, that ethnic divisions are far greater in the republics of Russia than in regions (*oblasts*) and territories (*krais*). Post-Soviet development in the

[59] M Farukshin, *Sovremennyi federalism: rossiiskii i zarubezhnyi opyt* (Kazan, Kazan University, 1998), p. 159.
[60] Mukhametshin & Isaev, *Respublika Tatarstan v zerkale obshchestvennogo mneniya*, p. 65.
[61] Farukshin, *Sovremennyi federalism*, p. 159.
[62] Loc. cit.

republics has been accompanied by ethnic conflict, and the republics are where the most serious violations of human rights, personal freedoms and democratic principles have taken place. Fish and Brooks suggest in their recent study of a large number of contemporary states (over 160) that, while the argument that mono-ethnic societies have comparative advantages is a powerful one, its logical corollary, that ethnically fragmented societies are intrinsically unstable, is ruthlessly exploited by undemocratic rulers the world over.[63] They cite the example of Singapore's longtime strongman, Lee Kwan Yew, who has long argued that his country's diversity makes democracy problematic. Also, the rulers of China, Burma and the five ex-Soviet Central Asian republics justify their dictatorships by the multinational nature of, and hence the potential for social strife in, their countries. According to their logic, democracy is inappropriate in diverse societies precisely because it is unsustainable: political opening-up will only spark mass conflict and thereby undermine even the scant rights and security that the populace enjoys under authoritarianism. Western leaders mostly accept this line – tacitly, at least – and expect less from multiethnic polities.[64]

James Fearon and David Laitin report that 'it appears *not* to be true that a greater degree of ethnic or religious diversity – or indeed any particular cultural demography – by itself makes a country a more prone to civil war'. Fearon and Laitin note that their finding 'runs contrary to a common view among journalists, policy makers, and academics, which holds "plural" societies to be especially conflict-prone due to ethnic or religious tensions or antagonisms'.[65] Their observation is logically followed by the conclusion reached by Thomas Fleiner and Lidija Basta Fleiner on the post-communist regimes in Eastern Europe and ex-Soviet states: 'When facing the climax of legitimacy crisis within their own regimes, the communists turned to another totalitarian legitimacy basis – that of national interests as universally valid in themselves. They generated and fomented interethnic conflicts in order to remain in power. Today all these regimes have a constitutional-democratic form, but no democratic civil society behind'.[66]

My findings match these conclusions. In most Russian republics, apart from Chechnya, ethnic or religious diversity was, and is, frequently used, on the one hand, as an excuse to restrict existing democratic institutions and prevent the development of new ones. On the other hand, it was used to demonstrate an assumed likelihood of conflicts and mass uprisings, even when the basis for such conflicts and aggression was in fact very slim.

[63] Fish & Brooks, 'Does Diversity Hurt Democracy?', p. 162.
[64] Loc cit.
[65] JD Fearon and DD Laitin, 'Ethnicity, Insurgency, and Civil War', *American Political Science Review*, Vol. 97, February 2003, p. 75.
[66] T Fleiner and LR Basta Fleiner, 'Federalism, Federal States and Decentralization', in Lidija R Basta Fleiner and Thomas Fleiner (eds), *Federalism and Multiethnic States: The Case of Switzerland* (Bale-Geneve-Munich, Helbing & Lichtenhan, 2000), p. 14.

Tatarstan falls precisely into that category, and is quite a typical example. Similar cases can easily be found not only in the authoritarian states of Central Asia but also on other continents. In Chechnya, however, we have a unique case[67] in which groups of bandits under the banner of democracy seized power, and the federal authorities made so many blunders when trying to restore order that they managed to antagonize much of the ethnically united population. This fundamental difference and the many distinctions demonstrated above render parallels between Chechnya and Tatarstan, which have, unfortunately become customary in the mass media, scholarly works and assessments by politicians, incorrect.

---

[67] 'A bandits' revolt the like of which has rarely been seen before', Sakwa, 'A Just War', p. 164.

4

The Chechen War in the Context of Contemporary Russian Politics

Emil Pain

In December 1994, the Russian federal authorities launched their first attempt to suppress Chechen separatism by military action. After fierce fighting, the Russian army brought practically the whole territory of the republic under its formal control. It was at this point, however, that a guerrilla war started, and the Russian forces began to suffer defeats and considerable losses. According to official figures (probably understated), the military action of 1994–6 cost the lives of more than 30,000 Chechens, and 5,300 Russian soldiers.[1] This war, the economic cost of which is estimated at $5.5 billion[2] (not including the cost of rebuilding the ruined Chechen economy and social sector), was among the main causes of the Russian economic crisis of August 1998, when the state found itself unable to honour its immense debts.

The two-year military operation ended with the signing of the so-called Khasavyurt agreement in August 1996, which allowed for presidential and parliamentary elections in Chechnya. The Russian authorities recognized the winner of the presidential elections, Aslan Maskhadov, as the legitimate head of a Chechen Republic as part of the Russian Federation; this was confirmed by a raft of legislation. In March 1997 Maskhadov went to Moscow and signed a treaty with the President of Russia, Boris Yeltsin, by which both sides committed themselves to seeking only peaceful solutions to disputes arising between the Russian Federation and the Chechen Republic.

[1] See V. Mukomel, 'International and Regional Armed Conflicts: Human Losses and Social Consequences', in *Identichnost' i konflikt v postsovietskikh gosudarstvakh* (Moscow, Moscow Carnegie Centre, 1997), p. 301.

[2] Mukomel, 'International and Regional Armed Conflicts'.

It appeared that there was no danger of another war breaking out between the two sides in the near future. In September 1999, however, another armed conflict broke out, which journalists dubbed 'the Second Chechen War'; the Russian authorities called it 'an anti-terrorist operation'.

From the First War to the Second

From the outset, Russian society took a radically different view of the second military campaign than of the first. As late as June 1999, the Communists and most of the other parties in the State Duma were clamouring for the removal of Boris Yeltsin from the presidency, the main reason for which was that he had 'started the war in Chechnya.' However by November, two months after the start of renewed military operations, there was almost unanimous support in parliament for the decision to launch the new war (with the single exception of the 'Yabloko' party).[3]

A radical change of mood had taken place among even the so-called liberal politicians, who had led the anti-war movement in the first war. In December 1994 Yegor Gaidar organized the first demonstration against the war in Chechnya in Moscow's Pushkin Square. In 1996 Boris Nemtsov, then governor of Nizhny Novgorod region, collected a million signatures calling for an end to the war; in this he was assisted by Sergei Kirienko.[4] The leading figure on the moderate right, Anatoly Chubais, effectively the team leader of the campaign for Yeltsin's re-election in 1996, persistently urged the President to end the war, as its unpopularity among voters was a significant obstacle to his winning a second term. However in 1999, all these figures supported the actions of the federal government in Chechnya. Anatoly Chubais expressed this most emphatically when he declared that 'the Russian Army is being reborn in Chechnya'.[5]

In 1994 the Russian press gave the war in Chechnya a hostile reception from the start, and the bombardment on Grozny provoked such fierce protest that the President was forced to declare publicly that he had ordered it stopped. In 1999, the situation was completely different: no passions were

---

[3] The democratic party 'Yabloko' was established in 1993. The name derived from the initials of the founding members: Yavlinsky, Boldyrev and Lukin. Soon afterwards, Boldyrev left the party. Between 1993 and 2003 Yabloko was represented on the party list in the Russian parliament (the State Duma), where it represented the liberal part of the political spectrum, together with the Union of Right Forces (SPS).

[4] Sergei Kirienko was one of the founders and leaders of the Union of Right Forces. In 1998 he became prime minister, dealing with the economic crisis that led to the partial default in August of that year. From 2000 he was president Putin's representative to the Volga Federal district. He has not criticized the second Chechen war.

[5] During a debate between Grigory Yavlinsky and Anatoly Chubais on the television programme *Glas naroda* (Voice of the People) on the NTV channel, 26 November 1999. Presented by Yevgeny Kiselev *http://www.yavlinsky.ru/said/interviews/discuss.phtml? id=621-36K.*

raised by the deaths of innocent people, and reports were dominated by a succession of official communiqués and mundane accounts of the army's victorious progress. The scale and speed of the shift in public opinion towards the war in Chechnya was staggering, and highlighted a shift to a far more belligerent attitude, as the following polls show:

Changes in Russian public opinion on the Chechen problem

Question	October 1995	November 1999
'Do you agree that the military operation in Chechnya is essential in order to prevent the disintegration of Russia?'		
Yes	20.4%	53.1%
No	64.9%	20.4%
'Which solution to the Chechen problem do you consider preferable?'		
To pursue military action all Chechen resistance is eradicated	3.2%	62.5%
To withdraw Russian troops from Chechnya and strengthen the border with the republic	51.1%	13.8%

This survey, conducted by the independent research centre 'Russian Public Opinion and Market Research' (ROMIR), clearly demonstrates how the mood of the Russian public underwent a complete reversal. The extent of this can be measured by the huge (almost twentyfold) increase in support for the pursuit of military action until Chechen resistance was eradicated. The ratio between support for and opposition to the preservation of the Russian Federation by military means was turned on its head. Although in 1995, a large majority (two thirds) were opposed to a military solution to the problem, four years later approximately the same percentage was now in favour of this course of action. These changes seem particularly striking when we look at the underlying trend in public opinion up to the beginning of the second war. According to the same research centre (ROMIR), in July 1998, only a year before the second Chechen campaign began, 82 per cent of Russians were prepared to agree to the secession of Chechnya from Russia (or at least were prepared to accept this).

What brought about these radical changes in the Russian mood? They were largely due to the disillusionment felt over the consequences of 'independence' for the Chechen Republic of Ichkeria. Most Russians regarded the republic as a training camp for Chechen terrorists, who were carrying out kidnappings and blowing up apartment blocks in Russian cities. Among the reasons why the Russian public took up such a belligerent stance, it is worth mentioning the government's propaganda campaign. In December 1999, in accordance with government resolution no. 1538, the Russian Information Centre was created especially to provide reports on the Second Chechen War. This Information Centre not only screened reports from the front, but also selected special journalistic clichés for further dissemination.

Meanwhile, NATO's military operation in Kosovo also played a distinct role in shifting Russian public opinion. Many thought that if, for the sake of political objectives, NATO was allowed to bomb civilian targets and kill innocent people in a non-member country, then surely Russia has every right to do the same in its own territory. At the same time, the Russian public viewed as hypocritical Western criticism of human rights violations in the Chechen war.

The main reason for the shift in public opinion, however, was widespread disillusionment with liberal reforms and the perception that they constituted a blow to the national psyche. The public, weary of economic, political and military failures, craved a victory. So when in September 1999 news came in from Dagestan that the bandits encroaching into the republic from Chechnya had been defeated, and the Russian government confirmed that the 'terrorist bases' in Chechnya were being bombarded in response to the terrorist attacks in Russian cities, public opinion was turned on its head. People began to believe that it was possible to solve the Chechen problem by force, and bring order to the country under an 'iron hand'. This approach, to the surprise of many, was epitomised by Vladimir Putin.

War and Power

It is well known that the second Chechen war has played an important role in Vladimir Putin's career. An obscure official, barely known as a politician even following his appointment as prime minister in August 1999, he apparently stood no chance of becoming the President of Russia. The fact that Boris Yeltsin named Putin as his successor in a television address ('I have now decided to name the person, who, in my view, is capable of consolidating our society')[6] did not help Putin at all, as Yeltsin was extremely unpopular at the time. Yeltsin's announcement that his successor would 'ensure the continuation of reform in Russia' also seemed to hinder rather than further Putin's prospects. Incidentally, opinion has it that Yeltsin did not choose Putin to continue reform, but to make sure that his own back was covered. 'The idea was', writes Irina Khakamada, 'to guarantee not only the safety of the "Family" (although this was important), but also the security of the existing structures of power, of the army, and of the country as a whole'.[7]

---

[6] See Galina Kozhevnikova and Vladimir Pribylovsky, *Biografiya Putina V.V*, http://ist.ist.md/index.asp?doc=17&doctree.

[7] See Irina Khakamada, 'Vozmozhen li odin kandidat ot vsekh demokratov v 2004g?', *Moskovskie novosti*, 22–28 July 2003.

Whatever the real motive for Yeltsin's announcement, Putin does not owe his popularity to Yeltsin; rather, growth in support for Putin can be linked directly to the start of the military operation in Chechnya, and to his emphatic statements on the issue. On 23 September 1999, in response to a series of attacks in Russian cities (the bombing of apartment blocks in Buinaksk on 4 September, in Moscow on 9 and 13 September, and in Volgodonsk on 16 September) declared to be the work of Chechen terrorists, Russian planes carried out air strikes on the city of Grozny. Such attacks had been ordered before; however, unlike Yeltsin, who had tried in every way possible to avoid responsibility for the strikes, Putin did not attempt to distance himself from them. On the contrary, on 24 September, speaking in Astana (Kazakhstan), he declared emphatically that the air strikes were aimed at terrorist bases '...and this will continue, wherever terrorists may be found...If we catch them in the outhouse, we'll wipe them out there too'.[8] As it turned out, these words went down extremely well with the public. All the public opinion polls indicated a great leap in Putin's popularity, at a time when the Russian people had been shaken by the terrorist attacks. And Putin built on this success. On 21 January 2000, the day before a group of his supporters put forward his official nomination as a presidential candidate, Putin, at a meeting with interior ministry officials, warned of the increasing danger of a new wave of terrorist attacks by Chechen separatists on Russian cities. Research has shown that increases in Putin's popularity coincide with periods when there has been popular reaction to issues connected with the Chechen War: in October 1999 (Putin's speeches following the September terrorist attacks in Russian cities and at the beginning of the second Chechen campaign); in January 2000 (the assault on Grozny), and in November 2002 (after the storming of the Moscow Dubrovka theatre, which had been seized by terrorists).[9] Only the seizure by terrorists of the school in Beslan in September 2004 dented the president's popularity. Support fell by 2–4 per cent, though within a month it had once again returned to pre-Beslan levels. Popular consciousness appeared to be affected by the traditional distinction, common in imperial Russia, between the 'good tsar' and his bad servants who were responsible for all the failings of the government.

The war in Chechnya remains the main factor capable of politically mobilizing the Russian public, and therefore it constantly engages Putin's attention. It occupies a prominent place in all his speeches to the Federal Assembly, and is always associated with the concept of a 'powerful state', the 'preservation of the country's territorial integrity' and 'restoration, law and order'. At the same time, the President varies his emphasis on this topic changes from speech to speech and, in my opinion, he clearly takes

[8] Khakamada, 'Vozmozhen li odin kandidat...'.
[9] *Obshchestvennoe mnenie – 2002: po materialam issledovanii 1989-202gg., Ezhegodnik* (Moscow, VTsIOM, 2002), p. 45.

fluctuations in the public mood into account. In his first state-of-the-federation address in 2000, when it was not in any way necessary to justify the military action taking place within the country (at the time it enjoyed the support of most of the population), Putin spoke of the lack of understanding abroad for Russia's Chechen policy: 'Russia has received a fundamental challenge to its sovereignty and territorial integrity. It has come face to face with a force striving to redraw the geopolitical map of the world. Our efforts to rid Russia of this danger are interpreted with a lack of objectivity, and from a one-sided viewpoint. They are subject to all kinds of speculation'.[10] In his second address, the President employed a clearly argumentative style, and this time his speech was aimed at his internal Russian audience. 'Until recently', claimed Putin, 'it was said that the army was falling apart, and that we could not count on any significant military achievements. And in the political sphere, it was alleged that we could not expect anything positive, as we could never find a single Chechen who would support the efforts of the federal centre to fight the terrorists and to establish constitutional order. Experience itself has shown both these ideas to be false'.[11]

In a later address the president clearly demonstrated his desire to claim complete success for all his policies in Chechnya: 'The referendum on the constitution held in the republic draws a line under the era of hardships... It is finished'.[12] The Russian leader's tone of bravado, however, is at distinct odds with the current state of public opinion. According to research carried out by the public opinion research organization VTsIOM, by January 2001, after eighteen months of war, 57–60 per cent of Russians did not believe official statements that Chechen resistance had been broken.[13] By 2002, only 0.8 per cent of those questioned believed that the war in Chechnya was over. Another 10.1 per cent believed that the war would last approximately another five years, but the largest group (36.6 per cent) thought it unlikely that the war would end even in 10–15 years' time.[14] This mood of pessimism grows with every passing year, a feeling strengthened by events in Beslan.

It should be noted that most of those questioned today do not think that bloodshed is necessary to keep Chechnya within the Russian

[10] 'Address of the President of the Russian Federation V.V. Putin, to the Federal Assembly of the Russian Federation', The Kremlin, Moscow. 8 July 2000; 'Vystuplenie pri predstavlenii ezhegodnogo Poslaniya Prezidenta Rossiiskoi Federatsii Federal'nomu Sobraniyu Rossiiskoi Federatsii', http://www.president.kremlin.ru/events/42.html.

[11] 'Address of the President of the Russian Federation V.V. Putin, to the Federal Assembly of the Russian Federation', The Kremlin, Moscow, 3 April 2001; RIA Novosti, 4 April 2001.

[12] 'Address of the President of the Russian Federation V.V. Putin, to the Federal Assembly of the Russian Federation', Moscow 16 May 2003, *Rossiiskaya gazeta*, 17 May 2003; *http://www.rg.ru/Anons/arc 2003/0517/1.shtm*.

[13] See The Russian Centre for Public Opinion and Market Research (VTsIOM) Press release No. 3. 30 January 2001.

[14] See VTsIOM survey: - EXPRESS – 7 (26.07-29.07.2002),// www.wciom.ru.

Federation: 15.5 per cent believe that the republic is already to all extents and purposes no longer part of the federation, and another 55 per cent would not object to Chechnya seceding from the federation, or at least would be prepared to accept it.[15]

This was, it should be noted, the state of public opinion after three years of war. The public mood was rather different in 1999–2000, however, when Putin's Chechen policies and his strategy of setting up a vertical system of power, subjugating the regions to the centre, were still taking shape.

Traditionalism – The Ideological Basis of War and Reform

At that time, there was a hope, widespread among the Russian public that it would be possible to put the country back on track after the failure of liberal reforms, by implementing tough or by simple administrative measures. The military successes during the initial phases of the second Chechen war did more than any theoretical arguments to nudge Russians towards this way of thinking.

At that time, the whole structure (or as it is now called, 'project') of Russian internal politics was beginning to change. While in Yeltsin's time this hinged on the confrontation between the 'democrats' and communists, under Putin, with the general decline in public participation in politics, political discussion is now centred instead on the confrontation between the traditionalist *derzhavniki* (supporters of Russia as a world power and the most influential political force), and the political minority in the shape of western-oriented liberals. The political majority, whose lead Putin has followed in internal politics, despite his cautiousness and constant attempts to maintain a balance of power, has determined the new course of politics. The main idea has been to construct a vertical system of power, with the presidential apparatus at the top, and to strengthen the role of the traditional Russian levers of power, such as the prosecutor's office, the police, the security services and others. Against this background, the setting up of federal districts, headed by presidential plenipotentiaries, appears not so much to indicate the continuation of the period of reform as a return to the Soviet tradition of appointing to the regions the direct representatives of the centre – the party secretaries. This is how the Russian public viewed it, and respect for Soviet tradition has made Putin's project more attractive as, since the end of the 1990s, a positive attitude towards the Soviet era has become prevalent among the Russian public.[16]

---

[15] see VTsIOM survey: - EXPRESS – 7 (26.07-29.07.2002),// www.wciom.ru.

[16] L. Gudkov, 'Russki neotraditsionalizm i soprotivleniye peremenam', in V. C. Malakhov and V. A. Tishkov (eds), *Multikul'turalizm i transformatsiya postsovetskih obshchestv* (The Institute of Ethnology and Anthropology and The Institute of Philosophy, The Russian Academy of Sciences (RAN), Moscow 2002), pp. 132–3.

In the opinion of experts and in accordance with several internal indicators, the organization of Putin's project and the use of propaganda are reminiscent of a Soviet-type party structure, the only difference being that the 'Bolsheviks, in their time, changed from an ideological organisation into a state-bureaucratic one, while today's party constructors are starting off from the latter position.'[17]

Generals at War and in Civilian Life

The Chechen war and the administrative reforms are the fruits of a single ideology, which some authors have termed 'neo-traditionalism', and others 'neo-Sovietism'. It is completely natural, therefore, that the same personalities should be involved in both campaigns. At the same time, the Chechen war, more than any other factor, has led to the growth of traditionalism in the country; this doctrine regards the state as supreme, and has strengthened the general desire for a 'strong hand'. The war has also boosted the influence of generals and senior officers of the army, Interior Ministry and security services in the political life of the country. It is no accident that the borders of the federal districts were drawn to coincide with those of the military districts of the Interior Ministry forces, and that five of the seven presidential plenipotentiaries in the federal districts are generals, two of which (General Viktor Kazantsev and General Konstantin Pulikovsky) served as commanders in the Chechen War. Other commanders in Chechnya have entered politics: General Vladimir Shamanov became governor of the Ulyanovsk region, and General Gennady Troshev became a presidential advisor. A whole plethora of 'the conquerors of Chechnya' can now be found among the top echelons of the Russian military. The Chief of the General Staff, Anatoly Kvashnin, who is extremely highly rated by the 'patriotic press', played a particularly prominent role. It has credited him with transforming the Russian General Staff into an 'essentially *Russian state* body'.[18] Academics have called the country's political elite under Putin a 'militocracy'. According to statistics compiled by Olga Kryshtanovskaya, the percentage of academics in today's political elite has fallen by two and a half times in comparison to Yeltsin's era (from 52.2 per cent to 20.9 per cent), while the number of military has risen at practically the same rate (from 11.2 per cent to 25.1 per cent).[19] These changes in the structure of the

---

[17] *Obshchestvennoe mnenie – 2002*, p. 43.

[18] See Vladislav Shurygin, 'Zvezdy generala Kvashnina', *Zavtra*, 13 July 1999. *http://zavtra.ru/cgi/veil/data/zavtra/99/293/31.html*.

[19] See 'Research on the Russian Elite', carried out by the Section for Research on the Elite, The Institute of Sociology, The Russian Academy of Sciences (RAN), from 1989 to 2002. Among the elite were included: members of the Security Council of the Russian Federation, deputies of both houses of the Federal Assembly of the Russian Federation, Members of the Russian government, heads of the regions of the Russian Federation in 1993 and 2002. For more detail, see: O. V. Kryshtanovskaya, 'Rezhim Putina; liberal'naya militokratiya?', *Pro et*

elite reflect to a great extent the shift in the public mood and changes in societal preferences.

Since the beginning of the 1990s Russia has embraced a set of values characteristic of a traditional society. Only three institutions are trusted – the leader (the person, not the presidency), the church, and the armed forces, including those serving in the Federal Security Service (FSB). At the same time, there is a distinct lack of trust in the government, in parliament and in the courts – not to mention political parties, and such exotic (in the Russian view) posts as a Human Rights Ombudsman.[20]

With the entry of generals into ruling circles, to what extent have the hopes of the Russian people been realized? The main task of the presidential envoy to the Southern Federal District is of course the pacification of Chechnya. Viktor Kazantsev should have been just the man for the job (he was in the post until replaced by Vladimir Yakovlev in March 2004; he in turn was replaced by Dmitry Kozak following the Beslan school massacre in September 2004). Kazantsev is a tough, direct man, with little time for intellectual scruples, and whom subordinates call simply 'the bear'. It is said that he is aware of this, but does not take offence.[21] In Chechnya they still remember how, on 13 January 2000, after Chechen fighters attacked the already 'cleansed' Argun and Shali districts, General Kazantsev issued an order that 'only women, children under ten years old, and men over sixty are to be considered refugees. All others are to be detained and subjected to scrutiny'. Although this led to uproar in the press, the only response was the torching of Komsomolskoe and the intensification of action by federal forces on all fronts of the counter-terrorist operation. Kazantsev has his own score to settle with the Chechen separatists. During the first war, in which the general himself did not take part, one of his three sons, Sergei, was seriously injured. The General-Governor, it is said, is the very last person to choose to hold peace talks with Chechen field commanders such as Basaev and Khattab, or with Aslan Maskhadov. Nevertheless, he was the very one entrusted with the task of negotiating with Maskhadov's representative, Akhmed Zakaev, in November 2001. This may have been done deliberately in order to sabotage the talks and to demonstrate that such negotiations with separatists are pointless. Kazantsev's basic responsibilities were gradually reduced, however, and he became a secondary figure. This occurred largely because his military experience did not help him resolve issues associated with implementing Putin's political decisions, something best illustrated by the circumstances surrounding preparations for the referendum on the Chechen constitution. The president attached enormous significance to this, entrusting its organization not to Kazantsev, but to the deputy director

Contra, Volume 7, No. 4, 2002, pp. 158–80. See also Olga Kryshtanovkaya and Stephen White, 'Putin's Militocracy', _Post-Soviet Affairs_, Vol. 19, No. 4, October-December 2003, pp. 289–306.
[20] _Obshchestvennoe mnenie – 2002_, p. 42.
[21] Ibid.

of his administration, Vladislav Surkov, and his assistant, Sergei Yastrzhembsky. Bypassing the general, they cooperated directly with Moscow's appointee in Chechnya, Akhmed Kadyrov, and achieved the desired result, which was to ensure that Chechnya's constitution was changed, thus formally depriving former president Aslan Maskhadov of any residual legitimacy.

The most notorious measure taken by Lieutenant-General Konstantin Pulikovsky – presidential envoy in the Russian Far-East Federal District until September 2004 – was his ultimatum of August 1996, in which he threatened to begin air strikes and an artillery bombardment on Grozny. It was in connection with 'Pulikovsky's ultimatum' that I handed in my resignation as the head of a working group appointed by the President to attempt to end military action in Chechnya, because these attacks threatened an inevitable tragedy, not only for thousands of the inhabitants of Grozny (who at the time were unable to flee the city) but also for Russian soldiers. In August, following the sudden recapture of Grozny by Chechen detachments, the front line ceased to exist, and it was impossible to determine in which apartments and houses Russian soldiers or Chechen fighters were occupying. Due to the street fighting, ordinary people could not even go out, let alone leave the city. Thanks to the legendary 'accuracy' of Russian bombing, Pulikovsky's plan presented far more danger to Russian soldiers than to the Chechen fighters, who knew all of the city's hiding places and underground lairs. No one doubted the resolve of the general, and his punitive impulse was linked in no small measure to the loss of his son Aleksei, killed in a Chechen ambush. Luckily for all concerned, the Secretary of the Security Council, General Alexander Lebed rescinded this mad strategic plan. Following this incident, Pulikovsky came to personify the recklessness of the General Staff.

Pulikovsky later made his attitude to the duties of a general quite clear: 'Generals with a great deal of experience and a good education had become used to carrying out the orders of the political leadership. There came a limit, however, and the generals realised that the time had come to stop carrying out stupid orders. They needed to go into politics and change the law, and through the law prevent the authorities from issuing crazy commands'.[22] This was the very path that Pulikovsky took. With two diplomas from military academies in his possession, and holding the post of Deputy Commander of a Military District, he resigned his commission ten years before the retirement age for generals. He began working in the Krasnodar territory for the regional office of the *Otechestvo* (Fatherland) party, which had been founded by a nationalist known throughout Russia, Batushka (old man) Kondratenko. During the presidential elections he became

---

[22] O. Vladykin, T. Likhanova, A. Kostyukov, 'Semero po lavkam: kogo president poslal ukreplyat' svoyu "vertical"', *Obshchaya gazeta*, No. 21, 25–31 May 2000.

Vladimir Putin's representative in the Kuban region, for which he probably received his present senior post. Pulikovsky is significant as a public figure, but as an administrator his role soon diminished.

The boldness and decisiveness of the general would seem to be particularly useful in crises that hold special significance for the prestige of the president and federal power. In such situations, however, Putin prefers to entrust the reins of power in the regions, including in the Russian Far East, not to the general, but to professional managers from his administration.

Chechen policy to a large extent defined the approach and methods used to resolve a whole raft of regional problems. It defined the new style and the new methods employed in Russian politics, above all the method of pressure (not necessarily military) and toughness that ensures the subservience of regional leaders to the Kremlin. This was apparent in the new law adopted by the Duma at the Kremlin's behest in December 2004 dealing with the nomination of governors by the president, and their subsequent ratification by regional legislatures; this in effect gives the president sole authority to appoint governors – at least, this is how this measure is perceived by most politicians and much of the press.[23] The adoption of this law, as with Chechen policy as a whole, is justified in terms of the struggle against separatism and terrorism.

There are today in Russia two counter-terrorist operations: one is in Chechnya and the other is in the rest of Russia. Hence it is not surprising that we encounter in both the same individuals, in particular the generals of the Chechen campaign. However, neither campaign has been crowned with success. The 'war against terrorism' in Chechnya has led only to its diffusion out of Chechnya to the rest of Russia. The starkest example of this was the assault by Chechen terrorists on certain towns in Ingushetia and their capture of the republic's MVD armoury on 22 June 2004, their capture of the middle school in Beslan on 1 September 2004, and their attack on the State Narcotics Agency and the seizure of its armaments in Nalchik (the capital of Ingushetia) on 14 December 2004. All of these attacks took place in the Southern Federal District, where in the space of a year, as noted, it has had three heads: first, General Kazantsev was replaced by the former governor of St. Petersburg, Vladimir Yakovlev; he in turn was replaced by Putin's most trusted lieutenant and his personal friend, Dmitry Kozak.

The 'war against terrorism' in the sphere of state reform has not helped establish order in the country. Experience has already demonstrated that the appointment, rather than the election, of regional leaders does not

---

[23] See, for example, the response of senator V. M. Zubov to a journalist's question when the law passed its second reading: *http://zubow.ru/page/1/17_1.shtml*. A typical article was 'Putin Proposes the Law on the Appointment of Governors', *http://news.barnaul-altai.ru/ citynews/?id=534&m=09*. Another was the article 'The Council of the Federation Has Adopted the Law on the Appointment of Governors', http://www.gazeta.ru/2004/12/08/ last141954.shtml.

improve the quality of the state actions. At the least, terrorists were less able to infiltrate Ingushetia under the elected president Ruslan Aushev than under the effectively appointed leadership of Murat Zyazikov. Moreover, this 'reform' strongly contradicts national traditions: for the peoples of the North Caucasus elections are a traditional institution and part of daily life. Here almost everyone is elected: from the *tamada* who presides over the festive table to the village elder, from the head of the local Islamic community to the republic's grand mufti. The appointment of the tsar's or the president's plenipotentiary usually only reflects formal authority, while real power is exerted by informal and elected figures. The greater the gulf between formal and informal powers, the greater are the chances of a breakdown of governance. This is illustrated starkly by the August 2004 events in Dagestan, where the mayor of Khasavyurt openly spoke out against the head of the republic, who remains in power only because of Kremlin support. Instead of supporting authoritative but 'inconvenient' leaders, the Kremlin favours weak but subservient figures. However, such leaders are unable to achieve political stability in their regions, as vividly demonstrated by the series of dramatic events following quickly one after the other between June and December 2004 in Ingushetia, North Ossetia, Dagestan, Karachai-Cherkessia and Kabardino-Balkaria.

Force and pressure has not helped win the Chechen campaign, and it is even more unlikely that they will help consolidate the role of the federal districts in Russian life, even if professional managers replace the generals. Professional managers, as experience has shown, can fulfil a supervisory role, above all by carrying out flying visits from Moscow, but they cannot win the support of the population. After the passage of a decade, the attitude of Russians toward the Chechen campaign has returned to that which prevailed at the time when the first campaign was already obviously failing.

5

A Multitude of Evils: Mythology and Political Failure in Chechnya

Robert Bruce Ware

Since it emerged from the Soviet Union, the Russian Federation has fought two wars in Chechnya, the first, from December 1994 to August 1996, and the second, from October 1999 to the present. During both these wars, Russia has committed political errors and military crimes that have merited the criticism that they have received from Russians and Westerners alike. Yet while focusing upon the faulty execution of these wars, many critics have failed fully to consider the deeper causes behind them. Some observers have based their analyses upon assumptions and sentiments that have much to do with the myths of another historical era and little to do with the realities that have haunted the North Caucasus throughout the last decade. Indeed, many have failed to consider the region at all, preferring to see the conflicts along a North/South axis running from Moscow to Grozny while neglecting the tensions between Chechnya and its Caucasian neighbours to the East and West. The result of this neglect has often been a mix of misconceptions and partial truths that have only made it easier for Russian officials to dismiss legitimate criticism of their errors and excesses. Because it inadvertently strengthens the hands of hardliners on all sides, an imbalanced critique can only serve to perpetuate instability in Chechnya.

Why has Chechnya spent the past 15 years lurching from one political failure to the next? The Chechen wars are mired within a multi-layered mythology that has flourished, in no small part, because this region is so little visited and so much misunderstood. Yet as the wars have nourished the mythology, so has the mythology nourished the wars. Any attempt to help the people of this region must begin with a balanced and realistic assessment of their situation. In turn, a balanced and realistic assessment of the situation in Chechnya must begin by clearing away the elaborate mythology that has sustained and perpetuated the history of political catastrophe in Chechnya. This essay offers a critical examination of ten myths at the heart of the Chechen conflict.

Myth No. 1: The Chechen Wars have been Separatist Conflicts[1]

While nationalist rhetoric has been a regular feature of both Chechen wars, while both wars have featured opposing claims to national sovereignty, while deep historical grievances have sometimes divided Russians and Chechens, while some people in Chechnya wish to live apart from Russia for reasons that are compelling, and while many Chechen rebels understand themselves as fighting to liberate their country from Russian domination, there are nonetheless two crucial anomalies that confront the common inference that the wars in Chechnya have been fundamentally separatist conflicts: first, extended periods of *de facto* Chechen independence preceded both wars, and second, Chechen independence was not the immediate cause of either war.

Nationalist mobilisation in Chechnya increased most rapidly from 1990 through 1992. In March 1992 Chechnya refused to sign the federation treaty and then declared independence. Yet there was no war in 1992. On the contrary, the last Russian military forces withdrew from Chechnya that June, leaving half their arsenal for the nominally independent Chechen government, strange behaviour if fears of Chechen separatism were the paramount cause of the subsequent conflict. Nor was there warfare during the next two years when Chechnya styled itself an independent state. Then why did Russian troops return to Chechnya in December 1994? By the late summer of 1994 Chechnya was mired in civil war, a civil war that followed a year of violent clashes and two years of extreme political instability.

In March 1993 Chechen president Djokhar Dudaev vetoed a resolution by the Chechen parliament to hold a referendum on Chechen sovereignty that might have resulted in Chechnya's peaceful integration in the Russian Federation. The parliament voted no confidence in Dudaev, after which he forcibly disbanded the parliament, causing death or injury to some members. Dudaev then ignored impeachment proceedings by the remnants of the legislature; he ignored efforts by the Chechen Constitutional Court to deny his authority, and he ignored demands for his resignation by coalitions of Chechen citizens. Thereafter Dudaev's erratic extremism could be

---

[1] For a discussion of related issues see Robert Ware, 'Will Southern Russian Studies Go the Way of Sovietology', *Journal of Slavic Military Studies*, Vol. 16, No. 4, December 2003, pp. 157–181. The article is also available at http://www.siue.edu/~rware/.

resisted only by violence, which is what immediately erupted and rapidly escalated among opposing Chechen groups. Meanwhile Chechnya became a haven for organised criminal activities that spilled across its borders into Russia. In 1994, there were a series of incidents in which Russian citizens were held hostage by Chechens, culminating that July, when Chechen terrorists commandeered a busload of Russian tourists near a resort in southern Russia.

The immediate cause for Russia's return to Chechnya in December 1994 was not Chechnya's declaration of independence two years earlier; rather it was the rapid escalation of political turmoil and civil strife within Chechnya, as well as the rapid escalation of the organised criminal activity and terrorism spilling beyond its borders into neighbouring republics. The critical intensification of these factors, and not an intensification of Chechen nationalism, was what distinguished 1994, when the Russians went into Chechnya, from 1992, when they pulled out of Chechnya. Faced with similar conditions of rampant criminality, hostage taking, and civil conflict on their southern borders many other powers would also have sent in the troops to restore order. For example, faced with much less extreme and threatening situations in Haiti, Grenada, Panama, and Mexico,[2] the United States did much the same.

In the case of Russia's 1994 invasion of Chechnya, there were contributory causes that went beyond the rapid escalation of criminality, violence and instability. These included oil reserves, oil routes, Russian political maneuvering, and Russian concerns about Chechen separatism. However, the immediate motive for Russian intervention was not Chechen separatism *per se*, but the fact that by the end of 1994 a period of de facto Chechen independence had culminated in a failed state that posed a serious threat to Russian citizens in surrounding territories. No power can accept a failed state on its border. Nevertheless, Chechen independence was sustained by the first Chechen war. Russia was obliged to negotiate the Khasavyurt Accord in August 1996, and once again to withdraw its troops from Chechnya by the following January. Why did Russian troops return to Chechnya three years later?

Again, the immediate cause was not Chechen separatism. Rather it was two irredentist invasions[3] of the Russian Republic of Dagestan from bases in Chechnya that were supported by international Islamist organisations and prosecuted by Islamist radicals from Dagestan and Chechnya, along with a spectrum of fighters from throughout the Islamic world. The attacks

---

[2] After Pancho Villa raided the town of Columbus, New Mexico, in 1916, General John 'Blackjack' Pershing led an American Army detachment southward into Mexico on a punitive expedition.

[3] Beginning 2 August and 5 September 1999. See Enver Kisriev and Robert Ware, 'Conflict and Catharsis: A Report on Developments in Dagestan following the Incursions of August and September 1999', *Nationalities Papers*, Vol. 28, No. 3, September 2000, pp. 479–522.

were led by Shamil Basaev, a Chechen warlord and former acting prime minister of Chechnya,[4] and a Saudi national known locally as 'Emir al Khattab'.[5]

The Islamist insurgents who invaded Dagestan were not attempting to liberate Chechnya. Chechen independence had been sustained three years earlier in August 1996. Rather the insurgents were attempting to impose radical Islamist rule upon populations who wanted no part of it, and who wished to continue their practice of traditional North Caucasian Islam as citizens of the Russian Federation. Those invasions involved approximately 2,000 insurgents, resulted in dozens of deaths, destroyed communities, displaced 32,000 Dagestanis, and were potentially genocidal in that they attacked mountain villages accommodating entire populations of small ethno-linguistic groups.[6] The incursions into Dagestan are properly

---

[4] According to the Chechen constitution, the Chechen president was also the prime minister. However, in October 1997, Aslan Maskhadov asked Shamil Basaev to accept this post. From 1 April 1997 to 10 July Basaev was also first deputy prime minister. Basaev served as acting prime minister of Chechnya from 28 October 1997 to 3 July 1999. Basaev resigned the post less than one month before the incursions that he led into Dagestan, beginning on 2 August 1999. Basaev's resignation also came more than two months after he was elected president of the 'Congress of Chechen and Dagestani Peoples' at a meeting in Grozny on 26 April 1999. Sponsored by Chechen foreign minister Movladi Udugov's Islamic Nation movement, which advocated the annexation by Chechnya of several raions of Dagestan, the Congress called for strengthening 'the unity of the peoples' of the North Caucasus. Addressing delegates, Chechen vice president Vakha Arsanov said that the congress' principal aim was 'to consolidate Islam in Chechnya and to spread it throughout the Caucasus'. The Congress also heard Basaev's account of his preceding organisation of an autonomous military force in Chechen camps that were receiving international Islamist support. The Congress passed a resolution stating the need 'to commence the process of the decolonisation of Dagestan'. During the two months after he accepted the presidency of the Congress in which Basaev continued to act, on Aslan Maskhadov's authority, as Chechen prime minister, there is no evidence that Maskhadov raised any objections. See Kisriev and Ware 'Conflict and Catharsis'.

[5] With experience in Afghanistan and Tajikistan, Khattab attracted attention when he led a contingent of foreign fighters in an ambush of Russian forces near the Chechen town of Shatoy on 16 April 1996. The attack killed 73 Russian troops and wounded 52. After the first war Khattab married a woman from the central Dagestani village of Karamakhi. The village was a fortified and heavily defended Wahhabi enclave that sustained Dagestani and federal attacks during September 1999. Khattab was fatally poisoned by Russian security forces in 2002.

[6] It is useful to compare this point to claims that Russia is waging a genocidal, or potentially genocidal, war in Chechnya. The incursions into Dagestan during August and September 1999 were potentially genocidal because they involved attacks upon 100 per cent of the villages and ethnic territories of some of Dagestan's smallest ethno-linguistic groups, for example, the Andi people with a total population of approximately 30,000. By contrast, Russian assaults against Chechnya have never involved attacks against 100 per cent of the villages and territories traditionally occupied by Chechens. This is because approximately 100,000 Chechen-Akkins, or about ten per cent of the total Chechen population are indigenous to Dagestan, where they have lived undisturbed by Russian forces throughout the recent conflicts in Chechnya. If Russia were interested in committing genocide against the Chechens it is unlikely that 100,000 Chechens would have been left to live peacefully in Dagestan.

described as terrorist attacks because they initially involved attacks against Dagestani civilians and police officers. Because the federal military response to the incursions was slow, and because it was initially fumbling and disorganised, all of the early resistance to the invaders, and much of the later resistance, was undertaken by Dagestani police, by spontaneously organised citizen militias, and by individual Dagestani villagers.[7]

Moreover, those invasions were only the latest in a long series of incursions from Chechnya that regularly involved attacks upon civilians and Dagestani police, and that, in December 1997, culminated in an attack on a federal military garrison (the 136th Motorised) near the Dagestani town of Buinaksk. During the same years, hundreds of Dagestanis were kidnapped and transported to Chechnya, where they were tortured and dismembered on videotape or sold into slavery, as were thousands of citizens from other Russian republics in the region.[8]

In 1999 the Russian Federation's defence of the Dagestani people was substantially different from a separatist conflict. Whereas the latter might aim at containing nationalist mobilisation and preventing secession, the former invoked the protection of loyal citizens from terrorism, from invasion, from hostile subjugation, and from human rights violations that were both massive and sustained over a period of years.[9] The latter suggests a potential for repression of popular movements, but the former is the moral duty of any responsible government. In 1999, officials in Moscow and in Chechnya's neighbouring republics were concerned with Chechnya not as an enclave of North Caucasian nationalism, but rather as a base for internationally supported irredentist attacks aimed at the violent separation of the

---

[7] The author had an opportunity to gather anecdotal accounts of these events while in Russia from 4 August to 17 August 1999, for purposes of planning and organising a Dagestani survey research project. See Kisriev and Ware, 'Conflict and Catharsis', and Ware, 'Report of the Helsinki Commission of the United States Congress', September 1999, pp. 479–522.

[8] There were more than 1,100 documented abductions involving Russian citizens. Citizens in republics bordering Chechnya suffered most. However, there are no complete figures for abductions during this period because many were not reported to the authorities due to concern for the victims' safety. Moreover, during the same period of Chechnya's *de facto* independence thousands Chechens were abducted by other Chechens. There are no authoritative figures for these intra-Chechen incidents, but some observers have estimated the total in excess of 10,000.

[9] The industries of hostage-taking and slavery that flourished in Chechnya during the inter-war years are also an indictment of all major international rights and relief organisations. Because foreign nationals were targeted by kidnappers, all such organisations, and most journalists, understandably, abandoned the region by early 1998. They returned only at the end of 1999 when the return of the Russian military afforded them with protection. Then they rightly criticised Russian troops for their human rights violations, while however neglecting to document the rights violations committed against the people of the region by groups in Chechnya prior to the return of the Russian military. The reader need only attempt to recall how many human rights or relief organisations she has seen reporting on the inter-war hostage industry or interviewing refugees from the 1999 invasions of Dagestan. In each case the number is zero.

North Caucasian republics from the Russian Federation and the imposition of Wahhabite[10] Islamist fundamentalism upon their unwilling inhabitants.

In March and April 2000, I led a group of researchers who conducted a population survey of 1001 respondents throughout Dagestan.[11] We asked respondents what sort of state they would prefer to inhabit. Fewer than 11 per cent wished to live in an Islamic state, while over 63 per cent preferred to return to a socialist state. We asked them to identify the greatest external threat to Dagestan: Russia, Chechnya, Eastern Countries, or Western Countries. Chechnya was identified as the greatest threat by far. Russia was least threatening for all Dagestani ethnic groups except Dagestan's indigenous Chechen-Akkins. When we asked 'Who would you trust in case of an acute crisis?', nearly two thirds of the Dagestani respondents said that they would place their trust in the 'Russian federal leadership', far more than those who would trust personal networks of family and friends, on the one hand, or Dagestani officials, on the other, and way ahead of those who would place their trust in religious leaders or leaders of social groups.[12] Our survey found that Dagestan and Russia respectively were the two most important referents of identification for most Dagestanis. All Dagestani ethnic groups, including (by a slight margin) indigenous Chechen-Akkins, wanted closer relations between Dagestan and Russia. Elite interviews conducted in Dagestan during the following month provide detailed support for these views. In the case of Dagestan, it is clear that Moscow was not resorting to force in order to forestall separatism. Dagestanis clearly view Chechnya as a threat and look to federal officials for help.

But what sort of threat was Chechnya? Were the invasions of Dagestan violations of the Khasavyurt Accord; were they acts of war; or were they simply criminal acts? Since the invasions of Dagestan were neither resisted nor supported by the legitimate government of Chechnya, headed by president Aslan Maskhadov, perhaps they should be regarded as criminal acts? If they were criminal acts they were clearly massive in their scale.

---

[10] North Caucasians commonly use the term 'Wahhabi' with reference to proponents of Islamist ideologies with radical political agendas, whether those proponents are local or foreign. However, proponents of radical Islamist ideologies reject the label, and are more likely to describe themselves as 'true Muslims'. Throughout this essay, the designation will be applied in accord with its common North Caucasian usage.

[11] The study was funded by the National Council for Eurasian and Eastern European Research (NCEEER) and by the National Research Council. Results are contained in a report to NCEEER, as well as in a series of papers and publications. See Robert Ware, Enver Kisriev, Werner Patzelt, and Ute Roericht: 'Dagestani Perspectives on Russia and Chechnya', *Post Soviet Affairs*, Vol. 18, No. 4, October 2002, pp. 306–31; 'Political Islam in Dagestan', *Europe-Asia Studies*, Vol. 55, No. 2, March 2003, pp. 287–302; 'Stability in the Caucasus: The Perspective from Dagestan', *Problems of Post-Communism*, Vol. 50, No. 2, March/April 2003, pp. 12–23.

[12] Personal networks of family and friends, as well as some religious leaders, have great importance in Dagestani society. Presumably, this result indicates that during acute crises, such as the invasion of Dagestan, families, friends, and religious leaders might not be able to offer much assistance. Russian federal officials, on the other hand, have demonstrated their ability to provide military and financial support.

Nevertheless prime minister Putin was prepared to avoid war by negotiating the crisis in essentially criminal terms prior to ordering troops to return to Chechnya. On 29 September 1999, Putin offered to open negotiations with the Chechen leadership, on condition (1) that Maskhadov condemn terrorism 'clearly and firmly;' (2) that he eject armed bands from Chechen territory; and (3) that he agree to the extradition of 'criminals'.[13] Far from using the invasions of Dagestan as a pretext for the subjugation of an independent Chechnya, Putin offered Maskhadov an opportunity to treat the preceding invasions of Dagestan as a criminal matter and to negotiate a peaceful solution. It seems unlikely that he would have done this had he been primarily concerned with Chechen separatism. Putin's terms were similar to those that President Bush offered the leaders of Afghanistan's Taliban government almost precisely two years later, when he sought the closure of terrorist training camps in Afghanistan and the extradition of Osama Bin Laden and other Al-Qaeda leaders.[14]

When a journalist asked Aslan Maskhadov why he didn't arrest Basaev, Raduev,[15] and Khattab, or at least deprive them of their bases, Maskhadov responded: 'I cannot simply have Basaev arrested as a gangster; people here would not understand that. After all, we fought together for our country's independence'.[16] Maskhadov, faced with an opportunity to prevent war by opposing Basaev, chose not to oppose Basaev, nor to restrict the military activities of these warlords, nor to close internationally supported terrorist training camps, nor to preserve his own government by joining with the Russians to restrict the terrorists.[17] Since these terrorists were, at the time, promising violently to separate the North Caucasian republics from the Russian Federation and forcibly to subjugate their inhabitants to radical Islamist rule, it is difficult to see that Putin had any choice other than a military return to Chechnya. Moreover, it is difficult to understand why Putin did not have a moral obligation to do so in order to protect Russian citizens, as they clearly wished to be protected, from further invasions from Chechnya. Certainly most heads of state would have made the same choice that Putin made.

Indeed, President Bush made a similar decision to invade Afghanistan when Taliban leaders refused to close terrorist training camps and extradite

---

[13] Matthew Evangelista, *The Chechen Wars: Will Russia Go the Way of the Soviet Union* (Washington, DC, Brookings Institution Press, 2003), p. 68.

[14] The ultimatums offered by Putin and Bush in these two cases are not only similar, but also at least marginally overlapping since Basaev and a contingent of Chechen fighters trained at one of those camps in Afghanistan in April 1994.

[15] In January 1996, Chechen warlord Salman Raduev led a party of fighters on a raid in which they commandeered a hospital in Kizlyar, Dagestan, where they held more than 3,000 men, women, and children as hostages. The raid appeared to mimic that of Basaev who held more than a thousand hostages in a maternity hospital in the Russian town of Budennovsk in June 1995.

[16] Joerg R. Mettke, 'Interview with Chechen President Aslan Maskhadov', *Der Spiegel*, No. 39, 27 September 1999; Evangelista, *The Chechen Wars*, p. 68.

[17] Again, the 1999 incursions into Dagestan are properly described as terrorist attacks because they initially involved attacks against Dagestani civilians and police officers.

terrorist leaders. If President Bush was justified in declaring the entire Taliban government to be a terrorist organisation because it refused to close training camps and extradite terrorists, then it is difficult to understand why the government of Aslan Maskhadov would not be regarded as a terrorist organisation on the same grounds.[18]

Nor was this the first time that Maskhadov was warned. When Major-General Gennadi Shpigun was kidnapped in Grozny in March 1999, Russian interior minister Sergei Stepashin cautioned that further 'terrorist acts' would prompt Russian military intervention aimed at the destruction of bases occupied by the 'criminal formations.'[19] Indeed, those who have urged Moscow to negotiate a settlement of the second conflict might recall that Shpigun was not the first high-level Russian official to be kidnapped in those years. The Russian presidential envoy to Chechnya, Valentin Vlasov, was also held hostage for six months. When Moscow attempted to negotiate with Chechen officials, its negotiators were taken as hostages. Following Shpigun's kidnapping, Stepashin, prime minister between May and August 1999, drew up plans for an invasion of Chechnya, and the formulation of these plans is one of the reasons that some have claimed that the invasions of Dagestan were a 'pretext' for renewed Russian efforts to eliminate Chechen separatism.[20] Yet alongside Stepashin's warning to Maskhadov, these should be regarded as the sort of contingency plans that most other governments would make under similar circumstances. Indeed, Dudaev had drawn plans for a war with Russia in 1992,[21] so it would seem that if planning can be equated with the intentional execution of a war then we must consistently hold Chechnya responsible for the first war and count Russia's 1994 'invasion' as a pretext for the realisation of Dudaev's war plans.

Some of the same observers would have preferred that the Russian military had actually followed Stepashin's plan, which would have limited its occupation to lowland Chechnya, north of the Terek River, or, alternatively, that it had created a *cordon sanitaire* along the Chechen frontier. Yet that is essentially what Stepashin tried to do in April 1999 when a series of killings and kidnappings in the Stavropol region, near Chechnya, prompted him to close the Chechen border.[22] That same month, in Grozny at the Congress of the Peoples of Chechnya and Dagestan, Shamil Basaev vowed to proceed with 'the decolonisation of Dagestan'.[23] The Congress was dedicated to the establishment of an Islamist state spanning the North Caucasus.

In 1998 and 1999, Russian officials did not seek a pretext to challenge Chechen separatism or revoke Chechen independence. Rather in the face of

---

[18] See Robert Ware, 'The Threat Within', *In the National Interest*, 28 July 2004.
[19] 'Stepashin Issues Ultimatum to Grozny As Opposition Warns of Reprisals', RFE/RL, *Newsline*, Vol. 3, No 47, Pt. 1, 9 March 1999; Evangelista, *The Chechen Wars*, p. 58.
[20] See, for example, Evangelista, *The Chechen Wars*, pp. 76–9.
[21] Evangelista, *The Chechen Wars*, p. 35.
[22] Evangelista, *The Chechen Wars*, pp. 59–60.
[23] Kisriev and Ware, 'Conflict and Catharsis'.

provocations that would have led most other powers to intervene, they repeatedly sought some means of avoiding a second war in Chechnya. Yet by that point, Islamist extremism and terrorism had proliferated in Chechnya to the point that a second war was virtually inevitable. War could have been prevented only by an act of political transcendence involving an alliance of Russian and Chechen moderates against the Islamists and hardliners. As Maskhadov explained, he and most other Chechens were unable to conceive of such an alliance. By contrast, a similar alliance was embraced by most Dagestanis, and was the means by which Dagestani society preserved itself in its confrontation with Islamist extremism.[24] Unlike their Dagestani neighbours, the people of Chechnya lacked the political resources to recognise that they faced threats much greater than those from Moscow. Ironically, this political failure was similar to that which occurred in the West during the same years, when many political leaders, analysts, journalists, and scholars preferred to cling to antagonisms of the past, involving nation states such as Russia and Iraq, rather than recognizing new and more serious threats from international Islamist extremism.

Myth No. 2: The War in Chechnya is Unjustified

What would happen if there were a sovereign, or semi-sovereign, country to the south of the United States that was kidnapping thousands of American citizens, including men, women, and children of all ages? Suppose that after being kidnapped from their homes in the United States, Americans were transported to this country where some of them were sold into slavery and treated thereafter in the cruelest conceivable manner. Most of the other American hostages were chained in dark holes, sometimes flooded, where they were regularly beaten, sometimes starved, and then tortured and dismembered on videotapes that were subsequently sent to their families in the United States in order to extort exorbitant ransoms. Now suppose that the United States government sent two high level emissaries to this country at different times to negotiate issues, including the kidnapping epidemic, and that both these emissaries were kidnapped. Suppose that nearly every day saw cross-border raids from this country into the United States resulting not only in kidnapping, but in plundering and other property crimes, as well as regular attacks upon American police forces, and, on one occasion, a US military base. Finally, suppose that two thousand gunmen invaded the United States

---

[24] For a discussion of the unique political system that the Dagestanis developed and its struggle with Islamist extremism during these years see Robert Ware and Enver Kisriev, 'Ethnic Parity and Political Stability in Dagestan: A Consociational Approach', *Europe-Asia Studies*, Vol. 53, No. 1, January 2001, pp. 105–32; 'Political Stability in Dagestan: Ethnic Parity and Religious Polarisation', *Problems of Post-Communism*, Vol. 47, No. 2, March/April 2000, pp. 23–33; 'After Chechnya: New Dangers in Dagestan', *Central Asian Survey*, Vol. 16, No. 3, Autumn 1997, pp. 401–12; 'The Islamic Factor in Dagestan', *Central Asian Survey*, Vol. 19, No. 2, June 2000, pp. 235–54.

from Al Qaida-supported terrorist training camps in this southern neighbour, murdering dozens and driving more than 30,000 Americans from their homes. Suppose that after all of this the American president asked the ruler of that southern country to extradite the leaders of those invasions and close the international terrorist bases in his country, and suppose the southern leader refused to do so. What would happen?

We all know what would happen. Russia had at least as much justification for going to war with Chechnya in 1999 as the United States had for going to war with Afghanistan in 2001, or with Japan in 1941. Indeed, the United States invaded Cuba, Haiti, Grenada, Mexico, Panama, and Iraq, in both 1991 and 2003, with much less justification. American interventions in Mexico, Japan, Afghanistan, and Iraq were preceded by periods of radical nationalism in each of these states. Yet who would claim that nationalist issues were of primary importance in America's conflicts? On the contrary, most Americans would be deeply and understandably aggrieved by any such characterisation. This does not deny that American occupations of Japan, or Afghanistan, or Iraq raised nationalist issues. It simply observes that nationalist issues were neither the immediate nor the principal causes of those conflicts.

Russian invasions of Chechnya in 1994 and 1999 invoked long-standing nationalist issues and raised questions about the independence that Chechnya had, in each case, sustained for more than two years preceding. It did as the American invasions of Mexico, Panama, Afghanistan, and Iraq did, invoking long-standing nationalist sentiments within, and raising questions about the sovereignty of, these countries. Yet in all of these cases issues of nationalism and local sovereignty were understood to be secondary to the immediate and principal causes of the conflicts.

The conventional view that the Chechen wars lack sufficient justification, and that they are primarily Russian efforts to suppress national liberation movements, are part of an elaborate mythology that has contributed to the intractability of these conflicts. The separatist myth, in turn, nourishes the romantic mythology of a small but proud warrior nation fighting to free itself from imperial control. Any realistic account of the Chechen conflicts must clear away the multiple layers of this mythology and face the less comforting reality of a proud but self-destructive nation that freed itself, and that sustained its independence for several years, only to degenerate into chaos, and to prey upon its neighbours in an orgy of lawlessness and human rights abuse.

Myth No. 3: Historical Grievances are to Blame for the War in Chechnya

Conventional wisdom holds that Chechnya's instability is due to the history of bitter grievance and brutal warfare between Russians and Chechens. Yet the Dagestani case seems to undermine this explanation. The Dagestanis led the Chechens in their long war against Russian expansionism in the early to mid-nineteenth century, but settled thereafter into a relatively comfortable accommodation with Moscow.

Then perhaps Chechnya's instability follows from the brutal deportation of the Chechen people to Central Asia in February 1944. Without question this deportation was a crucially formative experience for the Chechen nation and remains a source of deep resentment among Chechens today. Yet while the bitterness of this experience cannot be minimised, it also cannot be accepted as sufficient cause for Chechen instability since the neighbouring Ingush and other Caucasian nationalities (as well as the Crimean Tata,s. Kalmyks and Volga Germans) endured the same mass deportation without also suffering bloody conflicts throughout the last decade. While these historical grievances undoubtedly have contributed to Chechnya's problems they provide an insufficient explanation for Chechnya's recent conflicts. What is the fundamental cause of the conflicts in Chechnya?

Chechen society is traditionally organised around a complex, seven-level kinship structure, in which the *teip*, or clan, is the pre-eminent organisation. Chechen society lacks a tradition of an authoritative, overarching political structure that encompasses kinship groups and reconciles their differences. Instead it is chronically fragmented among more than 150 *teips*. This chronic social fragmentation breeds radicalism as competing leaders seek to justify their ambitions in ideological terms that transcend Chechnya's social cleavages, then escalate extremist rhetoric and commit extremist acts in order to attract attention, demonstrate prowess, and appeal for supporters. In the early 1990s this intra-Chechen extremist escalation was played out in nationalistic terms that exploited antagonisms with Russia and interfered with opportunities for compromise with Russian officials. In the late 1990s it was played out in terms of Islamist rhetoric and ties to international Islamist organisations. From 1991 to 1994, these dynamics favored, and thereby encouraged, the radical nationalist appeals of Dudaev and his supporters. From 1997 to 1999, similar dynamics favoured, and thereby encouraged, the Islamist extremist appeals of those such as Shamil Basaev and Movladi Udugov. In the case of their nationalist rhetoric or their Islamist rhetoric, Chechen leaders appealed to values that transcended the inherent fragmentation of Chechen society by emphasizing, and to some extent inventing, causes with which all Chechens might identify. In both cases, intra-Chechen social dynamics favored the most radical appeals.

These tendencies are exacerbated by Chechen warrior mythology, which fulfills and perpetuates itself through cycles of conflict. On the one hand, a defeat is a bitter and enduring affront to the Chechen self-conception, demanding violent retribution. On the other hand, a victory, such as that in 1996, affirms the mythology of Chechen culture, and thereby encourages further violence. Corollary mythologies are cherished by a host of journalists, scholars and other romantics who celebrate Chechens for fierce warriors when they win and innocent victims when they lose. Then there are those who wish to view Chechnya as a rightfully independent state at all times except when this would mean that the people of Chechnya would be held responsible for their actions. For example, human rights organisations say that they do not hold Chechens responsible for the abuses of the interwar years because they are concerned only with state-actors, which Chechnya, in their view, was not, even though some have also argued that Russia violated Chechnya's sovereign independence when it invaded in 1999. One would have thought that the events of 11 September 2001 might have demonstrated that substantial human rights abuses can be committed by non-state actors.

After the Chechen victory in 1996, as after the collapse of the Soviet Union in 1992, the endemic fragmentation of Chechen society prevented the consolidation of an overarching political structure capable of supporting the rule of law and the development of legitimate economic activity. From 1992 to 1994, Chechnya's traditional social cleavages were exacerbated by Dudaev's extremism. From 1997 to 1999, the regime of Aslan Maskhadov was never able to control the warlords and *teip* leaders who confronted one another. Hence, neither Dudaev nor Maskhadov was able to prevent Chechnya's rapid descent into chaos and criminality. Clearly there is reciprocity among these factors. If Chechen social fragmentation tends toward the radicalism that was a contributing cause of both wars, then the desperation, devastation, and bitterness resulting from both wars has also contributed to the fragmentation and radicalisation of Chechen society. Yet if there is truth in the preceding argument then Chechen society tends toward violent extremism by virtue of its inherent dynamics regardless of external factors.

It is unappealing to consider the prospect of inherent structural problems in a society that has suffered as much as that of Chechnya. Especially while some Chechens are suffering horrible abuse at the hands of Russian troops and Grozny militias it is easier to blame Moscow for all, or most, of the problems in Chechnya. This strategy may provide satisfaction to Western observers, but neither has it thus far contributed to peace in the Caucasus, nor is it likely to do so. There will never be a lasting peace without truth, and there will never be truth without a careful consideration of all reasonable possibilities. Our interviews in Dagestan, and anecdotal information from regular visits to the region, suggest that while many locals sympathise with suffering in Chechnya, most of them hold the people of Chechnya responsible for their situation. Many think that there will not be peace in Chechnya until the people of Chechnya accept responsibility for their society.

Myth No. 4: The Chechens are to Blame for the Apartment Block Blasts

Myth No. 5: Russian Security Services are to Blame for the Apartment Block Blasts

Ninety-four people died in their sleep when an explosion leveled a nine-story Moscow apartment building on 9 September 1999. Four days later, 118 died in another Moscow apartment blast. Just three days after that, 17 people died when a bomb exploded in a truck parked near an apartment building in the city of Volgodonsk, to the south. The recently appointed prime minister Putin saw a Chechen connection, though this was denied by Chechen president, Aslan Maskhadov. Further doubts were raised after 22 September when another suspected bomb, discovered in the basement of an apartment building in Ryazan, turned out to be part of a 'training exercise' sponsored by federal security services. The next day Russian aircraft bombed the Grozny airport, and a week later Russian troops re-entered Chechnya.

Vladimir Putin's reputation soared on his hardline prosecution of the conflict in the Caucasus, but there were lingering suspicions that the blasts had been the work of government authorities seeking to generate public support for an invasion of Chechnya. The Ryazan incident led to speculation that federal security services had planned an explosion there, and perhaps had planted the bombs in Moscow and Volgodansk. Earlier questions had been raised when the speedy removal of rubble seemed to preclude a full investigation of the Moscow blast sites. Some observers noted that Chechen leaders such as Shamil Basaev and Salman Raduev were usually quick to claim responsibility for their exploits. Would not Basaev have taken credit if the apartment blasts had been his work? Indeed why would any Chechen wish to enrage Russians by attacking civilians in their beds? And why did the explosions stop when Russian troops re-entered Chechnya? If Chechens were behind the blasts then would not the blasts have continued after warfare resumed? In later years, two Russian legislators who were investigating the blasts died in questionable circumstances. A Russian lawyer was arrested on a dubious weapons charge after investigating the case. Finally, in 2003, two Karachai men were convicted of perpetrating the apartment block blasts. However, their closed trial answered none of the questions about the explosions, while raising new questions about the need for secrecy in a trial of great public consequence. These and other troubling ambiguities have been explored in a series of publications suggesting that Russsian security services planted the bombs with the intent of blaming Chechens for the explosions and thereby mobilizing Russian society for a second war in Chechnya.[25]

Yet pending further evidence, the simplest, clearest explanation for the apartment block blasts is that they were perpetrated by Islamist extremists from the North Caucasus who were seeking retribution for federal military

---

[25] For example, see, Rajan Menon, 'Russia's Quagmire: On Ending the Standoff in Chechnya', *Boston Review*, Summer 2004; John B. Dunlop, 'The October 2002 Moscow Hostage-Taking Incident', in three parts, *Radio Free Europe/Radio Liberty*, 18 December 2003, 8 January 2004, and 15 January 2004; David Sattar, *Darkness and Dawn: The Rise of the Russian Criminal State* (New Haven, Yale University Press, 2003); John Sweeny, 'Take Care Tony, That Man Has Blood on His Hands: Evidence Shows Secret Police Were Behind 'Terrorist' Bomb', *The Observer*, 12 March 2000; Jonathan Steele, 'The Ryazan Incident', *The Guardian*, 24 March 2000; Jamie Dettmer, 'Terrorism: Did Putin's Agents Plant the Bombs?', *Insight on the News*, 17 April 2000.

attacks upon the Islamist enclave in the central Dagestani villages of Karamakhi, Chabanmakhi, and Kadar. There is much evidence for this hypothesis. On 4 September 1999, just five days before the first Moscow explosion, a truck bomb ripped through an apartment block in Buinaksk, Dagestan, killing 64 people. The building had previously housed military families. The next day Basaev and Khattab launched their second invasion of Dagestan in a month. Why the second invasion when Basaev had declared on 22 August, at the end of his first incursion, that the next stage in his Dagestani adventure would be 'political not military'? There is reason to suppose that the second invasion by Khattab and Basaev was intended to relieve the Islamist fundamentalists, locally known as 'Wahhabis', who were under Russian military attack in the central Dagestani village of Karamakhi, and in the two neighbouring villages of Chabanmakhi and Kadar. Together these fortified villages came to be known in Dagestan as the 'Islamic *Djamaat*'.[26]

Wahhabism spread to Dagestan from Tajikistan in the early 1990s, and its proliferation in Dagestan was generously funded by individuals and organisations in the Persian Gulf. By the mid-1990s, several Islamic 'charities', including the International Islamic Relief Organisation and Benevolence International, were operating in the republic.[27] In 1998, Dagestani officials accused those organisations of waging jihad against the traditonalist Moslems of Dagestan. Emir al Khattab, Abu Walid, and other Arab leaders of the Wahhabi movement served as intermediaries for much of the radical Islamist funding that came to region. Yet the puritanical Wahhabis were out of step with Dagestan's moderate, traditionalist Muslims. In August and September, when militant Wahhabis twice invaded Dagestan from Al-Qaeda-supported bases in Chechnya, Dagestanis rallied around their political leaders. They pushed the insurgents out with the help of the Russian military.

Between those two invasions of Dagestan, on 29 August 1999 the fortified villages of the Islamic *Djamaat* were attacked by Dagestani OMON security forces. Moscow initially exercised restraint due to the consequences that it feared might follow from attacks waged, not against Chechen insurgents along the Dagestani border, but against Dagestani villagers at the heart of the republic. However, in early September, when assaults by the Dagestani OMON ended catastrophically with the deaths of twelve servicemen who were killed during street battles in the villages, federal forces began an artillery assault. It was not the first violence the villages had seen.

Confrontations began in the summer of 1996 following the murder of a village mayor. On 12 May 1997 a quarrel between fundamentalist Wahhabis

---

[26] A *djamaat* is a village, or an historically connected group of villages, that constitutes the fundamental unit of Dagestani politics.

[27] For example, see Nabi Abdullaev, 'Dagestani Wahhabis Surrender to Russia', ISN Security Watch, 4 August 2004.

and moderate Sufi traditionalists over arrangements at a funeral led to a melee involving 600 people and resulting in a fatality. In December 1997 representatives from these villages, styling themselves 'Fighting Squads of the *Djamaat* of Dagestan' established a 'Military Mutual Assistance Treaty' with Chechen commander Salman Raduyev. The treaty affirmed that Chechen government forces and the Islamic *Djamaat* of Dagestan were unified in the struggle for an independent Islamic Caucasian state. On the night of 22 December 1997 Wahhabis from this *Djamaat* joined with Chechen raiders to attack the 136th Motorised Brigade based in the nearby village of Gerlakh, outside Buinaksk. The 'Central Front for the Liberation of the Caucasus and Dagestan' claimed responsibility for the incident, which resulted in 3 civilian fatalities and 14 casualties.[28]

In May 1998 the Islamic *Djamaat* defeated a contingent of 150 police officers who were despatched after gunmen seised the Karamakhi police station. On 5 July 1998 approximately 1000 gunmen gathered at a meeting near Karamakhi to demand the resignation of the entire Dagestani government, union with Chechnya, and the withdrawal of all federal troops from Dagestani soil. Having refused to recognise any government authority, and having successfully resisted government control, the Islamic *Djamaat* developed a reputation as a 'little Chechnya' in the center of Dagestan. In the winter of 2001, a Dagestani court credibly convicted five so-called Wahhabis from the Islamic *Djamaat* for the Buinaksk apartment explosion. One of them, who had worked as a cook for Basaev and Khattab, admitted that he had brought the explosives from Chechnya beneath a truckload of watermelons. Later he retracted his confession.

Could there have been a connection between the Buinaksk blast and the explosions in Moscow and Volgodansk? In an interview on 9 September 1999 Shamil Basaev said:

The latest blast in Moscow is not our work, but the work of the Dagestanis. Russia has been openly terrorising Dagestan... For the whole week, united in a single fist, the army and the Interior Ministry units have been pounding three small villages...And blasts and bombs — all this will go on, of course, because those whose loved ones, whose women and children are being killed for nothing will also try to use force to eliminate their adversaries. This is a natural process and it is yet more evidence of Newton's third law, that each action generates a reaction... What is the difference between someone letting a bomb go off in the centre of Moscow and injuring 10-20 children and

---

[28] For the history of Dagestan's Islamic *Djamaat*, see Robert Ware and Enver Kisriev, 'After Chechnya: New Dangers in Dagestan', *Central Asian Survey*, Vol. 16, No. 3 Autumn 1997, pp. 401–12; 'The Islamic Factor in Dagestan', *Central Asian Survey*, Vol. 19, No. 2, June 2000, pp. 235–52; 'Conflict and Catharsis'; 'Irony and Political Islam', *Nationalities Papers*, Vol. 30, No. 4, December 2002, pp. 663–90.

the Russians dropping bombs from their aircraft over Karamakhi and killing 10-20 children? Where is the difference?.[29]

Among those whose women and children were in Karamakhi during the Russian assault was Khattab, who was married to a Karamakhi woman. On 15 September 1999 Greg Myre, an Associated Press reporter, quoted Khattab as saying: 'From now on, we will not only fight against Russian fighter jets (and) tanks. From now on, they will get our bombs everywhere. Let Russia await our explosions blasting through their cities. I swear we will do it'. Yet in a subsequent interview with the Interfax news agency Khattab denied that he had anything to do with the Moscow attacks. 'We would not like to be akin to those who kill sleeping civilians with bombs and shells,' Khattab was quoted as saying.

Khattab and other Wahhabis affiliated with the Islamic *Djamaat* clearly had a motive for blowing up Russian apartment buildings. In September 1999, when the Islamic *Djamaat* was being bombarded, their motive was somewhat more crystalline and immediate than were those of other suspects, such as the Russian military and political establishments. Indeed, the last of the blasts, in Volgodansk, occurred on September 16, the same day that the insurgents were driven from Dagestan for the second and last time. If the blasts were connected to the fighting in Dagestan, then one might expect them to conclude at the same time that the fighting did. Moreover, the Wahhabis and Al-Qaeda would have had as much to gain from war as Russia's military and political leaders since warfare would also mobilise their own supporters and spur the international fund raising upon which they depend, much as did their attacks upon the United States.

There is also much evidence that Dagestani Wahhabis are responsible for a long series of subsequent terrorist explosions in Dagestan. The best-publicised of these occurred at a parade in the Dagestani town of Kaspisk on 9 May 2002, but there have been many other explosions. For many of these explosions, Dagestani officials have blamed Wahhabi gangs led by Rappani Khallilov and Shamil Abidov (a.k.a Abuyev). There is evidence for those allegations.[30]

Proponents of the view that Russian security services were responsible for the apartment blasts, such as David Sattar and Rajan Menon, have noted that the apartment block explosions involved hexogen, and have argued that hexogen is a highly controlled substance in Russia with availability tightly restricted outside of government circles. According to Menon, 'the bombs used in Moscow and Volgodonsk were made with tons of hexogen, which is manufactured under tight security in very few locations in Russia;

---

[29] Interviewed by Petra Prokhazkova, *Lidove Noviny* (Prague), 9 September 1999, p. 7.
[30] See Robert Ware, 'New Terrorist Offensive in Dagestan', *Radio Free Europe/Radio Liberty*, 22 December 2003. For an expanded discussion see Robert Ware, 'Renewed Terrorist Offensive in Dagestan', *Central Asian Survey*, forthcoming.

it would have been extraordinarily difficult to obtain it and transport it in such massive quantities.'

Unfortunately, this is another myth. Dagestani law enforcement officials sponsored a programme for the voluntary surrender of arms from 1 October 2003 to 1 December 2003. Among the weapons that were surrendered were 1 ton, 877 kg, 992 g of explosives, including large quantities of hexogen and ammonite. Also surrendered were 57 artillery rounds and missiles, 3 guided anti-tank rockets, 6,807 grenades, 1,256 detonators, 1,151,033 bullets, 962 rifles and pistols, 291 grenade launchers, and three flame throwers.[31] Siseable amounts of hexogen and large quantities of weaponry, both familiar and exotic, were, and still are, readily available in Dagestan. Dagestani officials estimate that the surrender programme recovered only a small fraction of the weapons, ammunition, and explosives circulating in Dagestan, since most of those wishing to dispose of these items would be better compensated on the black market. Certainly, the defenders of Karamakhi, Chabanmakhi, and Kadar, who were heavily armed and well fortified, had access to the full range of this ordinance.

Hence, the simplest, clearest explanation for the apartment block blasts is that they were perpetrated by Wahhabis from Dagestan, and perhaps elsewhere in the region, under the leadership of Khattab, as retribution for the federal attacks on Karamakhi, Chabanmakhi, and Kadar. If the blasts were organised by Khattab and other Wahhabis as retribution for the federal attack on Dagestan's Islamic *Djamaat*, then this would explain the timing of the attacks, and it would explain why there were no attacks after the date on which the fighting in Dagestan was concluded. It would explain why no Chechen claimed responsibility. It would account for Basaev's reference to Dagestani responsibility, and it would be consistent with Khattab's initial vow to set off 'bombs everywhere... blasting through their cities'. Yet if Khattab and other Wahhabis were responsible for the blasts then this would mean that the Chechens were blamed unfairly, and this injustice would have contributed to many injustices that followed. Vladimir Putin's suggestion that Chechens bore primary responsibility for the apartment block blasts appears to have been poorly grounded, and to have given rise to a dangerous and inequitable mythology of Chechen culpability.

At the same time, assertions that Russian security services are responsible for Russia's apartment block blasts appear to be at least partially incorrect, and appear therefore to have given rise to an obscurantist mythology of Russian culpability. At the very least, it is clear that these assertions are incomplete in so far as they have not taken full account of the evidence suggesting the responsibility of Wahhabis under the leadership of Khattab, who may have been seeking retribution for the federal assault upon Dagestan's Islamic *Djamaat*. Conversely, the Ryazan incident is not addressed by the evidence above. Hence, a further possibility is that

---

[31] Data published in *Novoe Delo*, 9 January 2004.

Khattab and his supporters (perhaps including Basaev) were responsible for the first blast in Buinaksk and for some or all of the following blasts, but Russian security forces, recognizing the utility of the blasts for purposes of social mobilisation, were then preparing to follow Khattab's lead with a blast of their own in Ryazan. A final hypothesis is that Khattab and his followers were responsible for all of the apartment block blasts, and the Ryazan incident had nothing at its base apart from the incompetence and confusion of some security officials.

Myth No. 6: The Chechen Wars are to Blame for Islamist Extremism and Terrorism in the Region

Russian officials have consistently characterised the second Chechen war not as an anti-separatist campaign, but as a struggle against international Islamism and terrorism. On the other hand, numerous observers have characterised the spread of Islamism and terrorism in Chechnya less as a cause of the second war, than as a consequence of the economic devastation, social dislocation, widespread desperation produced by both wars.[32] It is clearly true that both wars have contributed to the proliferation of Islamism and terrorism in Chechnya. Yet while war must be regarded as a contributory cause of this proliferation, there are two reasons why it cannot be regarded as a necessary cause: First, both Islamism and terrorism preceded

---

[32] See Evangelista, *The Chechen Wars*. Also see, Svante Cornell, 'Cloaking the Chechen War as Jihad: The Risk of Militant Contagion', *Central Asia Caucasus Analyst*, 21 June 2000. As a third example, US Ambassador Alexander Vershbow was asked: 'Should we understand the two wars in Chechnya as nationalist struggles, or as Islamist struggles? If the struggles are primarily the result of Chechen nationalism, then why did Russia withdraw all of its troops from Chechnya in 1992 and 1997? If the struggles are primarily the result of militant Islamism, then why isn't the U.S. doing more to help Russia against common enemies?' Vershbow responded: 'I think the Chechen conflict has evolved, even mutated, since the beginning. At is root, in the early 1990s it was a nationalist struggle, with origins going back centuries because of the historic enmity between the Chechens and Tsarist Russia. Those ill feelings were re-kindled during the Stalin-era deportations during the Second World War. But as time passed and the war escalated and human rights violations were committed by Russian forces, and also by the Chechens, this contributed to a radicalisation of the population and created fertile ground for radical Islamic ideas, which in turn attracted foreign terrorist and foreign Islamist elements to enter Chechnya. Thus, we saw a region with no Islamic fundamentalism to speak of when the Soviet Union broke up suddenly become a breeding ground for radical ideas. In that sense, we have indeed recognised that there is a danger that Chechnya could be a link in the chain of international terrorism. And we have tried to help the Russians with the external dimension. But, ultimately the Russians' ability to deal with the attraction of the new generation of Chechens to fundamentalist ideas lies in their own decisions in developing a more credible political process that can win the support of the population, rather than driving them into the hands of the radicals. Unfortunately, we think the process they have underway under Kadyrov is likely to fall short'. 'Q. & A.: Russia's Place in the World', UPI, 11 April 2004; *Johnson's Russia List*, No. 8163, 11 April 2004.

the first war in Chechnya. Second, both Islamism and terrorism proliferated in Dagestan, where there was no war with Russia.

Indeed in the early 1990s, Islamist extremism arrived *first* in Dagestan. From there it was brought to Chechnya by Dagestanis, such as Akhmed-Kadji Akhtaev and Bagudin Kebedov (a.k.a. Magomedov), who acquired considerable influence with Chechen leaders such as Zelimkhan Yanderbiyev and Movladi Udogov.[33] Moreover, the proliferation of Islamist extremism in Dagestan has been directly connected with numerous terrorist acts, despite the absence of hostilities with Russia. While problems of Islamism and terrorism would probably have been less severe in the absence of Russo-Chechen conflicts, it is likely that such problems would still have been substantial, and probable that they would, in any case, have led to war with Russia in much the way that they did in 1999. Certainly, Dagestani officials, who made numerous efforts and offered substantial concessions, in order to avoid conflict with Islamists, found that their efforts came to nothing, and that war was the inevitable consequence.[34]

Chechen groups committed acts of terrorism as early as 1991 (when Basaev hijacked a Turkish airliner), long before the first Chechen war. Islamist elements appeared in Chechnya as early as 1993, and had acquired influence by the spring of 1994 when Basaev and his followers trained at terrorist camps in Afghanistan. Four years later, Islamists were competing for control of Chechnya and were a serious destabilizing force in Dagestan, where they were involved in numerous violent confrontations, and where they established an enclave[35] that rejected the authority of Dagestani and Russian officials. In February 1999 Maskhadov placed Chechnya under the rule of Sharia law, an indication that he had effectively surrendered Chechnya to Islamist control. At that time, there were hundreds of Arab gunmen in Chechnya, especially near Urus-Martan and at a military training camp in Serzhen-Yurt.[36] Many of these fighters had Al-Qaeda connections, and international Islamist funding underwrote the camp's expenses. While there has been, until recently, a steady stream of foreign fighters into Chechnya, and while these fighters have played a significant role in the fighting especially since the fall of Grozny in 2000, international extremist organisations have primarily played a financial role. The scale of international support would have to be rated as substantial not only because it involved large financial transfers, but also because it sustained militant forces after 1995.

Here it is important to address a persistent misunderstanding about the nature and role of Islamist extremism in the North Caucasus. Many commentators have argued that the role of Islamist extremism in the

---

[33] Ibid. Also see Kisriev and Ware, 'Irony and Political Islam'; Ware and Kisriev, 'The Islamic Factor in Dagestan', *Central Asian Survey*, Vol. 19, No. 2, June 2000, pp. 235–52.

[34] Kisriev and Ware, 'Conflict and Catharsis'; Ware and Kisriev, 'The Islamic Factor in Dagestan'.

[35] In the proximate villages of Karamakhi, Chabanmakhi, and Kadar.

[36] Evangelista, *The Chechen Wars*, p. 73.

current Chechen conflict should be regarded as marginal because there are
currently few Arab fighters in Chechnya. These commentators often confine
their use of the term 'Wahhabi' to those foreign fighters, whom they distinguish from local fighters. The local fighters, they claim, are more often motivated by nationalist concerns. However, this usage is at odds with that of
people living in the region. Locals use the term 'Wahhabi' to designate anyone, whether local or foreign, who subscribes to a set of fundamentalist
Islamist views that are at odds with local Sufi traditions.[37] Hence, when they
say that they are fighting Wahhabism, or related forms of Islamist extremism,
they mean that they are opposing local adherents as well as their international supporters. It would, of course, be naïve to suppose that international
Islamist networks are confined to Arabs. On the contrary, it is well known
that these networks involve local people in many countries. Some commentators are simply missing the point when they attempt to take small numbers
of Arab fighters in Chechnya as grounds for their arguments that the war in
Chechnya has little to do with international Islamist extremism.

Myth No. 7: Aslan Maskhadov was a Moderate[38]

Who was behind the Nord-Ost hostage drama in Moscow in October 2002?
Shamil Basaev claimed responsibility, but Russian officials say that he did
so to shield Aslan Maskhadov. Maskhadov has denied involvement. At
stake are the credibility of the Chechen cause and the possibility of a negotiated settlement for the conflict. Both may depend on whether Maskhadov
is part of the problem or part of the solution.[39]

   After the first war Basaev opposed Maskhadov in Chechnya's presidential
election, then served as his acting prime minister. The two leaders were at
odds as often as not, and Maskhadov evidently was unable to prevent
Basaev's incursions into Dagestan in 1999, which precipitated the present
conflict in Chechnya. Yet while Maskhadov was unable to control radical
Islamist warlords such as Basaev, Arbi Baraev and Khattab, he was
regarded as a moderate secularist official by many in the West, who viewed
him not only as Chechnya's legitimate leader but also someone with whom
Moscow could negotiate towards a workable peace. Nevertheless there was

---

[37] In 2000, our survey research found that about ten per cent of Dagestanis sympathised with
the Wahhabi approach. See Robert Ware, Enver Kisriev, Werner Patzelt, Ute Roericht,
'Political Islam in Dagestan', *Europe-Asia Studies*, Vol. 55, No. 2, March 2003, 287–302.

[38] Much of the material in this section is contained in Ralph Davis and Robert Ware, 'Was
Aslan Maskhadov Involved in the Moscow Hostage Crisis', *Journal of Slavic Military Studies*,
Vol. 16, No. 3, September 2003, pp. 66–71.

[39] Since its tragic conclusion, the Dubrovka hostage incident has served to damage
Maskhadov's reputation, being written off as 'damaged goods'. According to an unidentified
US official, Maskhadov has 'forfeited any legitimacy he had…he's either unwilling to stand
up to terrorists or incapable of it', 'US Rejects Chechen Separatist Chief', *Los Angeles Times*,
30 October 2002. See http://groups.yahoo.com/group/RCWMC-Archive/message/1.

growing evidence of Maskhadov's radicalization, although just before his death on 8 March 2005 it appeared that he was looking for a new way out of the crisis by offering a ceasefire.

In an apparent effort to compete with Islamist warlords in Chechnya, Maskhadov disbanded parliament, signed a constitution resembling that of Sudan, and established Sharia courts in Chechnya.[40] These courts sentenced people to death, mutilation, and flogging. They executed people for crimes such as adultery and homosexuality. Children and pregnant women were not exempted from these punishments. The Chechen Shaira courts also sentenced Russian citizens. For example, Dagestan's popular Minister of Nationalities, Magomed-Salik Gusaev was sentenced *in-absentia* to death for his role in countering the propaganda of Chechen information minister, Movladi Udugov, during the invasions of Dagestan.[41] When the Russian Duma condemned the public executions, Chechen vice president Vakha Arsanov expressed indifference and promised to continue the executions. At the same time, a slave market flourished in Grozny, while another operated openly in the Chechen village of Urus Martan.[42]

At a 4 July 2002, conference chaired by Maskhadov and Basaev, Maskhadov presented a new formation of the Chechen wartime government. Basaev was appointed head of the Military Committee of the Majlis ul-Shura of the Chechen Republic of Ichkeria. Yet, while assigning military responsibilities to Basaev, Maskhadov retained his position as commander-in-chief of all Ichkerian forces. He foresaw that the new structure would establish centralised command over Chechen military operations that previously took the form of isolated guerrilla actions. Maskhadov ordered all commanders to increase the scale and tempo of operations within their districts, whether inside Chechnya or outside. Presenting the war as part of the Great Holy Jihad, Maskhadov concluded with assurances that freedom would return to Chechnya under Islamic law.[43] At the same meeting, the Ichkerian constitution was amended to bring it into conformity with the laws of Sharia.[44]

---

[40] See Nabi Abullaev, 'Puppet State or Failed State? As Russia's Engagement in Chechnya Drags on, it's Time for a Reality Check About What the Future Would Hold for an 'Independent' Chechnya', *Transitions On Line*, 13 August 2004.

[41] Gusaev was assassinated in August 2003. Dagestani officials blamed Dagestani Wahhabis for carrying out the sentence of the Chechen Sharia court. See Robert Ware, 'Renewed Terrorist Offensive in Dagestan', *Central Asian Survey* (forthcoming).

[42] See Nabi Abullaev, 'Puppet State or Failed State?'. Akhmed Zakaev, who represents Maskhadov in Britain, and Ilyas Akhmadov, who represents Maskhadov in the United States, were both ministers in this government. Britain and the United States have respectively granted each of them asylum.

[43] 'Rebel Chechen leader says situation to change by end of year', BBC Monitoring Service, 29 August 2002. See http://groups.yahoo.com/group/RCWMC-Archive/message/6.

[44] 'Chechen web site publishes amendments to constitution', BBC Monitoring Service, September 13, 2002. The text of the amendments as published by Kavkaz-Tsentr can be viewed at http://groups.yahoo.com/group/RMSMC/message/1441; also see http://groups.yahoo.com/group/RCWMC-Archive/message/7.

In an interview with Kavkaz-Tsentr on 14 August 2002 Basaev reiterated that all combat actions had become more co-ordinated due to the reorganisation of the Majlis al-Shura: 'Even groups of mojahedin which were unknown earlier and acted independently, are trying to establish permanent contact with us and coordinate their actions in line with the common decision.'[45] At an extraordinary session of the Majlis al-Shura held at the western front during August 2002, Maskhadov stated that all mojahedin were now under the provisions of the nisam (law), which are based upon the Koran and the traditions of the Prophet Muhammad, i.e., Sharia law. Furthermore, Maskhadov stated that combat missions have been established which would soon force Russia from Chechen territory. 'I hope,' said Maskhadov, 'that we will be able to change the situation by the end of this year and force the enemy to leave our lands. I am sure we will build our state - the Islamic state of Chechnya, God willing. Allah's law will prevail in our state. We will have no individual groups or disagreements. There will be a single nisam — nisam of Allah'.[46]

A militant video released after the downing of a Russian military helicopter on 19 August 2002 showed Maskhadov sporting the green epaulets of Islamist leaders while sitting in front of a banner saying 'Allahu Akbar'. On 14 October the regional headquarters of the North Caucasus intercepted radio communications from Maskhadov's message wherein he called for intensification of terrorist activities and sabotage in Russian territory.[47] Evidence of Maskhadov's complicity in the Nord-Ost hostage crisis was provided by interviews with its two principal perpetrators, Movsar Baraev[48] and Abu Said.[49] Furthermore, a report that Maskhadov's Baku representative, Ali Asaev, was able to contact and influence the hostage takers during the siege suggests complicity on the part of Maskhadov and/or his staff.[50] Hence there is evidence that: 1) Maskhadov

---

[45] 'Chechens launching coordinated operations against Russians, rebel commander'; Kavkaz-Tsentr news agency web site, August 17, 2002. See *http://groups.yahoo.com/group/ RCWMC-Archive/message/14*.

[46] 'Rebel Chechen leader says situation to change by end of year', BBC Monitoring Service, 29 August 2002. See http://groups.yahoo. com/group/RCWMC-Archive/message/6.

[47] 'Chechen outlawed leader's voice intercepted by federal forces – spokesman'; Interfax-AVN military news agency web site, 14 October 2002.

[48] NTV, 10-26-02; 'Russian NTV shows previously filmed interview with hostage-takers' leader', BBC Monitoring Service; 26 October 2002. This interview and much more coverage of the incident are available at http://groups.yahoo.com/group/RMSMC/message/1535. Also see http://groups.yahoo.com/group/RCWMC-Archive/message/2.

[49] 'Azeri daily publishes pre-assault interview with Chechen hostage-taker', BBC Monitoring Service, 26 October 2002. This interview and much more coverage of the incident are available at http://groups.yahoo.com/group/RMSMC/message/1535. Also see http://groups.yahoo.com/group/RCWMC-Archive/message/12.

[50] 'Hostage-taking in Moscow Gave Impetus to Closer Azerbaijani-Russian Relations', *The Central Asia-Caucasus Analyst*, Wednesday/November 6, 2002. See http://groups.yahoo.com/ group/RCWMC-Archive/message/10.

had undergone Islamist radicalisation; 2) Maskhadov was responsible for reorganising the militant command structure in July 2002 in order to centralise operations and give himself comprehensive oversight; 3) Basaev acquiesced to Maskhadov's centralisation of operations; and 4) Maskhadov ordered an increase in the tempo and scale of militant operations outside of Chechnya that would force Russia to end the war. The hostage takers repeatedly said that Maskhadov had authorised their actions, and Maskhadov's centralisation of the Chechen command structure suggests that this should have been the case. Moreover, if Maskhadov was not complicit in the hostage crisis then why did he fail to condemn it while it was in progress?

On the night of 21 June 2004 a series of attacks occurred in Ingushetia, the Russian republic on Chechnya's western border. The attacks killed 98 civilians and wounded 104 more. Approximately 20 civilians were taken hostage. The attacks had no military targets. The targets were police officers and civilians, some of whom were hacked to death. Because their targets were civilians and police officers, the attacks must be regarded as terrorist acts. Responsibility for the attacks in Ingushetia was initially claimed by Basaev. Maskhadov initially denied responsibility. However, in July 2004, Aslan Maskhadov publicly accepted responsibility for the Ingushetia attacks. Following Maskhadov's acceptance of responsibility for these attacks there can no longer be any doubt that he is a terrorist.[51] In the same month, Maskhadov promised more attacks like those in Ingushetia, and vowed to murder the winner of Chechnya's upcoming presidential election.

Despite the reputation that he established in the mid-1990s, Maskhadov was an Islamist terrorist. The fact that he used his power as Chechen president to impose a system of Sharia law upon a population that was, and is, largely opposed to Islamism and Sharia is an indication of how far down that road he had traveled prior to the beginning of the second war, and how weak was his claim to represent the Chechen people. The mythology of Maskhadov's political moderation has only served to obscure the situation in Chechnya. Demands that Russian officials should negotiate with Aslan Maskhadov were comparable to demands that American officials negotiate with Mullah Omar. Granting asylum or attention to Maskhadov's representatives is comparable to giving asylum or attention to representatives of the Taliban.

---

[51] The terrorists claimed that the attacks in Ingushetia were justified because Ingush police officials have been involved in abuses culminating in the abduction and murder of some Ingush citizens. In the United States, a staffer at the Jamestown Foundation published a similar justification, also claiming abuse by Ingush officials against Chechen refugees; see *Johnson's Russia List*, No. 8304, 23 July 2004. See also 'Powers-That-Be Shrink From Implications of Ingushetia Raid', *Chechnya Weekly*, Vol. 5, No. 26, 30 June 2004; reprinted on *Johnson's Russia List*, No. 8276, 1 July 2004. There is some evidence that supports these claims, though it is not conclusive. However, these claims are no more effective in justifying the Ingushetia attacks than were the claims that Timothy McVeigh offered as justification for his attack upon the Federal Building in Oklahoma City.

Myth No. 8: The Chechen Conflict has been Concluded

Despite declarations by the Putin administration that the conflict had been concluded, Chechnya had descended into civil war by the end of 2003, a civil war in which federal forces were fighting against one side. It was a civil war that had been brewing since the collapse of the Soviet Union, an internecine conflict that had already broken out prior to the first Russian invasion in 1994. In 1999 the invasion of Dagestan was, at least in part, an expression of the rivalry and competition among Chechen groups, whereby Islamists and other radical elements sought to seise the initiative from secularist and moderate elements in order to attract followers and international funding to their cause. Indeed, both of the Russo-Chechen wars that have occurred in the past decade have served to evade, and to postpone, civil war within Chechnya by uniting antagonistic Chechen forces against a common enemy, and this is among the reasons that radicals such as Dudaev, Basaev, Raduev, and Udugov have pursued aggressive policies.

The civil war in Chechnya is, much as it always would have been, a multifaceted conflict. All sides in the conflict are amalgamations of sometimes-contentious sub-groups. There are rivalries, competitions, and fluctuating antagonisms among groups constituting the federal forces. For their part, the militants have always fielded a highly fragmented force, which has augmented their resilience during periods of pressure by federal forces, but which has not greatly undermined their offensive capacity. Militant forces are arrayed along a motivational continuum with implacable ideologues such as Shamil Basaev at one end, and, at the other end people who are fighting on a mercenary basis or because fighting enhances opportunities for criminal enterprise. In between are fighters whose motives are essentially nationalist, and those whose military interests are primarily personal or retributive. This militant motivational continuum is highly fluid, with most fighters experiencing interests that overlap and fluctuate over time, and which lead some fighters into, and back out of, militant circles. On the whole however, militant motives are diverging toward the extremes of this continuum, with increasingly greater proportions of those who are fighting for radical Islamist objectives, on the one hand, and for personal or pecuniary objectives on the other.

Chechens opposed to the militants are being recruited and organised by those loyal to the Grozny administration, who are able to offer social, political, economic, and security incentives in exchange for their support. As these groups continue to expand they will become increasingly prone to internal fragmentation, rivalry, and antagonism. Those groups nominally within the Kadyrov/Alkhanov organisation are collaborating, competing and sometimes conflicting, with other groups that are regularly aligned with neither Grozny security forces nor the militants, and which are sometimes opposed to both. These groups include structures organised around either kinship or criminal interests, or both. Some individuals have affiliations with multiple groups.

Relations among all of these groups are chronically fluid, and are subject to shifting opportunities for conflict and collaboration. At the field level, there are opportunities for collaborations of an informal economic nature among even those groups that seem most directly opposed, such as federal forces and militants. The civil war in Chechnya is a maelstrom of all of these shifting interests and forces. Caught in its midst are many people who are, to varying degrees, alienated from, and exhausted with, all of these groups, and who are primarily interested in efforts to stabilise their private lives. This mix provides no immediate opportunities for a negotiated end to the conflict. Because the conflict is multifaceted, and because many of those facets are fluid and shifting, there is no one who controls forces sufficient to guarantee its resolution on any terms. Neither the administration in Moscow, nor that in Grozny, nor any militant leader is currently in a position to end the conflict regardless of concessions that might emerge from the other sides.

It must be emphasised that there are no militant leaders with whom Moscow can negotiate, not only because there are no moderate militant leaders, but also because there are no militant leaders with authority and responsibility sufficient to guarantee any agreement that might be reached. For all of these reasons an international peace-keeping force would be highly counterproductive. First, this force would face complexities and dangers many orders of magnitude greater than, say, those faced by American peace keepers in Somalia. Within a few months peace keepers would be kidnapped and held for ransom or mutilation. Second, most people in the North Caucasus are strongly opposed to a foreign military presence. There are many people in the region who fear that the United States will decide to treat Chechnya like Kosovo and start bombing them.

Ironically, one of the weaknesses that the militant strategy of terrorism shares with pressures being applied upon the Putin administration by international groups is that the Kremlin is no longer in a position to end the conflict even if it wished to do so. The perpetuation of the conflict is not in Putin's political interest. He is no longer popular because of the war in Chechnya, but rather in spite of it. The war is a substantial drain on the limited resources of his government, and the unpredictability of terrorist attacks is a political liability. Putin cannot afford capitulation, but he appears to be deriving little benefit from the conflict, and there are periodic indications that it provides him with considerable frustration.

The second Putin administration probably will attempt to distance itself gradually from the conflict, probably through a sustained programme of Chechenisation. Militant Islamists will surely continue a low-intensity campaign punctuated by high-profile terrorist acts, perhaps resembling the Moscow metro blast on 6 February 2004, the attacks in Ingushetia, on 22 June 2004, or the destruction of passenger aircraft on 24 August 2004, or the Beslan hostage tragedy of 1–3 September 2004. While militant operational capacity has weakened in Chechnya it has regained some of its former strength in neighbouring territories. As Chechen officials have applied greater pressures upon the militants, the latter have increased their operations in Dagestan and Ingushetia. In Dagestan they are cooperating with Wahhabis who are being released from prison following the 1999 incursions. Though the militants have little popular support, the economic and political frustrations consistently encountered by young men throughout the region, combined with steady, if somewhat diminished, funding from international Islamist organisations, ensures a constant stream of new recruits. There will be no lasting peace until there is genuine democratic reform and sustained economic development.

Myth No. 9: The Conceit of the Chechen Presidency

Moscow's political failures in Chechnya have a long and bitter history, dating from the eighteenth century. These failures include the sustained brutality of the nineteenth century Caucasus War, Soviet ethnic policies of the 1920s and 1930s that carved the North Caucasus into a series of titular ethnic republics,[52] and the brutal deportation of Caucasian and Crimean groups in the 1940s.

Moscow's failures in managing the Dudaev regime, especially in 1993 and 1994, have been extensively examined.[53] However, two points deserve emphasis. First, in December 1992, Boris Yeltsin offered Dudaev an autonomy treaty that had been drafted by Moscow officials in conjunction with the Chechen legislature. This treaty might have been the basis for negotiations similar to those which Moscow successfully concluded with Tartarstan, after Tartarstan, like Chechnya, refused to sign the federation treaty in 1992. Unlike Tartar leaders, however, Dudaev flatly rejected Yeltsin's offer. In March 1993, the Chechen parliament opened another window on a Tartarstan-style settlement when it resolved to hold a referendum on Chechen sovereignty. That was when Dudaev had the members of the parliament beaten and literally thrown out of the windows of their chamber, after which Chechnya descended into political chaos and intra-Chechen violence. After more than two years of the turmoil, Russia invaded.

---

[52] See Robert Ware, 'Conflict in the Caucasus: Historical Context and Prospects for Peace', *Central Asian Survey*, Vol. 17, No. 2, June 1998, pp. 337–54.
[53] See John Dunlop, *Russia Confronts Chechnya: Roots of a Separatist Conflict* (Cambridge, Cambridge University Press, 1998); Evangelista, *The Chechen Wars*; Carlotta Gall and Thomas De Waal, *Chechnya* (New York, New York University Press, 1998); Stanley Greene, *Open Wound: Chechnya 1994–2003* (New York, Trolley Press, 2003); Anatol Lieven, *Chechnya: Tombstone of Russian Power* (New Haven, CT, Yale University Press, 1998).

Yet, second, even after those two years, Russia's 1994 invasion was as confused as it was premature. In December 1994 Russian leaders were unable to clarify the reasons for their invasion to themselves, to the citizens of Russia and Chechnya, and to the world. The failure of the Russian leadership to elucidate the causes of the invasion is the primary reason why those causes became mired in a misleading mythology of separatism. The lack of clear moral purpose was part of the reason why Russian society, and therefore its military, never had the focus necessary for sustained mobilisation and sacrifice. Russian leaders would have done better to postpone any conflict until its cause, and perhaps its necessity, were clearly evident to all concerned. Given the trajectory of social disintegration along which Chechnya was then descending, such cause would probably have soon presented itself in terms of internal political chaos and organised criminality. Had Chechen leaders somehow managed to reverse these trends, then they might have reengaged Russian leaders in the negotiation of their relationship.

Yet, at a minimum, there should have been no invasion of Chechnya prior to a clear presentation of sufficient cause in domestic and international forums. Had Russian leaders made such presentations then they likely would have fostered the moral certitude and sustained the social mobilisation necessary for protracted conflict, much as these were achieved by Russian society in 1999. At the outset of the second war, Russian leaders were able to present their domestic audience with sufficient cause, in terms of the invasions of Dagestan, terrorism, organised criminality, and the chronic vacuity of Chechen politics. Still their efforts to present these causes in international forums were lost amid a flood of mythologies, propagated particularly by political leaders, journalists, and scholars in Western countries.

Yet if the case for war was clear in the autumn of 1999, it was once again muddled in 2000, the year that marked another important political failure in Chechnya. In 1999, many Chechens, who were exhausted and alarmed by the criminality, instability, and Islamist radicalism of the interwar years, were prepared to accept reintegration in the Russian Federation. Yet the indiscriminate brutality of invading Russian forces provided them with renewed cause for grievance and militancy.[54] A dozen years of relentless political failures, on the parts of both Russians and Chechens, set the stage for the events of 2003, and it was against this backdrop that those events initially appeared as opportunities for the people of Chechnya to make a new start. Yet a new round of errors began with the structure of the government that was ratified in Chechnya's constitutional referendum held in March of that year.

[54] See Evangelista, *The Chechen Wars;* Greene, *Open Wound;* Anne Nivat, *Chienne de Guerre: A Woman Reporter Behind the Lines in Chechnya* (New York, Public Affairs Press, 2001); Anna Politkovskya, *A Dirty War* (New York, Harvill Press, 2001); *A Small Corner of Hell* (Chicago, University of Chicago Press, 2003).

The chronic fragmentation of Chechnya's political system, particularly along the traditional lines of Chechnya's 150 (plus) *teips*, or clans, is incompatible with the imposition of a presidential system. An individual executive inevitably will benefit some groups over others.[55] In a political society as fragmented as that of Chechnya this can only exacerbate cleavages and increase political alienation. Instead of a presidential system, Chechnya needed some variety of consociational institutions, such as those that helped to stabilise Dagestan from 1994 until a presidential system was imposed there in 2003.[56]

In some states, consociational systems have assisted societies that are divided along ethnic or religious lines in making their transition to democratic institutions. While consociational systems have varied widely, they have shared some common features. Within a consociational system, political elites from each of the social segments cooperate in what Arend Lijphart, describes as a 'grand coalition.'[57] Political bodies guarantee proportional representation to all social segments, and veto powers permit a single representative from any group to sideline policies or legislation that are viewed as harmful to his group. Finally, consociational systems permit spheres of autonomy to all social segments.[58]

Chechnya's traditional social structure suggested numerous possibilities for consociational innovation. For example, Chechnya might have been served by a bicameral legislature with a lower house representing small single mandate districts determined strictly in terms of equal increments of the total population, along with an upper house that might have been constituted by one member of each *teip* regardless of the group's sise.[59] An executive

---

[55] For example, see Abdulla Istamulov, 'Chechnya Faces a Hard Choice', *MosNews*, 11–17 August 2004; *Johnson's Russia List*, No. 8324, 12 August 2004.

[56] For a discussion of consociational democracy in Dagestan, see Ware and Kisriev, 'Ethnic Parity and Political Stability in Dagestan'. For discussions of the recentralisation process that has undermined Dagestan's consociational institutions and imposed a presidential system, see Robert Ware and Enver Kisriev, 'Russian Recentralisation Arrives in the Republic of Dagestan: Implications for Institutional Integrity and Political Stability', *Eastern European Constitutional Review*, Vol. 10, No. 1, Winter 2001, pp. 68–75; Ware et al, 'Dagestani Perspectives on Russia and Chechnya'; Robert Ware and Enver Kisriev, 'Bending Not Breaking: Dagestan's Presidential Expedient', *Central Asia and the Caucasus*, No. 4, August 2003, pp. 54–61.

[57] Arend Lijphart, *Democracy in Plural Societies* (New Haven, CT, Yale University Press, 1977).

[58] Among the problems of consociational systems are tendencies toward brittleness and collapse. They have been most successful in societies undergoing sustained economic development (such as Austria, Belgium, the Netherlands, and Switzerland). In other countries (such as Lebanon and Nigeria) they have collapsed with catastrophic results. Nevertheless, Dagestan's consociational system had demonstrated remarkable resilience, and would probably have provided a better model for the Chechen constitution than the federal institutions, upon which the new Chechen government is based.

[59] In practice this would have opened the door to controversy since divisions among teips are not always unequivocal and some sub-groups have claims to membership in more than one *teip*.

might have been chosen by a plurality of the upper house for a two-year term, with the provision that members of no single *teip* could hold the executive office twice within a period of five years. Such a system might have built upon Chechnya's traditional social structures with a view toward transcending the cleavages among them, and binding them within a cohesive political framework. Were such a government successful in providing a stable political foundation for Chechen society, then subsequent economic development might have rendered traditional social cleavages less salient over time, so that a presidential system might have become more appropriate in twenty or thirty years. The problems with a system such as this were, first, that it would have produced a weak, and possibly brittle, government when Chechnya's desperate social circumstances called for a strong government. Second, at least in the short term, such a system would have tended to institutionalise, rather than eliminate, Chechnya's chronic political fragmentation.

Despite these broader concerns, Chechnya's constitutional referendum provided grounds for hope. Though electoral irregularities were evident,[60] and to some degree inevitable, it appeared that the result nonetheless reflected a broad consensus among the Chechen population that the time had come to move forward within the federal framework. In so far as this consensus ever existed it marked an important milestone, raising hopes that there might be sufficient political will to make the presidential system work.

These were the hopes that were betrayed in September 2003, when the presidential election was blatantly manipulated in order to extend new authority to Akhmad Kadyrov. Kadyrov was a former Mufti (Supreme Islamic leader) of Chechnya, who had fought against Russian forces in the first Chechen war, but had been disillusioned thereafter by the rise of Wahhabism and criminality that took place in Chechnya during its years of *de facto* independence from 1996 to 1999. When the second war began, Kadyrov opposed the militant forces led by Chechen President Aslan Maskhadov. Unabashed electoral machinations on behalf of Kadyrov deprived Chechen voters of a legitimate political process through which they might have influenced the terms of their political union. Instead the administration that emerged from this process dictated those terms in a sometimes brutal and arbitrary manner. What might have been the commencement of a process of political reconciliation and reintegration, proved

---

[60] There appeared to be massive ballot stuffing that inflated both the turnout and the support for the constitution. Opportunities for fraud increased after the October 2002 Federal census. Its figure of 1,088,000 clearly over-counted the residents of the republic, though it may have more nearly approximated the total number of Chechen nationals in all of the Russian Federation. Census procedures permitted each person to record all his or her family members whether or not they were resident in Chechnya. The actual number of Chechen residents was fewer than 650,000 and perhaps closer to 550,000. Hence, the real Chechen electorate was probably between 250,000 and 350,000. The voter lists, however, included 540,000 people.

to be a cynical plan to ensure political repression. Yet while the election failed to legitimate the presidency of Akhmad Kadyrov, his administration nevertheless achieved a measure of legitimacy, and increased popular support, through the partial efficacy of his efforts to stabilise Chechen society.

Those efforts were terminated by Kadyrov's assassination on 9 May 2004. Shamil Basaev claimed responsibility.[61] Kadyrov's assassination further exposed the weaknesses of electoral manipulation. By the time that he was assassinated, Moscow had grown to depend as much upon Kadyrov as Kadyrov depended upon Moscow. Indeed, Kadyrov was already taking advantage of that dependency in order to apply pressure upon Moscow.[62] Had there been a free and fair election in October 2003, it would have produced a field of serious contenders, and it might have precipitated some degree of power sharing within the Chechen administration that would, in either case, have left the Kremlin less dependent upon Kadyrov. The irony of these events is that Moscow weakened its own hand in Chechnya when it countenanced the manipulation of the Chechen presidential election.

In fairness, however, it is unlikely that any election result would have removed Kadyrov entirely from the administration of Chechnya. First, Kadyrov had substantial support and it is quite possible that he would have won a fair and open election. Yet no less significantly, there were at least three thousand armed men under Kadyrov's command by August 2003. Hence, any electoral victor would have had to make a deal with him. At one point, during that summer it appeared that Moscow was interested in opening a door to such a deal when Kremlin officials made a series of ambivalent remarks about Kadyrov, and then listed him among Moscow's United Nations delegation.

Yet whatever reservations the Kremlin may have had about Kadyrov in July seemed to have been resolved by 3 September 2003, when a meeting between Moscow businessman, Khusein Dzhabrailov, and Kremlin aide, Alexander Voloshin, was followed by the withdrawal of the former from the Chechen presidential race. The Kremlin enticed Chechen Duma

---

[61] The timing of the assassination is interesting: 9 May is the day that Russians celebrate their victory in world war two; 21 and 22 June are the days that Russians remember the Nazi invasion of Russia. Shamil Basaev and Aslan Maskhadov claimed responsibility for a series of attacks in Ingushetia on night of 21–22 June 2004. According to Basaev, Rappani Khallilov, a Dagestani Wahhabi leader, was among the leaders of the Ingushetia attacks. These must also be regarded as terrorist attacks because they strictly targeted civilians and police officials. On 9 May 2002 a massive explosion occurred at a Victory Day parade in Kaspiisk, Dagestan. It killed more than 40 people, of whom nearly half were children. Dagestani officials charged Dagestani Wahhabis who are led by Rappani Khalilov, and who are connected with Basaev. On 9 May 2000, a large bomb was discovered near the ceremonial platform that was set to hold most of Dagestan's leadership at a Victory Day ceremony scheduled to begin a couple of hours later in the main square of Mahachkala, Dagestan.

[62] For example, in proposals made by Kadyrov and rejected by Putin at the People's of the Caucasus Forum, held in Sochi at the end of March 2004.

representative, Aslambek Aslakhanov, from the race with the offer of an executive position, and then stood by as Moscow entrepreneur, Malik Saidullaev, was disqualified on a technicality. Saidullaev was Kadyrov's last serious challenger; it is also possible, if perhaps unlikely, that he would have won a fair election. The implications of Chechnya's current situation may be elucidated by comparison with the consequences that might have followed from Saidullaev's victory. Suppose, for a moment, that the presidential election had been fair, and that Saidullaev had won. Even with an electoral mandate of sixty or seventy per cent, Saidullaev would have lacked the strength to rule, in no small part because he lacked a personal militia. Even with popular support he therefore would have lacked leverage with Chechnya's numerous armed groups.

Hence, such a president-elect would have had little alternative but to yield to the necessity of a power sharing arrangement with Kadyrov. Yet regardless of his title, Kadyrov would have retained more raw power than the new president would have been likely to acquire during his first years in office. In such a situation, Kadyrov might have remained effectively head of the government, though perhaps on a nominally 'transitional' or 'emergency' basis. Hence, a hypothetical electoral victor, such as Saidullaev, might have amounted to little more than a minister of finance, or a ceremonial head of state, at least during the first years of his administration. Yet had Saidullaev been incorporated, even marginally, in some sort of power-sharing arrangement, his background in business and philanthropy suggests that he might have made a contribution to Chechnya's economic development and reconstruction.

Moreover any such arrangement would have been preferable to a brutal monopoly of power, and would have been preferable not only from the standpoint of many Chechens, but also, ironically, from Moscow's perspective. Chechnya needs someone with the entrepreneurial instincts of a Saidullaev to focus on economic and civic development. Yet Saidullaev, or anyone like him, would have needed someone not so dis-similar from Kadyrov to handle security. A second locus of Chechen administrative power, however much weaker than Kadyrov's, would have served nevertheless to limit Kadyrov's rule. At the very least, Moscow would have had an alternative toward which power could be shifted in the likely event of increasing friction with Kadyrov, or in the actual event of Kadyrov's assassination.

Throughout the summer of 2004, officials in Moscow and Grozny repeated the errors that they made a year earlier. In the run-up to the election of Kadyrov's successor, Malik Saidullaev was once again eliminated, this time on the basis of an absurd technicality concerning a detail in his passport. On 29 August Alu Alkhanov was elected by questionable polling procedures from a field that included no other serious contenders. At the age of 47, Alkhanov had served in the Kadyrov administration as Chechnya's top police official. He vowed to continue Kadyrov's policies for improving security in Chechnya, and he had the support of both the

Kremlin and the Kadyrov clan. Because Kadyrov's policies had substantial popular support, because Alkhanov hails from a respected Chechen family, and because he had built a reputation for personal decency, it is likey that he would have won an open and fair election. It therefore appears that the second elimination of Saidullaev's candidacy accomplished nothing, apart from depriving Alkhanov of the legitimacy that he would have won through a fair election, and thereby depriving Chechnya of the stability that only a legitimate government would have been able to provide.

The conundrum of Alkhanov's managed candidacy, was neatly encapsulated on 8 August 2004 when he addressed Russia's upper legislative chamber, the Federation Council. The Federation Council had never before invited a report from a candidate for a elective post in one of its constituent members. In his address, Mr. Alkhanov took advantage of this unprecedented occasion to make a crucial point. Interestingly, his speech ignored a second, closely-related and equally critical point. The neglected point was, however, underscored by Alkhanov's very appearance before the Federation Council. In his report, Alkhanov emphasised that security issues in Chechnya are closely connected to economic development. 'Unemployment and poor living conditions are forcing people to join criminal groups,' he said. He added that 'As long as social problems remain unsolved, complete stabilisation will be impossible'.[63] This is true in Chechnya and true throughout the North Caucasus, where there are few employment opportunities outside of law enforcement, narco-business, terrorism, and war.

Much of the time law enforcement, narco-business, terrorism, and war are essentially four branches of the same encompassing and self-sustaining enterprise. North Caucasians are turning to drugs to help them cope with their ample daily doses of anxiety, frustration, and despair. Narco-business is rapidly expanding in the North Caucasus through the growth of efficient, hierarchical, criminal organisations. The expansion of narco-business not only feeds other forms of organised crime, but also creates employment opportunities in law enforcement. Additional law enforcement jobs are created when militants and Islamist extremists pay young men to attack police stations and targeted police officials. More than 50 police officials were murdered in Dagestan in 2003 and 2004, many of them in the Department of Combatting Extremism and Organised Crime. Police officials were also primary targets in the 22 June 2004 attacks in Ingushetia.

Militants and Islamists make their money through criminal enterprises, such as narco-business, smuggling, kidnapping, and theft of metals and petroleum. They also receive funding from international Islamist organisations. When money becomes available, young men are hired to attack a police station. The next week some of the same young men apply for newly created

---

[63] 'Alkhanov: Chechnya Needs Help', Associated Press, 9 August 2004.

jobs at the same station. A month later more money becomes available and some of the same young men attack another police station. In Chechnya, where unemployment was hovering at 76 per cent in 2004, such work is sometimes all that is available.

Moscow has focused upon the security situation in the North Caucasus without seeming to grasp the extent to which it is connected with problems of economic development. Along with its big stick, Moscow has also offered carrots, in the form of budget subsidies for the North Caucasian governments. Apart from Chechnya, Dagestan has received the greatest federal support, regularly accounting for more than 80 per cent of the Republic's budget, nearly R11.3 billion ($384 million) for 2003. In Ingushetia, smaller federal subsidies provide 85 per cent of the budget. When this money is funneled into the upper echelons of local government hierarchies, little trickles down to the base. This was part of. Alkhanov's point in his report to the Federation Council. He told the Council that 'large federal resources ... are simply being mishandled'. He noted that of the 67 billion rubles ($2.3 billion) allocated for Chechnya's reconstruction, only10 billion ($344 million) reached Chechnya. More is lost to corruption within the republic. Hence, of the 88,000 applications made for cash compensation for destroyed housing, only 8,000 had been accommodated by the date of his report.

At the same time, North Caucasian officials are required to use part of these subsidies to purchase products for use by people in their republics from Moscow suppliers. Thus, instead of stimulating local economies and ensuring that a range of local industries are supported, part of the subsidies remains in Moscow. Both in the case of regional political elites and in the case of Moscow suppliers, the North Caucasian budgetary subsidies ensure that the rich get richer.

Throughout the North Caucasus, local business people are systematically discouraged, and tend to adopt a passive approach. They know that any significant success in their enterprise will attract the attention of local officials, who will seek to take as much of the business as they can by means of bribes and other diversions. A successful business will also become a target for extortion by criminal elements of the local society. Local business people see that they cannot succeed on any significant scale, so they waste little effort in trying to do so. This is doubly destructive because North Caucasian culture is socially proactive and economically entrepreneurial. The obstacles that prevent people from acting in order to improve their lives are creating a deep pool of frustration and anger.

There is anger not only because of economic obstacles, but also because of political obstacles. Throughout the last five years all of the North Caucasian republics have seen a contraction in the circles of economic and political elites that has narrowed both financial access and democratic participation. While this process of elite contraction has local causes, it has also been exacerbated, since the spring of 2000, by the recentralisation of Russian government, which has given the federal centre a greater presence throughout this region. Whereas regional elites were previously bound by their need for a local political base, Moscow's expanded influence has now become the basis for their power and has tended to insulate local elites from local accountability. This has alienated village leaders and other activists who previously constituted the core of local political bases, but who are now finding their roles to be increasingly redundant.

Historically, democratic traditions were more developed in the Caucasus than in Russia. Electoral fraud and arbitrariness on the part of officials has at times raised more protests in the North Caucasus than in other parts of the Federation. Hence, there is something deeply corrosive in Moscow's support for those North Caucasian leaders who display few virtues beyond their loyalty. North Caucasian tendencies toward enterprise and self-assertion, whether socially or economically, combine with the high spirits and the hot blood of local honor cultures to create a propensity for conflict. In an effort to reduce these tendencies to something more compatible with its own cultural traditions, Moscow tries to construct local hierarchies of power and obedience. These efforts only multiply local frustrations.

Yet these efforts were also the reason for Alu Alkhanov's unprecedented appearance before the Federation Council three weeks prior to his election. Alkhanov was correct when he told the Federation Council that economic development is closely linked to security in Chechnya. What he neglected to mention is that democracy is also closely linked to security, not only in Chechnya but throughout the North Caucasus. Perhaps he did not need to dwell on that point since his very presence before the Federation Council three weeks prior to his election was ample proof of democracy's failure. Despite the worthy content of his report, Alkhanov's appearance before the Federation Council was yet another illustration of the ways in which everyone involved in the Chechen conflict seems constantly to be working against himself.

This is particularly true of Vladimir Putin. On 13 September 2004 Putin announced sweeping changes in Russia's 89 regions, primarily the end of elections for governors. Putin presented these changes as his response to a series of terrorist attacks in Russia, including explosions in two passenger planes and a Moscow subway station, and the hostage tragedy at a school in the North Caucasian republic of Ossetia. Yet, unfortunately, Putin's changes are precisely the wrong response, and will eventually increase terrorism in southern Russia. Putin's changes will further undermine democratic procedures in the North Caucasus. His plan to begin appointing the previously-elected provincial governors will further restrict political access and expression; will further shift local political power away from popular control; will augment the region's endemic political corruption; will increase economic disparities, and will thereby multiply local resentment and frustration. These frustrations are already major factors in regional terrorism.

As a consequence of these changes, local governments will be even less legitimate than they are now. In the short term, regional elites will bide their time, but when the implementation of the new system eventually will close doors for most of them. Some of these elites will remain loyal and content themselves with economic and political crumbs. Others will give the appearance of doing so, while quietly undermining the system. Thousands of village leaders, local activists, bureaucrats, and local businessmen, will feel resentment as circles of power contract and their political access is further restricted. Currently, most of these people are loyal to regional governors and to Moscow, but as soon as the Kremlin begins appointing regional leaders it will close the door on most of them, and they will become increasingly anti-Russian. Some of them will initiate or increase contacts with local extremists. Wealthy locals who suddenly find themselves without access to power may contribute to radical causes. At the bottom of the political hierarchy, impoverished young men will continue to find that they have no economic prospects, no political means for improving them, and nothing to lose by joining the radicals, who may at least be able to offer 30 dollars for a night's work. The proposed political changes will eventually contribute to alienation and terrorism, and will loosen Moscow's hold on the region. The destabilisation of Ingushetia after Ruslan Aushev is an indication of what lies ahead for the North Caucasus if Putin's political programme goes forward without substantial economic improvement.

More than half of the people in the North Caucasus would gladly relinquish democracy, and would accept authoritarianism, if they could return to Soviet-style economic benefits and security. However, the latter are unlikely, and whether or not it proves possible to retract democratic reforms, it is surely impossible to eliminate the economic disparities and the Islamic revival that has accompanied them. Efforts to impose a quasi-authoritarian political structure upon the region's new social realities are unlikely to be successful.

Myth No. 10: The Reconstruction of Chechnya

A plan for Chechen reconstruction advanced by the Russian Audit Chamber in 2004 called for the creation of a special economic zone and the resurrection of the Chechen oil industry. The plan would provide Chechnya's leaders with direct access to revenues from natural resources together with a series of tax, customs, and other financial benefits. In the past, oil revenues went to the federal government and were partially returned to the region in the form of subsidies. Even under current conditions of local economic collapse, this sum amounts to 1.5 billion rubles a year, and could easily increase ten-fold given renewed economic development. The hope is that economic revival will create jobs and entice Chechen men away from militant, and other extra-legal, activities. Similar enticements, involving the extension of regional economic benefits, were instrumental in ending the Caucasian War of the nineteenth century.

This plan is sound in its basic premise. Many of Chechnya's current political problems, which have been exacerbated by conditions of social devastation and economic collapse, are likely to be gradually ameliorated by economic growth. The problem is that most of the money is likely to disappear into the pockets of local officials rather than being directed along channels most conducive to economic development. Auditors may prevent some of this, but more often they are likely to be co-opted, intimidated, eliminated, ignored, or out-maneuvered. Moreover, increased control of local resources will strengthen the hands of corrupt officials, and thereby entrench traditions of lawlessness. Hence, it is likely that the immediate results will bear little resemblance to the Audit Chamber's plan. Nevertheless, new sources and patterns of economic flow will help to consolidate new political structures and elites. Given Chechnya's recent history, the consolidation of nearly any political structure is likely to mark an improvement that will help to stabilise Chechen society around new channels of economic flow, however corrupt and undesirable these otherwise may be.

More effective still would be a plan for an incremental handover of local resource revenues, contingent upon verification of their legitimate appropriation. Under such a plan, patterns of misappropriation would be checked by an automatic reduction in subsequent transfers. Conversely, a record of legitimate appropriations would be rewarded with greater local control. The intent of such a plan would be to give officials a choice between benefiting themselves by misappropriating relatively small increments of revenue, or by legitimately appropriating larger increments—by skimming a lot from a little or a little from a lot. While this sort of incrementalist approach is unlikely to be adopted, it is possible that the plan will yield to other forms of compromise. Chechnya needs an effective programme for distributing reconstruction funds to families that have lost their homes. Even those fortunate enough to receive compensation often get less than their due, and then they sometimes become targets for robbery and extortion by their neighbours. Chechnya, and indeed all of the North Caucasian republics need programmes for assisting small businesses. The North Caucasus needs a micro-loan programme.

If there is one simple thing that would do real good in the North Caucasus right now, it would be the construction of highland fruit-processing plants. Unemployment is high in most of the highland villages of the North Caucasus. The chronic lack of employment feeds political alienation, inspires radicalism, and ensures recruitment for militant causes. Highland villagers usually survive by means of subsistence farming, harvesting excellent fruit and vegetables from their orchards and gardens. If they wish to market their produce, the impoverished villagers must travel over difficult roads for hours to reach a market. Usually some of the fruit is damaged in the journey. Some villagers stop trying, and simply trade their produce with neighbours, give it away, or conserve it for personal consumption. Hence, the construction of highland fruit processing plants would help to solve several problems at once. They would provide: a) local employment, b) a market for local produce, c) an incentive for additional agricultural production, and d) a buffer against alienation, radicalism, and militancy.

Why is it that western governments, who so frequently express concern for the people of Chechnya, have not offered to help fund programmes such as these? During the Cold War the United States rarely hesitated to go into less developed countries with economic development programmes. Even when the local political situation was unsavoury, the United States was rarely deterred because Americans were convinced that they were locked in an ideological struggle with communism, with which they were therefore obliged to compete in all possible venues. Today the United States is locked in an ideological struggle with Islamist extremism. For the past 14 years, Islamist extremists have been the only foreigners who are active in the North Caucasus. Why have the United States and other western entities failed to compete with Islamist extremism in the North Caucasus through economic development programmes such as these?

This failure results, in no small part, from the full range of mythologies, romantic fantasies, and other irrelevancies that have obscured the situation in the region. Westerners have been prevented from the deveopment of realistic programmes to help the people of this region because their understanding of it has largely been confined within the mythology of the noble freedom fighters and the evil empire. In fact, the militants and Islamists in Chechnya and elsewhere in the North Caucasus have little popular support. Most people in Chechnya are frustrated, exhausted, and disconsolate and are simply seeking elements of security and minimal prosperity in their daily lives. They long ago concluded that mililtants and extremists are not going to be of any help in this regard. If westerners really cared about the fate of these people they would stop catering to the irrelevant claims of small bands of isolated radicals, and commence efforts to provide the people of Chechnya and their North Caucasian neighbours with what they truly need.

Economic development, along with democracy and rights, are the keys to security, peace, and political stability in Chechnya. Moscow has made serious errors in recent years because it has attempted to focus upon security issues in abstraction from broader frameworks for human rights, democratisation, and economic growth. Because it generally has ignored economic development while undermining human rights and democratic practices, Moscow has made its own task much more difficult. Western governments, organisations, and commentators have also made serious errors by focusing narrowly upon the struggle between Moscow and Chechen militants in abstraction from, and usually in self-complacent ignorance of, the context of deep regional problems in which it occurs. All sides have fostered self-serving mythologies in place of the careful analysis that might have yielded policies both realistic and comprehensive. These mythologies have cast their shadows across a multitude of evils.

6

Chechnya and the Russian Military: A War Too Far?

Pavel K Baev

The second Chechen war, launched by Russia's leadership in autumn 1999, was intended to be a breakthrough in the revival of the Russian Army. Vladimir Putin, hand-picked by President Yeltsin as the successor, was generous with promises to make Russia proud again in its military might and to give the Armed Forces every support they needed for achieving the victory. Four years later, heading towards the well-prepared re-election in March 2004, Putin assiduously avoided the topic of the deadlocked war and insisted that there was no need for further military reform, since the Army was perfectly capable of performing its duties. For any unbiased observer, however, no amount of PR spin could hide the fact that the victory had not taken place, and the presidential denial of the Army's continuing degradation was not made any more convincing by the supporting roar from the top brass.

The war in Chechnya can rightly be seen as the 'original sin' of Putin's regime, determining such authoritarian features as closeted decision-making, obsession with control over every source of power and rigid censorship of the media.[1] At the same time, this war necessitates the building up of conventional military capabilities, both for suppressing the resistance and for engaging in other conflicts of this type. The maturing 'patriotic' ideology of the state-centric regime also places a heavy emphasis on the ability to project power as the ultimate argument in relentless geopolitical contests. Nevertheless, the increased financing of the Armed Forces has not brought any improvement in combat capabilities and the High Command, including the ambitious Commander-in-Chief, appears quite content with this

---

[1] See, for instance, Dmitri Trenin and Alexei Malashenko, *Russia's Restless Frontier: The Chechnya Factor in Post-Soviet Russia* (Washington, CEIP, 2004); Mathew Evangelista, *The Chechen Wars: Will Russia Go the Way of the Soviet Union?* (Washington, Brookings, 2002).

lack of a key element of state power. This inability to advance a serious modernization project for the Army requires a better explanation than the eternal lack of resources, the resistance of the arch-conservative military bureaucracy or just platitudes like 'you cannot reform your army in the middle of a war'.[2]

This chapter will attempt an evaluation of the impact of the Chechen war on the Russian military, seeking to find an explanation for the lack of interest among both the top brass and the ruling clique in learning its lessons and translating these into new guidelines for modernization. It starts with a brief examination of the evolving pattern of combat operations in Chechnya that seeks to identify the key impacts on various elements of the Armed Forces. There follows an assessment of the overall impact of the war on the integrity of the military structures and on the transformation of military culture. Finally, the influence of the prolonged hostilities on the relations between the military leadership and Putin's court will be examined, with particular focus on decision-making related to exploiting the Chechen War for all sorts of particular interests.

Experience Without Learning, Pain Without Healing

In retrospect, it is now possible to see that the start of the second Chechen campaign was the rare, maybe even unique, moment when the Russian Armed Forces were able to conduct operations according to their own plans and patterns. Unlike the first war, when the muddled political goals translated into confusing operational guidelines, in autumn 1999 the top brass received carte blanche from the Kremlin to engage the enemy as they saw fit. Nobody expected a low-casualty 'peacemaking' operation, there were few concerns about the 'collateral damage' and there was not much pressure to achieve a quick victory.[3]

The initial engagement of summer 1999 in Dagestan demonstrated once again all the familiar shortcomings of the rusty military machine: the deployment was slow and inadequate, the interaction between units was chaotic, the planning non-existent. It was, nevertheless, a victory – secured primarily by strong support from the local population, who were outraged

---

[2] For my earlier analysis of this apparent contradiction, see Pavel Baev, 'The Russian Army and Chechnya: Victory Instead of Reform?', in Stephen J Cimbala (ed.), *Russian Military into the Twenty-first Century* (London, Frank Cass, 2002), pp. 75–96.

[3] One remarkably thorough analysis of the performance of the Russian military in the first Chechen War is NN Novichkov et al., *Rossiiskie Vooruzhennye Sily v Chechenskom Konflikte* (Russian Armed Forces in the Chechen Conflict) (Moscow, Infoglob, 1995). My analysis is in Pavel Baev, *The Russian Army in a Time of Troubles* (London, Sage, 1996), chapter 6.

by the violent incursion from Chechnya.[4] The real war, however, was launched in a very different way: a massive grouping (up to 100,000 strong, of which more than half were military units) was assembled and moved slowly into the 'enemy territory' behind a barrage of artillery fire. Every point of resistance on the road towards Grozny was smashed by concentrated firepower, and the capital itself was destroyed thoroughly and systematically rather than stormed. After that, the forces deployed step by step into the mountainous parts of the rebellious republic, taking control of all towns and key villages (an objective that had never been achieved in the first campaign).[5] Consolidating this territorial control and sealing off the border with Georgia were tasks that took a heavy toll during the first year of the campaign,[6] but from spring 2001 the intensity of military operations began to subside. The troops settled in their fortified garrisons, leaving them only for infrequent raids into the mountains or more frequent 'cleansings' (the brutal term *zachistka* has entered not only Russian political discourse but even international vocabulary) of every town and village.

The Chechen rebels[7] suffered significant losses during the first year of the war and had to change their strategy of resistance. Most attacks were carried out by small groups of trained fighters (3–5 combatants) supported by a dozen or so local activists. These groups joined together in larger units only for particular operations, for instance a breakthrough into Georgia or an ambush on a lucrative convoy. Mine warfare became the main form of attack, further reducing the mobility of Russian forces so that could only move at an average speed of one kilometre per hour. While the Russian leadership presented this shift in the pattern of conflict as a 'victory' and proclaimed the war to be over, the command of the grouping of federal forces had no other choice than to try to keep the key roads under control with the fortified checkpoints (*blockposts*) and daily sweeps by combat engineers, placing the main burden of actual fighting on mobile detachments of special forces (*Spetsnaz*).[8]

---

[4] Despite significant losses, the core unit of some 400 fighters, led by Shamil Basaev, retreated to Chechnya; see Vadim Solovyov, 'New Invasion Reveals Flaws in Russia's Military Posture', *Nezavisimoe Voennoe Obozrenie*, 10–16 September 1999.

[5] For a positive evaluations, see Michael Orr, 'Second Time Lucky?', *Jane's Defence Weekly*, 8 March 2000, pp. 32–6.

[6] The most dramatic combat episode of this stage of the war occurred in late February 2000, when a company of the 76th Pskov Airborne Division was ambushed and completely destroyed. Nobody has been held responsible for muddled operational planning and the lack of support (see Andrei Riskin, 'Questions to the Leadership of Genshtab and VDV', *Nezavisimoe voennoe obozrenie*, 8 August 2003); however, a popular TV serial was made turning the blunder into a heroic moment, see Aleksandr Shuravin, 'A Serial on the Chechen War Based on Real Events', *Nezavisimaya Gazeta*, 2 April 2004.

[7] The term 'rebels' is used here as the most neutral identification, in order to avoid bias inherent in such labels as 'bandits', 'terrorists', or 'freedom-fighters'.

[8] See Mikhail Khodarenok, 'Only *Spetsnaz* is Hunting Fighters', *Nezavisimoe Voennoe Obozrenie*, 27 June 2003.

The transfer of the overall command of the grouping of federal forces in Chechnya in January 2001 from the military to the FSB appeared consistent with the changed pattern of conflict; it did not, however, address the key problem in adopting efficient counter-tactics: lack of intelligence. The military simply did not have the technical means for tracing the movement of small groups in the mountains, nor could they process crucial information in real time.[9] The FSB cannot compensate for this shortage with reliable 'humint' (human intelligence) due to its proven inability to build networks of agents and informers. One part of the problem here is the reluctance of the FSB spymasters to recruit 'untrustworthy' Chechens; another part is suspicion and mistrust towards the 'sources' providing information for Kadyrov's militia.[10]

Despite its dominance over and penetration into other security structures in Moscow, the FSB was also unable to organize effective interaction between various federal forces in Chechnya. The Unified Grouping of Federal Forces in Chechnya (OGV), which was devised to organize joint operations,[11] has not been able to integrate several independent chains of command. The Ministry of Interior relies on its own *Spetsnaz* to back the OMON units manning the *blokposti*, and the Border Troops, while subordinated to the FSB from early 2003, cannot expect any combat support from the Army for their units deployed along the border with Georgia.[12]

The total strength of the grouping was gradually reduced to about 80,000, of which only some 35,000 came from the military. That allowed the General Staff to change the pattern of deployment, discontinuing the rotation of composite units and organizing a permanent basing of the 42nd Motorised Rifle Division. All officers in the division, however, have been serving on 6-month postings, so that this combat experience has become widely spread throughout the Army officer corps.[13] The Chechen War also provided an opportunity for the Air Force to maintain at least a minimum level of readiness: while in most units the number of flight hours throughout the 1990s was way below the standard requirements, combat missions in Chechnya, despite their risk, helped develop

---

[9] Experiments with night flights of modern helicopters Ka-29 were abandoned as too complicated, see Viktor Velichkovsky, 'Horned-Owls over Chechnya', *Nezavisimoe voennoe obozrenie*, 21 June 2002.

[10] See on this Andrei Soldatov and Irina Bogoran, 'Experts on Terror: FSB Turns into an Army', *Versiya*, No. 49, December 2003.

[11] On the tasks and structure of this body, see Colonel-General MI Karatuev, 'Features of activities of the united grouping of federal forces in the counter-terrorist operation', *Voennaya mysl*, No. 3, May–June 2000, pp. 64–9.

[12] A thorough examination of the problems with coordination and command can be found in Mark Kramer, 'The perils of Counterinsurgency: Russia's War in Chechnya', *International Security*, vol. 29, no. 3, Winter 2004/5, pp. 1–57. I had the privilege of reviewing an earlier draft at the PONARS academic conference in May 2004.

[13] See Vladimir Mukhin, 'Chechnya as an All-army Test Site', *Nezavisimoe voennoe obozrenie*, 28 November 2003.

professional skills.[14] Since 2003, however, the intensity of the air campaign has been significantly reduced, particularly as far as fixed-wing aircraft are concerned. The character of key operations that have been conducted since spring 2001 require a wide use of combat and support helicopters, so one would have expected that the Army Aviation would receive prominence and priority attention. That, however, has not been the case: after a series of accidents and casualties, this branch was detached from the Army and subordinated to the Air Force, where its interests are often neglected.[15]

A further shift in the pattern of the Chechen War took place from autumn 2002 with a sharp rise in the number of terrorist attacks, first of all suicide bombers across the Northern Caucasus and, most significantly, in Moscow. It was the 'Nord-Ost' (Dubrovka) hostage-taking tragedy in October 2002 that marked a watershed of sorts in this development. The parallel with the escalation of the terrorist dimension in the Palestinian resistance is too striking to be overlooked.[16] President Putin ordered the military to focus on the threat of terrorism but, unlike the Israeli army, the Russian Armed Forces had capabilities neither for lightning raids nor for high-precision strikes.[17]

It was this functional inability to conduct efficient counter-terrorist operations (in the real, not the propagandistic, sense of the word) that convinced the Kremlin to alter its strategy in the Chechen War. One manifestation of this was the formal transfer of responsibility for maintaining 'order' in Chechnya in July 2003 from the FSB to the MVD, which in September that year duly took over the Regional Operational Staff that supervises the activities of the OGV.[18] The major change, however, was the recognized need to build a local power base – and not just a 'puppet regime' – that would supplement the military occupation. This power-building had to involve, and even rely upon, many 'pardoned terrorists', and resources were channelled accordingly. Through a series of carefully staged electoral 'operations', Akhmad Kadyrov emerged as a confident leader with a considerable

[14] A competent analysis of the performance of the Air Force is in Benjamin Lambeth, 'Crisis of Russian Air Power', in John Andreas Olsen (ed.), *From Manoeuvre Warfare to Kosovo?* (Oslo, The Royal Norwegian Air Force Academy, 2001), pp. 164–95.

[15] It was the crash of transport helicopter Mi-26, which was shot down in Grozny on 19 August 2002 with up to 120 casualties, that led to this 'organizational conclusion'; see Aleksandr Chuikov, 'The Blame for the Mi-26 Catastrophe is Allocated', *Izvestiya*, 22 September 2002; on the flawed logic of denying the Army its own air support, see Valentin Rog, 'Malignant Opportunism', *Nezavisimoe voennoe obozrenie*, 6 December 2002.

[16] For a careful examination of the connections between the Chechen resistance and international Islamic movement, see Julie Wilhelmsen, 'When Separatists Become Islamists: The Case of Chechnya', *FFI Report* (Oslo, February 2004).

[17] Putin's directive of November 2002 was quietly buried and already in October 2003 he proclaimed that the period of military reforms was over and only 'normal modernization' would happen in his second term; see Vadim Solovyev, 'MoD Returns to 1984', *Nezavisimaya gazeta*, 2 April 2004.

[18] The explanations for this presidential decision were provided by the FSB Director Nikolai Patrushev and the Minister of Interior Boris Gryzlov in 'FSB Relinquishes, MVD Takes Over', *Trud*, 30 July 2003.

(and experienced) local militia under his control. The military command, however, has been at best ambivalent about this scheme for the 'Chechenization' of the conflict but does not have much say in these matters. Putin then decided in late 2003 to retire General Viktor Kazantsev, the presidential envoy in the Southern federal district and a veteran of the Chechen campaign, who had insisted on keeping Kadyrov on a short leash.[19] The newly formed militia began to claim control over various profitable sectors of the war economy, for instance illegal oil production or refining, or drug trafficking, provoking an increasing number of clashes with the military and OMON.[20] The strategy of 'Chechenization' suffered a heavy blow in May 2004, when Akhmad Kadyrov was assassinated in Grozny; Putin, however, insisted on continuing with the existing arrangement, appointing Alu Alkhanov as the next president, but keeping the militia in the hands of Kadyrov's son Ramzan. Summer 2004 saw an unprecedented escalation of terrorist attacks culminating in the raid on Beslan, North Ossetia, with schoolchildren among the massive casualties.

Overall, the direct pressure from Chechnya on Russia's military has gradually but significantly diminished; the remaining 30,000 troops are no longer required to conduct large-scale operations. Other militarized structures (some 40,000 strong) are now carrying the main burden, such as the OMON and SOBR units and Interior troops, which struggle to maintain control over key cities and main roads, while the Border troops try to monitor every mountain path. However, the negative impact of Chechnya cuts deep into the institutional cohesion and professional culture of the Armed Forces.

'Chechenization' of the Russian Military

Defeat in the First Chechen War shocked and humiliated the Russian Army. Historically, such defeats, for instance in the Crimean War of 1853–6 or in the Russo-Japanese War of 1904–5, stimulated deep structural reforms in the military. This was not the case in 1997–8, however. Yeltsin did approve a small-scale package of reforms, but the financial meltdown of August 1998 undermined even that minimal gesture. Instead of focusing on its own capabilities, the top brass complained about the quality of political leadership and the lack of support in society.[21] Vladimir Putin, as the up-and-coming commander-in-chief, was hard pressed to provide guarantees

---

[19] See Konstantin Kazenin, 'Papa is Sent Packing', *Gazeta.Ru*, 10 March 2004.
[20] Most of these clashes are reported as 'counter-terrorist' operations, for a rare insight, see Aleksandr Kots and Andrei Rodkin, 'The Ambush', *Komsomolskaya Pravda*, 3 March 2003.
[21] The first candid and competent analysis of the impact of the failure appeared on the very eve of the second war, see 'Chechnya and the Posture of the Russian Army', *Voenny vestnik* No. 6 (Moscow, MRFIT, October 1999).

against any new 'betrayals'.[22] For a few crucial months, the electorate was skilfully rallied behind a 'war cause', which helped to restore a measure of harmony in civil-military relations.

The chance to cover the shame of defeat with a decisive victory also provided a strong mobilizing impulse within the Armed Forces that generated enough of a sense of unity to overcome the multiple internal divisions that had opened up by the late 1990s.[23] That impulse, however, proved to be even less durable than popular enthusiasm for the war in society.[24] Already, in late summer 2000, the embarrassing public row between Minister of Defence Sergeev and Chief of the General Staff Kvashnin revealed the depth of disagreement in the High Command over key strategic priorities. Whatever the personal acrimony, the main focus of that quarrel was resource allocation, with Sergeev advocating priority financing of the most cost-efficient strategic forces, while Kvashnin demanded more money for the war.[25] On that occasion, the Chechen 'bill' was indeed covered in full, and Kvashnin saluted his rival into retirement. However, from early 2003 a new strong drive for increasing the share of resources allocated to strategic forces has emerged, spearheaded this time by the command of the Navy. Despite a series of spectacular failures, from the *Kursk* tragedy in August 2000 to the aborted missile launches during the 'presidential' exercises in February 2004, Admiral Kuroedov, Commander of the Navy, was able to claim new funds, exploiting Putin's 'soft spot' for the naval traditions established by Peter the Great.[26] Sentiment aside, it can be argued that it is precisely the deadlock in Chechnya that prompts the Russian leadership to increase its reliance on nuclear forces to underpin its 'Great Power' ambitions.[27]

The row between Sergeev and Kvashnin in summer 2000 was also a manifestation of a remarkable clash of cultures within the Armed Forces.

---

[22] While the rumours about threats of resignations allegedly issued by top generals were probably 'spinned' by the media, the attitude in the High Command towards political 'interference' is clear in the remarkable memoir by Gennady Troshev, *Moya voina: Chechensky dnevnik okopnogo generela (My War: the Chechen Diary of a Trench General)* (Moscow, Vagrius, 2002).

[23] I examined this unifying momentum in Pavel Baev, 'The Challenge of "Small Wars" for the Russian Military', in Anne C Aldis and Roger N McDermott (eds), *Russian Military Reform, 1992–2002* (London, Frank Cass, 2003), pp. 189–208.

[24] For a more elaborate analysis of the shifts in the public attitude towards the war, see Emil Pain's chapter in this volume.

[25] For a sympathetic view of Sergeev's agenda, see Aleksandr Golts, 'The Last Chance for a Technocrat', *Itogi*, No. 30, 28 July 2000; for support for Kvashnin's performance, see Mikhail Khodarenok, 'By no Means a Saboteur', *Nezavisimoe voennoe obozrenie*, 22 March 2002.

[26] See Vladimir Kalinin, 'The President is Sea-sick', *Grani.Ru*, 17 February 2004 (http://www.grani.ru/War/m.60598.html).

[27] For a recent analysis of this trend, see Vyacheslav Baskakov and Aleksandr Gorshkov, 'Moscow has not Formulated a New Strategy and a Nuclear Concept', *Nezavisimoe voennoe obozrenie*, 2 April 2004.

Absorbing the bulk of the USSR's enormous military machine, Russia inherited the traditional Soviet military culture, which was quintessentially bureaucratic. This moss-covered tradition, however, was sharply challenged. It was engagement in numerous local conflicts throughout the 1990s, coming on top of the experience of Afghanistan, which resulted in the growth of a new, warrior-type, professional culture, primarily in the Army officer corps.[28] The First Chechen War was a major factor in the consolidation of this culture, which crystallized around Kvashnin's General Staff, while Sergeev's Ministry of Defence remained a bastion of the military bureaucracy. Kvashnin's personal triumph, nevertheless, did not grant a victory to the war-fighting culture because the new minister, Sergei Ivanov, who has been reshaping the Ministry of Defence since spring 2001 to achieve simultaneously wider control and more efficiency, is by no means a warrior.[29] Putin himself is in essence a product of a bureaucratic culture (in its rather peculiar KGB variant) and is highly suspicious about the unavoidable spread in the ranks of the Army of battlefield camaraderie and readiness to cut across rules and borders.[30]

Whatever the end result of the fusion of old and new professional cultures in the military, it is already clear that this process has been accompanied by a sustained deterioration of the social atmosphere in the barracks.[31] The First Chechen War, unpopular as it was, created a deep popular resentment against the draft and made draft-dodging a socially acceptable norm. At the same time, the barracks became infested with ethnic tensions and unprecedented brutality, which itself reflected the nature of combat operations in Chechnya. The pattern of rotation of composite units exposed a large proportion of soldiers, first of all in the ground forces, to the extreme violence typical in that 'dirty war'. The short interval between the wars did little to eradicate this effect, and with the start of the Second War it has gained in strength. Even during the first year, when the war enjoyed broad 'patriotic' support, attitudes to the draft did not change in any significant way.[32] The motivation for soldiers was nearly non-existent and expectations were very low. The escalation of terrorist attacks from 2002 resulted in the widespread dehumanization of the

---

[28] I examined this cultural transformation in Pavel Baev, 'The Plight of the Russian Military: Shallow Identity and Self-defeating Culture', *Armed Forces & Society*, Vol. 29, No. 1, Fall 2002, pp. 129–46.

[29] On Ivanov's mixed record in streamlining the military bureaucracy, see Vladimir Mukhin, 'Sergei Ivanov Goes Against Fradkov', *Nezavisimaya gazeta*, 6 April 2004.

[30] A penetrating analysis of Putin's bureaucratic instincts can be found in Dale Herspring and Jacob Kipp, 'Understanding the Elusive Mr. Putin', *Problems of Post-Communism*, Vol. 48, No. 5, September–October 2001, pp. 3–18.

[31] For an elaborate analysis, see Joris Van Bladel, 'Russian Soldiers in the Barracks: A Portrait of a Subculture', in Aldis and McDermott, *Russian Military Reform*, pp. 60–73.

[32] See on that Aleksandr Golts, 'The Social and Political Condition of the Russian Military', in Steven E Miller and Dmitri V Trenin (eds), *The Russian Military: Power and Policy* (Cambridge, American Academy of Arts and Sciences, 2004).

'enemy', which was again reflected in an escalation of violence in the barracks. Besides suicide and fratricide, group escapes, often armed and sometimes violent, of soldiers from their units have become a common feature of the Army's 'normal' life.[33]

The prolonged combat operations in Chechnya have sharpened debates on the contentious issue of manning the Armed Forces, which are driven not only by the firm rejection of the traditional draft system by society, but also by the steadily worsening demographic situation.[34] One the one hand, it has been proven beyond doubt that teenage conscripts should not be exposed to the high-risk environment of this war, not least because they simply cannot handle their tasks efficiently under such stress.[35] On the other hand, the 'experiments' with hiring soldiers on the basis of short-term contracts have brought mixed results, as the units of *kontraktniki* (contract soldiers) appear motivated only by the prospect of looting, and show a tendency to break discipline and disobey orders. Besides, the Ministry of Defence has discovered that the failure to deliver on its side of the contract (the delays with salaries and bonuses are widespread) brings an avalanche of expensive lawsuits.[36] There have been many well-reasoned recommendations about keeping seasoned veterans in the Army as professional sergeants and warrant officers,[37] but the inescapable fact is that most of the officers perceive soldiers as cheap unqualified labour and would have no idea about how to manage specialists. Only the Airborne Troops (VDV) have managed to preserve a modicum of esprit de corps, rotating its regiments in Chechnya and seeking to build up combat experience.[38] However, the shrinking VDV cannot compensate for the shortage of light infantry and mobile armour, and their 'professionalization' remains an uncertain proposition. In fact the key role in the war has been delegated to the elite *Spetsnaz*

[33] General Alekseev, the Moscow Military Prosecutor, revealed that some 20,000 men were listed as 'escapees' from the army; see '20,000 Have Run from the Army', *Grani.Ru*, 4 December 2003 (http://www.grani.ru/War/Draft/m.52920.html).

[34] This issue was one of the key political proposals of the Union of Right Forces (SPS) championed by Boris Nemtsov (see, for instance, Grigory Okhotin, 'Army is Pushed Again to the Back-burner', *Polit.Ru*, 27 May 2003, http://www.polit.ru/publicism/country/2003/05/27/zweiter.html); this party, however, failed to cross the 5% barrier at the December 2003 parliamentary elections, which in essence means the end of these debates.

[35] See Pavel Felgengauer, 'The Russian Army in Chechnya', *Central Asian Survey*, Vol. 21, No. 2, June 2002, pp. 157–66.

[36] According to Deputy Defence Minister Lyubov Kudelina, up to 800 million roubles (some USD 27 million) was spent from the 2003 defence budget on covering the fines and other legal expenses, related primarily to the Chechen contracts; see 'Lyubov Kudelina: MoD Paid 3 Billion Rubles', *Grani.Ru*, 15 April 2004 (http://www.grani.ru/War/Mil_spending/m.67274.html).

[37] See, for instance, Igor Rodionov, 'Transformation of the Army Should Start with Sergeants', *Nezavisimoe voennoe obozrenie*, 17 January 2003.

[38] The VDV Command encourages ties with the Orthodox church to strengthen the morale of its troops; see Pavel Korobov and Sergei Petukhov, 'Officers of the Lord' ('Ofitsery Gospoda'), *Kommersant-Vlast*, No. 12, 29 March 2004.

and SOBR units that have demonstrated the ability to perform combat duties in various 'unconventional' situations.[39]

Overall, it is clear that many branches of the Armed Forces, such as the Navy or the Strategic Forces, are not directly affected by the war in Chechnya. However, the mainstream culture and social climate in the Russian military have always been determined by the ground forces, which have been deeply affected. The implicit impact of Chechnya goes much deeper than immediate exposure would suggest, and the self-perception as well as the reputation of the Army are shaped to a large extent by the degradation arising from the brutal and never-ending war.

Putin's *Siloviki* and the Top Brass

Rushing along the fast track to the Kremlin in late-1999–early 2000, Putin went to great lengths to demonstrate his personal involvement with the army in combat. Never a man of words, he flew to Grozny in a fighter jet to deliver Christmas presents to troops.[40] There was, however, little of real substance behind the skilfully created PR façade of presidential concern for the heroic military; in fact, Putin has always been uncertain about the viability of military instruments for his policy, and has been unwilling to build them up. In the 2004 presidential campaign, there was typically scant attention paid to military problems and even less to Chechnya. Besides the cultural disagreements and the traditional mistrust between the army and the KGB, there are serious political reasons for this estrangement.

Initially, Putin had to build his power from a very narrow base, and support from the military was crucial for advancing his bid for presidency.[41] This dependency, however, was perceived by the up-and-coming leader as a vulnerability that had to be reduced and eventually eliminated. With his background in the special services and limited but painful political experience, Putin had learned to value personal loyalty above all other qualities and qualifications, and he had reason to suspect that the prime loyalty of

---

[39] There is perhaps too much propaganda to 'heroise' *Spetsnaz* (including a TV serial), but according to one trustworthy view, SOBR units, with their 'easy camaraderie and spontaneous discipline', do possess 'a spirit out of which something could be made for the future – if they were given a state and a cause worth fighting for.' See, Anatol Lieven, *Chechnya: Tombstone of Russian Power* (Yale, Yale University Press, 1998), p. 55. However, the court case against the *Spetsnaz* GRU unit that massacred six civilians during a mountain patrol on 11 January 2002 tells a different story; see Aleksandr Shapovalov 'Spetsnaz Awaits the Verdict', *Nezavisimaya gazeta*, 27 April 2004.

[40] Visiting the 76th Airborne Division in August 2000, he placed the symbolic cornerstone for a monument to the paratroopers ambushed in February; the grandiose monument was indeed erected in August 2002, see Andrei Riskin, 'Generals as Art Critics', *Nezavisimaya gazeta*, 20 August 2002.

[41] See Mark Kramer, 'Civil-Military Relations in Russia and the Chechnya Conflict', *PONARS Memo* 99 (Cambridge, Harvard University, December 1999).

the 'Chechen generals' was with the cause and not to him personally. Carefully constructing several narrow circles of aides and advisors, residing on a vast bureaucratic pedestal, Putin did not include a single military general in his court.[42]

That cadre policy effectively reduced the political influence of the top brass, who had not had much influence in the autumnal years of Yeltsin's era but expected an improvement under his successor. Pre-empting their disappointment, Putin in early 2001 placed his most trusted lieutenant, Sergei Ivanov, into the key position of Defence Minister with the limited mandate of maintaining a reliable relationship with the military leadership. Ivanov refrained from a massive reshuffling of this bureaucratic behemoth and from any direct interference in the activities of the General Staff, while watching carefully for any sign of discontent in the top brass. On the basis of this information, Putin methodically moved the most active generals from Chechnya into peripheral political positions. Thus, General Shamanov was made (through firmly managed elections) the governor of Ulyanovsk *oblast*, General Pulikovsky became the presidential envoy in the Far Eastern federal region, and the scandal surrounding the removal of General Troshev from the North Caucasus was quickly extinguished.[43]

Significant new features appeared in this uneasy cohabitation by the end of Putin's first presidential term. The extraordinarily closed nature of decision-making in the Kremlin has reduced political analysis to processing rumours and guesswork;[44] nevertheless, some available hard facts provide a basis for reconstructing this top-secret reality. One remarkable set of data emerged from political sociology, which uncovered a steady growth of a particular group in the bureaucratic population, comprising officials with backgrounds in all kinds of military and paramilitary structures. Olga Kryshtanovskaya, who has pioneered this research, proposed the term 'militocracy' to characterize this new rising elite.[45] This catchy term was quickly picked up by the media,[46] but it is in fact rather misleading, since the essence of the phenomenon is the penetration into the upper and middle echelons of the civil service of personnel from the special services,

---

[42] I examined these relationships in Pavel Baev, 'Putin's Court: How the Military Fit In', *PONARS Memo 153* (Washington, Council on Foreign Relations, December 2000).

[43] See Sergei Konovalov, 'We Have too Few of the Likes of General Troshev', *Kommersant*, 23 December 2002.

[44] As one astute critic of the 'entertaining detective work' known as Kremlinology noted, 'Vladimir Putin's consolidation of power is giving Kremlinologists another chance to get Russia wrong'. See Peter Lavelle, 'Kremlinology's Resurrection', *Untimely Thoughts*, Vol. 2, No. 40, 22 March 2004.

[45] See, for instance, Olga Kryshtanovskaya, 'Putin's Regime: A Liberal Militocracy?', *Pro et Contra*, Vol. 7, No. 4, Autumn 2002 (*http://www.carnegie.ru/ru/pubs/procontra/67060.htm*).

[46] A good example is Adrian Karatnycky, 'Jobs for the Boys: Putin's New "Militocracy"', *Wall Street Journal*, 13 June 2003.

above all the FSB (*chekisty*). They are building extensive horizontal ties across ministries and agencies, but by and large the retired military officers in these structures are not involved in these networks.

After the extensive reorganization of the government and the presidential administration at the start of Putin's second term, the alliance in the Kremlin between *chekisty* from St Petersburg and the leadership of the FSB succeeded in further consolidating the political influence of both groups.[47] The top brass, on the contrary, have lost a few outspoken supporters (like General Nikolaev, head of the Defence Committee in the State Duma of 1999–2003), and can hardly rely on a couple of symbolic figures (General Troshev and General Burutin) who hold the position of presidential advisers yet lack access to the ear of the chief. Sergei Ivanov alone personifies the link between the Commander-in-Chief and the High Command, but this is essentially a one-way connection, since he is much more the president's watchman than a channel for the military to pursue their agenda. The minister remains quite isolated in the defence establishment, even after his carefully prepared 'triumph' over the arrogant Kvashnin, who was forced into retirement in July 2004.[48] Often portrayed as a possible successor to Putin in 2008, he has no intention of spoiling his chances and so is generally content with the limited role of a national security spokesman, which includes being an international advocate of the war in Chechnya. It means that nobody close to the Kremlin would bother himself (adding 'or herself' would be unnecessary in this male-dominated environment) with operational routines and details of the ongoing war.

One litmus test of the relative influence of various branches of the executive power and their 'delegates' in Putin's court is the annual tug-of-war over the allocation of budget resources – and the military do not have an impressive record here either. The bulk of the growth in the military budget has been spent on (badly needed) increases in officers' salaries, but since 2002 the military have received no extra funds for counter-terrorist operations.[49] In Chechnya as well, the military has no access to the lucrative 'restoration' funds and are increasingly elbowed out by Kadyrov's militia from such 'shadow' businesses as semi-legal oil production and the 'black' market of kidnapping for ransom.[50] While the war economy is growing on a par with Russia's economic 'miracle', the military invariably find themselves at the back of the queue and cannot any longer compensate

---

[47] See Olga Kryshtanovskaya, 'Putin-2: Towards Napoleonization', *Gazeta.Ru*, 19 March 2004 (http://www.gazeta.ru/comments/tendency/96742.shtml).

[48] My analysis of this tug-of-war can be found in Pavel Baev, 'The Decline of the General Staff leaves Reform in Limbo', *Jane's Intelligence Review*, October 2004, pp. 48–9.

[49] The FSB, in contrast, has found a positive response to its requests, swiftly receiving, for instance, an additional 3 billion rubles for expanding its anti-terrorist efforts (plus 1.9 billion for the Border Service) in mid-2003; see 'The FSB is Granted Extra 6 billion Rubles', *Grani.Ru*, 16 June 2003 (http://www.grani.ru/Politics/Russia/Parliament/m.35792.html).

[50] See Tatyana Lokshina, 'Chechenization and De-Chechenization', *Polit.Ru*, 24 March 2004.

Chechen veterans with a 'relaxing' and well-paid tour of duty in the Balkans.

Overall, the sociology of the elites and the economics of the budget both point to the same conclusion: that the Armed Forces are consistently marginalized in the Byzantine intrigues of Putin's court. While the president relies on 'power structures' to advance his centralizing political project, the top brass are not among those *siloviki* who enjoy his trust and convert their domains into profitable business empires. Chechnya, where the military are stuck with a dirty and endless war that the President would prefer to become invisible and forgotten, is certainly a major factor in this estrangement.

Conclusions

The war in Chechnya, protracted and deadlocked as it is, cannot be characterized as one of those violent conflicts that have no military solution. The difference in the power potential of the two sides is just too great, and the war can be won in at least two ways. The first way involves a massive application of deadly force, including 'carpet bombing', aimed at sustaining the tempo of destroying the 'enemy home territory' for a sufficiently long time to make the southern half of this territory (some 7,000 sq km) into *terra nullis*.[51] The second way involves exterminating the 'mountain guerrilla' with mobile special units and high-precision airstrikes, and the 'urban guerrilla' with efficient muscular policing.

In essence, the choice is between traditional genocide and modern peace enforcement; Moscow, however, has opted for building a local force that is expected to conduct most of the hard work. From the point of view of the military commanders, Kadyrov's militia is not that different from Basaev's 'mojahedin' (the peculiar combat slang term 'chekhi', literally meaning the Czechs, is applied to both). At the start of the second war, they revealed a readiness to pursue the 'scorched earth' option, but are incapable of delivering the 'hunt-and-guard' option without significant modernization.

This brings us back to the question raised at the beginning of this chapter: Why have the lessons of Chechnya not been translated into a military modernization project? The somewhat paradoxical answer from our analysis is this: self-preservation and fear. The high command and most of the generals (and it is a very top heavy structure) have good reason to believe that any serious modernization would immediately reveal their inefficiency and incompatibility with a flexible and computerised organization of combat operations. A new generation of experienced and motivated leaders is necessary, and can be found in the numerous and still growing cohort of

---

[51] I examined this Stalinist option in Pavel Baev, 'Will Russia go for a Military Victory in Chechnya?', *PONARS Memo* 107 (Washington, Council on Foreign Relations, February 2000).

'Chechens'. Here, however, the fear factor comes into play, and it is concentrated in the only place that matters in Russia – the Kremlin. Putin, surrounded by triumphant bureaucrats and with only a handful of loyal *chekists*, is extremely worried about any shadow of real competition, and a tightly knit and hard-driven military 'opposition' would be perceived as a mortal danger. 'Modernization' and 'competitiveness' are his favourite clichés, but investing in an efficient and usable military machine that would be controlled by ambitious generals with questionable loyalty is a proposition too far. The slow-moving debacle in Chechnya in fact serves perfectly the political purpose of controlling the military: why fix a disaster that works?

7

The Chechen Wars and Human Rights in Russia

Alexander Cherkasov and Dmitry Grushkin

The second Chechen war has been continuing for over half a decade.[1] The tenth anniversary of the start of the first Chechen war has come and gone.[2] Even before the Russian intervention in December 1994, latent post-Soviet ethno-social conflict in Chechnya had been articulated as a separatist Russo-Chechen confrontation.[3] Russian society has now become used to regular despatches from this 'hot spot' about battles and terrorist acts. The Chechen war has become part of everyday reality, and has affected the lives of all Russians. It has made an indelible impact upon the lives and destinies of hundreds of thousands of people – the inhabitants of the republic, refugees and servicemen.[4] During this time, international perceptions of Russia

[1] There is no generally accepted date for the start of the war. Federal forces occupied the border heights on 29 September 1999. The bombardment of Grozny began on 21 September. Extremist bands invaded Dagestan on 6 September in Novolaksky district and on 8 September in the Botlikh district. In practice, military activity began in Tsumadin district on 2 August.

[2] Federal forces entered Chechnya on 11 December 1994. Two weeks earlier, on 26 November, Grozny was unsuccessfully stormed by soldiers recruited by the Russian security service.

[3] The Chechen National Congress met in Grozny on 23–25 November 1990. The Congress elected an Executive Committee, which later became the Executive Committee of the All-national Congress of the Chechen People (OKChN), the main political structure of the extremists. Its chair was Major-General Dzhohar Dudaev. OKChN adopted a declaration creating the Chechen Republic Nokhchi-Cho. On 27 October 1990 the first secretary of the Chechen-Ingush Communist Party organization and chair of the Chechen-Ingush Supreme Soviet, Doku Zavgaev, signed the republic's declaration of state sovereignty.

[4] Let us give one example. Viktor Droznik from the town of Monchegorsk in Murmansk region fought in Chechnya and received the Suvorov medal. After being demobilized and returning to his home town he was unemployed, and joined one of the local criminal bands. In 2003 Droznik was killed during a conflict with a rival group.

have been significantly influenced by the interminable war in the North Caucasus. In this chapter, we will first look at some of the ways the conflict is perceived at home and abroad, and will then examine the role of human rights organizations in the settlement of the armed conflict in Chechnya.

The International Context of the Chechen Wars

Both Chechen wars were accompanied by a massive violation of human rights by the warring sides, by military crimes and crimes against humanity. In both cases the federal side sought to place these actions outside the context of law, both national and international. In both wars, as in all developments in Chechnya over the last ten years, the trend has been from 'bad to worse'.

However, there is a clear difference between the two Chechen wars. The first claimed more lives, but the second was undoubtedly more brutal. Both wars were provoked, to a considerable extent, to enhance the political standing of the federal executive authorities. However, the first war provoked general indignation, and actors in the Russian political system played a substantial role in bringing the war to an end. Defenders of the rule of law, the anti-war movement and the free media played their part in forcing an end to the war. By contrast, the second war has been supported by the majority of the Russian people, as well as by a large section of the political spectrum and the mass media. This war played a key role in the successful election campaign of the Russian president, Vladimir Putin. The Russian authorities have succeeded in marginalizing not only the anti-war and legal rights activists, but also any significant discussion of the events in the Caucasus.

Another difference between the two conflicts is that the international community took an active part in trying to resolve the first Chechen war, with the Organization for Security and Co-operation in Europe (OSCE) acting as mediator. In the second conflict the OSCE and other intergovernmental bodies have been more restrained, and journalists reported more information from the scene of events in the first conflict than they do now. The attitude of the international community towards the conflict in the North Caucasus, and towards Russia in the context of this conflict, is contradictory and changeable, while the attitude of Russian commentators towards the West, by contrast, is stable and decisive. They usually represent the 'West' as a homogeneous entity, without distinguishing between the opinions of politicians, leaders of mass protest movements or representatives of the human rights community.

One aspect of the difference in the West's reaction to the events of late 1994 and Autumn 1999 is associated with changing attitudes towards Russia's leaders. Another is that during the 1990s and into the 2000s Western attitudes towards 'humanitarian intervention' have oscillated as a result of failures in Somalia in late 1993 followed by effective intervention after the massacre in Srebrenica, with Nato's bombardment from July 1995 forcing the participants of the Bosnian conflict to sign the Dayton agreement that Autumn. The perception of the efficacy of 'humane intervention' rose drastically. However, this did not affect the situation in Chechnya. By this time the 'first' Chechen war had already moved from the borders of the republic to Grozny, then up into the mountains and from there to Budennovsk in Stavropol region. The assistance group from the OSCE had already started to work in the region, beginning with its officials' participation in closed negotiations between the sides. In June 1995 negotiations between the delegations of the federal centre and the separatists in Grozny were conducted under the aegis of the OSCE. Leaders of the Allied powers visited Moscow in early May 1995 to participate in the celebrations marking the fiftieth anniversary of victory in World War 2. The Russian leadership did not question the minimal participation of the world community in the settlement of the conflict; in turn, the latter did not expect to achieve too much.

Belief in the positive impact of 'humanitarian intervention' remained strong through the second half of the 1990s, partly due to a widespread overestimation of the effectiveness of high precision weapons, which could allegedly lower the ratio of loss of lives between enemy troops and innocent populations to 10:1, reversing the typical twentieth century proportion and thereby lowering the human cost of intervention to an acceptable level. In Spring 1999, after the ethnic cleansing carried out in Kosovo by the Yugoslav leadership against the Albanian population, Nato intervened, disregarding the rules established by international law. A solution to the Balkan crisis was achieved in Spring 1999: Serbian forces withdrew from Kosovo and the genocide of Albanians was brought to an end. However, it became clear that the capabilities of 'high-precision' weapons had been grossly overestimated: the ratio of casualties between the military and the civil population came to about 1:1.

The second Chechen war began a few months after the armed conflict in Kosovo. European public opinion had sided with the 'victims' – Croats, Muslims and Albanians in Kosovo for whom independence and self-determination seemed the panacea. These views of 'right' and 'wrong' were by analogy projected on to Russia and Chechnya. It seemed easy from a distance to make judgements regarding the conflict; typical examples being the influential French left-wing philosophers André Glucksman and Bernard-Henri Lévy. They defined the actions of the federal forces in Chechnya as 'genocide' and considered 'independence' the solution, a perspective that was clear-cut and intelligible to public opinion. An equally simple solution, for these philosophers, would be the participation of international forces in settling the problems of the Caucasus. In this, public opinion and human rights organizations were poles apart. The latter, while informing the world about the mass violation of human rights in this or that region, simultaneously warned states and organizations against hasty actions that could infringe norms and procedures established by international law.

In Chechnya, human rights activists acknowledged the events and occurrences that acted as the *casus belli*; that is, kidnappings, hostage-taking and the invasion of Dagestan. In contrast to Chechnya, however, the separatist enclaves in Dagestan did not produce so much criminal activity, terrorist attacks or armed invasions of neighbouring regions. Second, human rights activists accepted the possibility and even the necessity of the state's use of force to protect the lives, rights and freedoms of its citizens, but only in accordance with domestic laws and the international obligations of the state. Third, when discussing the actions of the state in Chechnya, they used the terms 'military crimes' and 'crimes against humanity' because the existence of genocide has not, strictly speaking, been proved. Fourth, concerning the necessity and desirability for Russia of the internationalization of the Chechen conflict, they insisted that the core issue was Russia's fulfilment of its obligations in the framework of the OSCE and the Council of Europe, as well as the implementation by these international organizations of their own rules and procedures: mediation between the sides, sending delegations to the conflict zone, activating the mechanisms of the European Court of Human Rights (ECtHR) in Strasbourg, and so on.

Chechnya and the 'War on Terror'

In the last five years Russian discussions on Chechnya have been full of references to the Balkan, Afghan and Iraqi experiences. For patriots, Chechen separatism was seen as representing a threat to the dissolution of Russia, repeating the scenario acted out in Yugoslavia. Second, any talk of human rights in Chechnya was considered the equivalent of calling for the bombing of Russia; anybody questioning this was considered an enemy of Russia. Third, paradoxically, the proclaimed unlawful bombardment of Yugoslavia by Nato was viewed as a precedent for the use of force in Chechnya.

There is, perhaps, another paradox in this: the federal forces, their roles and actions, can be compared with those of the Yugoslav army and police. Although the level of violence against the civilian population did not reach Bosnian or Kosovan proportions, there were incidents of mass murder of civilians by Russian federal forces in Alkhan-Yurt, Staropromyslov region and Novy Aldy. Thousands of people became victims of violent and non-voluntary disappearances and extra-judicial executions. The mass and non-selective bombardment of populated areas and roads in Chechnya cannot be compared with the attempted pinpoint strikes of US or Nato forces. There is after all an analogy here. One of the declared reasons Moscow gave for starting the war was the squeezing of ethnic Russians out of Chechnya when Dudaev and Maskhadov were in power. The restoration of the peaceful co-existence of ethnic communities may well have been the aim of the federal centre. The achieved outcome was however opposite to that aim. As a result of the two wars Chechnya has practically become ethnically homogeneous: everybody – Russian and Chechen – fled from the war, and now only Chechen refugees return to the republic.

After the events of 9/11, which happened two years after the second Chechen war started, President Putin joined the 'war on terror'. Russia was presented with an opportunity to emerge from the international isolation in which it had found itself with the onset of the second Chechen war; this, however, was the road back to political rather than legal legitimacy. The threat of terrorism is presented by the USA above all, as a unique threat that demands the rejection of the existing system of international law, or at least extending its boundaries to deal with this threat. Since no general definition of terrorism has been agreed, states have received extensive freedom of action but are not always capable of using their extended powers responsibly.

After 11 September Russia became accepted as part of the war on terror, but the country exists in two parallel legal spaces at the same time, governed by principally different imperatives. The Shanghai Co-operation Organization, whose members include China and the former republics of Central Asia, was founded on Russian initiative and on the principle that a state's violation of human rights can in no way justify interference in its internal affairs. Here, a distinction is drawn between the complex of norms of international law – presupposing the primacy of human rights – and the view that the violation of these rights is the internal affair of a state. The view among the member states of this agreement on Russia's part in the 'antiterrorist coalition' is based on mutual exchange: Russia's role in Chechnya is ignored; in turn, it overlooks internal abuses of its fellow members of the Organization.

In 2003 another example of 'humanitarian interference' on a far larger scale followed in Iraq. Here on the diplomatic front Russia is on close terms with France and Germany against its trans-Atlantic ally in the 'antiterrorist coalition'; as a result, there exists a tacit acceptance of Russia's activities in Chechnya. If the war in Iraq did not bury the system of international law, then certainly the idea of 'humanitarian intervention' has been weakened. The military victory was achieved quickly, but considerably more American soldiers were killed after the end of hostilities than during them. The same can be said about the Russian victories and losses in Chechnya. The political settlement process seems to have started, there appears to be a civilian government, but the terrorist underground remains a permanent threat. Chechnya remains true to form.

The Role of Human Rights Organizations

In August 1999 the actions of the federal forces enjoyed all-round support in Russia. This is quite understandable, since society wanted to feel positive towards the authorities and the army. There was no reason to feel that way at the end of the 1990s until the invasion of Dagestan by detachments led by Basaev and Khattab, which was repulsed by federal forces. The Russian authorities could not close their eyes to the crisis situation in Chechnya and the neighbouring regions. The Russian army finally acted as liberator. The state not only has the right but has the duty to use armed force to protect its citizens. For the first time since the Second World War servicemen, who considered themselves defenders of the people, behaved correctly towards them.[5] It should be noted that the military conducted themselves with unusual openness during the operation in Dagestan. All this led to a situation where in the first weeks of the second Chechen war the actions of the federal forces were supported by most of the Russian mass media, the majority of the electorate and practically the entire political spectrum.

The war hysteria that overwhelmed the Russian media after the explosions in Buinaksk, Moscow and Volgodonsk, with the Chechens held responsible by the authorities, did not permit any room for doubt. This explanation of events has not been sufficiently confirmed, but neither has the parallel version blaming the Russian special services for the explosions. It became the main instrument of the pre-election campaign for the pro-Putin forces during the elections to the State Duma in December 1999. Later, Russian society was not given the opportunity to see whether the positive image of the federal forces remained valid once they had invaded Chechnya's territory. An information blockade of the zone of the armed conflict was established, one that was far more rigid and effective than the regime imposed during the first Chechen war.

All this made the work of human rights activists in the zone of armed conflict in Chechnya much more difficult and impeded attempts to use the information gained to improve the situation. For Soviet human rights defenders the main problem was individual political repression, but when this stopped with the disintegration of the USSR numerous 'hot spots' emerged. For non-governmental organizations (NGOs) work became far more complex. During Yeltsin's rule the relationship between the government and the human rights movement existed in another dimension than civil society. The authorities used the language of human rights, which they inherited from the democratic movement, but there was no dialogue between the power system and society. To all intents and purposes, human rights activists became invisible.

With the introduction of a free press in Russia in the 1990s the human rights movement had to change the way it operated. Expert and specific legal work became its main activity. After the dissolution of the USSR the view emerged that the issue of the 'hot spots' was not a pressing one. Not only had Russia won democracy but it had allegedly separated itself from the local conflicts, now across national borders. This illusion was shaken after the conflict between North Ossetia and Ingushetia in 1992 and the conflict between Yeltsin and the Russian parliament in 1993, and was conclusively dispelled at the beginning of the first Chechen war in 1994.

---

[5] This was in evidence in Dagestan during the storm and 'cleansing' of the Wahhabi enclave of Karamakhi, where the militants conducted themselves as if they were on foreign territory.

During the first Chechen war (1994–6), from 15 December 1994 human rights representatives of the Russian Federation worked in the war zone, but no law regulated their activities. Sergei Kovalev was appointed by the State Duma to the post, but he did not have any real power or rights. That is why a number of non-governmental human rights organizations, above all the 'Memorial' society, joined in to help the work of human rights representatives and sent their members to join its staff. Founded in 1987, Memorial was effectively the first and undoubtedly the largest non-governmental organization in the USSR during the *perestroika* period. Its initial goal was to commemorate the victims of political repression in the USSR, studying and revealing the crimes of the past as part of Gorbachev's *glasnost* (openness). However, history and the present are always woven together. The human rights work of Memorial began in 1989. It was impossible to talk about the past and to be silent about the present.

For the human rights movement of the Soviet Union during *perestroika* and post-Soviet Russia, the theme of 'hot spots' took on a special significance right from the outset. It turned out that the integrity of the USSR was based on repression, and when that stopped the ethnic tensions surfaced and numerous bloody ethno-social conflicts flared up. The Union centre used force to try to prevent dissolution, and again blood was shed. Refugees started fleeing. It was precisely these issues, 'hot spots', refugees and discrimination, which became central to the work of the human rights centre Memorial. Sergei Kovalev's group was active until March 1995, when Kovalev lost his job as representative through a vote of deputies in the State Duma.

However the activities of the human rights activists did not stop in the conflict zone. In the same month an observation mission of human rights public organizations, headed by Kovalev, was set up on Memorial's initiative. The group included representatives of human rights activists from the branches of Memorial in Moscow, St. Petersburg and Ryazan, the Central-Chernozem research centre on human rights, while deputies of the State Duma worked as part of the mission as observers. The human rights activists – both Kovalev's group and the observation mission – managed to obtain tangible results. Their reports were actively used by the mass media and influenced society. The observation mission and Memorial prepared and published a number of reports devoted to particular episodes of the war and aspects of events from the zone of armed conflict, including studies of the living conditions of detainees, the condition of captive servicemen, the practice of taking hostages, the use of the population as a 'live shield', and much more. The single most important work was the volume, edited by O. P. Orlov and A. B. Cherkasov, entitled *Russia-Chechnya: Chain of Mistakes and Crimes*, published in 1998.[6]

---

[6] OP. Orlov and AV Cherkasov (eds), *Rossiya-Chechnya: tsep' oshibok i prestuplenii* (Moscow, Memorial/Zven'ya, 1998).

Human rights activists were active in helping negotiate the resolution of the Budennovsk crisis, helping save the lives of over a thousand people taken hostage by Basaev and to halt the war for half a year. In August 1996 Alexander Lebed ended the war by implementing the ideas of the human rights movement, namely, by negotiating with the insurgents. However, later, in 1997–9, civil society in both Russia and Chechnya were incapable of withstanding the parties in favour of renewed war. The beginning of the second Chechen war in 1999 not only coincided with the change of power in Russia but, as we have seen, became one of its main mechanisms, the main feature of pre-election PR.

According to the official, formally legal point of view, since 1999 nothing special has been happening in Chechnya. Apparently, the Russian constitution is effective there, since no state of emergency or martial law has been introduced that would allow the restriction of human rights. What is more, the Chechen republic has its own constitution, president and government. Russia, the signatory of numerous international pacts on human rights, did not announce to the United Nations or the Council of Europe its intention to suspend its commitments to uphold civil and political rights and the operation of the European Convention on Human Rights in Chechnya. From the point of view of the authorities, there are no hostilities: the Russian Federation insists humanitarian rights norms do not apply in Chechnya.

So what is actually going on? Since 1999 there has been a 'counter-terrorist operation'. In 1994–6 there had been 'restoration of the constitutional order' and 'disarmament of illegal gang formations'. All these linguistic contrivances sought to place the federal forces in Chechnya beyond any kind of control, parliamentary or international, and to free them from any restrictions. To achieve this aim a legal vacuum was artificially created. As a result, there have been mass and indiscriminate bombardments that have led to the loss of the lives of tens of thousands of people. The Russian city of Grozny was practically destroyed. Brutal multiple 'mopping up' operations (*zachistki*) of built-up areas were often accompanied by the premeditated murder of peaceful inhabitants. Behind the façade of the official system of agencies called upon to maintain legality and order, an unofficial punitive system emerged where detained and 'vanished' people are cruelly tortured and extra-judicial executions take place. There is the impunity of the '*siloviki*' (force personnel), who have committed crimes against civilians. There is the halving of the population of the Chechen Republic, basically due to migration, and the emergence of hundreds of thousands of forced migrants. There is the imitation of a process of political settlement, the carrying out of a referendum and presidential elections. The 'eternal engine' of terror is at work in which an explosion set off by fighters is reciprocated by mass indiscriminate violence by the power structures, which in turn stimulates new 'avengers'.

Data on the War

How many people have died in the two Chechen wars? The Russian government has made no realistic attempt to count the loss of the civil population either during the war of 1994–6 or after 1999. There are no lists – even incomplete ones – with the names of victims, and any intelligible discussion about accurate figures (accurate to within tens of thousands, that is), is impossible for the Russian authorities. Thus, on 17 September 2002 the Chechen public figure Salambek Maigov told journalists that during the second Chechen war 80,000 peaceful dwellers had been killed, citing Human Rights Watch and the human rights centre Memorial, although neither of them had ever reported figures like this. The following day Abdul-Khakim Sultygov, the president's special representative on human rights to the Chechen Republic, responded by noting that that the estimate was too high, and anyway, 'all the numbers that human rights organisations announce are subjective, providing data that bear no relation to the real situation'.

In the course of the first Chechen war there was only one attempt to calculate the number of inhabitants of Grozny who perished in the fighting from December 1994 to March 1995. Associates working with the Memorial watch mission cross-examined more than a thousand refugees from Grozny concerning first-hand cases of the loss of relatives (close relatives and cousins) and acquaintances during the fighting. While processing the evidence, family structures were taken into account, as were the general number of relatives of different degrees of kinship and the width of the circle of acquaintances, while adjustments were made for double counting. On the whole the methodology used by Eduard Gelman, research fellow of the Kurchatov Institute, in 1995 is typical for calculating the number of victims in regional conflicts. On the basis of the data obtained the conclusion was reached that some 25,000 inhabitants of Grozny lost their lives.

In January 1996 Vladimir Rubanov, deputy secretary of the Russian Security Council, declared in an interview with 'Interfax' that no official statistics were available. In spring 1997, during the preparation of the Russian-Chechen treaty (Appendix 2), the question about the possible amount of compensation to be paid to Chechnya for the damage and the loss of life was discussed. Boris Brui, head of the demographic statistics section of the Russian state statistics agency (Goskomstat), turned to Memorial to discover the number of civilians killed. He had previously asked the International Red Cross Committee, who referred him to Memorial. As a result, based on the same data, Goskomstat concluded that about 30,000–40,000 people had been killed. In turn Memorial, realising the possible inaccuracy of similar evaluations, used the formula of 'fewer than 50,000'.

The only definite evaluation of the number of civilians lost during active operations in the second Chechen war was made by human rights activists from Human Rights Watch using an analogous method. Having collected and analysed detailed information about 1,300 people killed during the first nine months of the conflict, they came to the conclusion that their sample covered between one-eighth and one-fifth of the total number of victims. That is to say, the number of civilians killed during those months totalled between 6,500 to 10,400.

It is possible to calculate the number of citizens of the Chechen republic who died during the armed hostilities using as a basis for assessment *The Chronicle of Violence*, which has been kept by Memorial since July 2000. The number of people whose death is recorded in the *Chronicle* changes for different periods: from 489 during the second half of 2000 up to 559 for the whole of 2002, excluding insurgent losses and Chechen militiamen. The outcome of this monitoring is notoriously incomplete. Memorial records perhaps a quarter of such cases and certainly not more than half, as is shown in comparison with official MVD statistics for 2002. Extrapolation of data in the *Chronicle* makes it possible to conclude that between 6,300 to 11,700 civilians have lost their lives since the official end of active combat operations. In addition, during the second Chechen war around 4,000 people disappeared following detention by federal power structures. The bodies of some vanished people have been found, but the great majority have disappeared entirely. Thus, the total number of civilians who have perished during the second Chechen war, including the 'disappeared', is somewhere between 15,000 and 24,000. A conservative estimate, without taking into account the people reckoned to be missing, is between 10,000 and 20,000.

Where did the other, much larger, estimates of deaths come from? During the first Chechen war there was talk of about 80,000–120,000 deaths. These numbers are politically motivated and have little connection to reality. In Winter 1996, soon after Rubanov's declaration, some politicians, including Alexander Lebed and the veteran oppositionist Valeriya Novodvorskaya, declared that if the government talks of between 25,000 and 30,000 deaths, then in actual fact there must be at least three times more, giving a total of 80,000–100,000. Another estimate is connected with an incorrect interpretation. Lechi Saligov, who worked for the pro-Russian Chechen administration during the first war, asserted that in 1995 in the Grozny region alone more than 120,000 people perished. This was calculated by the difference between the pre-war population and those counted after the cessation of hostilities by door-to-door visits. Saligov interpreted this disparity as the number of deaths, although migration would be a more natural explanation.

If the losses among the civil population were, as a rule, exaggerated in statements of politicians, then the military and official propaganda underestimated or denied it altogether. In August 2001 General Valeri Manilov declared that in the second war no more than a thousand peaceful dwellers had been killed. A year later, in August 2002, Kostyuchenko, the Public Prosecutor of the Chechen Republic, repeated the same figure. Even at that time, this evaluation was easily refuted, not by estimates and extrapolations but by directly recorded deaths.

At the same time, the military and propagandists regularly declared their success in exterminating Chechen fighters, although their number was growing into tens of thousands. These numbers, it appears, are not plucked from the air but are obtained as a result of the work of the bureaucratic machinery, though they have nothing to do with reality. The number of victims published by the authorities is also political and is barely connected with reality. However, the numbers of fighters killed, quoted by the military and usually exaggerated, correlate with the losses of the civilian population. Thus, the total number of people who lost their lives in the two wars in the Chechen republic may reach 70,000 people. Although, the accuracy of our estimates is not precise, the government has not counted and still does not count the number of civilians who have died during the course of the 'counter-terrorist operation' and the 'restoration of constitutional order'.

Legal Issues

The federal law of 25 July 1998 'On the Struggle against Terrorism', used in the Chechen Republic for the significant restriction of human rights, has repeatedly been subjected to criticism, both in Russia and abroad. The complaints of the Council of Europe against the Russian Federation focus on the incompatibility of the law with generally accepted European standards. This criticism stresses the possibility of human rights violations due to the provisions laid out in this law. The potential for the arbitrary and broad interpretation of the law also provoked much concern, and allowed prolonged, large-scale military operations to be carried out, accompanied by mass and indiscriminate bombardments and firing conducted within the framework of the 'counter-terrorist operation'.

In the 2000s, however, the main human rights violations by federal power structures in the zone of hostilities in Chechnya were associated with 'cleansing', 'filtering' and the disappearance of people; that is, with mass unsanctioned house searches, indiscriminate detentions, keeping detainees in unlawful places, cruel treatment, torture and extra-judicial executions. These actions, carried out in the framework of the 'counter-terrorist operation', obviously contradict the law 'On the Struggle against Terrorism'.[7] According to Article 25 of the Russian constitution, officials and their representatives may enter the houses of civilians against their will only 'in cases set out by federal law'. Only federal law may restrict the inviolability of a dwelling (Article 55.3 of the constitution), including during a state of emergency (Article 56).

The federal law 'On the Struggle against Terrorism' in operation in Chechnya is less harsh in comparison with the law on the state of emergency

---

[7] See SA. Pashin, a member of the Independent Expert Legal Council, in his note 'On the Legality of the Mass Unsanctioned Entrance of Power Officials into Houses' of 19 March 2002.

dealing with the conduct of counter-terrorist operations. Nevertheless, according to section 4 part 1 article 13 of the former law, those conducting the operation have the right 'to enter without impediment into housing, and other properties belonging to citizens' only when the following two conditions pertain:

1. Dealing with a terrorist act as defined by Article 3 of the law (that is the direct criminal act of a terrorist nature in the form of an explosion, fire and such like acts endangering people's lives, causing significant loss of property or other socially dangerous consequences; or dealing with people suspected of having conducted a terrorist act).
2. If delay would create a real threat endangering the life and health of people.

The forces taking part in a counter-terrorist operation are limited by law and are obliged to have adequate reason for an unauthorized entry into a house; this covers not just any piece of land (populated area) in general but the actual dwelling in question, which is protected by law. The following constitutes a significant breach of human rights: unauthorized intrusion by servicemen into a citizen's dwelling against his will, following a terrorist act, after it had been averted or when the real threat to people's lives and health has diminished. This is an unlawful action violating the constitutional right of a human being and a citizen to have a sacrosanct living space.

The issue here is the arbitrary and broad interpretation of the law; not the inadequacies of the legal act but the way it is implemented. The law 'On the Struggle against Terrorism' was initially intended to regulate the local and short-term use of force where an immediate reaction was required and where there was no time to gain parliamentary sanction. The counter-terrorist operation provisions were used in August 1999 to allow the use of armed force without introducing a state of emergency or martial law, which would have required the sanction of parliament. In the event, this law on the struggle against terrorism has been used for many years in an area that covers many thousand square kilometres.

To justify mass unsanctioned searches and arrests in the course of 'zachistki', and also in 'special operations', service personnel cite Article 13 of the law. This article allows people to enter property during a counter-terrorist operation and in general overrules the inviolability of inhabitants. It basically allows, as in the law on the struggle against terrorism itself, the rule of 'hot pursuit' of Anglo-Saxon law. In hunting a criminal, if he hides in a building the police can immediately enter without special permission, thereby infringing habeas corpus. Earlier, when the law was adopted, human rights activists were concerned about the broadening of the powers of security structures during counter-terrorist operations, especially since under current conditions of discipline in the security forces, their general application inevitably leads to massive human rights violations. However, the arbitrary and broad interpretation of the law intensified this outcome. The law itself assumes 'the unity of place and time', but its substantial application in space and time leads to outcomes (the activities of security agencies) from causes (the activity of terrorists) that in effect renders the cause irrelevant.[8]

Security agencies have been granted wide powers without any serious normative base to control and regulate the use of these powers. This has been recognized in particular, by the military procuracy.[9] Therefore, in using the law on the struggle against terrorism and the system allowed by 'counter-terrorist operations' to limit civic rights in the zone of armed conflict in the Chechen Republic, the Russian authorities consciously created a legal vacuum. This artificially created vacuum is filled with legal practices based on the arbitrary interpretation of laws, and often on their conscious infringement. The results of this 'judicial experiment' have been the mass infringement of human rights.

There has unfortunately been no reaction to this in Russia. The political atmosphere has changed dramatically. If in 1994–6 we could talk about a 'peace movement, today only isolated politicians allow themselves to express their views. Taking into account changes in public opinion, condemnation of what is going on would give parties little if any electoral benefit. Of the two 'democratic' electoral blocs, one, the Union of Right Forces (SPS), supported the war and in the December 1999 State Duma elections crossed the five per cent threshold. The other party, Yabloko, was the only one to come out with a clear anti-war position and lost many votes. Both failed to cross the five per cent threshold in the December 2003 election. Deprived of political support, human rights activists found themselves marginalized.

The Work of Human Rights Organizations in the Second Chechen War

This situation forced human rights activists to conduct their work in a different way to that which was possible in the first Chechen war, and we will now turn to a brief review of their activities. In the months before the war Memorial[10] was working in the North Caucasus, including regions next to

---

[8] For example, a village may undergo an unsanctioned *zachistka* on the basis of the destruction of a petrol tanker miles away.

[9] A representative of the military prosecutor's office noted in a speech to a meeting in Znamensky on 28 February 2002 that 'There is no real legal basis regulating the conduct of "special operations", or even the counter-terrorist operation as a whole. There is only the general law 'On the Struggle against Terrorism' allowing us to detain individuals, but the terms and length of that detention are not stated'.

[10] The executive director is TI Kasatkina. The address of the central office is Moscow 103051, 12 Maly Karetnyi Pereulok. Email: memhrc@memo.ru.

Chechnya: in Ingushetia, Stavropol, North Ossetia and Karachai-Cherkessia. Work in the conflict zone began from the very start of the war.[11] In September 1999 in Dagestan there were Memorial workers in Novolaksky district (the area attacked by the Chechen units led by Basaev and Khattab) and in the war zone in the village of Karamakhi. Thereafter groups worked in Ingushetia and Chechnya, presenting their findings to press conferences in Moscow.

In the first year of the second Chechen war the human rights organiza-tion Human Rights Watch continuously monitored the situation in the region. At that time it was probably the leading human rights organization on the Chechen question.[12] In the winter of 2000 a permanent Memorial office was established in Nazran in Ingushetia, the base for all work in the conflict zone. In October 2001 sub-offices were opened in Grozny and Urus-Martan and later in Gudermes. Free legal consultation was provided by the group 'Migration and Law' in the displaced persons' camps and in other temporary camps in Ingushetia. These camps were also visited by social workers, while the organization 'Civil Support', which works closely with Memorial, provided humanitarian help. At the same time, the condition of forced migrants was monitored, as well as – more broadly – the human rights situation in the conflict zone.

Memorial does not conduct detailed monitoring accompanied by daily news reports or the placing of general news online. This is because of the way that Memorial has learnt to work over the years: accuracy comes first and speed second. All information is checked from as many angles as pos-sible. Its website regularly carries informational materials and reports on the situation in the region.[13] Since July 2000 Memorial's *Chronicle of Violence* publication has provided information about all human rights infringements by both sides in the conflict. The list of those disappearing without trace is constantly updated, and on the basis of our information a tally can be kept of those killed and kidnapped in Chechnya. As in the first war Memorial issues reports dealing with various aspects of human rights abuses and humanitarian norms in the Chechen conflict.[14] At first the authorities con-demned these breaches of the informational blockade, demanding to know why material about criminal activity was given to the mass media and not to the procuracy? Later, however, these criticisms abated. Memorial annu-ally sends the General Procurator and the procuracy of Chechnya hundreds of appeals, to which they are not able to respond.

---

[11] Work in this region is conducted within the framework of the programme 'Hot Spots' directed by OP Orlov.

[12] For its numerous reports on the conduct of the war in Chechnya, see http://www.hrw.org.

[13] http://www.memo.ru/hr/.

[14] Recent books include U Baisaev and D Grushkin (eds), 'Zdes' zhivut lyudi': Chechnya, khronika nasilie ['People Live Here': Chechnya, a Chronicle of Violence], Part 1 (Moscow, Memorial, 2003), and SA Gannushkina, O polozhenii zhitelei Chechni v Rossiisskoi Federatsii [The Condition of Chechen Citizens in the Russian Federation] (Moscow, Memorial, 2004).

At the present time a few other Russian human rights organizations conduct permanent human rights monitoring in Chechnya. Among them is the Russian-Chechen Friendship society.[15] In 2001 the Committee of National Salvation of Chechnya, based on forced migrants living in Ingushetia, was created and has conducted monitoring work.[16] There are a number of active human rights associations in Chechnya, for example groupings of relatives of those who have disappeared, those detained by federal security forces and disappearing without trace. These include 'Dog Teshar' ('Heart's Hope') in Grozny and 'Zhertvy voiny' ('Victims of War') in Urus-Martan. During the war many foreign human rights organizations have sent representatives to the North Caucasus and issued materials devoted to the situation in Chechnya. These include Amnesty International and the Federation International des Ligues des Droits de L'homme (FIDH). The work of many international humanitarian organizations working in Chechnya and Ingushetia also has a human rights dimension.

A few days before the terrorist act in Dubrovka in October 2002 the new staff members of the president of Russia's commission on human rights were announced. Ella Pamfilova had already been appointed its chairman in July; the other members were Svetlana Gannushkina (Memorial), Ludmila Alekseeva (Moscow Helsinki Group), Aleksei Simonov (Glasnost Defence Foundation), Alexander Auzan (Konfop), Svyatoslav Zabelin (Social-Ecological Union), and Valeri Borshchov. At the president's first meeting with the human rights commission on 10 December 2002, the plight of forced migrants became the main topic. The key point of discussion was Ingushetia, where the forced migrants were under pressure to return to Chechnya. At that time the refugee camp 'Iman' near the village of Aki-Yurt was forcibly broken up. As a result of the negotiations with the president the closure of camps and forcible repatriation of the refugees was halted. A commission was sent to the North Caucasus to clarify the situation. Apart from Stanislav Ilyasov, minister for Chechen affairs, and General Igor Yunash, deputy head of the migration agency, the commission included Alekseeva, Gannushkina and Ella Pamfilova. However, in summer 2004 all the camps in Ingushetia were closed; the process could not be stopped in any way.

International Organizations

Throughout the conflict human rights organizations have appealed to international agencies, sending them their reports, meeting with their

---

[15] The organization was established in Nizhny Novgorod on 17 April 2000. The head of its organization in the Caucasus is I Ezhiev, and it works in close partnership with the Moscow Helsinki Group headed by Ludmila Alekseeva. It site is http://www.uic.nnov.ru/hrnnov/friend.

[16] The organization is headed by R Bardalov and it works closely with the movement 'For Human Rights' headed by L Ponomarev.

delegations in Russia or lobbying their headquarters in Strasbourg or Geneva. Numerous intergovernmental organizations have examined the human rights situation in Chechnya. There is a common view that international society has dropped the question from its agenda, since the second Chechen war is considered a Russian domestic matter, an attitude that appears to have been held by the leading international organization, the United Nations, and above all its commission on human rights. At least this is what Russian officials declare – and surprisingly enough, many human rights activists agree with them. Probably both are wrong: the situation is far more complex. The potential of appealing to international society is not exhausted. It is another matter that it is getting much harder to be heard. The human rights situation in Chechnya has frequently become the subject of discussion by international organizations. This problem disappears and then returns to the agenda, and various documents have been adopted, sometimes inclining towards human rights and sometimes towards *Realpolitik*.

The approach taken by the Council of Europe to the Chechen question is typical. By late 2001 Chechnya appears to have disappeared from the agenda. There are various explanations for this, including the changed global situation after 9/11 and the beginning of the international 'war on terror', in particular after Russia joined this coalition. This silence from international society, however, was not sudden. International organizations had long been distancing themselves from what was going on in Chechnya. From the very beginning of the conflict in the North Caucasus human rights organizations, when appealing to international society, above all turned to European structures. It was here that Russia committed itself to observing human rights and to resolving conflicts by political means, and there were legal and political mechanisms to control the observance of these obligations. In January 2000 the Parliamentary Assembly of the Council of Europe (PACE) discussed the Chechen question for the first time. In spring of that year a fundamental resolution was adopted demanding that Russia respect human rights. The Russian delegation was stripped of its voting rights and Council of Europe member states were advised to apply international complaints against Russia to the Strasbourg EctHR, while the EU Council of Ministers called for Russia's membership of the Council of Europe to be suspended.

This appeared to be a victory of human rights over *Realpolitik*. However, the Assembly is filled with representatives of parliaments, while the decision was to be taken by the executive branch. In May the Council of Ministers, consisting of foreign ministers of Council of Europe member states, refused to accept this recommendation. The Committee, of course, did not openly declare this but noted 'significant progress in the observance of human rights'. Not a single European country appealed to the Strasbourg court. There was much unofficial talk about which country would join such an appeal – long as some other country took the initiative. No such country was found. After these two recommendations were not fulfilled, in January 2001

PACE restored full authority to the Russian delegation, once again of course noting an improvement in the situation.

In subsequent years the Council of Europe's commissioner of human rights, Alvaro Gil Robles, and the General Secretary of the Council of Europe Walter Schwimmer made many a sharp comment about the situation in Chechnya. One should note the report on the human rights situation in Chechnya by the secretary of the Council of Europe's Committee on legal questions and the human rights situation Rudolf Bindig, which recommended that 'if not enough efforts are made to try those accused of human right abuses in Chechnya and the situation where no one is punished continues we propose that the international community creates an ad hoc tribunal to deal with military crimes and human rights abuses in Chechnya on the model of tribunal of the former Yugoslavia, responsible for trying all criminal acts committed in Chechnya after 1 December 1994'.

Similarly, voting at the 59th Session of the UN Commission on Human Rights did not determine the future resolution of this issue. Much depends on the statutes of this or another inter-governmental organization and on the work of NGOs. Thus, in its announcement of 16 May 2003, the UN Committee Against Torture's 'conclusions and recommendations' on the questions of Russia's observance of the 'convention against torture, cruel, inhuman and other humiliating forms of behaviour and punishment' dealt at great length on the human rights situation in Chechnya, and formulated its views clearly and without ambiguity. In October 2003 a no less unambiguous statement on Russian policies and practices in Chechnya was entered into the conclusions and recommendations of the UN Committee on Human Rights.

The 'Civic Forum' and Order No. 80

Because the situation of human rights observance in Chechnya repeatedly became the subject of discussion in forums of intergovernmental organizations, whose delegations visited the region many times, the Russian authorities had to react. One form of reaction was to create state-inspired 'public' and 'human rights' organizations. An example of this activity without purpose was the creation in the State Duma of a 'commission to promote the normalization of the socio-political and socio-economical situation and observance of human rights in the Chechen Republic'. Its interaction with the PACE rapporteur on Chechnya, Lord Frank Judd, resulted in the creation of a joint group 'Duma-PACE' ('Judd-Rogozin'), which twice took part in the Duma's hearing on the Chechen problem, in September 2000 and in June 2001. Perhaps the European parliamentarians decided that at last the Russian state and society realised the seriousness of the crisis, and active debates were conducted to find a way of resolving it. For official Russian organizations, these hearings remain unique in the broad range of participants and the sharpness of discussions. In the event, the commission of the State Duma was effective only in propaganda terms and little substantive was achieved.

The same can be said about another state institution that is called upon to defend human rights in the conflict zone. The official human rights ombudsman in the region, the special representative of the president of the Russian Federation on human rights and freedoms in the Chechen Republic, was created on the initiative of the Council of Europe. From its establishment in February 2000 until 2002 it was headed by Vladimir Kalamanov, then (from July 2002 onwards) by Abdul-Khakim Sultygov; in 2003 the post was dissolved. The institution turned out to be incapable of decreasing the level of violence and defending the civil population from the arbitrariness of power structures, but it was quite useful in receiving numerous international delegations visiting the conflict zone in the North Caucasus.

Also worthy of mention is the official human rights organization created on recommendation of the UN Commission on Human Rights. The 2000 resolution adopted by the 56th session of the Commission called on the Russian government to investigate immediately the human rights violations and the norms of humanitarian law in the Chechen Republic, to create urgently an independent commission in accordance with acknowledged international standards. Soon afterwards, as if spontaneously created by popular initiative, the National Public Commission was created, headed by Pavel Krasheninnikov, the former Russian Minister of Justice. However, neither the procedure of its creation nor its membership conform to international standards applied in relation to similar commissions. We do not know whether anything concrete has been done by this commission for the investigation of crimes and for bringing the guilty parties to justice.

This process cannot stop: political technologists have to engage in new projects to keep their jobs. The government's next move, which seemed inevitable, was to establish control over the structures of civil society, including non-governmental organizations. This undertaking was – at the first attempt, at least - unsuccessful. In 2000 non-governmental organizations, sensing a change in the situation, attempted to band together. Non-governmental organizations with branches in many regions, like Memorial, the Moscow branch of Helsinki groups, the Confederation of Societies for Consumer Protection, the Socio-Ecological Union, the Glasnost Protection Fund, and so on, initially formed a round table called 'People's Assembly' with the purpose of working out a common approach in certain areas (such as access to information) and to improve interaction between regions and their local organizations. When in May 2001, having completed its work in eviscerating NTV, the Kremlin political technologists got down to work on civil society, and this grouping of social organizations showed its viability.

Initially, it was evidently intended to single out certain NGO leaders who could represent the whole third sector as a corporation. An attempt had been made to invite, among others, Alexander Auzan, leader of the Konfop social organisation, to a meeting with the president. He noted that his coalition colleagues should also be invited. He was told that only he was a true defender of human rights and all the rest (Memorial and so on) were needed in the past to overthrow the communists but now their work was done. Auzan repeated his request, and he was then also dropped from the list to meet the president. Later they tried, unsuccessfully, to get Ludmila Alekseeva (Moscow Helsinki Group) involved in the same manner.

In June 2001 political technologists headed by Gleb Pavlovsky, the head of the Effective Politics Foundation, began preparations for the 'Civic Forum', which was conceived as a congress of a few thousand NGO delegates selected as corporate representatives. It was already clear that without some organizations from the People's Assembly the Forum would be by definition unrepresentative, yet splitting the organizations had proved impossible. During negotiations with Vladislav Surkov, the deputy head of the presidential administration, conditions for participation in the Forum's organization were drawn up. Its purpose had changed. Now it was a dialogue with the authorities on several dozen themes, with corresponding discussion platforms. The authorities were part of the Forum's organization committee, as were NGO representatives. No elections were planned at the Forum; the formation of a corporation was postponed. The main thing was that Chechnya became the main theme for discussion.

The Civic Forum took place in Moscow on 21–22 November 2001. Besides the plenary session in the Kremlin Palace of Congresses, dozens of discussions took place. One of them was called 'Chechnya – our common pain and concern: ways of achieving peace and agreement'. A corresponding 'discussion platform' began work. In Chechnya consultations and meetings were conducted between NGOs and representatives of the military command, the commandant's office of the Chechen Republic, heads and deputy heads of the federal agencies of the Chechen Republic. Four meetings took place (under the name of the 'permanent working group') on 12 January, 28 February, 25 April and 8 July 2002. In Moscow the NGO representatives had one meeting with representatives from the presidential administration and federal agencies (procurator's office, MVD, Ministry of Defence, FSB and others) after the Forum, on 22 March 2002. This relationship with 'power' continued for six months, after which representatives from non-governmental organizations abandoned the process since they could see that it was not going anywhere.

Sergei Yastrzhembsky, an aide of the Russian president, and Vladimir Kalamanov, the president's special human rights representative to Chechnya, took upon themselves the task of organizing meetings on behalf of the authorities. In the intervals between these meetings, contacts with the procurator's office, special representative and the military commanders were maintained. On behalf of all the NGOs, the meetings were organized by a number of them, including Memorial, the Union 'Women of the Don', the Moscow Helsinki Group, the Society for Russian-Chechen Friendship, and the Chechen Committee for National Security. A number of other NGOs working in Chechnya as well as compulsory migrants in Ingushetia were drawn into the discussion process. Memorial became the coordinator among the NGOs.

During the first phase of the work of 'the discussion platform', it seemed that it would be possible to reach concrete constructive results. During the preparations for the first meeting in Chechnya, there was close interaction with the Public Prosecutor's office of the Chechen Republic. It was agreed that Memorial would send faxed enquiries to the Chechen Republic's Public Prosecutor, V Chernov, about human rights violations, requiring immediate response. As a result, twenty people managed to be freed after having been unlawfully detained by internal troops. However, this episode remained unique. At the very first meeting in Chechnya, on 12 January 2002, between NGO representatives and state agencies serious differences in the evaluation of the situation of human rights in Chechnya were revealed. One could hardly have expected any other outcome. With all these differences it was possible, at the most, to try and work out jointly real measures for the defence of the population against unlawful violence, or at least, to make it easy for NGOs to get information about the investigation of crimes, what the authorities were doing to improve the situation, and so on.

The majority of NGO ideas were rejected by the authorities. Only one proposed package of concrete measures was approved by all government representatives, including the North Caucasus high command led by General Vladimir Moltenvoi:

- Armoured vehicles must be clearly numbered on their sides;
- After a 'cleansing' was over, lists of detained people with the name of the unit that detained them and the location to which people had been taken was to be given to the head of the local administration;
- The leaders of the search groups entering houses must introduce themselves.

However, at the next meeting in Chechnya on 28 February it became clear that no one was going to turn these ideas into a concrete order. On 22 March in Moscow Yastrzhembsky was asked the same question, and the human rights activists received full support. As a result, on 27 March Order no. 80 of the united group of forces in the North Caucasus was issued, 'On measures to enhance the activities of local organs of government, population, RF law protective agencies in the struggle with the violation of the lawfulness, on the responsibility of the officials for the violation of the lawfulness and law and order while carrying out special operations and house raids in localities of the Chechen republic'.[17] Our suggestions had been incorporated into the document:

2. In the course of carrying out special operations ... military commandants from centres and regions of the republic, heads of administrations in populated areas, clergymen, elders, heads of village police stations,

---

[17] See the Memorial website for the full text of the document.

military public prosecutors of administrative centres (regions), heads of RF FSB agencies of administrative centres (regions) are to be involved ...

After the house raids ... a document is to be drawn up signed by the head of the special operation, head of administration of the town (region, populated area), the public prosecutor of the administrative centre (region), head of FSB agency of the administrative centre (region), chief of the temporary military group, head of the village police station ... The document is to be confirmed by the head of the united group of forces in the North Caucasus. Lists of the detainees, of the confiscated weapons, ammunition, explosives and narcotics, documents, money, property and so on, are to be attached to the document ...

3. The heads of the search parties ... are obliged to introduce themselves to the owner of the household, stating clearly their military rank and surname as well as the aim of the search. The use of masks is prohibited out unless strategically needed ... The search is to be carried out with tact, restraint and politeness ...

4. State registration signs and very clear side numbers ... are required on all means of transportation and military vehicles.

Two points of Order No. 80 were devoted to improving discipline:

1 ... special operations and house raids ... are to be carried out only by personal permission of the head of the united group of forces in the North Caucasus and in accordance with plans approved by him.

5. During the preparation and carrying out of special operations ... additional organizational and educational measures are to be taken to exclude cases of looting, physical and moral insult of civilians. ... every case of looting is to be thoroughly investigated, reported to the united group of forces headquarters, and criminal proceeding are to be instituted...

The Order, if carried out and observed, would help to stave off serious crimes against the peaceful inhabitants of Chechnya and to improve the human rights situation there. Order No. 80 was the only real achievement after six months of meetings, and even this single outcome made the negotiating process worthwhile. The Order could have been a major step towards improving the human rights situation in the Chechen Republic, and was presented by the authorities as a significant breakthrough in the human rights cause in Chechnya. However, within three months it became clear that the Order was universally and maliciously unfulfilled. None of the 'cleansing' was carried out in accordance with its provisions. People in masks would burst into houses without introducing themselves, insult and beat people, loot, and finally would drive people away in an unknown direction in armoured vehicles without number plates. Detained people were beaten and tortured, and no lists of the names of the detainees were passed to the heads of administration. Corpses of some of them were found with signs of torture and were often blown up. True, now at the end of a 'cleansing' incident servicemen demanded that heads of the local administration sign a no-claim document stating the operation had been conducted in conformity with the order. In the light of these and other breaches, active co-operation and discussion between human rights activists and the authorities lasted barely half a year and then the former withdrew. Was it a defeat? Possibly. But the formulations of Order No. 80 read like a judgement pronounced on the authorities themselves.

The Situation Today

In October 2002 the war once again came to Moscow itself with the Dubrovka siege. Human rights activists were not called upon to play a role in negotiations; only later were they brought on by the authorities and accused of inappropriate talk about peace. Seven years earlier in Budennovsk, after the unsuccessful assault on the hospital captured by Shamil Basaev, human rights activists, including Oleg Orlov and Sergei Kovalev, entered negotiations and not only secured the release of hostages but also the beginning of a peace process that managed to put the war in Chechnya on hold for half a year. At Dubrovka, however, human rights activists were not involved and nothing managed to prevent the assault.[18] As in Budennovsk, over 100 people were killed as a result of the terrorist act and 'counter-terrorist operation'.

All talk of a peace process in Chechnya was buried. What was the reason? What had changed? The release of hostages in Budennovsk became possible only because of continuous attempts at getting the peace process going, with Kovalev's group emerging as an effective mediator. During the second Chechen war, the sparse dotted line of peace initiatives did not turn into a process. There are several reasons for this. During the first Chechen war, human rights activists and peacemakers were denied any support, even symbolic, from the authorities, and were not taken seriously as mediators either by the Chechens or the generals, yet their influence was continuously felt. By contrast, Putin's power machine shows determination and does not need negotiations or, consequently, mediators. This is in sharp contrast with the inconsistency shown by the government under Yeltsin, which combined negotiations with coercion.

It is not only the Russian political system that has changed. Although Maskhadov has declared many times that he is willing to start negotiations, this desire coincides less and less with his real ability to control the insurgency. The negotiating capacity of the Chechen leadership has declined considerably during the long years of war. In particular, Shamil Basaev is certainly a major strategist. Basaev denounced any negotiations, even sending Movsar Baraev to Moscow to seize the Dubrovka theatre to make negotiations

---

[18] Tatyana Popova, *Nord-Ost glazami zalozhnitsy* (Moscow, Vagrius, 2002).

impossible. Meanwhile, beginning in 2002, terrorist acts in Russia are perpetrated with terrible regularity. At the end of August and beginning of September 2004 Basaev undertook a series of new terrorist acts: explosions on the ground and in the air; the seizure of the Beslan school and the deaths of children. After Basaev took responsibility for these crimes, Maskhadov declared that he was ready to hand him over to answer for his crimes 'at the end of the war'. One feels that the time of legitimate Chechen independence and statehood is coming to an end, if not already over, and that the last grains of sand are pouring out of the timer.

The terrorists have succeeded in achieving this, and the Russian 'war party' can celebrate the victory with them. Among the defeated are the dead hostages and the people of Russia and Chechnya. During the first Chechen war there was no total mutual bitterness, in contrast with many 'hot spots' of the former USSR. In spite of their best efforts, the 'special propagandists' from both sides did not succeed in imposing the image of the enemy on the people of Russia and Chechnya. As a rule, Russian journalists and soldiers' mothers could move about freely in Chechnya, and Chechen citizens could leave the republic. As before, both saw not so much an enemy as a human being 'on the other side'. This alone, it seems, made it possible to stop the war in 1996. 'Occupied by people' – such inscriptions can still be found in the Chechen ruins, but neither politicians nor journalists are willing to notice them, together with practically all, if not the majority, of the citizens of Russia.

After the monstrous terrorist act in Beslan on 1–3 September 2004, in which more than 300 people – mostly children – died, the Russian federal authorities made another attempt to strengthen the hierarchy of power by limiting the voting rights of citizens by appointing rather than electing regional governors and by abolishing single-mandate districts in parliamentary elections. Public opinion surveys reveal that for the last three years more than 60 per cent of Russians want to begin peaceful negotiations with Chechnya. Paradoxically, however, the prevalence of the anti-war mood does not develop into a mass anti-war movement. At the biggest mass meeting on 23 February 2000 in Moscow, there were far fewer participants than, for example, in Paris on the same day. The anti-war club (coordinated by Anna Karetnikova) and the Committee for Anti-war Actions (with Andrei Naletov as coordinator) function in Moscow and carry out regular picketing (up to twenty participants), occasionally organize small meetings (a few hundred people), but do not have any influence on public consciousness. When sociologists ask the question: 'With whom are we to conduct negotiations?', it becomes clear that only a quarter of the respondents mention negotiations with the opponent: the armed separatists. The rest think of negotiations with their own puppets, which is seemingly an obvious absurdity. What is the reason for this? One reason may be that latent anti-war moods have not been adequately articulated and reflected. Discussion of Chechnya and other problems associated with it have been marginalized, to put it in the most optimistic terms.

One of the reasons for this failure is that right from the beginning of the second Chechen war the authorities successfully imposed Orwellian language. Who could object to a 'counter-terrorist operation' in the course of which 'precision strikes' are dealt against bandits, while peaceful inhabitants escape to 'secure areas' along 'humanitarian corridors'? These combinations of words speak for themselves, and do not require proof or even commentary. A lot was left out of the frame and not broadcast: that rocket, artillery and air strikes claiming hundreds of lives were carried out on trusting people trying to escape along the 'security zones'. No mention was made of the fact that 'humanitarian corridors' only existed on paper, and that neither the population nor the military were, it seems, informed about the 'corridors' by the high command. People died trying to escape. Although soldiers were killed in the second Chechen war in the same way as in the first, only now they were called 'small losses'. Society was ready to agree with this as well.

The change in understanding concerning hundreds of thousands of people escaping from 'selective strikes' was no less successful. The declaration of the UN commissioner for refugees that there was no humanitarian catastrophe in the forced migrant camps, while people died of starvation, cold, thirst and illness on a grand scale, was interpreted by Russian propagandists almost as if the refugees had found heaven on earth. The very existence of the refugees was questioned: the authorities refused to give them the formal status of forced migrants. Apart from that, they were forced to return to another 'heaven' – the Chechen one. In the Russian virtual parallel reality these refugees have returned to Chechnya, and all of those who have perished have come back to life. How else can one explain that in the 2002 census 1.8 million people were found to be living in the republic whereas the true figure is well below a million. Nearly half a million dead souls counted in the census were active during the March 2003 referendum on the new constitution and the two presidential elections of October 2003 and August 2004.

In his report of February 2003 Rudolf Bindig stated that the impunity of the authorities was the 'permanent motor' of 'the death machine'. There are many tens of thousands of appeals to official bodies, with complaints about serious crimes committed by the federal security services. There have been over a thousand criminal cases begun by the Russian procuracy, although only after heavy pressure from European organizations on Russia. A few dozen criminal cases have gone to trial, about which the Russian procuracy has talked of with great pride. But only a handful of soldiers and militiamen have received genuine punishments for particularly terrible crimes committed in Chechnya. Impunity triumphs and provokes new crimes.

Here once again we encounter the problem of lack of objective information. It is impossible to struggle against that which is not openly discussed. Journalists have written about the psychology of servicemen who have been in Chechnya and have talked of a 'Chechen syndrome', comparable to that of Vietnam veterans. Chechen veterans on returning home often join criminal groups and nationalist extremists. However, there are no trustworthy statistics or a serious discussion; it is as if the problem does not exist. More is written about corruption or that Chechnya is a 'black hole' of the economy, sucking in huge economic resources intended for military operations or for restoration. But here equally seriously enormously different figures are cited, from billions to hundreds of billions of dollars, which does not allow serious discussion of the problem to take place. But one thing can be stated with certainty: the continuation of the conflict is destroying both Russian and Chechen society. The experience of unpunished violence will not be forgotten. In Russia and in Chechnya, a 'Caucasian war' generation is being formed. As Brodsky writes, in contemporary tragedy it is not the hero but the choir that perishes.

8

Dynamics of a Society at War: Ethnographical Aspects

V. A. Tishkov

From the beginning the Chechen conflict has in essence been an armed revolt against the Russian Federal authorities by one of the country's ethnically based autonomous republics, which in 1991 declared unilaterally that it was seceding from Russia and setting up an independent state.[1] Similar armed conflicts in the form of 'wars for self-determination' emerged at the end of the 1980s and beginning of the 1990s in several regions of the former USSR (in Nagorno-Karabakh in Azerbaijan, in South Ossetia and Abkhazia in Georgia, in the Transdniestria region in Moldova). Almost all of these ended in a victory of sorts for the separatists, but not one of these conflicts has produced an independent state, nor has a political solution to them yet been found.

Context

The federal authorities' attempt to put an end to the separatist regime in Chechnya by force spilled over into the drawn-out and destructive military campaign of 1994–96, culminating in the withdrawal of troops from the republic and the signing of peace agreements in August 1996 and in May 1997. According to official figures, in the first Chechen campaign the federal forces and police alone lost around 4,000 dead. The 1994–96 war in Chechnya led to enormous human and material losses: around 35,000 people were killed, more than one third of the republic's population (almost 450,000, including those who had left before the war) became forced migrants and refugees, while Grozny and many other places suffered severe destruction. The war was a tragedy for the Chechen people and post-Soviet Russia's worst crisis.

[1] Material for this chapter is taken from V. A. Tishkov, *Obshchestvo v vooruzhennom konflikte: Etnografiya chechenskoi voiny* (Moscow, Nauka, 2001), pp. 7–9, 40–56, 531–36.

The conflict between the Russian federal authorities and the Chechen separatists remained unresolved, and its consequences were not eliminated. In 1997–99 Chechnya experienced internal social chaos under a regime of rival armed factions. These attempted to gain legitimacy through radical Islam, and acquire material resources via human trafficking and terrorist activities for external clients. The breakdown of the social order in a self-proclaimed and unrecognised state, the destabilisation of neighbouring republics in the North Caucasus, the critical condition of the Russian state in a period of transformation, and external manipulation, including Western sympathy for Chechen separatism and direct support from Islamic radicals, eventually led to a new cycle of mass violence.

In August 1999, in order to widen the zone of armed separatism via the promotion of 'true Islam' and the war against the infidel (the jihad), armed incursions were made into western Dagestan from Chechen territory, and terrorist attacks (apartment block bombings) were carried out in Makhachkala, Moscow and Volgodonsk. In the autumn of 1999 federal forces, along with the Dagestani police and armed militia, responded by launching a huge military campaign in Dagestan and wiping out the radical Islamists. Forced migration within the combat zone dealt the unique ethno-cultural mosaic of Western Dagestan a severe blow, but overall the republic emerged from the crisis more united in its loyalty to Russia, and was able to overcome the effects of the conflict fairly rapidly, with the exception of the devastation caused in the so-called Kadar zone (the settlements of Karamakhi and Chabanmakhi).

Vladimir Putin, the Prime Minister between September and December 1999 and later Russian president, adopted an uncompromising position towards the separatist regime in Chechnya. This was in contrast to former Russian prime minister Sergei Stepashin, who had presented the leaders of the separatist regime in Chechnya with monogrammed pistols, praised the activities of the religious extremists who had taken over several Dagestani villages, and finally uttered in public the astonishing comment: 'We can afford to lose Dagestan!'. The autumn of 1999 saw the launch of a large-scale military campaign aimed at destroying armed groups in Chechnya, and re-establishing federal control over the republic. This action was officially termed a counter-terrorist operation.

The country was again plunged into an armed conflict with thousands of federal troops, Chechen fighters and innocent civilians killed or wounded. By June 2001 the second war had already cost the lives of around 3,000 Russian servicemen, with approximately 8,000 wounded. Even higher numbers of Russian citizens in the shape of innocent civilians and Chechen fighters were killed in Chechnya. Around 150,000–200,000 people left the republic, with only some returning after the most intensive fighting ended.

Having lost control of most of the republic with serious losses, the armed separatist groups switched to using guerrilla and terrorist tactics against both the federal forces and local inhabitants loyal to Moscow. The mass presence of the army and other federal forces in Chechnya was accompanied by attempts to set up an effective and legitimate local administration, to get life back to normal, and to rebuild post-war Chechen society. The Russian government initiated a special programme aimed at restoring both the Chechen economy and public life. However, the military had already lost the vital support of a local population suffering from the war and from gross human rights violations.

The Chechen war remains among the most serious problems facing Russian society. For various reasons it has drawn the attention of the world community. It has often been the focus of journalistic and academic research, usually in the form of political analysis. My own contribution looks at the Chechen War mainly in terms of socio-cultural anthropology. It is not a description of the war itself, but of its ethnography – a topic that has been neglected, but one that definitely deserves attention.

Chechnya and the Concept of Self-determination

The most difficult concept to evaluate in my research has been that of self-determination, which is mainly associated with the fields of political theory and the law, especially international law. Its essence and historical origins are generally well known, emerging from Woodrow Wilson's understanding of self-determination as government with the agreement of the majority of the population.[2] From the beginning this doctrine was used by the winning sides in the global military and political-ideological conflicts of the twentieth century to impose their own will. It has never been employed by its spiritual fathers and political initiators simply for its own sake, but has always been intended for external consumption. The doctrine received a new lease of life with the radical restructuring of the post-communist world, especially with the disintegration of such states as the USSR, Yugoslavia and Czechoslovakia.

The rhetoric of self-determination has always been basically an emotional political argument to justify disintegration and violent conflict. The post-communist world, especially the winning side – the liberal West, has taken to self-determination with enthusiasm. Many experts, especially specialists on the Soviet Union, have called for the principle of self-determination to be reassessed and updated in the light of the new geopolitical situation. Due to the overt ideological prejudices of those campaigning against the last empire (i.e. the USSR) and the new 'mini-empire' (i.e. Russia), this reassessment has not been directed at removing the old fundamental contradictions

---

[2] For more on self-determination, see H. Hannum, 'Autonomy, Sovereignty and Self-Determination: The Accommodation of Conflicting Rights' (Philadelphia, 1990); T. D. Musgrave, *Self-Determination and National Minorities* (Oxford, 1997); G. Starovoitova, 'National Self-Determination: Approaches and Case Studies', Thomas J. Watson Jr. Institute for International Studies, *Occasional Paper* (Providence, 1997), No. 27.

in the doctrine, but at increasing their legitimacy. Russian experts have also played an active role in this process, the overwhelming majority similarly committed to the damaging Soviet doctrine of limited self-determination aimed at subjugating ethnic groups to the state (the heterogeneous nation).[3]

Nevertheless, even the most thorough research into the contradiction between the right to self-determination and the state's territorial integrity, as well as into the interrelationship between self-determination and minority rights, has not led to any serious re-evaluation in the last decade. The author of one of the most recent works on the issue of self-determination and national minorities, while acknowledging the various opinions and interpretations that contribute to the understanding of the topic in the West, the former Soviet bloc and the so-called Third World countries, arrived at the following conclusion:

> The extent to which self-determination has become a legal right has still not been definitively established, because the term 'people' has never been defined in any precise manner, and because international practice with regard to self-determination has been inconsistent. Although decolonisation has been universally accepted as an integral part of the law of self-determination, the legal status of other aspects of self-determination remains unclear. The theory that self-determination entails representative government is widely acknowledged by Western states and by the majority of the former Soviet bloc states. However, this understanding of self-determination is not accepted as a part of international law by many states in the Third World. The status of ethnic self-determination remains even more uncertain. Although it is widely claimed as a legal right by many ethnic groups throughout the world, it is not accepted as such by most states.
>
> Ethnic self-determination does not fit easily into the system of international law... The primacy of the state in international law has meant that a state's population has been considered simply as an attribute of that state. The traditional primacy of the state in international law is therefore fundamentally at odds with claims of ethnic groups seeking self-determination, because such groups in effect seek to subordinate the position of the state to that of the group.[4]

I have always been amazed at how precisely and determinedly the Soviet and post-Soviet mind has linked the right to 'national self-determination'

[3] For more on the law and the freedoms of nations, see R. A. Tuzmukhamedov (eds), *Pravda i svobody narodov v sovremennykh istochnikakh prava*, collection of documents (Kazan, 1995); A. Kh. Abashidze, *Zashchita prav men'shinstv po mezhdunarodnomu i vnutrigosudarstvennomu pravu* (Moscow, 1996). For more on specific issues of self-determination in the context of minority rights, see S. V. Sokolovskii, *Prava men'shinstv: antropologicheskie, sotsiologicheskie i mezhdunarodnopravovie aspekty* (Moscow, 1997); Starovoitova, *National Self-Determination*, op. cit.
[4] Musgrave, *Self-Determination and National Minorities*, pp. 256–57.

with ethnicity. I should not be surprised, since I was after all the editor of the extensive encyclopaedias *The People's of Russia* (1994) and *Peoples and Religions of the World* (1998), adding more weight to the ethnic sense of the word 'people'. A more precise term would have been 'ethnic groups' rather than 'peoples', but such is the Russian tradition in academic and socio-political language. I well remember the words of Pierre Trudeau from my studies of Canada in the 1970s and 80s:

> A state that conducts its affairs mainly in line with ethnic and religious considerations will inevitably become chauvinistic and intolerant. Nationalists are political reactionaries, as they govern according to the common interests of an ethnic group or religious ideal, and not in the interests of the 'entire nation' independent of individual characteristics.[5]

The former General Secretary of the UN Boutros Boutros-Ghali hit the nail on the head when he stated in his programme document: 'The world cannot allow itself the luxury of permitting every culturally distinctive group to set up its own state, it is completely unworkable'.[6]

In Chechnya's case the rhetoric of self-determination is all-pervasive: from the main argument of Chechen separatist leaders to the language of ordinary Chechens. However, as our material demonstrates, the use and meaning of this word is often in conflict with the inconsistent interpretations of politicians and academics. Interpreting the Chechen crisis as a manifestation of the Chechen people's national liberation movement and the attempt by imperialist forces to suppress this has always been popular among some Russian and the overwhelming majority of foreign specialists.

Practically all studies of the history of 'the Chechen Revolution' and the war in Chechnya are based on holistic categories such as 'nation', 'freedom', 'sovereignty', 'the state', 'religion' and so on, and also on explaining fundamental 'historical rules'. Perepelkin was one of the first to come to the conclusion that 'The peculiar modern political development of Chechnya was predetermined by a unique combination of historical, socio-economic, ethnic, demographic, psychological and other factors, which due to historical chance are concentrated on the territory of this small republic'.[7] Petrov and his co-authors, analysing the course of the Chechen War also very much in terms of the geopolitical situation, state categorically that: 'The secession of Chechnya from Russia is now inevitable, whatever happens', and that 'The Chechen people have paid for their freedom in blood'.[8]

---

[5] P. Trudeau, 'Against Nationalism', *New Perspectives Quarterly*, Vol. 7, 1990, p. 60.
[6] Boutros Boutros Ghali, *An Agenda for Peace* (New York, 1992).
[7] L. S. Perepelkin, 'Chechenskaya Respublika: sovremennaya sotsial'no-politicheskaya situatsiya', *Etnograficheskoe obozrenie*, No. 1, 1992, p. 5.
[8] N. V. Petrov et al, 'Chechenskii konflikt v etno- i politiko-geograficheskom izmerenii', second edition, revised with additional material, *Politicheskii landshaft Rossii: byulleten*, January 1995, p. 21.

Western experts have demonstrated emotional and political prejudice when evaluating events in Chechnya. A pro-Chechen stance has been combined with an unexpectedly strong relapse into anti-Russian sentiments. This positive view of separatism within Russia was and still is characteristic of former Cold War warriors, who through inertia continue the struggle with the 'Evil Empire'. It can be seen, for example, in a report based on the findings of a mission sent to Chechnya in autumn 1992 by the non-governmental organisation International Alert. Its main author was Paul Henze, a former employee of the RAND Corporation. The main content of the report is a history of the Chechen and entire North Caucasus 'liberation movement against Russian colonisation', and a description of the radical cultural distinctiveness of the Chechens and their exceptional internal solidarity in working to achieve an independent state. Much of this interpretation is a product of the Western historiographic tradition of Russian Islamic studies, set out by Alexander Bennigsen, a historian of Russian extraction.[9] The main conclusion of the report contains a warning against attempts to resolve the conflict by force, but its general tone is resolutely in favour of Chechen independence as an accomplished fact. For Western experts like Paul Henze, to say nothing of many Western journalists, there was absolutely no doubt that in 1991 under Dudaev's leadership a national democratic revolution had been launched against the imperial centre and the local nomenclature. The 1994–95 war was neo-imperialist Russia's response.

The author of the report believes that Chechnya and in fact the entire North Caucasus region does not belong to Russia or even to the Russian Federation. Here is the document's conclusion, which for the Chechen radicals became a kind of moral sanction for secession:

> The Chechen republic has made an impressive start towards setting up state and governmental structures. Chechen society is characterised by a significant level of political openness and freedom of expression. All sides must shoulder the responsibility of preserving this favourable environment. In certain respects the political system does not always run smoothly, as it has evolved in a limited period. Chechnya's more prominent citizens constantly raise legitimate concerns over elections, the transparency of the government, and Chechnya's relations with its neighbours. The leadership must find ways to respond to such misgivings.
>
> Chechnya cannot resolve the issue of its status and relationship with Russia and other parts of the former Soviet Union by force. Russia cannot 'solve' its Chechen problem or wider related issues – of stability and positive political evolution in the Caucasus – by political intrigue, subversion, or economic sanctions. The Russian government has a duty

---

[9] A. Bennigsen and S. E. Wimbush, *Mystics and Commissars: Sufism in the Soviet Union* (London, 1985).

to inform the people of the real nature of the problems in the Caucasus, and of the realistic choices available to tackle them. In order to prevent the situation becoming even worse, and to avoid further human suffering, it is essential that all sides be patient and willing to negotiate.[10]

It is extremely rare for advocates of radical-democratic or anti-imperialistic interpretations to go in for re-evaluations. Such a critical reassessment was much more clearly demonstrated by the well-known Russian political analyst, Igor Klyamkin, when questioning why Dudaev was confirmed in office in Chechnya thanks mainly to politicians in Moscow:

It seems that it was not so much the man himself as the idea the rebellious general represented, an idea that made him appear to be a hero. I am referring to the idea of the 'national-liberation' (i.e. separatist) movement, which is claimed to be the natural and only way for non-Russians to achieve their democratic aspirations. From the emergence of the first 'Popular Front' in the republics of the USSR, this idea was so well-received by Russian democrats that it somehow became a habit to turn a blind eye to the nationalists' sins, both grievous and petty, and to forgive them first for their mildly unlawful activities and later for their open violence.

There is no doubt that in the *perestroika* era struggle with the yet unvanquished Soviet communist system, democratic movements quite often developed under an ethnic guise. But after the fall of Communism and the break-up of the Soviet Union, when the former union republics themselves became the centre and the 'national liberation' baton was passed on to their own autonomous regions, the true essence of separatism was exposed in its original form. And you had to be blind or deeply politically prejudiced not to perceive the calls to 'fight for the self-determination of indigenous peoples' as the basic striving of local leaders, freed from Moscow's grip, to direct the national frustrations of ethnic minorities to their own ends, far removed from the interests of democracy and national rebirth. Examples of such political blindness litter the history of post-Soviet liberalism.[11]

Civilisational-ethnographic Romanticism

I have identified another approach to explaining the nature of the Chechen conflict, which may be referred to as *civilisational-ethnographic romanticism*.

[10] *Chechnya: Report of an International Alert Fact Finding Mission* (London, 1992), p. 56.
[11] *Izvestiya*, 7 February 1995.

It has been adopted by many academics and commentators, and is often used by politicians. The core of this approach is found either in the 'clash of civilisations' between Islam and Christianity (from Samuel Huntington's weakly constructed theory), or in the incompatibility of ethnic systems and in Russian politicians' ignorance of the deeply rooted specifics of Chechen society. This is how Aleksei Malashenko, a leading orientalist, explains the situation:

> The Chechens have their own way of life and of thinking, their own codes of behaviour and beliefs. They have developed a unique social system, which the ethnologist Chesnov calls 'Vainakh democracy'... Two social-cultural systems with conflicting histories and outlooks will always repel each other. There has never been peace in Chechnya under any political system... It seems that Chechnya will always be radically different from Smolensk *oblast* or Primorsky *krai*. For this reason it will one day gain its independence, and God knows, we need at least one more friendly state on Russia's borders.[12]

As for the ethnologist Chesnov, his definition of modern Chechen society as one based on deeply traditional social structures is an example, often encountered in the field of ethnography, of a specialist constructing a set of cultural parameters mainly through a historical excursion into the realms of 'how difficult it is to be a Chechen' under the burden of *teip* coalitions and egalitarian personal relationships.[13]

The work of academic romantics always contains a treatise on 'the need for every mountain-dweller to bear arms', on 'the Chechen national military culture', on the absence of a tradition of submission to the authorities and written laws, on the decisive role of the elders, and so on. Traditional Vainakh military democracy theory to explain the high level of Chechen mobilisation in time of conflict is also found in the work of Sergi Arutyunov, a leading expert on the Caucasus region. He argues as follows: 'Actually, the processes that we encounter have much deeper roots. An intense re-awakening of the early-feudal and pre-feudal way of life is taking place in the region'.[14] The above-mentioned authors have, however, undoubtedly made an important contribution towards explaining the Chechen crisis.

The element that I call ethnographic romanticism is more deeply rooted and influential than it may appear. The Chechen crisis has given rise to or made popular a rich pseudo-scientific mythology about a people's history and modern image that has made the transition from academic and literary texts to the mass consciousness, including that of the Chechens themselves.

---

[12] *Nezavisimaya gazeta*, 31 December 1994.
[13] *Nezavisimaya gazeta*, 22 September 1994.
[14] S. A. Arutyunov, 'Zakony gor vne zakonov ravnin', *Itogi,* 19 January 1999, pp. 14–16.

One of these prevailing myths is of the people's unique nobility and love of freedom, which they have demonstrated throughout their entire history, but especially during two centuries of resistance to Russian colonialism. To a great extent this myth was developed in literature, and one of its main creators was Leo Tolstoy, for whom the story *Hadji Murat* was a kind of personal atonement and a creative exposé of autocratic despotism. Fashioning 'an image of otherness' in the shape of the utterly noble and brave Chechen Hadji Murat, the author was actually writing about the problems in Russian society, and about the constant search for the human ideal among the 'vulgarity of everyday life'. Through the power of his pen Tolstoy presented 'an image of a people' to the modern generation of Chechen readers, who in time became part of their mass consciousness.

Another powerfully imposed myth is of the unique antiquity of the Chechen nation. This draws its arguments from the historical and linguistic research of academics in Moscow and St. Petersburg, and also from the local region, on the lineage between the modern Vainakh languages and the Hurrian and Urartian languages, which were widely spoken in the second and first centuries BC in the Trans-Caucasus region, Eastern Asia Minor and Northern Mesopotamia.[15] With reference to this purely academic hypothesis, President Dzhokhar Dudaev created a political slogan that read: The Chechens, as the 'oldest nation of the Caucasus', should by right be given the role of Pan-Caucasian leader.

If we leave aside political and ideological motives, all these interpretations are limited in terms of objectivity, preferring to seek out deeper reasons and a historical pattern in the social process (or in events). Such an approach ignores modern-day personal strategies or motives, the role of individuals' constantly changing moods, including in inter-governmental relationships, and finally the role of accidental, emotionally subjective and moral motives and actions. Major social upheavals, and even more so large-scale military conflicts, appear too important to be ascribed to a seemingly superficial set of circumstances, such as the leaders' personal ambitions or the desire for revenge after a collective trauma.

It is no longer the done thing to engage in critiques of Huntington's 'clash of civilisations' theory, as it has never been clear what a civilisation is according to him, and because the concept is now politically well established. The crux of the theory is that one 'large battle' follows another, and that the time has come for the West to defend itself from 'enemy civilisations' (above all Islamic and possibly also Orthodox).

It seems that in Chechnya's case the breach between civilisations is clear-cut: Orthodox Russians face Chechen Muslims. My own analysis, however, rejects this theory even in its most tenuous form. There are far more similarities between the Chechens and the other peoples of the

---

[15] For more detail see, for example, S. Kh. Nunuev, *Nakhi i svyashchennaya istoriya* (Yaroslavl, 1998).

Russian Federation, most of all the Russians, than there are differences. This harmony of values, personal strategies and even cultural behaviour existed before the conflict, and is still in place now.

Obviously, the war greatly alienated the Chechens from other groups and strengthened the feeling that Chechens are different, not only in terms of their own self-consciousness. I cannot agree, however, that my colleagues and the people whom I have interviewed belong to a different civilisation. My research does not bear this out. There is no doubt that Chechen living conditions are radically different. Several important cultural distinctions are also apparent. But I have found that a Russian professor in Moscow and his Chechen counterpart from Grozny have more in common than a Chechen professor and a Chechen fighter from the same mountain village. The cultural divide is a result of a conflict within society, which exists both for those who live in 'war-torn' societies, and for those who live outside them or on their fringes.

Other Explanations

There is also a place in Chechen war literature for conspiracy theories. In other words, various actions and pronouncements, both from the federal and Chechen sides, can be viewed as nothing more than camouflage for the hidden motives and interests of more powerful forces, manipulated by politicians and generals. Alternatively, the war is seen entirely as a plot by foreign powers.

One dominant theme is the search for some powerful hidden economic motive or 'true cause' of the war in Chechnya. Experts usually identify these reasons as money and oil. This is what Edvard Ozhiganov, a former expert of the State Duma's Analytical Centre, believes:

> If we view the matter dispassionately and without prejudice, fear or favour, then despite the apparent difficulties everything is really extremely simple. There are currently only two routes for exporting strategic commodities from Russia: via the Baltic or through the Caucasus, passing mainly through Chechnya. The entire struggle is for control over these routes, and more precisely, over the exports themselves. Therefore, any changes in the leaders or personnel, or in the course of the conflict itself are merely a distraction from this struggle. The root of the conflict is found not in Grozny, but in Moscow. The Russian state mafia has already sought out the goods and raw-material export route through the Baltic, and no further problems are emerging there. In Chechnya the situation is completely different. Dudaev's regime was not happy to play the role of 'client'; it was much more interested in being the patron. All the more so as there were truly fantastic amounts of money at stake. 'Business' developed in three directions: arms sales, oil products and stolen cars. There was also the

opportunity to export currency freely from the republic, and then distribute it among foreign bank accounts. For this reason Dudaev's team chose a certain moment to simply claim exclusive rights to these revenues, and closed off Russia's 'Chechen route'. It was this action that caused the crisis.[16]

We should not ignore the fact that economics, including the criminal aspect, certainly played an important role in the evolution of the Chechen crisis. The description of Chechnya as a 'free criminal zone', provided by Sergei Shakhrai, a Russian deputy prime minister, is well known. Emil Pain and Arkady Popov, from the president's Analytical Centre, compared Chechnya and Dudaev's regime to the Medellin cartel in Colombia and to general Manuel Noriega's regime in Panama.[17] The 'criminal' nature of activities in Chechnya became the official line of the federal authorities, or rather of the president and his entourage, in the president's annual address to the Federal Assembly. In his speech Boris Yeltsin stated that 'as a result of an armed revolt, a genuine dictatorial regime has been set up on Chechen territory. The fusing of the criminal world with the authorities – which both politicians and journalists have consistently described as the main danger for Russia – has become a reality in Chechnya. It was the testing ground for the expansion of criminal authority to other regions of Russia'.[18] An almost identical assessment of the Chechen crisis is provided by Russia's extreme right-wing nationalist forces. On 14 December 1994 the Central Committee of Russian National Unity (the Barkashovtsy) passed a declaration on events in Chechnya, which contains the following passage:

> It is also no secret that the actions of Dudaev's regime have caused almost all economic activities in Chechnya to cease. This has led to an expansion of Chechen criminal groups throughout Russia, which is encouraged by the current Chechen administration as practically its only source of revenue. The present administration has turned Chechnya into a parasitical-predatory conglomerate, and by the same token consigned its people to the early Middle Ages.[19]

Another approach to the conflict is to explain it as an unsuccessful blitzkreig against a self-proclaimed independent Chechnya. The centre, and especially the president and his entourage, launched the war in order to resolve a series of political tasks associated with strengthening and preserving their own power at a time of deepening economic and political crisis in Russia. This view of the Chechen crisis was formed mainly by the

---

[16] *Obshchaya gazeta*, 9–15 February 1995.
[17] *Izvestiya*, No. 23–26, 7, 8, 9, 10 February 1995.
[18] *Nezavisimaya gazeta*, 17 February 1995.
[19] *Russkii poryadok*, No. 1–2, 1995, p. 8.

political and intellectual opposition, regardless of their political loyalties. For politicians and specialists of a radical-democratic persuasion, Chechnya was a conspiracy by the security forces, the president's closest aides and even his 'bodyguards', aimed at putting an end to democratic changes and setting up an authoritarian regime, based on 'supreme power' and national-patriotic ideology. As Yegor Gaidar claimed, resolving the Chechen problem by force was a practical step towards turning Russia into a police state.[20] 'Hands off Chechnya!' has always been the slogan of the radical democrats, although their arguments are somewhat subject to change. At first the emphasis was on sympathy for Chechen 'national self-determination'. Once the war started, and again on its return in autumn 1999, the focus was on gross human rights violations, mainly by the Russian army.

In my view, alongside the historical, cultural, social and political aspects of the Chechen conflict, there are also decisive personal, emotional and moral elements that cannot be explained in the usual terms of positivist causality. Here is just one example of how the conflict acquired an extremely personalised nature, precisely at the decisive moment. It concerns the personal relationship between Yeltsin and Dudaev. During an interview Mintimer Shaimiev, the president of Tatarstan, made a seemingly insignificant but in my opinion extremely important comment: 'Yeltsin was more or less ready to enter into negotiations with Dudaev in the same way he had over Tatarstan, but then he found out that Dudaev had made a negative comment about him'. It was obvious that at a certain moment Yeltsin (no doubt influenced by his aides and some members of the government working on his ego), decided not to have any further contact with Dudaev, and promoted him to main enemy after all other foes had been tamed or pacified. The best conformation of this came from another politician who was in contact with the president. When Valery Vyzhutovich, a journalist from *Izvestiya*, asked Sergei Stepashin, the director of the Russian Intelligence Service (then called the Federal Security committee, FSK, the precursor to today's FSB), which issue the president had raised with him most often recently, the answer was: 'It's usually the same one: "When are you going to catch Dudaev?"'[21] I chose this factor as the dominant theme for a review of events and the social-cultural context of the conflict.[22]

In addition, it is impossible to understand the Chechen War, especially its internal logic, intensity and drama, without considering the influence of the modern mass media on the conflict, as it was the first 'televised war' on the territory of the former Soviet Union. I am not so much interested in the media's coverage of the war as in its participation in the conflict – the creators of video images and newspaper articles produce a market-orientated

---

[20] *Moskovskie novosti*, 25 December 1995.

[21] *Izvestiya*, 2 March 1995.

[22] V. A. Tishkov, 'Chechenskii krizis: sotsial'no-ku'lturnyi analiz', in V. A. Tishkov (ed.), *Ocherki teorii i politiki etnichnosti v Rossii* (Moscow, 1997), pp. 405–77.

dramatised version (or versions) of the war, which is then served back to the participants themselves, not only influencing them, but also at times affecting their behaviour to a greater extent than military orders. In an interview I held in Ingushetia on 23 February 1995, the field commander of the 'Afghan battalion' in Chechnya referred to the radio and television many times ('although we don't have them on the front-line'), indirectly confirming the role of the media as an active participant in the unfolding drama. Here are some of his more typical comments:

'Even when Dudaev announced full mobilisation of the armed forces on television people sat at home and laughed'. (In connection with the federal authorities' view of the setting up of a regular army in Chechnya – V. T.);

'They say on television that the bombardment has stopped, but we drove round the city and saw for ourselves the effect the intermittent bombing was having on innocent civilians'. (On the lack of trust in the media – V.T.);

'If the politicians say to me, if they announce on the radio... that they've stopped the war, that I should lay down my weapons... then I will do it'. (Here an example of complete faith in the media – V.T.).

In modern conflicts the mass media is a powerful mobilising and belligerent force. It is as much a military resource as tanks and artillery. The television and press can help to achieve such vital goals as recruiting and motivating the troops, and gaining public and international support for the warring sides. During the second war, especially after they managed to film the helicopter of a Russian general being shot down in Dagestan, the Chechen commanders, according to some reports, never went out on a major operation without television cameras, in order to quickly show footage of their latest victories. Having employed the primitive procedure (used during the Second World War) of dropping leaflets from aircraft, the head of the FSK made a characteristic admission:

Yes, the Russian authorities have lost the information war. How brilliantly the Chechen information minister Movladi Udugov has gone about his task, how artfully and skilfully he provides the press with all kinds of lies, distortions and manipulations of the facts!... Meanwhile we kept the journalists at arm's length: 'always keep quiet, give nothing away!' Yes, I myself have avoided speaking for a long time.[23]

Experts have already pointed out the enormously influential role of the mass media in conflicts. This was especially obvious in Bosnia, when one of the stars of television war journalism, Christiane Amanpour, began filing

---

[23] *Izvestiya*, 2 March 1995.

reports for CNN, openly siding with the Bosnian Muslims. Her inflammatory dispatches not only won over world public opinion to the Bosnian side, but also provided the Bosnian Muslims, glimpsed on both their own television screens and on others around the world, with a powerful motivation to fight.

What explains the special role played by the mass media in post-Soviet conflicts? First, people in the former USSR have continued in their habit of believing the information and interpretations delivered by the time-honoured authority of television and the press to a far greater extent than those living in more advanced societies. Second, the citizens of the former Soviet Union are fully literate and are avid readers, making them far more susceptible to external influence than people in other countries where open conflicts and internal wars take place, such as Somalia, Mexico and India. In this respect the former Soviet Union can only be compared to other former socialist countries, including Yugoslavia, where the levels of literacy and education are high. Finally, the era of perestroika in Russia saw the emergence of a completely new generation of young and ambitious journalists, attempting to make a name for themselves in this dangerous and important profession, including via the slogan 'my war'. Russian journalists do not yet possess a set of generally accepted rules on the reporting of wars and conflicts. There were attempts to establish certain rules during the second military campaign, but they were dealt a serious blow, as for example, in the case of the *Radio Free Europe* journalist Andrei Babitsky.

Demodernisation as an Anthropological Phenomenon

Within the historiographic and theoretical context of my research, I would like to highlight and explain one of the fundamental concepts of this article, i.e. the idea that a society experiencing an intensely violent conflict is subject to demodernisation. The well-known theories of modernisation and post-modernism for all their various forms originate from the common epistemology of society's incremental development. This does not concern the situation under consideration here, which is more akin to what anthropologists call anomie, but only superficially. The situation in Chechnya is not one of rapid changes with which society cannot cope, causing it to descend into a state of anomie, but one of chaotic changes in which the very concept of society is swept away. During the armed conflict the Chechen 'nation', and even Chechen 'society', ceased to exist as an agent of social action. Attempts have been made to explain this, most of them reduced to simplified slogans and myths invented mainly by middle-ranking activists. These varied and even incompatible simplifications have entered the public consciousness, motivating personal strategies and actions, and sometimes existing side by side in the minds of individual people.

Since 1990 Chechnya has been living in a state of contradictions and torment, of serious disorder and disintegration, despite the dominant view of Chechnya as a place of unique solidarity and purpose, supposedly demonstrated by the Chechen people during the war. One only need read the lengthy book written by one of the leading ideologists of Chechen separatism, Zelimkhan Yandarbiev, to understand that the 'Chechen people', who appear on every page, 'the only ones able to stage major events and make their own choices',[24] are here something mythological and indefinable, because if you exclude from 'the people' all those whom the author calls communist bureaucrats, the rotten intelligentsia in their suits and ties, Zavgaev's supporters, the servants of Moscow and imperialism, the bewildered cowards, the treacherous hangers-on, the provocateurs and others who have no links to the 'Chechen people' as the agents of destiny, you are left with an extremely small group of those falling into the category of 'us'. This category, therefore, refers only to those bearing arms, who during the whole war did not exceed 5,000, but who grew considerably when the conflict ended in 1996.

During the war and in its wake the ordinary people were subject to an almost all-encompassing level of mass propaganda, which in turn was erected on simplified myths, appropriated from Soviet mythology, or partly borrowed from the 'national liberation' rhetoric of the outside world. An already feeble concept of political life and government by the people, of the state and its destiny, and of the essence of transformation, was subject to such further degradation that in the end it made only one alternative seem viable – armed struggle. Yandarbiev writes: 'The outcome of the independence struggle was predetermined. The people know what they are doing... A people desiring to be free and to build an independent state must be able to act decisively and be ready to make sacrifices. Every father, every mother, must, as our epic songs proclaim, be prepared to give up their son for the people's cause'.[25]

In my own study of real life stories I did not meet a single father or mother of a Chechen fighter who would go along with this idea, but such radical positions have certainly limited the scope of available information, and narrowed the range of options for Chechens down to one of 'dying for the people'. The psychologist Paul Stern has explained this phenomenon specifically in these terms, rather than by some 'basic' instinct or human need.[26] It is extremely difficult for an individual to break free of such constraints. This is not simply the logic of collective behaviour in action, when by following the crowd each person receives a share of the common gain. There are far more powerful agents at work in armed conflicts, including

---

[24] Z. Yandarbiev, *Chechenya – bitva za svobodu* (Lvov, 1996).

[25] Yandarbiev, *Chechenya*, pp. 15, 43.

[26] P. Stern, 'Why Do People Sacrifice for Their Nations?', *Political Psychology*, Vol. 16, No. 2, 1995, pp. 217–35.

violent coercion. An important characteristic of demodernisation, therefore, is the usurpation of people's minds by a simplified and restricted version of events, both past and present.

Another feature of demodernisation is the emigration from a society of those who offer an alternative, and who are capable of setting the necessary agenda for that society, providing it with such essential elements as economic and political administration, education, cultural activity and social care. This exodus has various reasons and takes various forms, but in general it carries an element of rejection or protest. In Chechnya the first to be forced out were the overwhelming majority of non-Chechens, along with some of the most well-educated and successful Chechens. The armed conflict then pushed out of the towns and villages many people suffering as a result of the destruction. At the same time, however, others left who did not wish to stay, and especially did not want their children to live in a society plunged into violent conflict. Finally, after the war, others departed who could not or did not want to be associated with building the new Chechen state. As a result more than half the population of Chechnya, and furthermore its more dynamic half (mainly in terms of education and qualifications), left the war-torn republic.

The size and make-up of this exodus is crucial in comparison with the entire population of the republic, as it altered the social and cultural nature of the group itself. Instead of a Chechen people in tune with its own culture and identity within a multi-ethnic environment, we now observe an ethnically homogeneous Chechnya, whose leadership has been usurped by its armed element. Similar scenarios have often occurred in history, and are present in a number of well-established conflicts today, but they have never been viewed in the context of demodernisation.

Demodernisation entails a radical change in social ties and institutions, in which people appear to lose all their normal ability to organise themselves. This of course does not mean complete social chaos, as society still retains such fundamental institutions as the family and even leadership on the local community level, although such communities are also greatly eroded. Families are torn apart, relationships change, morals and the psychological climate are conditioned by the trauma and by new problems. In small communities the elected or appointed leaders have to contend with impostors dictating their will through the barrels of Kalashnikovs. At a higher level, authority is also based not on elections and legitimacy, but on armed force.

In a large-scale conflict pseudo coalitions and mythological social structures typically emerge, potentially able to prevent chaos, or to provide new controls and social strategies. In Chechnya such coalitions (i.e. only those resulting from the war) were formed not only of groups operating within the 'warlord territories' and on the 'front-line', or of combat veterans, but also of those camouflaging themselves as traditional clan (*teip*) coalitions. My research has shown that such armed coalitions are extremely short-lived, and that solidarity among the fighters does not extend beyond the members of small individual groups, usually from a single village, that may be led by a commander from 'the city'. As for the teips, these are a metaphor always more easily and better defined as either the members of an enlarged family group, or as a collective based on place of birth or residence, or indeed as a combination of both.

Another distinguishing feature of Chechen society during the conflict is excursions into the past to find arguments for defending current activities, and also parodies (copies) of borrowed (foreign) projects. Virtually all the arguments for Chechen resistance (or Chechen revolution) have been built on a dramatisation of the past, and specifically, on the nineteenth century war in the Caucasus and the collective trauma of deportation by Stalin. The search in the past for a supposedly lost ideal (a kind of idealised Chechen society that never existed) is still the main theme of intellectual debates in post-war Chechnya. Local newspapers from 1996–1999 were full of articles written by historians, folklorists, archaeologists or journalistic notes on this subject.

As for the foreign borrowings, these were present in Chechen society before, during and after the war. At first texts were lifted from the documents of Sajudis in Lithuania and the Estonian Popular Front, in order to build a local political platform. Then the activities and attributes of armed combatants from other Islamic regions, and not only these, were copied. Finally, Sudanese Sharia Law Codes were borrowed in order to establish a similar model in Chechnya.

Such activities indicate a lack of competence in a society wishing to escape from the existing system. This is often seen in periods of radical change. Borrowings that clearly do not correspond to the norms and values that have been accepted by a society and shared by its people over a long period can be viewed as demodernisation. The general norms for Chechnya are European, even though they were established in distorted Soviet forms and existed side by side with so-called traditional institutions and values. As Dzhabrail Gakaev and Arutyunov have pointed out, however, Chechen society has absorbed a reasonably high number of values conditionally labelled 'Asiatic', although the norms and customs in question are mainly connected with Islam. The main drawback of past ideals and borrowings is that they deprive a society of its creativity and of the kind of innovation that emerges mainly from local conditions. Conflict demodernisation is a consequence of a society's inability to overcome a crisis without outside assistance. This, for example, affects how people earn a living, as wars destroy the official economy, and people are forced to find alternative ways to survive. This phenomenon has been observed in practically all armed conflicts,[27] and Chechnya is no exception.

---

[27] For more on the problems related to the post-conflict reconstruction of a society, see G. Carbonnier, *Conflict: Post-war Rebuilding and the Economy - A Critical Review of the Literature*, The War-torn Societies Project Occasional Paper, No. 2, Geneva, 1998.

Yet another characteristic of demodernisation is a state of apathy and a disregard for human life and common codes of behaviour. A domineering sense of helplessness is widely observed in post-conflict situations. I saw this for myself in Tskhinvali (in South Ossetia, Georgia) in spring 1992, and especially in Chechnya in October 1995. Social psychologists highlight post-conflict trauma or post-traumatic stress, which is a medical condition and a psycho-analytical concept. I focus on the broader social context of this phenomenon. A sense of apathy is especially prominent in the years immediately following a destructive war. In Chechnya it became prevalent and is expressed as a rejection of home-grown politics and the willingness to accept any type of 'order', even in the most unlikely form of a saviour from afar, for example, the British. Apathy affects the whole population, but especially the men, although women may also often express similar feelings.

A very good example of this was provided by Marina, an inhabitant of Grozny, in 1997. Here we see the whole spectrum of post-conflict apathy, but one thing is very important: unlike most men, including from her own family, Marina still manages to carry on working. She is a market trader.

As before I'm selling goods in the market. These days all we feel is a sense of helplessness, there are no prospects, no money, and everything is getting more expensive. I don't think it could be any worse... Wahhabism is also just a game, a political show. During the war it was said that we would be handed over to Britain. We were happy that there would be order. But so far we've seen nothing of the kind. We can't expect anything from Moscow. Maskhadov visits America, Turkey, but people aren't finding it any easier. Maskhadov has had his day. The people really believed in him, but he has disappointed them. We now need somebody else, someone uncorrupted. They're all connected: there isn't any difference between Maskhadov and Basaev. The Wahhabists have got some good features – unity mainly, they respect each other, and they've got money. People are already saying, let them come. Maybe then things will get better; the children will go to school. We'd be satisfied with an average of a hundred dollars a month per family to buy the bare essentials. That's just a dream now. We can't even dream of luxuries. You don't even think about yourself, there's no self-improvement, we've all become numb. We're going backwards, the people have slipped back fifty years. It's hard to say where it will all end.

Finally, a distinctive interaction can be observed between intolerance and conformism. During the war demonstrations of Chechen courage and generosity for the mass media appeared particularly effective when federal army soldiers were released from captivity. This looked especially dramatic when the soldiers' mothers were present. The mothers' own movement emerged in the wake of these releases. Subsequent events in Chechnya revealed an enduring cruelty, especially towards armed antagonists and even towards non-combatants (for example, the killing of police officers in Dagestan and the Stavropol region, the execution of prisoners, the maiming of hostages), and exhibition of enemies begging forgiveness (quite possibly genuinely) in the most humiliating manner. All these factors add up to a society in a condition that can be called demodernisation. It is a state in which social institutions and ties are destroyed by war, and in which society's resources are radically weakened, preventing it from restoring the status quo, let alone developing, a state that leads to the use of long forgotten ideals or inadequate foreign borrowings.

To be fair, no society is guaranteed against a return to past ideals, but demodernisation does not necessarily mean a return or movement backwards. It may also entail inventions, or the borrowing of inappropriate projects and rules currently existing in other societies. Social demodernisation may well occur when the most advanced technology is available and is used. For example, electronic communications and the mass media, including audio-visual recordings as part of the technology are used in modern-day human trafficking (prisoners-hostages for ransom). It is extremely difficult but not necessarily possible for a society to extricate itself from a state of demodernisation. It has never been proven that a society always evolves in a 'progressive' direction. Moreover, war and political violence have never belonged to this category, unless they have later been re-interpreted as 'liberating', 'revolutionary', or 'justified', in order to acquire historical legitimacy.

Proposals for Post-conflict Reconstruction

What external recommendations can be made by those studying wars and conflicts? In whose name and for whom is the research carried out, in a genre which is defined as 'public anthropology', i.e. anthropology of urgent importance to society which from a scientific and public platform strives to find the ways and allies necessary to overcome a grave crisis? What follows are notes prepared for a meeting with the resident of the Russian Federation, Vladimir Putin, at the Russian Academy of Sciences on 8 February 2000:

> The post-conflict reconstruction of Chechnya will be a long and arduous process. At the moment it is difficult even to take in the scale of the problems involved in restoring Chechnya to a functioning economic, social, cultural, and politically autonomous community-territory within a federal Russian state. From economics and the environment to medicine and psychology – all these can be tackled only through the collective efforts of Russian society with at least the minimum of agreement and it will be necessary to address the problems of reconstruction. A key issue is the whether the Chechens themselves will be willing to participate in efforts to restore a peaceful existence.

It is essential to involve the people, including the people of Chechnya, who have been hijacked by armed factions and extremist politicians in an attempt to destroy the Russian state system, and the Chechen autonomy that existed within it. The top leadership of the country must show contrition for those killed, not only for members of the armed forces, but also for civilians, including Chechen civilians. Both the Russian state and Russian society must express their determination to do everything possible to overcome the consequences of this destructive conflict and return Chechnya to normal life. There have been cases in recent years when even the most brutal conflict has been resolved thanks to sensible leadership and post-conflict development programmes. This work involves several basic tasks.

1. The elimination of bankrupt doctrines and projects that both lead to and perpetuate violence. Chechen independence and self-determination are two separate issues. Full independence from the Russian Federation is not feasible for many reasons.

   Full Chechen self-determination is feasible and should be granted, including state recognised status and a high degree of self-government. It should even be possible to introduce Chechen banknotes valid on the territory of the republic (as in Northern Ireland), federal and local laws could exist in tandem (legal pluralism), the republic could set up direct links with and even join international organisations and associations (as has Catalonia). A great deal is possible under the modern concept of federalism, those who were promoting the mistaken project of precipitous independence were either ignorant of this or were unwilling to look into it. A very high price has been paid for this mistake, a mistake made by leaders, ideologists and foreign instigators, but it is unwise to try to crush trampling Chechen self-determination when it is inevitable anyway.

   The people of Chechnya should receive immediate assurance that their sovereignty will be preserved with the support of the whole country, that it is they who will be in charge and not a governor or military commander, and that they will be able to re-establish the basic conditions for civilian rule. Bearing in mind the tragedy of the war and the extremely acute problems to be faced, additional (external) guarantees of Chechen sovereignty should be permitted. These could be joint assurances from CIS countries that they will respect the status and rights of self-governed territories within their borders (Abkhazia, Nagorno-Karabakh, Transdniestria, Chechnya and others).

2. Measures aimed at changing the social climate after two terrible wars in which around 40,000 soldiers, fighters, non-combatant Russians, Chechens and other nationalities have been killed (it is this more accurate figure that should be used officially, rather than those of 100,000 or 120,000!). A general reconciliation (a genuine peace and not simply an

end to the war) is feasible and essential. Many countries have been through this process and in a reasonably short period of time. The country needs to attend to the health and future lives of 'our boys', not just the federal troops, but also those who are currently living in Chechen towns and villages under the spell of primitive propaganda, deprived of their families and relatives, sick or wounded. Those who took part in this civil war need to find a common cause and set of interests – from work and study to sport and cultural activities and organisations providing assistance to those traumatised by war.

The more enlightened non-combatants should set an example of reconciliation, by providing specific help to those currently in distress. Many Russian families have the durable goods, spare books (including textbooks) and financial resources that the victims of the war in Chechnya need. We urgently require a nationwide campaign to provide assistance to both Chechnya and to Chechen refugees. This would be more than just help, but a source of self-healing and collective atonement for past sins. We cannot simply stand aside and continue the mutual accusations, or look for the 'original culprits' of the war. The Chechens want reconciliation just as much as the rest of Russia. The work must begin at the most basic level, with children, especially at school. Chechen children and adolescents need to be treated properly and in the same manner as school children in Moscow, Nalchik or other Russian cities. Despite the difficult conditions, teachers could come (or return) from other Russian regions. We need a home-grown 'Peace Corps for Chechnya', which would involve young people in various hands-on professions (doctors, social workers, those working in the cultural sphere, agriculturists, engineers and other specialists). Without such an organisation the troops, police and traumatised and socially disoriented locals alone will not be able to solve the problems of reconstruction. Similar volunteer organisations have played a positive role in many regions affected by civil wars (El Salvador, Guatemala, Nicaragua, and certain African countries).

3. Social therapy aimed at returning various categories of Chechens to civilian life and work. The most serious consequence of the war, apart from the human losses and devastation, is the demodernisation of Chechen society and the destruction of traditional institutions that regulate society. Today's Chechnya sees the revenge of the village on the town, barely literate armed youths set above their elders, thieves and bully boys more successful than honest workers, village mullahs usurping the law. This was unheard of in Chechnya before 1991, when the adult population lived and worked by the same rules and laws as the rest of the country, however good or bad those may have been. The Chechens had preserved their own customs, culture and language, as had other peoples in Russia, but in their basic behaviour they were not radically different from anyone else. The idea of 'otherness' (hostile or

romanticised) was created during the conflict, but it was just as perverse as the war itself.

It will be difficult to rebuild the foundations of public life in a half-depopulated Chechnya, but not impossible. The main support here ought to be the men and women of middle age. There is no point in idealising the role of the *teip* (largely semi-mythological) and the clergy (largely self-appointed) in rebuilding the social order. We need to re-establish the leading role (from the local to the higher level) of mature, educated and publicly active people regardless of sex, age and family. To be fair, even before Dudaev and his invented '*teip* assemblies' there were other innovations that were destroying both the law and the state.

The Russian government should desist from issuing harshly worded ultimatums demanding recognition of the Russian constitution. The Chechens have the right to their own constitution, and even to one that contradicts the Russian version (as do those of other republics). Dudaev's original constitution minus its preamble could serve as the basis for Chechen law, and at the same time leave the dignity of the local people intact. A key measure could be the setting out of a supplementary agreement on the delimitation and joint delegation of power. Work was carried out on this from 1992–1994 as part of federal-region relations between Moscow and Grozny. Official agreements were even put in place, but these were torn up by Dzhokar Dudaev.

Apart from re-establishing authority and at least a minimum of order, the main difficulty will be in overcoming the people's post-war apathy towards rebuilding the apparently unrebuildable ruins. Post-conflict apathy is a common syndrome, but it can be vanquished by the first fruits of success. Grozny should be rebuilt for this very reason, along with municipal life in general in Chechnya – this element is the basis for the vitality of modern societies. The village may have served as an anchor during the war, but in peacetime it is the town that provides support for everyday life and cultural integrity.

4. To restore Chechen confidence in the idea that they, and not outsiders, are the ones who can and should address their own issues. To achieve this it will be necessary to defend a wounded and weakened society from outside provocation and shameless manipulation. Foreign ideologists, including Chechen émigrés, will continue to wage their own war against 'the empire' and for 'Chechen freedom'. There will also be instigators in Moscow, including Chechens living in comfort and radical human rights activists. The Chechen people have already paid a high price for these external influences and for the actions of leaders imported from the military. They now need professional assistance and resources, which should be used according to general agreement and not as Moscow or foreign officials think fit. All activities and programmes must be discussed first with the Chechens. Consultation on peacetime plans and activities is itself part of the peace process. Let the

Chechens choose less than ideal reconstruction programmes if they wish, at least these will be their plans and projects that they will be willing to carry out according to their own understanding of what is involved.

5. Russian society, and especially the mass media, should not make the mistake of ignoring Chechnya. A Chechen channel should be set up immediately on Russian television (broadcasting in both Russian and Chechen). There are many Chechen intellectuals in Moscow, including journalists, who could become involved in this project. It would be easy to broadcast to Chechnya, and to provide assistance in the shape of a television set for every Chechen home that does not already have one. What should be covered? – mainly the issues that have already been described, along with many others, including those affecting the Russian Federation as a whole.

   Chechnya is a fundamental issue of nationwide importance, it is a test of the new Russia's ability to correct its own tragic mistakes and respond to external threats. If we can pass this test we can avoid a Third Chechen War. The 400-year old enmity between Chechnya and Russia dreamt up by Yeltsin and Maskhadov is pure illusion.

6. To establish basic norms and rules in the army and in other federal military and civilian structures operating within Chechnya, to be observed when dealing with local people, fighters and foreign mercenaries. Such regulations should also apply to internal relationships. There is an urgent need for a ban on alcohol for servicemen during their tour of duty in Chechnya (the Russian peacekeeping force in Bosnia has managed to observe this). It is essential that all non-combatants be treated humanely, and also that national and international regulations as regards combatants and terrorists be observed. Amnesties should be declared immediately. It is equally important that brisk and thorough investigations be carried out into serious crimes. It is worth considering allowing the armed resistance leaders to leave the country, along with those Chechen fighters who do not wish to remain in Russia. This would entail the loss of citizenship and a permanent ban on returning to the country. The question is whether countries sympathetic to Chechen separatism would provide quotas for such emigrants.

7. It is essential that moral sanctions be applied, and possibly also legal action taken against Russian politicians and public activists who have been openly calling for Chechen independence and continued armed resistance. Such calls encourage others to violate the Russian constitution, have an immoral and confusing effect on the Chechen population and on most anti-separatist Chechens, and are disrupting the army. The media must change tack and begin discussing the serious problems involved in the post-war reconstruction of this part of the country, as well those related to post-war trauma as a whole, including that suffered by Russian servicemen and their families.

8. Wide-ranging measures on the international stage are urgently needed to safeguard the Russian government's activities in Chechnya, to clarify the local situation, and also to work out ways in which useful outside participation could be facilitated and harmful foreign activities prevented. Russian diplomats and academics are not doing enough in these areas; they are either absent from many key international structures or play only a passive role. The Russian Press Ministry does not provide information in foreign languages for external consumption, and pays little attention to the activities of the foreign media in this area.

9. Events in Chechnya indicate the complete failure of the Chief Public Prosecutor's Office and the country's other legal institutions. No results have been achieved, nor is there even any information available on the progress of investigations into mass terrorist attacks and crimes committed by Chechen terrorists. Nothing has come of actions taken against Russian servicemen. The impression has been created that all Chechen fighters will be released without punishment if resistance ceases, and that servicemen may carry out their own form of justice. This is turning both a brutal war and the actions of the separatists into a dangerous, but profitable game of amnesties. We need to include the most loathsome separatists and foreign mercenaries on a list of especially dangerous criminals, who will face trial no matter what happens.

10. We need do more to present Chechens living both within Chechnya and beyond its borders as fellow citizens of the Russian Federation. We should stop referring to them as 'noble savages', and focus more on those who are resisting the fighters, on Chechens who are building a life for themselves, and so on. Something urgently needs to be done for Chechen children, adolescents and young people both in Chechnya and elsewhere, to shut off the supply of fighters and terrorists. International organisations, if they are genuinely interested, can assist in this effort. This means equipment for schools, medical and psychological help, food and clothing, admission to technical and military academies and so on.

9

Chechnya: The Breaking Point

Tom de Waal

On 15 May 2004 Russian economics minister German Gref visited the city of Grozny and was shocked by the sight. 'What we saw today at Minutka (a square in the south of the city) looks almost like a set from a Hollywood movie', Gref told reporters. Russian president Vladimir Putin had expressed something similar when he flew over the city four days before. 'Despite what's being done, from the helicopter it looks horrible', he told a meeting of the local Chechen government. It is worth considering the words of these two men, both of whom carry enormous responsibility for the state of the city they were visiting. The majority of the destruction they saw had been carried out by the Russian government more than nine years before, with more inflicted by Putin himself almost five years ago. Yet somehow both men had either forgotten or discounted the importance of the fact of this mass devastation of a Russian city until being physically reminded of it. In a way, like most of their compatriots, they had accepted the ruination of Grozny as normal.

The appalling condition of Grozny is of course no secret. The dozens of journalists and aid workers who visited the city over the preceding decade had repeatedly seen its ruins and tried to reflect on its meaning – not to speak of the tens of thousands of Chechens who have to live in these conditions and experience the meaning of it every day. Many others had used the same sort of language, such as Lord Frank Judd, who as rapporteur for the Parliamentary Assembly of the Council of Europe (PACE) on Chechnya, also said he was simply 'shocked' by his first visit to Grozny.

Point of Rupture

The nature and persistence of the conflict in Chechnya has been analysed and reanalysed over the past few years within the context of Islam, international terrorism, Russian federalism, oil politics, the condition of Chechnya's North Caucasian neighbours. The main contention of this chapter is that many of the analysts who work with these categories – some of whom have never been to Chechnya – have missed the point that Judd grasped immediately and that Gref and Putin were reminded of all too briefly. The central key to understanding the Chechen conflict was literally before their eyes. It lies in the massive violence that all but destroyed the city of Grozny, and to a lesser extent, other Chechen towns and villages in 1994–5. Rarely has there been a conflict in which the means used were so vastly disproportionate to the scale of the problem nominally being tackled. That means the cleavage between before and after the bombing – roughly situated in time that means before and after New Years's Eve 1994 – separates two entirely different situations, with Russia's bombers having left behind, as well as their craters and graves, a sociological and political hole that has still not been filled. Or, to put it another way, there were many possible remedies to the problem of Chechnya, a complex network of relationships tying together Chechnya and Russia, before the point of cleavage, up until December 1994; but even if Russia had stopped its military campaign and sat down to serious mediation with all parties in Chechnya in February 1995, the extent of the bombing campaign of the preceding weeks had changed things so irreversibly that something entirely different was – and is – needed to put Chechnya back together again.

Looking at the ruins of Grozny, any sane person who was familiar with the dispute that led to the Chechen war of 1994 was inclined to say, 'if this is Russia's solution, I would prefer the problem'. It is the most destroyed city in Europe, having suffered far in excess of Balkan war-zones like Vukovar or Sarajevo. The first and most devastating bombardment of the city, by artillery and heavy bombers, began in the first week of January 1995, following the catastrophic attempt to send tank crews into the city on New Year's Eve, and lasted until the end of the month. Almost no effort was made to have the 100,000 or so civilians still sheltering in the city evacuated, despite pleas from Russian human rights activists such as Sergei Kovalev. The veteran aid worker Fred Cuny estimated that he heard 4,000 detonations an hour in Grozny – compared to around 3,500 detonations a day in Sarajevo.

By the time Russian forces had control of Grozny in early February 1995, almost the entire central square mile of the city with its turn-of-the-century buildings and Soviet-era concrete tower-blocks, had been devastated. Casualty figures are notoriously hard to estimate, but 10,000 civilians could easily have died, while some Russian human rights monitors estimate that 27,000 people died there. Whatever the true casualty figures, it has to be said they were far in excess of anything perpetrated over the last ten years by the 'rebels' who the bombardment had been designed to suppress. In the autumn of 1999, the federal government again bombarded Grozny. Civilian casualties were less the second time around, although in one particularly sickening rocket attack several hundred may have died in the central market. This time, other areas of the city, such as Minutka Square, visited by German Gref, which had been spared bombardment in 1994 That means the cleavage between before and after the bombing – roughly situated in time that means before and after New Years's Eve 1994–5, were badly destroyed.

The sheer human tragedy of the killing of Grozny's inhabitants traumatized Chechen society. Most current and former inhabitants of Grozny lost close relatives in the bombing. The effects on Chechnya's social structures were just as devastating. Grozny was a Russian-built city and up until the 1960s had a very small Chechen population. Many Chechen workers used to be bussed into work in the city from surrounding villages. Slowly a Chechen professional class began to emerge, which also treated the city as its own. As a result, the city centre in 1994 was home mainly to ethnic Russians and more professional Chechens and it was they – particularly the most vulnerable and elderly – who took the brunt of the bombing and formed the mass of the killed and injured. Chechnya's main urban centre was also home to its university and oil institute – totally destroyed – and its museum and archive, which were badly damaged. The result of the bombardment of Grozny was therefore physically to destroy and drive out the very constituency of Chechnya's residents who were most sympathetic to political accommodation with Russia and who also were agents of modernization inside society. At a stroke Russia's bombers set back Chechnya two generations, from an urbanized republic with an educated elite to a rural village economy.

If all this is the case – if Russia's 'solution' was far worse than the 'problem' – it follows that retrospective analysis has magnified the gravity of the Yeltsin–Dudaev dispute of 1991–4. Knowledge of what came after has distorted perceptions of the scale of the drama surrounding what went before. In the Russian narrative of the Chechen dispute this means that the seeds of 'terrorism' and 'Wahhabism' are now adduced to have been dangerously present in prewar Chechnya; while the Chechen nationalist narrative exaggerates the threat posed by Russian neo-imperialism to Dudaev's regime, thereby justifying implacable resistance to a Russia with which most Chechens actually had deep ties.

A more rigorous analysis confirms that both sides have, for different reasons that suit their political agendas, talked up the divisions between them that led to conflict, while in fact up until 1994 they were tied together by innumerable threads that they themselves sundered. At the same time, if Chechnya's 'independence' of 1991–4 must be taken less seriously, then the violence used against Chechnya in December 1994 becomes more shocking and inexplicable and the central issue that comes into focus is the state of Russia's elite and its armed forces. The implications for a lasting solution to Chechnya are therefore part reassuring, part challenging and part deeply unpalatable for Russia. The political links tying Chechnya to Russia are probably reparable given the pragmatic attitude of most Chechens; but Russian society has yet to own up to the enormity of the tragedy it has inflicted on Chechnya and the enormous scale of physical reconstruction and legal and moral reparation that Chechens require from them if they are to become part of the Russian Federation. Otherwise the cleavage caused by war will remain and the potential remains for Chechens in the future to be tempted by a genuine de-colonial struggle.

Dudaev's Regime

The strange system presided over by Dudaev in Chechnya in 1991–4 was generally regarded as an anomaly within the new Russia, but in actual fact it had many similarities with what was going on in the rest of the country. Dudaev was inspired by the nationalist 'spring-time of nations' that overtook the Soviet Union in 1989–91 and led to the creation of Popular Fronts striving for independence in the Baltic and Caucasian republics. He in particular took inspiration from Estonia, where he himself served as the commander of a bomber division in Tartu, and on whose constitution he modelled his own. This was the symbolic side of Chechen 'independence'. For the All-National Congress of the Chechen People, of which Dudaev was elected chairman in 1990, the main issues were: respect for the rights of a people who had been downtrodden and persecuted for generations; the revival of their culture and language; greater control of their own economy; and, most importantly, recognition of the crimes of the Stalinist deportations of 1944. On coming to power in September 1991, Dudaev gave free expression to this upsurge of national pride by giving Chechnya all the paraphernalia of an apparently free nation: a constitution, flag, national anthem and public memorials.

The reality was rather different. According to every real indicator, Dudaev's Chechnya remained firmly part of the Russian state. Its borders to the rest of the North Caucasus remained freely open, gas and oil flowed in and out of the republic, flights went to and from Grozny airport to the rest of Russia, pensions were paid out of the Russian budget, the currency naturally was the rouble and the Terek Grozny football team continued to play in the Russian league. Chechnya's one foreign border, with Georgia, was hard to traverse across the mountains. To any sober outside observer, the question was not if Chechnya would return to being part of the Russian Federation, but how and when.

Chechnya of course had many deeply individual traditions that set it apart from Russia. Yet it is useful to think of Chechens as having a 'double identity' of both ancestral traditions retained within their local society and of a Russified identity acquired through proximity to the Soviet and Russian states. Many analysts have delved deep into Chechen history to explain Chechnya's peculiarity in terms of *teip* culture, Sufi brotherhoods and *murids* or the tradition of the *abrek* (bandit). In fact to most citizens of Chechnya in 1991, these were probably social and cultural elements in their lives that they were happy to have retained through the Soviet period, but were hardly defining characteristics. Aslan Dukaev has written:

> Clan affiliation can no longer be considered a major determinant of social relations. Clan ties are increasingly viewed as a historical or anthropological curiosity, especially in urban areas...Contemporary Chechen nationalism never fed on Sufi mysticism, which is too removed from real life to be used as a viable ideology. Neither was it underpinned by semimythical clan solidarity and pride. Abuzar Aidamirov's 1970 novel *Long Nights*, a powerful description of the Caucasian wars of the 19th century and the exodus of thousands of Chechens to the Ottoman Empire, was able to arouse more nationalist sentiment in the 1970s and 1980s than all the Sufi preachers in Chechnya. The song that later became Chechnya's national anthem... first appeared in this novel.[1]

The new Chechen elite around Dudaev, though semi-estranged for historical reasons from the high political class in Moscow, was also recognizably Sovietized and Russified. Dudaev – who had never lived properly in Chechnya, spoke the Chechen language poorly and had a Russian wife – is a prime example. As Georgi Derluguian has pointed out, 'Not one of the Chechens who in September–October 1991 overthrew the local nomenklatura was a traditional honourable bandit (*abrek*) or Sufi mystic. But all of them were graduates, or at least drop-outs, from Soviet higher education, both civilian and military'.[2]

History also cuts both ways. Certainly the mass Stalinist deportations of Chechens in 1944 were a bitter memory and a common wound; they served to remind Chechens of their traditions of resistance and alienation from the Russians and probably encouraged many Chechens, when faced with the Russian army in 1994–5, to pick up weapons and fight. However, in less extreme times, an experience such as mass deportation also teaches habits of accommodation and survival. The pragmatism that goes with being a small threatened people is an often-overlooked Chechen historical trait. The tsarist history of the colonial wars in the North Caucasus has at its heart the figure of Imam Shamil, who was not a Chechen and who fought Russian armies for more than 30 years. But it also contains the figure of the Chechen Haji Murat, who was immortalized by Tolstoy and who offers a rather different model. Haji Murat chose to cross over to the Russians, believing he was saving lives by doing so. In 2004 he had a latter-day counterpart in Magomed Khambiev, former defence minister to the rebel government,

---

[1] Aslan Dukaev, 'Grozny's Pyrrhic Victory', *Transitions*, Vol. 5, No. 5, May 1998, pp. 83–4.
[2] Georgi Derluguian, 'Che Guevaras in Turbans', *New Left Review*, No. 237, September/ October 1999, p. 20.

who surrendered, freely acknowledging that many people he respected would call him a 'traitor' but deciding that this was the least bad option.

Even Dudaev, who all too often projected dangerous levels of self-belief and romantic delusion, was not immune to this kind of pragmatism. In his more candid moments he made it clear that he did not want to cut ties with Russia and on occasion called himself a 'Russian patriot'. In January 1993 he said in an interview that 'Relations with Russia have not only not been broken off – neither economic, political, cultural or spiritual – but they are becoming stronger and firmer. And the fact that the Russian leadership is putting up unlawful barriers is I believe the misfortune of the Russian leadership itself'.[3] On a practical level, several other regions of Russia had almost as much autonomy as Chechnya did in the 1990s. They had either enthusiastically embraced the 'parade of sovereignty' begun in 1991 and used their autonomous status to bargain for more power, or simply used local revenues to keep Moscow at bay and run their own show. The criminalized fiefdoms of Yevgeny Nazdratenko's Primorsky Krai, Kirsan Ilyumzhinov's Kalmykia, Mintimer Shaimiev's Tartarstan, Murtaza Rakhimov's Bashkortostan and even in many ways Yury Luzhkov's Moscow had much in common with Chechnya.

None of the criminal problems associated with Chechnya were unique to Russia, only the blatant way in which the criminality was flaunted. In Russia Boris Berezovsky bought much of the automobile industry in a highly dubious manner but with a veneer of legality; in Chechnya, stolen cars were openly driven through the streets. In Russia the Western Group of Forces failed to account for thousands of pieces of heavy weaponry it had evidently sold off; in Chechnya you could buy small arms in the bazaar. In Russia, the bodies of victims of criminal hits would be disposed of discreetly; in Chechnya severed heads were left by the roadside. To visit Chechnya was to see the hidden mechanisms of the Russian black economy on open display.

Of course the security situation in Chechnya was several degrees worse than in the rest of Yeltsin's Russia. There were train robberies, two plane hijackings, barely a functioning police force. Again, however, this is better seen as a symptom of the lawlessness of Russia as a whole, magnified by Chechnya's political problems, than as a situation unique and contained to Chechnya. There were plenty of steps the federal government in Moscow could have taken to rein in the criminality of Dudaev's Chechnya without sending a single armed man into Chechnya itself. They included curtailing the corruption within Russian air traffic control that allowed international flights to leave and arrive in Grozny airport unmonitored; cracking down on the rampant corruption by officials in Chechnya's neighbours who were complicit in its illegal activities; and, most usefully of all perhaps, cutting

---

[3] *Megapolis Ekspress*, January 20, 1993, reprinted in *Ternisty put' k svobode: pravitel'stvennie dokumenty Chechenskoi Respubliki - stat'yi, interv'yu* (Vilnius, Vaga, 1993), p. 141.

off the tight links between Chechen organized crime in Moscow and the Moscow city government of the time.

Chechnya was therefore primarily different, not in the scale of its security problem, but because of the politics that lay behind it. The economic links between Chechnya and the rest of Russia were even more opaque than the black economy in the rest of Russia and less amenable to pressure from the Kremlin. In the case of Nazdratenko or Rakhimov, it was clear that this was a fight in which political differences were a cover for a quarrel over economic resources and in which the Kremlin had enough leverage to get most of what it wanted. Once the purely economic deal had been done and the allocation of revenues had been decided on, nominal political loyalty was easily bought. All of the five men named above ended up backing Yeltsin for president in 1996.

In Chechnya, the deal was much harder to do, with Dudaev refusing to play by the same rules and Yeltsin's government lacking the leverage it had elsewhere. Crucially, both leaders lacked political flexibility. The dispute was to a large degree the clash of two personalities; both were extremely proud, impulsive and disinclined to compromise. To Yeltsin, Dudaev's open rebellion was an affront to his attempt to project himself as the leader of a new Russian state. Others kept their subversion more discreet, while Dudaev mocked him openly. To Dudaev, Yeltsin and his cronies did not deserve compromise until they paid due respect to the Chechens' resurgent national project. There was also between Dudaev and Yeltsin the instant distrust of someone who remained, in many ways, a Soviet patriot and a man who had overthrown the Soviet system. Dudaev's Communist-era faith in the Soviet command economy and hatred for economic reforms put him on a level with Yeltsin's opponents in the Supreme Soviet. The Chechen leader told an interviewer in 1992:

> The economic reforms of the government in Moscow have already placed the country on the edge of a precipice, below which glimmers the spectre of civil war. I want Russians to understand us correctly and not to condemn us: we do not want to go along with Russia when it is being lead along a road ending in a sheer cliff. An outcome like that will not be better either for us or for you, so separation now is a mechanism of self-defence, the natural reaction of the living organism, which our peoples are, to a deadly danger.[4]

Again, the retrospective bias of analysis has obscured the fact that in 1994, Dudaev's hand was weakening and the prospects for a peaceful resolution of the Chechen issue were improving. This was because the internal contradictions of Dudaev's regime were driving down his popularity, as his failure to pay salaries and pensions or heat homes weighed more heavily

---

[4] From interview reprinted in *Ternisty put'*, p. 132.

with most Chechens than his rhetoric about the de-colonial struggle. In August 1994 a number of Chechens told me that Dudaev's days were numbered. However, in a memorable phrase, Chechen writer Said-Khamzat Nunuev, explained why the president still enjoyed loyalty out in the villages – though this too, he believed, would diminish: Nunuev said, 'After suffering tsarism and Communism, the people have not breathed the air of freedom enough'. To see off Dudaev, sheer patience and restraint was still required in Moscow.

The year 1994 instead saw Moscow up the stakes in the Chechen dispute. By the end of the year Western news agencies were using the formula that Boris Yeltsin had 'lost patience' with Chechnya. This was in fact rather comparable to President George W Bush's 'loss of patience' with Saddam Hussein in 2003. The timetable for the developing crisis was set in Moscow, rather than on the ground. While Dudaev's biggest critics, the Chechen professional classes, kept their silent counsel, armed internal dissent to Dudaev began, but it was entirely artificial, funded and organized by Moscow and with little popular support. The three men principally involved, Ruslan Labazanov, Umar Avturkhanov and Beslan Gantemirov had nothing in common except Russian money.

This rebellion should not be classified as a civil war or even a proper armed insurgency. Visiting two of the 'rebels', Labazanov and Avturkhanov, one day in August 1994, I found that they had not set up checkpoints, built defences or even amassed large amounts of weaponry, while having put only a few dozen men under arms, mostly their relatives and friends. The political conditions for conflict were simply not there in a Chechnya that under Dudaev was highly decentralized; and although Chechnya was plagued by violence between individuals, there were still strong sociological deterrents against mass violence. Even the peak of this insurgency in November 1994 ended in extremely light casualties. As late as August 1994, moreover, the Russian president was actually using his proxy insurgents as a reason to rule out the use of federal troops in Chechnya. 'Armed intervention is impermissible and must not be done', Yeltsin said on 11 August. 'Were we to apply pressure of force against Chechnya, the whole Caucasus would rise up and there would be such turmoil and blood that no one would ever forgive us'.

Yeltsin's move towards war was in fact dictated by two factors beyond the main drive of events inside Chechnya: the failure of the proxy insurgency led by Avturkhanov and Gantemirov, and Russian domestic politics. The insurgency ended in a humiliating defeat, which enraged and embarrassed the Kremlin, while inside the Kremlin a hardline faction led by the chief presidential bodyguard Alexander Korzhakov, which wanted to remake Yeltsin as a new semi-authoritarian leader, was gaining ascendancy. By crushing the Dudaev regime, they believed they would finally squeeze out the 1991-era 'democrats' who were still clinging precariously to posts in the presidential administration, trump the perceived threat of nationalist opposition leader

Vladimir Zhirinovsky (who had done remarkably well in the December 1993 parliamentary elections), and finally, they believed, follow the example of Bill Clinton in Haiti and win a 'small victorious war' to improve Yeltsin's flagging ratings.

As options to avert conflict narrowed, neither Yeltsin nor Dudaev was prepared to do a deal which involved a loss of face – not, that is, until the very last moment when Dudaev made desperate telephone calls to the Kremlin begging for a call from the Russian president, but was told he was too late. The mistake of using military force in Chechnya was colossal. At the time many foreign journalists who saw the bloodshed it caused believed that the mistake was so hideous that it would bring the Yeltsin administration down. Even one of the crimes committed in isolation, the killing of ethnic Russians, should, it was reasoned, have provoked intense fury amongst the voters. It was after all an immeasurably worse abuse of the rights of Russians than ones committed in the Baltic States, which exercised many parts of the Russian elite. And in 1994–5 – as opposed to the media management in 1999–2000 under Vladimir Putin – the relatively robust Russian media and in particular the NTV television channel showed footage of this killing.

Of course, the first war in Chechnya was unpopular and its unpopularity was a major reason why Yeltsin chose to seek peace in 1996. NTV's coverage did make an impact. But the political repercussions of the attack on Chechnya were far less devastating than they would have been in most countries. Why the tolerance for this violence amongst the population? Much of the answer lies in Russian political culture and the lack of a tradition of accountability of the ruler before the ruled, even in what was a nominal democracy. The men who took the decision to go to war were not put under any real scrutiny, either in parliament or the media, and defence minister Pavel Grachev was not even forced to resign after the debacle of New Year's Eve in Grozny. Another part of the explanation lies in what can, for want of a better word, be called a 'tradition' of violence in Russia. Within living memory, Russia had suffered unprecedented loss of life and mass destruction during the Great Patriotic War, and its repetition on a limited scale in Chechnya was perhaps less shocking than it would have been in other countries.

I would also suggest that Yeltsin had also broken a taboo on the use of violence the year before and got away with it, thus allowing him to try again. The differences and similarities between October 1993 and December 1994 are instructive. In October 1993 Yeltsin responded to an outbreak of serious – but almost entirely unarmed – disorder in Moscow by his opponents from the Supreme Soviet, by ordering the army to bombard the parliament building, the White House. If the interior ministry troops who shot down demonstrators at the Ostankino television station on 3 October were frightened and provoked, the same excuse cannot be given for the order to use tank-fire to bombard a building in the centre of Moscow the next day.

Political expediency here blatantly over-rode concern for human life, with 146 people killed according to official statistics, and a precedent for the political use of violence was set.

In both cases Yeltsin was in a position where the peaceful option would involve negotiating personally with opponents he strongly disliked, and contemplating losing certain powers. In both cases a hardline faction within the Kremlin, led by his chief bodyguard Korzhakov, took charge and in both cases his hapless, loyal and corrupt defence minister Grachev had his arm twisted and was persuaded to order the army into action. Finally, in both cases the Yeltsin administration and its spokesmen, such as foreign minister Andrei Kozyrev, were able to frame the decision to use force in a way that persuaded Western governments that it was expedient.

The Long Shadow of Violence

The key difference about the violence of December 1994 was that it remains ongoing. In Chechnya violence long ago replaced politics as the main arbiter of disputes and consumed pretty much everything that regulated prewar life. The main agent of violence has been the Russian armed forces, and what is seriously lacking from the literature of Chechnya is the sociology of their behaviour. The frightful state of the federal forces is perhaps the factor least appreciated by both Western and Russian commentators in Chechnya, some of whom persist in regarding them as an agent of security rather than mass insecurity.

Even a sensitive commentator like Valery Tishkov, seeking to describe 'Life in a war-torn society' while giving instances of soldiers' uncontrolled behaviour in Chechnya, gives them much less space in his analysis than he does to Chechen fighters. Yet this is the wrong way round: the federal troops exceeded their Chechen enemies both in actual numbers and in the scale of their destruction they committed in Chechnya and it is they, above all, who disfigured and deformed this society. The culture of violence that originated within Russian society, from Kursk to Khabarovsk, deserves thorough investigation if we are to understand what has happened in Chechnya in the last decade.

It was obvious that the Russian forces were not going to be welcomed as liberators. From the first day there were also enough young Chechen males inspired by Dudaev's nationalism to attack them and make them fearful. The number of ethnic Chechens who fought on the Russian side barely runs into double figures. Yet mass resistance by Chechen rebels was slow to start and the evidence suggests that it was inspired less by Dudaev than by a reactive decision to defend against marauding soldiers. It was the rampant behaviour of the Russian federal soldiers themselves that was the trigger to the escalation of the war. Reports from the war in Afghanistan suggested a Soviet army that was seriously demoralized, plagued by drug abuse and alcoholism and inclined to be as brutal to itself as to the 'enemy'. However in a large mountainous country far from the eyes of the media and with infrequent contact with the local population, that army's exploits did not come under the full scrutiny of others.

My own experience suggests that the behaviour of the 'federal forces' in Chechnya in 1994 had probably declined several degrees further from the men who fought in Afghanistan. The conscript soldiers I encountered thought only of going home, were eminently receptive to bribes, were poorly dressed, underpaid, rarely given hot meals or even tea and, if pressed, were ready to describe the Yeltsin government as 'criminal'. The *kontraktniki* were less forthcoming but evidently more brutal, and saw their service in Chechnya as a way of making large amounts of money from special payments, looting and extortion. Of course there were professional military men, especially among middle-ranking officers and special forces, who had higher standards of behaviour, but they were a minority within this environment.

It is important to point out that the random violence meted out by the Russian forces in Chechnya was something they seemed to find *normal*; it appeared to be only a more extreme form of the daily brutality that was part of army life in general, with its beatings, bullying and disregard for elementary safety. One of the most disturbing statistics to emerge from the first Chechen war provided by British military expert Charles Blandy was that for every one soldier who died in combat, five more died from carelessness or other reasons.[5] In March 2004, a *Moscow Times* reporter in Chechnya, Simon Ostrovsky, noted that 'officials conceded that the situation with morale, friendly fire and desertion is bad but no more alarming than on military bases outside the republic...I'd say this is a problem inherent to the whole army today'. FSB colonel Ilya Shabalkin, spokesman for federal forces in Chechnya, told Ostrovsky: 'It's no worse here than in units in other regions'.[6]

In this sense, although it was formally the enforcer of state security, the mass of the Russian army in Chechnya is best understood as a marginalized and economically underprivileged social group in society, for whom violence was a currency of economic and social survival. Although formally acting on behalf of the state, they were more of a 'non-state actor', a criminalized group of armed men who generally acted in despite of or in outright defiance of the declared goals of the Russian leadership. Again, examples of mass corruption suggest how everyday practices entirely undermine stated goals. In Chechnya in 1995 I was witness to how men, nominally sent to 'disarm bandit formations', ended up arming the Chechen fighters by selling them their weapons; how men supposedly sent to protect Chechen civilians from the Dudaev regime looted their homes and abused their inhabitants.

---

[5] Charles Blandy quoted in Carlotta Gall and Thomas de Waal, *Chechnya, A Small Victorious War* (London, Pan, 1997), p. 208.

[6] Simon Ostrovsky, 'A Soldier's Tale of Fear and Loathing', *The Moscow Times*, 17 March 2004.

Corruption has undermined the Russian campaign and Russia's national security on countless occasions. Bribes enabled Shamil Basaev and a convoy of heavily armed men to penetrate far beyond Chechnya to Budennovsk in June 1995. More recently this is the only plausible explanation as to why forty armed Chechens were able to evade capture and seize the Dubrovka theatre in Moscow in November 2002, and how 200 fighters were able to cause havoc in the centre of Nazran in June 2004. No checkpoint is impassable; it simply has its price.

Writ large, the result has been that a military operation whose expressed aim was to reintegrate Chechnya into Russia has, on a massive scale, achieved the exact opposite: Chechnya has been treated as an enemy land fit for pillage, Chechens not as compatriots but as 'the other', a people to be treated with contempt and hostility. Perhaps this kind of degradation can only be talked about in moral terms. It had its counterpart in the behaviour of the army elite and the impunity that accompanied the use of heavy artillery and aviation against civilians in Chechnya. The decision to carry out mass killing of its own citizens from the air was an easy choice for a military high command, which was strategically unable to rely on its ground troops, which had no political sense of responsibility and which was too corrupt to care about any military code of ethics. The nadir of Russian military behaviour may have come with the abrupt decision, apparently taken at Grachev's drunken birthday celebrations, to send unprepared tank crews to their deaths in Grozny on New Year's Eve 1994. Later, *Izvestia* reported, Grachev had vetoed a plan put forward by his Kremlin colleague Oleg Lobov to evacuate citizens from Grozny before beginning a bombing campaign. Voices were raised against this behaviour and a string of high-ranking resignations from generals and deputy defence ministers, such as Boris Gromov and Eduard Vorobyov, shows that others severely censured this kind of conduct. However, the painful truth is that the higher arbiter – President Yeltsin and his administration – chose to back the Grachevs over the Vorobyovs and allowed the killing to go on.

Chechen reaction to this violence took different forms, but all were affected by it, whatever their political persuasion. Many Chechens left the republic. Pro-Moscow politician Salambek Khajiev tried to complain about it in Moscow to no effect. Another 'opposition' figure, Beslan Gantemirov, while maintaining loyalty to his paymaster the Russian government, basically maintained his own armed group, which hit back hard at any violence by Russian troops. Others took up arms and resisted. At first the Chechen response appeared to confirm Dudaev's most fervent rhetoric. Hundreds of young men picked up weapons and went to fight. With their marching songs and Chechen flags they seemed to be enacting Dudaev's vision of a people rediscovering their history of resistance. It could be said the colonialist model of conquest and resistance, beloved of Dudaev, began to make sense at this moment and many Chechens started to think about independence for the first time.

Many, including Dudaev's chief of staff Aslan Maskhadov, were fairly scornful about Dudaev and his nationalist risk, seeing the struggle in far more down-to-earth terms. Taus A, a 30-year-old general under Dudaev, told Tishkov's research team:

> The war wasn't won by Dudaev, but by the people. When they saw that the Russian soldiers were doing, they understood what was in store for them, and their blood boiled. The people's militias were the main force behind our victory, and Dudaev had little to do with it, except by sending some commanders to the front. I saw them: our guys would prevail in an operation by their own wits, then a commander would pop up from nowhere.[7]

If defence of home and tradition was an initial motivation, gradually, in this war of unintended consequences, Chechen armed resistance began to erase the very traditions it was supposed to be defending. Chechnya's complex traditions of *teip*-membership, of decision-making by elders and communities, of unobtrusive Sufi Islam, could not withstand the rude impact of warfare. Mairbek Vachagaev has noted that attempts to form 'regiments' of fighters based on *teips* did not work and that the council of elders fell apart as war broke out.[8] The theatrical *zikr* dance performed in Grozny was, said traditional Chechens, a travesty of a religious tradition designed for quite other purposes.

Moreover the Chechen 'cause' attracted dozens of volunteers and supporters who sometimes had a different agenda from the locals and sometimes a completely contrary one. Hussein, the leader of a group of fighters in the village of Samashki, who is at the centre of Thomas Goltz's book *Chechnya Diary*, is a classic case of a 'diaspora nationalist', a Chechen resident in Kazakhstan who returns to fight for his people. Hussein said he did not know which *teip* he belonged to and was ignorant of many aspects of Chechen tradition.

Radical Islam was virtually unknown in Chechnya before 1995–6. Saudi-funded Islamists had made inroads into neighbouring Dagestan, but Chechnya's tight-knit society was resistant to their efforts. Chechens' Sufi traditions, their traditions of shrines, pilgrimages and holy men, were entirely antithetical to the newcomers. In a 1992 interview Dudaev said:

> I would like the Chechen Republic to be a constitutional secular state. This is what we are striving for, this is the ideal we are pursuing. Religion as a spiritual environment ought to play an exceptionally

---

[7] Valery Tishkov, *Chechnya: Life in a War-Torn Society* (Berkeley, University of California Press, 2004), p. 144.

[8] Frédérique Longuet Marx (ed.), 'Mille et une nuits', in *Tchétchénie: la guerre jusq'au dernier?* (Paris, 2003), p. 112.

important role in the spiritual enrichment of the people in the development of its morals and humanity. If religion takes precedence over the secular constitutional order, the Spanish Inquisition and Islamic fundamentalism in a strongly expressed form will appear.[9]

This was news to the foreign jihadis, who came to Chechnya believing that they were coming to fight for Islam.

The adventures of the American Islamic volunteer Aukai Collins are especially revealing because Collins is a kind of Candide-with-a-gun, who came to Chechnya with minimal understanding of what he would find there. What he found – and describes in his memoir *My Jihad* – was a confused society in which Russian brutality was the only unifier. He moved as a self-confessed 'wanderer' between different armed groups, who had different tactics for dealing with the Russians and little trust for one another. He spent time at the camp of the Saudi-born warrior Khattab and felt at home there because 'the Arabs... were more religious'. By contrast, he disapproved of some of the Chechens smoking cigarettes – just as 150 years before the devout Dagestanis around Imam Shamil had disapproved of Chechens smoking. The cruel behaviour Collins meted out – the shooting of Russian prisoners for example – was in contrast to the self-conscious 'nobility' aspired to by other Chechen fighters, who took pride in their high morale and good treatment of captured Russians (indeed many of them would keep in touch with the Russian Soldiers' Mothers' Association and call in mothers to rescue their sons). The jihadis, like Collins, were the other side of the coin to the Russian soldiers committing atrocities in the sense that they also saw an enemy, an 'other' on the opposing side. The continuing laceration of Chechen tradition caused by the war paved the way for a whole young generation of Chechen young men to turn to the 'Wahhabis' and inflict this kind of cruelty, first on Russians and then on other Chechens.

The high point of the Chechen independence project came in January 1997 with the orderly and impressive election, monitored by foreign observers, in which Chechen voters turned out in high numbers and elected Aslan Maskhadov as their president. However it was not clear even at that point to what degree the electors were voting for Maskhadov the victorious commander or Maskhadov the peacemaker and negotiator. Yet this pragmatic constituency was again overruled. From 1997, the brutalized young men who had grown powerful by war now turned to kidnapping and, with Russian help, all but institutionalized and formalized the informal violence that had gripped Chechnya for the preceding two years.

The second war in Chechnya that began in 1999 is more understandable in narrow security terms: the Russian federation faced the problem of an unstable and violent region within its southern borders and some of its extreme elements had also attacked another troubled region, Dagestan. However, the

---

[9] From an interview in *Literaturnaya gazeta*, 12 August 1992, republished in *Ternisty put'*, p. 115.

above description of cause-and-effect in 1994–6 should make it clear that the military method was again bound to exacerbate, rather than cure the 'problem', even if its narrow definition is taken at face value and the murky uncertainties that surround all the events of 1999 in Russia are left to one side. Chechen elder Alkhazur Sugaipov told the BBC in an interview late in 2003, 'If the Russians had been just a little civilised and decent to the ordinary working man, then the people would have welcomed them with open arms. But so many completely innocent people have been tortured and killed. Everybody knows that hundreds of people just disappear. Where are they?'[10]

As war begets more war, the second Chechen conflict has taken the violence there to new depths. The young men fighting on both sides have experienced or heard about cruelties inflicted on their friends and relatives that encourage them to commit further cruelties. In Chechnya in particular a generation has grown up that has known nothing but violence for more than a decade. The killings at Aldy and Alkhan-Kala, the *zachistki* and filtration camps, were even more cruel than the atrocities of 1994–6. As a result of the renewed violence, the silent pragmatic constituency has almost certainly grown larger. The pragmatic fluid links that connect many Chechens with diverse agendas demonstrate that self-preservation is now a higher priority than smaller political differences. Even a man like Magomed Khambiev, having spent almost a decade fighting, made the decision in 2004 that it was not worth carrying on – even as he acknowledged to *Kommersant* that he still believed in the idea of Chechen independence and respected Maskhadov's commitment to fight on.

Yet the process is now bigger than even an overwhelming majority opposed to it. To be a player in contemporary Chechnya you must be a man of violence. This is what gives a place in the game to Ramzan Kadyrov, Alu Alkhanov, the officers and men of Russian federal forces, the Yamadaev brothers, Aslan Maskhadov the warrior and Shamil Basaev. Others with merely political ideas, such as Ruslan Khasbulatov, Malik Saidullaev, Russian liberal politicians such as Boris Nemtsov or Yevgeny Primakov, Maskhadov the negotiator, Akhmed Zakaev and Ilyas Akhmadov are not players. If the challenge of peacemaking is to empower the second group above the first then violence has to be de-legitimized in Chechnya.

Conclusion

The Chechen–Russian relationship is an extremely subtle and complex one that endured many vicissitudes. In a conflict full of ironies and contradictions, perhaps the most outrageous paradox of the last decade is that a military intervention nominally designed to restore an apparently separatist Chechnya to the Russian Federation has profoundly alienated

---

[10] *Hot Spots Chechnya*, dir. Paul Mitchell, BBC 4, 4 July 2004.

ordinary Chechens and Russians from one another. Views that would have been profoundly unacceptable ten years ago have now become mainstream.

A disturbing example of this phenomenon is the book *Conversation with a Barbarian* (*Razgovor s varvarom*) by the late Pavel Khlebnikov in which Khlebnikov, a Western-educated Russian, prints his conversations with Khozh-Akhmed Nukhaev, a Russianized former Chechen Mafioso who now professes to be an Islamic ideologue. Both men eschew their common heritage to expound agendas that are equally intolerant, of a Russian 'civilization' that must rediscover order and purge itself of Islam (Khlebnikov), and of a rural Islamic society that must reject urban Western values (Nukhaev). Khlebnikov, in line with many other Russian commentators, writes about the Chechen tragedy with only the briefest reference to the suffering of Chechen civilians, glosses his mention of the Stalinist deportations with the historically inaccurate remark that 'many Chechens collaborated with the Germans during the war',[11] and portrays the activities of the Chechen mafia in Moscow as an ethnically motivated assault on the Russian people ('russkii narod'):

How many Russian boys the Chechens killed to assert their supremacy!...

How many Russian girls they beat and raped to draw them into the slavery of prostitution!...

How many Russian boys and girls they addicted to the needle to earn money!...

The Chechens played the most important role in destroying the statehood and civic life in Russian society and the Russian people is still suffering from the consequences of this.[12]

Nukhaev in his turn asserts that he actually welcomes the destruction of Grozny:

When the first war ended in 1996, the Russians had to return. Because Grozny remained, civilisation remained, their bastion of empire remained in Grozny. Like any city, Grozny was a nest of depravity and corruption, of mixing and assimilation, it brought us the rotten breath of civilisation... Today Grozny is destroyed. And if there is no Grozny, there is no bastion of empire. In 1996 Ivan left Chechen soil, but his bastion of empire, Grozny, was left behind. And now Ivan is still there, but there is no Grozny.

---

[11] Pavel Khlebnikov, *Razgovor s varvarom* (Moscow, Detektivpress, 2003), p. 15.
[12] Ibid, p. 65.

Now we have won and Ivan will leave all the same. There is nothing for him to do there. The main point is that Grozny is destroyed. Inshallah. That is the grace of the All-Mighty.[13]

Thus, the destruction of Grozny, a Russian-speaking urban centre, has played to the prejudices of the extremists, with the most bellicose on each side retrospectively seeking to justify the first Chechen war as a necessary conflict against an implacable enemy.

Yet the last thing a weak and corrupt state needs if it wants to reform itself is to cultivate mass violence that it cannot properly control. My emphasis in this chapter on the central role played in Chechnya by Russian informal violence is not a mere reckoning for the historical record, but to highlight the important implications for efforts to seek a way out of the Chechen tragedy. The overarching imperative is for the Russian federal authorities to take responsibility for the killing and destruction they have inflicted on Chechnya. This means two priorities: for the rule of law to be brought to defend Chechen civilians and for socio-economic reconstruction to begin in earnest so that the damage can be undone. In Chechnya this means with engaging with several constituencies that are being ignored: ordinary Chechen families, whose young men are tempted into radicalism by their treatment by federal paramilitary forces or *kadyrovtsy*, and who suffer from mass unemployment because there has been no serious reconstruction work; the Chechen professional classes, without whom society cannot be rebuilt; Chechen entrepreneurs, whose help is needed to rebuild the economy; and the international community, who can monitor the rights of Chechen civilians and help pick up the vast bill for reconstruction work.

But the message is broader than that ; it is about changing the whole discourse of how Chechnya and Chechens are perceived within Russia as a whole. Russia in Chechnya must confront its doublespeak, its talk of 'security', 'constitutional order' and 'anti-terrorist operation' that provokes only the grimmest laughter amongst Chechens. This is at its starkest when Chechnya is proclaimed to be a full part of the Russian Federation, even as the practice and the rhetoric has been about Chechnya as an 'other'. It has been called a 'bandit enclave' within an otherwise normal state, a 'security threat' to a responsible government, an 'ulcer' that needed to be cured or a boil to be lanced. The problem of Chechnya cannot be externalized in this way: it is better seen as Russia's dark subconscious brought to the surface, the most extreme manifestation of the violence, racial hatred and corruption that are deeply rooted within Russia as a whole. For Russia to face up to the tragedy of Chechnya means to face the titanic challenge of confronting its own failures in building a society fit for all its citizens.

---

[13] Ibid, p. 38.

10

Globalization, 'New Wars' and the War in Chechnya

Peter Shearman and Matthew Sussex

In May 2004, at a ceremony in Grozny commemorating victory over Nazi Germany, an explosion ripped through the main stands, killing Akhmad Kadyrov, the Moscow loyalist Chechen President. One could argue that this meticulously planned assassination was part of a conflict very different in its roots, reasons, rationale, and even results from the war whose end was being observed that day. World War Two was a 'modern' war pitting state against state with territory and power as the key factors. Conversely, the war in Chechnya that began in 1994 – half a century after Germany's defeat – has been identified as a postmodern or 'new' war, in an era of globalization in which traditional notions of power, space and conflict seem not to apply. But are wars changing so radically? In this chapter we deal with two central concepts: 'globalization' and 'new wars'. The first has become a cliché and suffers from multiple and unworkable (indeed, sometimes contradictory) definitions. The second is more recent. Its adherents claim that 'new wars' differ from earlier low-intensity conflicts and guerrilla warfare. We deal with these concepts together because those that have developed ideas on new wars explain them with reference to processes of globalization.[1]

---

[1] The key figures in developing theories of new wars are Mary Kaldor, *New and Old Wars: Organised Violence in a Global Era* (Cambridge, Polity, 1999); Kalevi Holsti, *The State, War, and the State of War* (Cambridge University Press, 1996); Chris Gray, *Postmodern War: The New Politics of Conflicts* (London, Routledge, 1997); Martin van Creveld, *The Transformation of War* (New York, The Free Press, 1991); Edward Rice, *Wars of the Third Kind: Conflict in Underdeveloped Countries* (Berkeley, California, University of California Press, 1988). Much of this literature focuses on wars between or, more often within, 'third world' countries or countries in transition. For an excellent overview of warfare in the third world see Robert E Harkavy and Stephanie G Neuman, *Warfare in the Third World* (New York, Palgrave, 2001). Van Creveld is cited on the cover of Harkavy and Neuman's book, comparing their work to Quincy Wright's classic *A Study of War* (Chicago University Press, 1942).

A variety of theories assert that we have entered a new era, one in which modernist notions of violent conflict between political communities are moribund. Mary Kaldor, for example, argues that we can only understand what she terms a 'new type of organized violence' as '...one aspect of the current globalised era',[2] in which political processes are undergoing radical change as the territorial state gives way to new forms of political organization. It is assumed that, as new types of polity are emerging and as new conceptions of democracy are being developed at the post-national, global level, the traditional state is being transformed. The institution of war in the modern era has been associated with the growth and expansion of the state.[3] Now, as the state system is being challenged by forces both at the global and local levels (both of which are, simultaneously, unifying and fragmenting forces) war is becoming, according to Kaldor, an 'anachronism', or, in the words of John Mueller, war is becoming 'obsolete'.[4] It is argued that since war in the modern era has been associated with the growth and expansion of the state, traditional war is becoming irrelevant as the state transforms.[5] Instead, violent conflict between organized political groups is increasingly associated with militias, warlords and transnational criminal groups.

In this chapter We test the main assumptions of the 'new wars' literature in the context of the war in Chechnya and, in doing so, We adapt the variables employed by Kaldor in her book *New and Old Wars*. We look at the goals of warfare; the posture of main actors in the conflict; the methods or processes of the war; the role of external actors; and finally the economics of warfare.[6] In a growing literature on the subject, Kaldor's approach represents the most sophisticated for assessing claims of new wars theories, since it identifies key factors that differentiate modern war from postmodern conflicts, thereby providing a more rigorous framework for analysis

---

[2] Kaldor, *New and Old Wars*, p. 1.

[3] See Philip Bobbit, *The Shield of Achilles: War, Peace and the Course of History* (London, Penguin, 2003) and MS Anderson, *War and Society in Europe of the Old Regime 1618–1789* (London, Fontana, 1988). Although the development of the modern state is closely associated with the waging of war, war (as organized political violence) has been a feature of human relations in all of recorded history. As John Kegan puts it: '...war antedates the state, diplomacy and strategy by many millennia'. Kegan, *A History of Warfare* (London, Pimlico, 1994), p. 3.

[4] John Mueller, *Retreat From Doomsday: The Obsolescence of Major War* (New York, Basic Books, 1989); and John Mueller, 'Is Major War Obsolete?', *Survival*, Vol. 40, No. 4, Winter 1998–9, pp. 20–38.

[5] Francis Fukuyama made this thesis popular with his article 'The End of History', in *The National Interest* (Summer 1989, pp. 3–17). His views were expanded into a book – see Francis Fukuyama, *The End of History and the Last Man* (New York, Free Press, 1992). Michael Mandelbaum has more recently made the linkage between free markets and democracy and the decline of warfare among the major powers. See Mandelbaum's *The Ideas That Conquered the World: Peace, Democracy, and Free Markets in the Twenty-First Century* (New York, Public Affairs, 2002).

[6] Although these are useful categories to guide our analysis, there is some overlap. Clearly it is not possible, for instance, to assess economics without also considering goals.

than those studies based simply on *ad hoc* observations relating to the amorphous concept of globalization.

I find that there are dangers involved in accepting assumptions about globalization and new wars, and how much of this literature misunderstands the extent to which war has become globalized. In demonstrating that contemporary conflicts in the North Caucasus are best understood through the prism of history and traditional thinking on warfare, We unearth three main findings. First, 'new' wars are not new at all. Second, local conflicts are opportunistically manipulated by internal and external actors for instrumental purposes. Third, prescriptions for conflict resolution, based on understandings of 'new wars', actually exacerbate their severity if pursued. We do not provide a detailed narrative on the history of the Chechen conflict, nor do we give a detailed evaluation of the flow of events during the two recent wars: these issues are covered fully by other chapters in this volume. This chapter, in contrast, is concerned with how war is conceptualized, and ultimately how academic analyses can and should engage with practical policymaking.

The Goals of Warfare

Errol A Henderson and J David Singer have noted that identifying a war's goals is always tricky.[7] What was the purpose of the two world wars of the twentieth century? The answer is not self-evident. If one can identify a clear original objective, it often becomes blurred by the 'fog' of war in which goalposts change.[8] Traditional understandings claim that interstate warfare generally has clear strategic goals linked to territorial conquest, balances of power and geopolitics. John Mearsheimer suggests that combatants are motivated by a security dilemma relating to power politics, prompting wars of territorial expansion.[9] Yet this does not accommodate the possibility that war can be transformed. Kalevi Holsti maintains that a transformation in warfare occurs when two out of three main features of warfare (which he

---

[7] Errol A Henderson and J David Singer, '"New Wars" and Rumours of "New Wars"', *International Interactions*, No. 28, 2002, pp. 165–90.

[8] This is as true of World War Two as it is of the more recent war in Iraq. The allies went to war in 1939 to save Poland and Europe from German Nazism; the end of the war saw Poland and much of Eastern and Central Europe effectively abandoned to the Soviet communist bloc. The stated reasons for the war in Iraq were to stem the proliferation of weapons of mass destruction and break Saddam's links with Al-Qaeda, yet neither WMD nor ties with Al-Qaeda were discovered.

[9] Those who make claims about new wars would see as quaint and tired the idea that war should still be seen through a Realist lens such as that of Mearsheimer in his *The Tragedy of Great Power Politics* (New York, WW Norton, 2001). It should be noted, however, that Mearsheimer's book is strictly about the causes of 'Great Power' wars – about inter-state wars of the Great Powers, and not intra-state or extra-state wars of weaker powers (the focus of the writings on 'new wars').

identifies as the types of participants; patterns of prosecution; and the purpose of war) are radically altered.[10] Analysts of postmodern war claim that contemporary conflicts lack obvious strategic objectives and are linked to identity politics, culture, religion, and instrumental political manipulation of elites. These elites might represent ethnic or tribal groups, or even criminal networks, but the point is that they are not engaged in a war with clear goals that can be won or negotiated. Often no end goal is sought, as the war becomes an end in itself for those waging it.[11]

Kaldor also claims that '[w]hat has become clear in the post-war period is that there are few causes that constitute a legitimate goal for war, for which people are prepared to die'. [12] In those instances where they are inclined to fight, Kaldor argues, the main goals are framed in terms of the politics of identity. This idea is perhaps supported by Samuel Huntington's argument that 'faith and family' and 'blood and belief' – in other words, the essential components of identity – have become the principle motivations for war, rather than traditional notions of national (for which read 'state') interests.[13] Whether they take place between civilizations or tribal groups, the mode of warfare reinforces similar types of goals: under such identity-driven conditions conflicts grow in their intensity as the enemy is portrayed as evil, alien, and a threat to the core beliefs of each protagonist.

At first glance this seems to be true of Chechnya. Both sides have inflicted horrific abuses upon the other, and both the Russian state-sanctioned media and the Chechen resistance movement have portrayed the violence as necessary in order to secure their respective cultures and political identities. However, all wars, irrespective of their origins or original purpose, have always demonized the 'other'. In inter-state, extra-state, or intra-state wars, the politics of identity have been paramount in the mobilization of the civilian population: as trained, traditional soldiers representing the state, or as guerilla groups fighting for liberation. Identity politics are undeniably important in understanding contemporary conflicts; but such was the case too in old wars. It is therefore an overextension of identity to argue that 'new wars', based upon narrow identities, reflect deliberate contestations with cosmopolitanism as a primary goal.

A far more compelling explanation is that that the objectives of contemporary conflict remain rooted in notions of power and interest. The war in Chechnya demonstrates that states and people are still willing to go to war

---

[10] Holsti, *The State, War, and the State of War*, p. 27.

[11] This is a point made by Jessica Stern in relation to Al-Qaeda: 'The Protean Enemy', *Foreign Affairs*, Vol. 82, No. 4, July/August 2003, pp. 27–40. Stern argues that the missions of this terrorist group are malleable, with objectives changing over time, and allies (of convenience) also shifting.

[12] Kaldor, *New and Old Wars*, p. 27.

[13] Samuel Huntington, *The Clash of Civilisations and the Remaking of World Order* (London, Simon & Schuster, 1997). Of course it should be noted that Huntington's level of analysis is at the wider cultural level of civilizational identity, and that the state remains the dominant actor.

for pragmatic purposes, and that both sides are willing to bear substantial losses in order to successfully prosecute the war. Russia has accepted large numbers of casualties in the war in Chechnya, and has also been willing to inflict huge casualties on the Chechens. Whilst the actual number of soldiers killed remains contested, and figures from Itar-Tass and advocacy groups (such as Soldiers' Mothers of Russia) differ significantly from official statistics, the Defence Ministry's total of 4,572 deaths with around 13,000 injured between the end of 1999 and 2002 shows that Russian losses have been significant. During the first war, from 1994 to 1996, it is estimated that 14,000 Russian military personnel lost their lives.[14] This is more than three times the rate of fatalities borne by coalition forces in Iraq from May 2003 to June 2004, with 1036 casualties over this twelve-month period.[15] It also does not account for the civilian losses, which Sergei Kovalev, one of Russia's leading human rights activists, has put at over 50,000 dead from 1994–6 alone.

Russia has firmly prosecuted the war in Chechnya for clear material rather than ideational reasons. The need to keep Chechnya within Moscow's orbit is seen as important for a number of reasons. It is vital for maintaining the territorial integrity of the Russian Federation. By the same token, instability and insurgency from Chechen rebels have prompted fears of conflict spillover to the neighbouring republic of Dagestan, and the possibility of new independence claims from republics in the economically vital South Caucasus. The loss of Chechnya would also seriously dent Russian prestige at a time when policymakers have come to regard maintaining the trappings of 'great power' status as a vital Russian interest.[16] Finally, Chechnya remains central to Moscow for geostrategic and geoeconomic purposes. Russia's economic recovery from the stagnation of the Yeltsin years has been largely underwritten by high oil prices, and Russia's eagerness to exploit vast petroleum reserves in the Caucasus and the Caspian Sea.

Power and interests at the domestic political level have also been important in framing Russian goals. High casualty rates during the unpopular first Chechen war were problematic for an ailing Yeltsin, who was lagging badly behind a strong CPRF challenge from Gennady Zyuganov in the election year of 1996. The peace deal ultimately brokered by the late Alexander Lebed and Chechen leader Aslan Maskhadov helped alleviate the pressure on Yeltsin, who later used Lebed as a third-party spoiler, coupled with a highly visible Western-style campaign to scuttle Zyuganov's bid for the

---

[14] See http://www.cdi.org/Russia/245-14.cfm.

[15] The official coalition casualty list has its own website: http://icasualties.org/oif/.

[16] This is evident from the discourse of the Russian foreign policy establishment. Perhaps it is best articulated by one of the doyens of this elite, Yevgeny M Primakov, in his recent book *A World Challenged* (Washington DC, The Brookings Institution, 2004). See also Peter Shearman, 'The Sources of Russian Conduct: Understanding Russian Foreign Policy', *Review of International Studies*, Vol. 27, No. 2, 2001, pp. 249–63.

presidency. Yet public opinion is fickle. The ceasefire between Russian and Chechen forces was routinely broken over the intervening years, and Yeltsin's Kremlin made it clear that, while it would make some concessions, any notion of full independence for Chechnya was out of the question. Just three years later, during Putin's campaign to succeed Yeltsin, the 'second' war proved immensely popular with voters (despite international condemnation at the time), coming as it did on the back of apartment block and railway station bombings in Moscow and other cities. While political interests were important at both the domestic and state levels of analysis, the goals of the conflict did not change significantly. Thus, between 1996 and 1999, normative factors pertaining to the Russian population's ideas about the conflict certainly changed. However, although political interests were important at both the domestic and state levels of analysis, the goals of the conflict did not change significantly during this time. In the Chechen case, therefore, it is difficult to construct explanations founded on ideas and the politics of identity. But, more importantly, there is a demonstrable link between ideational change and elite politics that marks shifts in public opinion as the product of instrumental rather than normative factors. Put simply, the Russian population's views on the conflict shifted due to elite manipulations that had more to do with political interests (such as winning the war and remaining popular with voters) rather than any wholesale shift in identity.[17] Given that Russian interests throughout the period remained static, one can confidently claim that, on the Russian side, traditional goals provided the main motives for the conflict.

Nor is it true that Chechen insurgents have been fighting merely as a result of their radicalized identities. For a world engaged in a highly popularized 'war on terror' it has become almost customary to include groups such as Al-Qaeda and Chechen freedom fighters under the same rubric. The assumption has been that such groups have few (if any) clearly articulated goals, and they employ violence as a visceral backlash against modernity and cosmopolitanism. However, the homogenizing role of globalization on long-held cultural norms and Muslim patterns of belief is not a persuasive 'root cause' of the war in Chechnya. Self-determination remains the main goal of insurgents, in which ideational changes are the product of alterations in material conditions, rather than representing underlying motivations for behaviour. Under these conditions, identity serves as a powerful instrument to mobilize and motivate fighters – it is a means rather than an end in itself.

---

[17] See for instance Stephen Brooks and William Wohlforth, 'Power, Globalisation, and the End of the Cold War: Reevaluating a Landmark Case for Ideas', *International Security*, Vol. 25, No. 3, 2000–1, pp. 5–53; Matthew Sussex, *Power, Interests and Identity in Russian Foreign Policy*, PhD dissertation, The University of Melbourne, 2001; and James Sofka, 'American Neutral Rights Reappraised: Identity or Interest in the Foreign Policy of the Early Republic?', *Review of International Studies*, Vol. 26, No. 4, 2000, pp. 599–622.

Statements by Chechen resistance leaders confirm this characterization. When Shamil Basaev, the field commander and leader of the Sabotage Battalion of Chechen Martyrs (RSMB), received 22 per cent of the vote in the 1997 elections, he refused to join the victorious Maskhadov's administration, but stated that 'we [he and Maskhadov] have a common goal – Chechnya's independence'.[18] Later, in June 2001 the commander of the Special Purpose Islamic Regiment (SPIR), Arbi Baraev, claimed responsibility for executing the mayor of Gekhi, identifying him explicitly as the head of the 'occupation administration'. The language used by insurgents in public statements therefore also more closely befits a liberation campaign than any united global Wahhabi movement. Akhmed Zakaev, the Deputy Prime Minister of the Chechen Republic of Ichkeria, claimed from political asylum in London that '[t]oday a prayer for Iraq, Palestine and Chechnya is offered in a single breath in every mosque in the world'.[19] It is also acknowledged that in the second Chechen war the Islamic influence has increased. According to Matthew Evangelista:

[E]very powerful man in Chechnya, starting with President Aslan Maskhadov, scrambled to acquire a degree of Islamic discourse and representation – beards grew longer, prayers became conspicuous, women were expelled from the remaining offices.[20]

Yet religion was not a factor in the origins of the post-Soviet wars. Dudaev, a former Soviet general, was influenced by the national liberation movements in the Baltic Republics where he served as air force commander in the late Soviet period; and his goal was sovereignty for Chechnya. Maskhadov and others have used symbols of Islam for legitimacy in the pursuit of sovereignty objectives associated with traditional, modernist notions of power and territory.

In old wars well-organized and well-disciplined military groups, motivated by political objectives, used violence as a means to an end. In new wars ill-disciplined militias rampage through society inflicting unprovoked violence often for no other purpose than to instill fear.[21] Winning is not the objective in any notion of new warfare: the ends and the means are one and the same. Yet this has been shown not to be the case in relation to intra-state ethnic conflicts; and it is certainly not the case in the Chechen war. Theatre-goers might be subject to terrorist acts, but the objective, whatever one thinks of the means, is to further the end of independence for

---

[18] Basaev's statement can be found in *Russian Regional Report*, Vol. 2, No. 4, 29 January 1997.

[19] Akhmed Zakaev, 'Chechnya: We Are Not Your Enemy in the War on Terror', *International Herald Tribune*, 18 June 2004.

[20] Matthew Evangelista, *The Chechen Wars: Will Russia Go The Way of the Soviet Union?* (Washington, DC, The Brookings Institution, 2002), p. 72.

[21] See Robert D Kaplan, 'The Coming Anarchy', *The Atlantic*, No. 279, February 1994, pp. 44–76.

Chechnya.[22] It should be noted that Chechnya is not the only case in which power and interests remain important rationales for war. It became a truism after Vietnam that the USA had lost the will to fight wars, and that normative considerations on the domestic level would prevent American presidents from sending troops into combat. This misunderstands the lessons of Vietnam, in which US interests and goals were internally contested from the outset. Any norm of war-avoidance – the so-called Vietnam syndrome – did not endure past 1990, after Saddam Hussein invaded neighbouring Kuwait in order to spread Iraq's influence in the world's most important oil-producing region. American casualties in the thousands were expected in 1991 when President George Bush launched Desert Storm, and American citizens were prepared to accept this price to ensure US interests were maintained. Then 9/11 demonstrated that a US President was once again willing to wage war, and that the US population was willing to see US troops sacrificed in the pursuit of American interests and to ensure national security. At no time in the interim, from Vietnam through to the Gulf War, did the defence of US interests or national security really warrant going to war. If their interests are seriously challenged, then states are willing, insofar as they are able, to wage war. Russia's war in Chechnya must be seen in this light.

The Main Actors in Warfare

According to Holsti, contemporary wars are no longer characterized by conflict between armies of the state. Now participants are mixed and there is a blurring between combatants (soldiers in uniform) and noncombatants (civilians). Holsti's primary focus is on third world postcolonial wars, or what he terms 'peoples' wars', which are what would more traditionally be called 'civil wars'. Now, he argues, insurgents, militias and others are the main participants, with higher levels of civilian casualties than in earlier wars. Mary Kaldor makes a similar claim:

> [W]hat was proscribed according to the classical rules of war and codified in the laws of war in the late nineteenth century and early twentieth century, such as atrocities against non-combatants, sieges, destruction of historic monuments, etc, now constitutes an essential component of the strategies of the new mode of warfare.[23]

This is a remarkable statement in light of the atrocities committed in wars during this same period. Henderson and Singer have shown that similar

---

[22] For relevant works on intra-state ethnic conflict see Michael E Brown, 'The Causes of Internal Conflict: An Overview', in Michael E Brown, Owen R Cote, Jr., Sean M Lynn-Jones and Steven E Miller, *Nationalism and Ethnic Conflict* (Cambridge, Mass, MIT Press, 1997), 3–25.
[23] Kaldor, *New and Old Wars*, p. 8.

ratios of high civilian-to-military casualty rates can be found in nineteenth-century wars fought outside Europe in the colonies. They cite as an example the second Philippines War of 1899–1902, in which 4,000 US troops were killed, along with 20,000 *insurrectos*, and about 200,000 civilians. This is a ratio of 10 to 1 civilian to military deaths (civilians making up an astonishing 89 per cent of the total).[24] Earlier still, in the seventeenth century, during the Thirty Years War (1618–48) fully 50 per cent of the civilian population perished in some areas, and it has been estimated that one-third of the German population died, with the Empire's population depleted by between 20 and 40 per cent.[25] One might claim that different kinds of protagonists will fight wars differently: traditional conflicts see set-piece battles between legitimate and disciplined armies, whereas 'new wars' are characterized by guerrilla forces using unconventional strategies. But old wars used guerrilla tactics too, and new wars use conventional ones. Indeed the term 'guerrilla' itself (coming from the Spanish for 'small war') originated with the irregular Spanish forces in the Peninsula War in support of Wellington in the first decade of the nineteenth century.[26]

There is clearly a threat to international security from transnational networks, especially from loosely linked Islamic terrorist groups. Many of these have grown out of previous policies of the main state powers, especially those of the USA during the Cold War period. One cannot fully explain the terrorist threats emanating from Al-Qaeda and the 9/11 attacks without going back to the conflicts in Afghanistan in the latter part of the twentieth century.[27] Hence local wars in the 'global south' have come to have wider ramifications for international security, in what Chalmers Johnson refers to as 'blowback'.[28] Tarak Barkawi has gone as far as to suggest that with the end of the Cold War '...the axis of threat has shifted from great power and superpower contests to a much older struggle: that between North and South, between the powerful and the weak'[29] More controversially, Barkawi states that Al-Qaeda should not be seen as a fanatical

---

[24] Henderson and Singer, '"New Wars" and Rumours of "New Wars"', p. 175.

[25] Philip Bobbitt, *The Shield of Achilles: War, Peace and the Course of History* (London, Penguin, 2002), p. 119. During this war the city of Magdeburg with its entire population (20,000 inhabitants) was annihilated: see Mueller, 'Introduction', *Retreat From Doomsday*.

[26] For a short but concise definition see Graham Evans and Jeffrey Newnham (eds), *The Penguin Dictionary of International Relations* (London, Penguin, 1998), pp. 214–15.

[27] The United States under Ronald Reagan was supporting 'freedom fighters' (the mujahadin) in their war against the Soviet-imposed regime in Kabul; yet once that regime was overthrown, the US lost interest in Afghanistan, the Soviet Union disintegrated, and the country was left to fester. In a chain of actions going back to US support for the overthrow of the Iranian government in 1953, through the Soviet war in Afghanistan, American interventions are seen as being directly linked to 9/11.

[28] Chalmers Johnson, *Blowback: The Costs and Consequences of American Empire* (London, Time Warner, 2002).

[29] Tarak Barkawi, 'On The Pedagogy of Small Wars', *International Affairs*, Vol. 80, No. 1, 2004, pp. 19–37, at p. 21.

extremist organization nor as a 'terrorist threat', but as a 'hybrid form of anti-colonial resistance', and that '[a] potentially global resistance movement has been called into existence, made possible by the centuries-old spread of Islam around the world'.[30]

Likewise, the wars in the former Yugoslavia were not based upon new postmodern (or post-nationalist) phenomena, but on the very old idea of the nation and, linking this to power and territory, of the nation-state. As with Yugoslavia, so too with the former Soviet Union, communist regimes were forced ultimately to acknowledge the power of the national idea in the construction of their federal political systems. Only authoritarian control could ensure that these national identities would not become the instrument for political contestation. Kaldor's claim that the form of nationalism existing in the member states that made up Yugoslavia is 'new' does not stand up to scrutiny. In a circular argument she claims that nationalism in Yugoslavia (and by extension in the former USSR, and contemporary Chechnya) is not linked to state-building, but to the disintegration of the state. Yet it was communism and dictatorship that disintegrated, a consequence of which was the resurgence of old nationalist sentiments and the political project of statehood for national groups.[31] Kaldor argues that the 'upsurge in particularistic identities cannot be understood in traditional terms'.[32] But in Chechnya as in Yugoslavia, Kaldor's 'particularistic identities' fit neatly within Anthony Smith's definition of nationalism: the 'pull' of demographic, industrial and economic forces around a central idea that permits identities to cohere, with territory playing a fundamental role as a primary requisite of national identity.[33] And, as Jack Snyder has pointed out, such nationalism takes on more aggressive forms where clear inequalities, such as poverty, economic crisis, and political uncertainties, are manifest.[34]

There is nothing new about resistance and struggle for national liberation. The French have resisted foreign occupation, as have Algerians, Indians and many others, while Jews in Palestine and, later, Palestinians in Israel have fought to build nations. The composition of main actors in the Chechen war shows that the conflict can be included in this category as an intrastate, civil war, and more specifically, a war of national liberation.[35]

---

[30] Barkawi, 'On The Pedagogy of Small Wars', pp. 22, 24.

[31] See Peter Shearman, 'Nationalism, the State and the Collapse of Communism', in Sarah Owen Vandersluis (ed), *The State and Identity Construction in International Relations* (New York, St. Martin's Press, 2000), pp. 76–108. See also Michael Cox and Peter Shearman, 'After the Fall: Nationalist Extremism in Post-Communist Russia', in Paul Hainsworth (ed), *The Politics of the Extreme Right* (London, Pinter, 2000), 224–46.

[32] Kaldor, *New and Old Wars*, p. 69.

[33] Anthony Smith, *National Identity* (London, Penguin, 1991).

[34] See Jack Snyder, *From Voting to Violence: Democratisation and Nationalist Conflict* (New York, WW Norton, 2000).

[35] In the edition of the Cassell *History of Warfare*, edited by John Keegan, that deals with this type of warfare the war in Chechnya is so defined: Daniel Moran, *Was of National Liberation* (London, Cassell, 2002), p. 25.

Hence the actors in this war are not new. They are the traditional actors in a form of conflict that has been manifest right through the state system. In the enthusiasm to link extremist Wahhabi Muslim groups together, US analysts and others have overstated the extent to which the major players in the Chechen conflict comprise organized criminals that supply weapons to jihadists from outside the region, united by common beliefs. The US State Department, for instance, lists SPIR, the RSMB, the International Islamic brigade co-founded by Basaev and the Saudi-born Ibn-al Khattab, and the Kavkaz Tsentr News Agency as groups with links to Al-Qaeda. The State Department notes that Khattab had met bin Laden in 1994 and had received financial support to mobilize 'Afghan Arab' fighters from Ingushetia, Ossetia, Georgia, and Azerbaijan to take part in combat operations against the Russians in Chechnya and Dagestan. Basaev had trained in Afghanistan in 2001, and the US alleges that both he and Khattab sent Chechens to serve in Al-Qaeda's '055' brigade, fighting alongside the Taliban against the Northern Alliance in Afghanistan.[36] In a similar manner, Rohan Gunaratna claims that with the defeat of the Soviet-backed regime in Kabul, and the subsequent victory of the Taliban, Afghanistan was lost as a 'liberated theatre of jihad' and that there has been 'a partial diversion of support to Chechnya', which has become a training base for future attacks against the West.[37]

Even if Gunaratna is correct, it is surprising that Russian officials have not made more of the apparent ties between Al-Qaeda and leading figures in the Chechen resistance. Indeed, it was the Chechen conflict that provided the impetus for the Bush administration to declare, shortly after 9/11, that Russia was playing an active role in fighting terrorists at home and abroad. In reality, foreign fighters make up only a small fraction of the Chechen resistance effort. As John Dunlop has noted, an *Izvestiya* interview in October 2001 with Sergei Yastrzhembsky (Putin's official spokesman), put the total number of Wahhabi fighters in Chechnya as 'not more than 200'.[38] Dunlop went on to point out that the core of the resistance effort is composed of at least 70 to 80 per cent secular nationalists loyal to Maskhadov. The problem is, however, that the focus of global attention, led by the US, has been on these smaller groups, which helps facilitate their growth, rather than the main independence movement that precipitated the conflict in the first place. In a televised address to the nation in the wake of the tragic end to the hostage-taking in Beslan, North Ossetia, in September 2004, Putin did not even mention Chechnya (despite the fact that the majority of the

[36] 'Patterns of Global Terrorism', Office of the Coordinator for Counterterrorism, US State Department, June 2003.

[37] Rohan Gunaratna, 'The Al-Qaeda Threat and The International Response', in David Martin Jones (ed.), *Globalisation and the New Terror: The Asia Pacific Dimension* (Cheltenham, Edward Elgar, 2004), pp. 51–69, at p. 64.

[38] John B Dunlop, 'The Second Russo-Chechen War Two Years On', *American Committee for Peace in Chechnya*, 17 October 2001.

terrorists were Chechens whose political demands all related to the war in Chechnya). Rather he portrayed these events as being part of a global war on terrorism.[39] Putin's immediate policy response was to strengthen his own position within the power structure of the Russian Federation, hence undermining an already precarious transition to democracy. Neither portraying the war in Chechnya as part of a global war on terror, nor undermining democratic development in Russia, will provide any possible avenues for resolving the Chechen war.

Whilst groups such as criminal gangs and extremist fighters have featured prominently in 'new' contemporary conflicts in the Caucasus, they do not represent the majority (or even the most influential minority) of actors in the conflict. As Stathis N Kalyvas has argued, the same has been true of 'old' civil wars. This is simply because, within the broader conflict between two opposing sides, war provides groups (whether criminals, old political foes seeking revenge, or other cleavages) with the opportunity to pursue their own objectives that might not have been possible in other circumstances.[40] Despite numerous reports in the Russian, European and US media concerning Chechens fighting the global jihad overseas in Iraq and Afghanistan, little solid evidence ever given to substantiate such claims. It would be surprising if there were not some Chechens involved in such activities, or that Chechnya itself was not a magnet for a minority of transnational Islamic militants. But it would be incorrect to attempt to link the war in Chechnya to the global war on terrorism. UK, US and Australian citizens have also been actively engaged in various parts of the world, including Afghanistan, in supporting the 'resistance' to foreign intervention and the global 'jihad'. Zakaev makes the point that, given their very limited resources, in terms of finance and manpower, and their primary objective of gaining independence for their nation, Chechens would hardly be deeply involved in Iraq or elsewhere.[41]

Given these constraints, the claim of proponents of the 'new wars' thesis – that a new type of polity has emerged that transcends the nation-state – is also bizarre given the significance increase in the number of states since the establishment of the state system. Chechens are not fighting for cosmopolitan justice or a new type of polity. They are fighting for statehood: for independence from the Russian Federation. Likewise, Russian authorities are not fighting an international war on terror in Chechnya; rather, they are struggling to prevent the Russian state from fragmenting, and refusing to acknowledge the aspirations of the Chechen people for independence. Before 9/11 the problems in Chechnya were perceived by outside forces as part of a wider post-Soviet (essentially postcolonial) issue, and Russian authorities were criticized for human rights abuses and waging an illegal,

---

[39] *Johnson Russia List*, 8371, No. 6, 17 September 2004.
[40] Stathis N Kalyvas, '"New" and "Old" Civil Wars: A Valid Distinction?', *World Politics*, Vol. 54, 2001, pp. 99–118, at p. 113.
[41] Zakaev, 'Chechnya'.

unjustified war on the Chechen nation. Following 9/11 the George W Bush administration superimposed the 'global war on terrorism' onto the conflict in Chechnya, thereby transforming it into a broader conflict between the West and extremist Islamic terrorism. In so doing it played into the hands of Putin, who himself sought to delegitimize the Chechen fighters as part of a global struggle against transnational terrorism.

Applying the 'war on terror' discourse to the Chechnya conflict therefore leads to a situation whereby the rhetoric becomes reality for those that employ it: the fighters in Chechnya are 'terrorists', 'foreigner Islamic groups', and so on. An imagined war becomes real, and we are left with a conflict that cannot end because the terms on which it is waged – its origins and roots, the political objectives of those that started it, are no longer recognized. They are not merely illegitimate; they are not actually acknowledged at all. This has similarities with the US war in Iraq. Opponents to the US occupation are described as 'foreign terrorists', remnants of Saddam's inner circle, and so on. As long as the enemy is not identified for what it is, and as long as the enemy's actual objectives are under-evaluated, there is little hope for a lasting resolution. This is true also of Russia under Putin. The application of the same logic to the Chechen war runs the risk of a self-fulfilling prophecy, as the global forces of radical Islamic fundamentalism take root in Chechnya, and spread further throughout the Caucusus.

Methods of War

'New wars' theorists see the seemingly arbitrary violence of militias as being disconnected from political objectives. Looting, rape, random killings, kidnapping and extortion appear to indicate a style of war with no 'rules of the game', no respect for established conventions on the conduct of war; rather, violence appears to be pursued almost for its own sake. As a result, 'new wars' are distinguished from old or conventional wars on the basis of the methods employed and the logic behind them. Old wars were conflicts between well-organized and disciplined troops or military formations that engaged in logical tactics in pursuit of a clear strategy. In contemporary conflicts like Chechnya and the Yugoslav wars of the 1990s, so the argument goes, protagonists use entirely different tactics that make no distinction between civil and military targets. The consequence is increased 'collateral damage' amongst noncombatants, since it is difficult to tell friend from foe, while the deliberate targeting of civilians by insurgents with limited military resources becomes a legitimate tactic. Yet the empirical evidence for this suggests otherwise. Old wars, both interstate and intrastate, were often extremely bloody and cruel, involving forms of violence not apparently necessary within a strategic framework linked to established political goals. There were many bloody examples of wanton violence in the American Civil War, and civil wars have always involved the most horrendous forms of bloodletting.

Certainly, blanket bombing during the World War Two hardly recognized the distinction between soldiers and non-combatants. In one night in February 1945 the German town of Pforzheim lost one-third of its population in a single air bombardment; overall it is estimated that 600,000 German civilians died in air raids, 3.5 million homes were destroyed, and at the end of the war there were 7.5 million Germans without homes.[42] There is much to compare between Dresden and Grozny in terms of the nature of warfare employed and the horrific suffering and destruction of civilian communities. Kaldor draws what has become a common but flawed distinction between old and new wars in relation to the ratio of military to civilian casualties in war, claiming that the ratio of military to civilian casualties of war has gone from 8:1 at the turn of the twentieth century, to 1:8 at the end.

This is simply incorrect. As noted above, a number of studies from the Correlates of War (COW) project have demonstrated that civilian casualties were often much higher during modern conflicts, especially considering that the vast numbers of deaths that occurred in Hiroshima and Nagasaki at the close of World War Two were virtually entirely civilian.[43] The problem here is that most data on civilian to military casualties in warfare is not properly documented, and is difficult to collate in the first place, since it often relies on second- and third- hand accounts from individuals and groups (both governmental and non-governmental) that have vested interests in pushing the limits of casualties either to the upper or lower ends of the spectrum. The International Committee of the Red Cross has acknowledged that it is unable convincingly to substantiate the various claims made about casualty figures amongst civil populations. Of the thousands of people treated for war injuries since 1991 by the Red Cross '…only 35 percent were women, children under 16, and men over 50', even though these groups together make up a large majority of most populations.[44]

It should be noted also that looting has been a recurrent phenomenon in all wars, including amongst even the most 'disciplined' participants. Looting of art treasures in warfare has been rampant over the centuries, leading right up to the looting of Baghdad in 2003. Looting as a form of taxation has been manifest in civil wars and inter-state wars alike (the USSR called it 'reparations' after the Second World War). Uncontrolled violence, torture and mass rape have also been common in wars.[45] Chechens have been the victims of bombing from the air, shelling from the ground, arbitrary arrest, torture, rape, and have had their treasures looted. All of

---

[42] WG Sebald, *On The Natural History of Destruction* (London, Hamish Hamilton, 2003), p. 3. Sebald notes that the Royal Air Force alone dropped 1 million tons of bombs on enemy territory in the war, and for Dresden there were 42.8 cubic metres of rubble for every inhabitant (p. 3). One should not forget, of course, the terrible fates of Hiroshima and Nagasaki.
[43] Henderson and Singer, '"New Wars" and Rumours of "New Wars"'.
[44] See Joshua S Goldstein, *War and Gender* (Cambridge University Press, 2001), p. 400.
[45] Goldstein, *War and Gender*, p. 400.

these things took place in World War Two. Coventry, Dresden and Darwin were bombed, Japanese citizens were detained in the USA, victims of Nazi concentration camps were tortured and many millions were murdered, while hundreds of thousands of women in Berlin were raped by Soviet troops when they captured the city in 1945. Similar activities have occurred in the 2003 Iraq war, even if on a much lesser scale. For example, there has clearly been systematic abuse of Iraqi detainees by US troops at the Abu Ghraib prison, as well as numerous rapes of Iraqi women.[46]

A further factor regarding modes of warfare concerns the level of popular support for the kind of conflict in question. Old wars are associated with mass support for the actions and objectives of the fighters (soldiers fighting for a noble cause); new wars are associated with smaller bands of warlords instilling fear in the masses in order to create the anarchic circumstances that facilitate their own personal ambitions and criminal activities. Old wars required winning the hearts and minds of the wider population; new wars require divisions and the fostering of hatred. These are said to be the main components of a new trend in asymmetric warfare. Yet again, there is little that is new about this concept, which has been a feature of conflict even before Napoleonic times. In more recent years, the Jews in British Palestine and French resistance movements in occupied France during World War Two, not to mention the Vietcong, have all used asymmetric tactics. This is simply because, given the radical discrepancies in power capabilities, such groups utilize what resources they possess to inflict damage on the foe, whether striking vulnerable targets such as civilians or military supply dumps. Asymmetric warfare is thus a reflection of the weak versus the strong, with the weak being forced to use *matériel* and methods that provide them with the possibility of waging war against the more powerful. These are rational responses in warfare where a protagonist's goals are not necessarily matched by the means in their possession.

This is demonstrated in the Chechen case by the apparent attempt to acquire and use Weapons of Mass Destruction (WMD), or at least threaten to use materials that can cause mass civil unrest, disturbance and disruption. What has been called the 'most important sub-state use of radiological material' occurred when Basaev informed the Russian television network NTV on 23 November 1995 that four cases of radioactive material had been hidden around Moscow at the entrance to a park.[47] Russian emergency teams roamed the city with Geiger counters, and located several canisters of Caesium stolen from a Russian hospital following a raid in which Chechen guerrillas seized 1,500 hostages at Budennovsk in June 1995.

---

[46] Rape in warfare has been historically linked to total conquest, a crime of domination that is the 'ultimate humiliation'. See Goldstein, *War and Gender*, p. 362.

[47] Gavin Cameron, 'The Chemical, Biological, Radiological and Nuclear (CBRN) Threat: Exaggeration or Apocalypse Soon?', in Jones (ed.), *Globalisation and the New Terror*, pp. 88–118, p. 99.

Chechens have also threatened to attack nuclear facilities in Russia on a number of occasions, including a plan to strike the four huge nuclear reactors at the Balakovo nuclear power plant. The carefully orchestrated seizing of Russian hostages at the Dubrovka theatre in Moscow in October 2002 was also indicative of the use of asymmetric warfare by Chechen fighters.

However, regardless of the level of the attackers' hatred and the civilian nature of their targets, asymmetric tactics do not equate to blind and irrational violence. For instance, in April 2000 the Dagestani Interior Ministry claimed that Russian special forces suspected Chechen rebels of possessing four containers of the biological agent anthrax.[48] Whether or not the claims were true, and taking into account the difficulties faced by unskilled fighters who lack access to sophisticated laboratories for weaponizing biological agents, no organized militia group, either in Chechnya or elsewhere, has yet used biological agents in a deliberate attack. Although the attractions of biological weapons are obvious, since the target population spreads the agent for the attacker, they are notoriously difficult if not impossible to control. Simply put, biological weapons kill at an indiscriminate level unmatched by any other WMD. The risk of a highly contagious agent infecting the attacking population as well as the target (a problem compounded by the close territorial proximity of combatants in civil wars) makes the use of biological weapons less rational than chemical weapons released within a contained target envelope before becoming harmless, or 'dirty bombs' that irradiate a given pre-selected geographic area.

In assessing the methods of war in traditional as opposed to postmodern conflict, we therefore find that there is little to differentiate the new from the old. Asymmetric warfare has been an enduring phenomenon, one that could even be identified as the norm in conflict situations. The ideal type of two protagonists, each with rough strategic parity in terms of material capabilities, was an unusual occurrence, even during the Cold War era. The fact that most wars are not symmetrical means that actors will, rationally enough, routinely seek advantages through different tactics to compensate for disparities in capability. This is certainly the case in the conflicts in Chechnya. While the bloodletting in that region has been terrible, it has been no more so than in other conflicts, either between states with established laws of war, or in numerous civil wars throughout history.

External Actors

At first glance assessments of the role of external actors – states – in conflicts do not differ significantly in relation to the discourse on 'new' and 'old' wars. Traditional conflicts are perceived to incorporate patterns of shifting

[48] Cameron, 'The Chemical, Biological, Radiological and Nuclear (CBRN) Threat', p. 105.

alliances as a war either gained momentum or dropped off in intensity, and other nations rushed to bandwagon with the anticipated victor. States, therefore, were seen as the main external actors in conflict.

Proponents of the 'new wars' theory define the role of 'external actors' along similar lines. However, Kaldor and others suggest that attempts to identify the players in postmodern wars should not be limited in scope merely to states, and that a host of organizations (and even individuals) can be listed as potential external actors. These include, for instance, NGOs working on the margins of the conflict in refugee camps – indeed, she claims that the refugees themselves are actors in the conflict due to the pressures they place on governments – as well as groups that provide funding and/or aid to combatants (on either side of a conflict). The rapid spread of information, emergent global human rights norms pertaining to civil society, porous borders in 'failing' states, and the capabilities of modern NGOs mean that processes of globalization increases the significance of such groups' involvement in contemporary conflicts.

On the issue of refugees, it is clear that population displacement due to war predates the state system in world politics. More recently, massive forced and voluntary movement of populations was a characteristic of twentieth century wars, including those between Turkey and Greece in the early 1920s, the Spanish Civil War, Russia and China during their revolutions and the Vietnam War, not to mention the displacement of peoples during wars of imperial expansion in the nineteenth century, culminating in campaigns between mass armies during World Wars One and Two. The war in Chechnya is no exception, prompting a tide of refugees to move to neighbouring republics of the Russian Federation, especially Ingushetia. The last remaining refugee tents were dismantled in 'Satsita', the large camp in Ingushetia, in June 2004. Clearly Russian authorities were keen to demonstrate that the problem was now over, as the vast majority of the camp's residents (576 out of 666) decided to return to Chechnya.[49] But removing large concentrations of Chechen refugees from such camps has not resolved the problem. Ivan Sukhov in *Vremya novostei* quotes figures obtained from migration officials that show there are still 18,610 Chechens '...living in some 148 compact settlements such as warehouses or factories rented by Russia's Federal Migration Service'. Chechen human rights advocates also maintain that another 1,000 refugees still live in tents in smaller, less visible, concentrations throughout Ingushetia.[50] The point, however, is that while refugees place a strain on an actor's capabilities, they rarely have a significant impact on policy decisions, particularly at a strategic level. Moreover, the risk of conflict 'spillover' due to the tragic plight of displaced people has long been identified as a potential danger.

---

[49] *Chechnya Weekly*, Vol. 5, Issue 24, 16 June 2004, p. 1. From the Jamestown Foundation: *brdcst@jamestown.org.*
[50] Cited in *Chechnya Weekly*, Vol. 5, Issue 24, 16 June 2004, p. 1.

One might argue that although refugees and NGOs concerned with their welfare have had little effect on the approaches of the main protagonists in the Chechen conflict, there is some evidence that NGOs have attempted to act in specific instances to influence the war. In Russia's repeated attempts to capture and try Akhmed Zakaev, Aslan Maskhadov's representative to Europe, human rights groups have played an important part in lobbying the legal authorities in the UK, Denmark, Germany and Norway, each ultimately rejecting requests for his extradition (see Chapter 12). Russia argued that Norway was obliged '...as a participant in the anti-terrorist coalition' to arrest him.[51] In Norway human rights groups, including the Norwegian branch of the Helsinki Committee, met with Zakaev on his visit to Oslo. Again, however, the fact that external actors other than states can influence conflict, particularly civil conflict, is nothing new. Some have direct ties to states and their interests, such as the French Foreign Legion. Others have taken part on a more personal level, but their achievements have been regularly used to achieve political goals. A classic example can be found in the impact of Che Guevara in Latin America, who quickly became a pin-up figure of revolutionary struggle, and has remained so to this day. The same was true of George Orwell, who published *Homage to Catalonia* in the late 1930s, an account of the time he spent fighting with the Spanish militia during the civil war. The details Orwell provided on the machinations of the Communist Party within the Republican movement were later used to great effect by the anti-communist movement in the USA.

In the war in Chechnya one can also identify a number of states as fitting the roles of external actors. The members of the European Union, as standard-bearers of good international citizenship and the 'soft' (non-military) power benefits (such as prestige) that such a stance conveys, played a peripheral role by berating Russia for repeated human rights abuses, once having threatened to expel it from the Council of Europe. In the aftermath of 9/11, official EU criticism of Russia's handling of the war has largely dissipated now that Putin is identified as a key Western ally in the struggle against global terrorism. Iran has played a role by supporting Muslim fundamentalists in places, but again this has been done for reasons of pragmatic national interest. In order to preserve its own influence in the Middle East, Iran has sought to keep the area inhospitable for others with designs on the region.

One must therefore question the extent to which postmodern conflicts capture the hearts and minds of external actors. Kaldor claims that the war in Bosnia-Herzegovina '...impinged on global consciousness the way no other recent war has done'.[52] The assumption here is that other actors on the global stage affected the course of the war. Here she refers to the international media, NGOs, a range of international institutions, and other 'major

---

[51] *Chechnya Weekly*, Vol. 5, Issue 24, 16 June 2004, p. 2.
[52] Kaldor, *New and Old Wars*, p. 31.

governments'. Kaldor states that '...the war in Bosnia-Herzegovina is likely to turn out to be one of those defining events, in which entrenched political assumptions, strategic thinking and international arrangements are both challenged and reconstructed'.[53] This exaggerates and misunderstands the role and functions of other transnational and international actors in wars, and misperceives the interests of Western governments as somehow representing a 'global consciousness'. It was not global civil society that intervened in Bosnia in pursuit of global cosmopolitan aims; it was the major state powers that intervened for their own perceived national interests. No global institutions have participated in the Chechnya conflict; while the major powers have, again for their own material interests, turned a blind eye to Russia's war against the Chechens, especially since 9/11. Moreover, it is inconceivable that the USA or NATO could even contemplate intervening in Russia, because doing so would escalate the conflict from an internal struggle to a war between nations.

The Economics of Warfare

The final feature of 'new wars' relates to changes in the economics of warfare. According to Kaldor, the economics of old wars were linked to national mobilization and state taxation policy, operating within a highly structured relationship between the government and the civilian population, in which the focus was on the end political goals to be achieved by war. In contrast, the economics of 'new wars', it is argued, revolve around the radicalized identities of the participants, and the interests of external actors who can provide assistance to one side over the other. As a result, while the economics of traditional war could be characterized in terms of state power and capabilities, the economics of postmodern war are much more fluid, typified by organized criminal gangs, international/transnational drug syndicates, and routine kidnappings and hostage-taking for economic purposes. This is assisted by the labelling of the 'other' as evil, thereby seeking not a negotiated solution to war, or even a final military victory, but rather to ensure the continuation of conflict for continued economic gain.

We characterize the economics of war rather differently, arguing that portrayal of the ethnic 'other' as responsible for disorder, anarchy, crime and uncertainty in times of economic crisis and political turmoil are not new phenomena, and are not unique to Chechnya. It is certainly true that Chechnya was by a large margin one of the poorest communities in Russia, and one with a real historical grievance that was easily manipulated by new nationalist elites. The relative poverty of Chechnya was clearly evident as the USSR collapsed. It had the most rural population of the USSR; at 73 per cent

[53] Kaldor, *New and Old Wars*, p. 32.

the highest birth rates (at 16.1 per 100,000 compared to the Russian average of 2.2 per 100,000); and was the least multilingual population in the Russian Federation. Chechens also possessed generally low levels of education. Some 15 per cent of the population had little or no formal education, 13 per cent had completed elementary schooling, 23 per cent had not completed secondary education, and only 4 per cent had gone on to higher schooling. Chechnya's health system was the poorest in the USSR, with only 112.6 doctors per 10,000 people (compared with 586 per 10,000 in Stavropol), and the region was beset by high unemployment.

In a comprehensive review of the literature on the causes of internal conflict, Michael Brown identifies structural factors, political factors, economic/social factors and cultural/ perceptual factors as playing a part. Internal conflicts can be triggered by mass-level factors inside the state, by factors external to the state (bad neighbours) or by internal or external elite-level factors (bad leaders).[54] Chechnya was faced with factors at each of these levels, while structural domestic anarchy, as the post-Soviet state was collapsing, led to a number of internal security dilemmas. This situation was exacerbated by the relative poverty of Chechnya compared to other regions in the Russian Federation, and the instrumental political goals of 'bad' leaders, both in Moscow and Grozny. In addition to these proximate causes for war in Chechnya, there were also the remembered crimes against the Chechen people inflicted by Stalin in the 1940s, giving a perceptual sense of victimhood that made war even more likely. Race riots in the UK or USA take place in the poor inner city slum areas, not in the middle class or wealthy areas of Chelsea or Georgetown. And while it is stretching a point to identify economics as the root cause of contemporary violence, including international terrorism (since the 9/11 hijackers were largely from the wealthy middle classes of Saudi society), it is nonetheless true that violent conflict is much more likely to take place in poor communities. The Chechnya conflict does not reflect a new phenomenon of organized criminal networks employing war as means of accumulating wealth. A stronger case can be made for linking the origins of the conflict to relative economic deprivation in a collapsing federal political structure in which there is a history of violence perpetuated by the former 'colonial' power.

Conclusions

Proponents of the 'new wars' theory claim that postmodern conflict is fought by different actors, using different means, in the pursuit of fundamentally different goals than in 'old wars'. An examination of the Chechen war, we argue, shows the exact opposite to be the case. Here we return to the most important aspect of war: its purpose. As noted above, identifying

---

[54] Brown, 'The Causes of Internal Conflict', p. 4.

the purpose of war is not easy. But we do know from the literature on war that the major triggers at the interstate, intrastate and extrastate levels have been territory, and the power struggles linked to security dilemmas. This has been shown to be true in the case of the wars in the former Yugoslavia (Kaldor's 'new wars') and in the Third World after 1945 (Holsti's people's wars). It is certainly true in the case of Chechnya, where the war is fundamentally over territory. Yet in Chechnya conflict has also been triggered by a potent cocktail of economic dislocation, profound social changes, historical antagonisms and elite-level manipulation during radical political transformation. The conditions for war were permissive as the USSR unravelled, and elites on both sides took advantage of the situation by mobilizing the masses around nationalism and historical grievances.[55]

Kaldor claims that the '...main implication of globalisation is that territorial sovereignty is no longer viable', suggesting that new wars are motivated by labels based upon identity 'rather than an idea'.[56] But surely there is no more potent an idea than that of the 'imagined community' of the nation: it is the idea of national identity that has proven to be potent. The claim that '...new wars take place in a context which could be represented as an extreme version of globalisation' does not match empirical reality.[57] If we are to take seriously President Bush's rhetoric about spreading democracy and freedom, dignity and human rights, this should lead logically to support of the legitimate political struggle of the Chechens for independence. That the US does not support the Chechens is to do with calculations of national interest and power. Furthermore, since 9/11, placing the conflict in Chechnya in the framework of the global war on terror plays into the hands of minority radical transnational terrorist groups, and risks making what is an anti-colonial national liberation movement also into an anti-American, anti-Western movement.[58]

How, then, should we go about resolving conflicts such as these? Many experts have put forward proposals for resolving the Chechen conflict. Apart from the Russian authorities, most call for a political solution. There is little confidence that Russia can win the war through military might, yet it can compromise any Chechen claim for full sovereignty for some time. In wars, original aims often change due to unexpected outcomes stemming from unforeseen circumstances, and due to the shifting and turbulent nature of fortunes involved in violent conflict. Thomas de Waal points out

---

[55] For the difficulty the Russians had in incorporating the peoples of the Caucasus into the Empire see Andreas Kappeler, *The Russian Empire: A Multiethnic History* (Harlow, Essex, Pearson Education, 2001), pp. 179–84.

[56] Kaldor, *New and Old Wars*, p. 98.

[57] Kaldor, *New and Old Wars*, p. 101.

[58] The following works provide detailed analysis of how US actions are actually undermining its power and real interests: Michael Mann, *Incoherent Empire* (London, Verso, 2003); Immaneul Wallerstein, *The Decline of American Power: The U.S. in a Chaotic World* (New York, New Press, 2003); and Chalmers Johnson, *Blowback: The Costs and Consequences of American Empire* (London, Time Warner, 2003).

that two constituencies have been largely absent from the politics of Chechnya: the Chechen people themselves and the 'international community'.[59] He suggests that a 'Loya Jirga' for Chechnya be arranged to glean a common view amongst the Chechens, and for this to be facilitated by outside, international mediation. It is not, de Waal claims, consistent for Putin to say both that the war in Chechnya is part of a wider global war on terror and then that it is a strictly domestic issue, and others should keep their noses out.[60]

To prescribe cosmopolitan law enforcement as a solution is not only utopian, but also a dangerous diversion. Kaldor unconvincingly maintains that the '...the right wing militia groups in the United States are not so very different from the paramilitary groups in Eastern Europe or Africa',[61] and continues by suggesting that the violence in the inner cities of Europe and the USA can also be described as new wars. On this basis we could conclude that *all* violence constitutes manifestation of 'new wars'. We would thus be led down the path of being able to explain everything, and hence actually being able to explain very little. Kaldor maintains that any long-term solution to new wars cannot be found within the framework of identity or on the 'basis of particularistic politics'.[62]

Yet surely this is exactly where the solution lies, linked to the origins of conflicts and the goals of the participants, tied to territory, interests and power. Scottish and Welsh devolution (although peaceful) was based not on ideas of cosmopolitanism, but on those relating to the national community. The solution to the Northern Irish problem, a long bloody conflict relating to the English imperial experience, acknowledged in the Good Friday Agreement, is linked specifically to the politics of identity. In the case of Chechnya, any solution will need to be negotiated within a framework that places national territory – the essential stimulus for identity politics – at its core. Primakov recently wrote: '...the problem of Chechnya will not be resolved by purely military means. At this stage it is not primarily a military problem'. He went on to state that '...this is a war that can be stopped only through negotiations'.[63] The lessons are clear: to recognize the local source of conflict and then to formulate a political solution that deals effectively and fairly with the issue of concern. There should be no skirting around this issue under a blanket of global legalism advocated by

---

[59] He made this point in a briefing paper presented at a meeting in London on Chechnya presented by the Institute for War and Peace Reporting. See *ICPR Caucasus Reporting Service*, No. 238, 16 June 2004. Info@iwpr.net.

[60] Indeed, Russia was willing to cede substantial powers to Kadyrov so long as he was not seeking full independence. See Thomas de Waal, *ICPR Caucasus Reporting Service*, No. 238, 16 June 2004. Info@iwpr.net.

[61] Kaldor, *New and Old Wars*, p. 11.

[62] Kaldor, *New and Old Wars*, p. 10.

[63] Primakov, *A World Restored*, pp. 118–19.

cosmopolitan notions of a mainly western elite, as good as intentions might be. Notwithstanding the Arab-Israeli dispute, all wars do eventually end; either through military victory for one side, or a negotiated solution. It is now widely acknowledged that there is no military solution to the Chechen conflict. A negotiated solution will necessitate compromise, and this will inevitably involve compromise over the essence of the conflict: over the control of territory. A very modern phenomenon indeed.

11

Western Views of the Chechen Conflict

Mike Bowker

There have always been differences in Western policy towards the war in Chechnya, but among Western governments, at least, the differences have been in emphasis rather than substance. Thus throughout the crisis Western governments have always publicly backed Moscow's policy on Chechnya. The West has refused to recognize Chechnya's claim of independence, and has accepted Moscow's right to defend its territorial integrity, if necessary by force (*jus ad bellum*). On the other hand, the West has occasionally spoken out against Russia's conduct in the war and the violation of human rights by the Russian authorities (*jus in bello*), but it has always been reluctant to back such rhetoric with any kind of meaningful sanction. Post-9/11, the West has also become more willing to accept Moscow's argument that Russia's struggle in Chechnya has become a war against militant Islamism as much as a war against separatism. As such, Western leaders have stressed the need for an end to terrorism before any political solution might be viable.

The Western media, on the other hand, tend to portray the Chechen conflict as primarily a war of national liberation. Although rarely spelled out in these terms, the implication of much of the coverage is that the Chechen cause is just. The Chechens have been oppressed by the Russians for the last two hundred years and deserve their independence. The use of force by the Russian authorities is heavily criticized, with the media focusing in particular on the war crimes and human rights violations perpetrated by the Russian forces in Chechnya. The media do not ignore the terrorist atrocities committed by the Chechen rebels, but they are generally explained in terms of a response to Russian brutality and intransigence. The majority in the media is also far more sceptical than Western governments that the conflict in Chechnya can be categorized as part of the international war against terrorism. They are equally sceptical of Putin's so-called 'normalization' process, a process backed by Western governments that has included the new constitution for Chechnya of

March 2003, and the election of the pro-Kremlin leader Akhmed Kadyrov as Chechen president in October 2003. The Western media have also been highly critical of Western government support for Moscow, which is usually explained in terms of cynical *realpolitik*. In other words, according to the media, Western governments have always viewed relations with Russia as far more important than the fate of a few thousand Chechens in the North Caucasus.

In a democracy, the public needs the media to adopt an independent and critical attitude towards government; indeed, this is acknowledged as a key role of the fourth estate. Therefore, the media are merely carrying out their responsibilities in critically analysing Russian policy in Chechnya and Western governments' response to it. Moreover, the media have been right to highlight the violation of human rights in Chechnya – not only out of a concern for common humanity, but also on the wholly practical grounds that the brutality of the Russian forces has made it more difficult to find a compromise solution in the troubled republic. Western leaders have prioritized relations with Moscow over the interests of ordinary Chechens, but it is still fair to say that the Western media's coverage of the conflict is scarcely less partial than that of governments. To some extent, this relates to the nature of the media who are searching for new and newsworthy stories, relevant to their readership at home. This leads to short reports that frequently lack, by necessity, much in the way of historical background and political context. This fact can help explain the media's preoccupation with terrorist attacks and human rights issues, which can be understood (and condemned) in the context of universal liberal morality. No context or background is required to elicit a human response. The response can also lead to demands that 'something be done', when in fact any possible solution will always be highly complex and long drawn-out, if not impossible to achieve. This is rarely the sort of story the media want to report, although this, almost certainly, is the story in Chechnya.[1]

The Issue of Secession

The first post-communist Chechen leader, Djokhar Dudaev, declared independence in November 1991 and, insofar as the Western media had a

---

[1] Although this chapter might at times appear to adopt a rather critical view of some media reporting of the Chechen conflict, it is important to note that the general liberal thrust of most serious news reporting from Chechnya is supported by the majority of Western academics and commentators. See, for example, Vanora Bennett, *Crying Wolf: The Return of War to Chechnya* (London, Pan, 2000); Carlotta Gall and Thomas de Waal, *Chechnya: A Small Victorious War* (London, Picador, 1997); Robert Seely, *Russo-Chechen Conflict, 1800–2000: A Deadly Embrace* (London and Portland, Frank Cass, 2001); and Matthew Evangelista, *The Chechen Wars: Will Russia Go The Same Way as the Soviet Union?* (Washington, Brookings Institution, 2002). One of the few critical of much of the Western news reporting on Chechnya is Anatol Lieven; see his 'Through a Distorted Lens: Chechnya and the Western Media', *Current History*, October 2000, pp. 321–8.

view, they have tended to support his claim.[2] Russia forcibly integrated Chechnya into the Tsarist empire in the nineteenth century, and has frequently used force since to prevent it seceding. In 1944 Stalin infamously exiled virtually the whole Chechen population to Kazakhstan, and the conditions of the deportation were so bad that almost a third were reported to have died *en route*. Although the survivors were allowed to return under Khrushchev, the Chechens suffered continued persecution inside the Soviet Union. Almost alone amongst the Soviet nationalities, ethnic Chechens were prevented from being Party leaders in their own republic.

Despite these historical claims to secession, Moscow refused to recognize Chechen independence, and was supported in this by virtually the whole international community (only Afghanistan under the Taliban formally recognized Chechnya's sovereignty).[3] However, for three years, the Dudaev regime was allowed to remain in office, despite the fact that the republic quickly became a centre of criminality. Apart from the usual robberies and kidnappings inside and outside the republic, Chechnya thrived on state-sponsored gun-running and the drugs trade, and over time became known as a safe haven for criminals. To the leadership in Moscow, the Dudaev regime represented a clear and present threat to the security of Russia. Military force was an obvious option to deal with the problem, but certainly not the only one. According to opinion polls at the time, the majority of Russians, including some leading political and military figures, believed that peaceful alternatives had not been exhausted in December 1994 when Yeltsin finally decided to launch the military campaign to overthrow the Dudaev regime. Yet Western leaders were ready to reiterate their view that Russia had a right to defend its own territorial integrity against nationalist rebels in Chechnya, and in April 1996, President Clinton expressed his support for the war in surprisingly fulsome terms when he compared Boris Yeltsin to Abraham Lincoln: 'I would remind you that we once had a civil war in our country over the proposition that Abraham Lincoln gave his life for – that no state had a right to withdraw from our union'.[4]

Although few leaders wanted to repeat Clinton's analogy (including Clinton himself, it seemed), the official Western position was in line with international law, which opposes anything other than mutually agreed and democratically determined secession. Thus the 1970 UN Declaration of

---

[2] For typical accounts that generally support the Chechen cause, see Deborah Orr, 'For Once, Vanessa Redgrave Could Do Some Good', *The Independent*, 23 December 2002: www.indepedent.co.uk/story.jsp?story = 360175: pp. 1–2; BBC 3: *Conflicts: Chechnya*, Friday 30 April 2004: www.bbc.co.uk/bbcthree/tv/conflicts.shtml; Peter Reddaway, 'Chechnya: An Apology', *The Guardian*, 30 June 2003, p. 17.

[3] It should be noted that historical claims alone are not generally perceived as sufficient grounds for secession in much liberal theory on secession. See, for example, Allen Buchanan, *Secession: The Morality of Political Divorce from Fort Sumter to Lithuania and Quebec* (Boulder, San Francisco and Oxford, Westview Press, 1991).

[4] Quoted from Thomas de Waal, 'America's New Hard Line on Chechnya', 3 November 1999 www.bbc.co.uk/1/hi/world/europe/503804.stm, p. 1.

Friendly Relations and Cooperation Among States declared quite explicitly that 'the territorial integrity and political independence of every state is indivisible'. Even in cases where domestic law permits secession along federal lines, as in the former Soviet Union, international law discourages the reconsideration of borders. In the words of one scholar, there should be 'no secessions from secessions'.[5] The 1993 Russian constitution confirms that its constituent units have no legal right to secede, a position confirmed, specifically in relation to Chechnya, by the Russian Constitutional Court in July 1995. Even political theorists who believe the current law is too restrictive do not argue that there should be an absolute right to secede.[6] There are a number of reasons for international law being so cautious, but essentially theorists worry about the possible outcome of secession.

Secession, involving the loss of population and territory to the state as well as anything of economic value on that territory, is always a major step, which should never be undertaken lightly. If there were an absolute right to secession, there is a fear that this could lead to essentially trivial demands for secession by minority groups whenever they fail to get their way at national level. Furthermore, there is a concern that secession for one state could lead to a domino effect, with ever-smaller groups seeking independence. At some point, there is a concern that these small states would cease to be viable and unable to carry out the most basic of functions of the state, including the security and welfare of its citizens. Moreover, this domino effect might be more likely to occur if the secession process leaves so-called 'trapped minorities' within the newly independent state. If independence leads to the under-representation, or even repression, of a new minority, then the value of the whole process of secession is cast in doubt. International law does allow for 'national self-determination', but this does not require the creation of a separate state for each nation or discontented ethnic group. Instead, the international community tries to encourage the granting of special cultural rights and political autonomy for ethnic minorities within a state. Thus, the international community prefers to promote a democratic state with a commitment to the rights of minorities, rather than secession for a minority whose nationalist demands might lead to intolerance and dictatorship.[7]

In its coverage of the conflict in Chechnya, the Western media generally seemed to underplay liberal concerns over secession, and the fact that Chechnya had no right in law to secede from the Russian Federation.

---

[5] Margaret Moore, 'On National Self-Determination', *Political Studies*, Vol. XLV, 1997, p. 903.
[6] Harry Beran, one of the more permissive theorists on secession, accepts this point. See his 'A Liberal Theory of Secession', *Political Studies*, Vol. 32, No. 1, 1984, pp. 21–31.
[7] For a discussion of some of these issues, see, for example, Beran, *op cit*, Buchanan, *op cit*, Anthony H. Birch, 'Another Theory of Liberal Secession', *Political Studies*, Vol. 32, No. 4, 1984, pp. 596–602; Lee Buchheit, *Secession: The Legitimacy of Self-Determination* (New Haven, Yale University Press, 1978); Daryl J. Glaser, 'The Rights of Secession: An Antisecessionist Defence', *Political Studies*, Vol. 52, No. 2, 2003, pp. 369–86.

In truth, many journalists have acknowledged that independence for Chechnya is unrealistic in any meaningful sense for the foreseeable future, but then appear to ignore the fact that Moscow has always been ready to grant Chechnya a considerable level of political autonomy within the Russian Federation. Although the media are critical of Russia's imposition of a new constitution on Chechnya, political autonomy is still central to the political compromise on offer. To the disappointment of many liberal secessionist theorists, however, political autonomy has never been sufficient for the more militant rebels in Chechnya. Others, of course, question whether such a solution is possible after two brutal wars since 1994.

Another reason for the international community to reject Chechen independence was the repressive nature of the Dudaev regime itself. In fact, Dudaev always lacked support in the republic and the way Dudaev came to power in September 1991 owed more to Bolshevik tactics in 1917 than to any norms of elective democracy. It was also doubtful whether there ever was majority support for independence. There was never a referendum on the issue in Chechnya, and the election of Dudaev in October 1991, which he referred to as ratification of his independence policy, was deeply flawed. A number of anti-secession regions were denied the vote, and there were reports of Russian voters being harassed at the polling stations.[8] Certainly, a substantial minority remained implacably opposed to secession, and indeed, Chechnya was rarely united on any issue of substance. The republic was deeply divided along ethnic, religious and clan lines, and this has always made it difficult for any leader to find consensus in the republic. Russians made up a quarter of the population of Chechnya in 1989 but many sought to leave the republic after the election in 1991, fearing they might become a persecuted minority under the Dudaev regime. The Ingush people were equally concerned about the future and seceded from Chechnya in July 1992 to 'rejoin' the Russian Federation. As political opposition grew in Chechnya, Dudaev abandoned the last remnant of democracy in June 1993; he closed down parliament, banned all opposition groups, and introduced direct presidential rule. When the Chechen people came out onto the streets in protest, Dudaev used force to repress the demonstration, killing up to fifty people in the process.[9] Dudaev's takeover of power, ostensibly to liberate the people of Chechnya, ended in dictatorship, widespread criminality, the break-up of the Chechen-Ingush Republic and thousands of refugees searching for new homes outside the republic.

In law, Moscow had a right to defend its territorial integrity. Yet Yeltsin was heavily criticized inside Russia for launching the war against the Dudaev regime in December 1994. Critics argued that Yeltsin could have sought a compromise settlement more actively. Yeltsin's own nationalities minister, Galina Starovoitova, suggested that if the Russian president had

---

[8] *Delovoi Mir*, 25 February 1995, p. 2.
[9] *Moscow News*, 16–22 December 1994, pp. 1–2.

agreed to face-to-face talks with Dudaev the war might have been avoided.[10] Others have argued that Russia should have been more open to the idea of Chechen independence, with Chechnya often seen in the West as a special case.[11] Writers such as Matthew Evangelista and Thomas de Waal have convincingly argued that secession, contrary to what some leaders in Moscow were saying, would never have led to the disintegration of Russia.[12] On the other hand, such arguments do seem to underestimate the republic's potential for destabilizing the Caucasus and perhaps even the country as a whole. Certainly, it would appear such thoughts were in Yeltsin's mind when hostages were taken for ransom in May 1994 in Mineralny Vody, a town outside Chechnya, in southern Russia. It has been widely reported that this action, which seemed to prove that rebels were willing to act outside the republic, was the catalyst for Yeltsin's decision to overthrow the Dudaev regime once and for all.[13]

The First War, 1994–6

When the West supported Moscow's right to use force, it was hoped the war would be short, but despite a massive superiority in numbers and *matériel*, the war was a disaster for Russia. It was poorly organized and incompetently led, and the result was heavy casualties on both sides. After initially being thrown back, the Russian forces finally captured Grozny, the capital of Chechnya, in January 1995 and the last rebel stronghold, Samashki, in April. But whilst Moscow declared the war won, the rebels simply retired to the mountains and turned to terrorism and guerrilla warfare. It soon became apparent that there was an impasse: the rebels were unable to drive the Russians out of Chechnya by force, whilst Moscow was unable to pacify the republic. While few Russians supported Chechen independence, the majority came out in clear opposition to the war.[14]

The West became embarrassed over its initial support for Moscow as casualties on both sides rose inexorably, and reports of Russian brutality in Chechnya became impossible to ignore. President Clinton articulated his concern over the war personally to Yeltsin in February 1995, while the Council of Europe and the OSCE publicly condemned the vicious nature of the war.[15] On a visit to Moscow in May 1996, Clinton said Chechnya was an

---

[10] Evangelista, *op cit*, p. 5.

[11] See, for example, Nick Paton-Walsh and Jonathan Steele, 'Putin faces Long Battle to Tame Chechnya', *The Guardian*, 10 May 2004, p. 13.

[12] Thomas de Waal, 'Introduction', in Anna Politkovskaya, *A Dirty War: A Russian Reporter in Chechnya* (London, Harvill Press, 2001), pp. xiii–xxxii; and Evangelista, *op cit*.

[13] Robert Service, *Russia: Experiment With a People* (Basingstoke and Oxford, Macmillan, 2002), p. 157.

[14] In a poll in early 1995, 66% were opposed to the war, but only 11% supported Chechen independence, *Moscow News*, 24 February–2 March 1995, p. 3.

[15] Evangelista, *op cit*, pp. 144–5.

'internal matter' but argued that the use of force was 'incommensurate with the provocation'.[16] The comparisons between Russia's actions in Chechnya and the Serbs in Bosnia were deeply uncomfortable for the West. While President Clinton pressed for increased military action against the Serbs, he restricted himself to mild admonition of Moscow in Chechnya; moreover, the West had invested too much in the success of Yeltsin's domestic reforms to abandon him over Chechnya. The conflict scarcely slowed the flow of aid to Russia in the 1990s. Indeed, on 11 April 1995, the IMF approved a loan of $6.8 billion to Russia, the second biggest in its history, and the head of the IMF, Michel Camdessus, actually went out of his way in an interview to deny that the fund had ever withheld loans to Russia for any reasons other than purely economic.[17]

There was a basic difference between the views of the media, which emphasized the human rights violations perpetrated by the Russians, and those of most Western governments, which focused on Moscow's right to defend its territorial integrity. Yeltsin was forced, however, to sue for peace in August 1996 in the face of public opposition to the war and his inability to pacify the republic. The West played no part in negotiating the Khasavyurt peace agreement, but was clearly relieved that the war was finally over. The agreement committed Russia to the withdrawal of all its troops by November 1996, and offered Chechnya political autonomy until a final decision was reached in 2001 on its ultimate political status, either as a republic within the Russian Federation or as an independent sovereign state. New elections were held in January 1997 in line with the Khasavyurt agreement, and the former Chechen chief-of-staff, General Aslan Maskhadov, was elected president on a pro-independence ticket. Unlike the Dudaev election of 1991, this election was deemed free and fair by independent observers, even though the turnout was low and anti-independent candidates were not allowed to stand. More importantly, the result was initially welcomed in Moscow – Maskhadov was viewed in the Kremlin as a moderate, at least in comparison to some of the other presidential candidates, such as Shamil Basaev and Zelikhan Yandarbiev.

The Inter-war Period, 1997–9

The 1996 Khasavyurt agreement gave grounds for hope that some level of stability and order would soon return to Chechnya. However, Maskhadov faced similar problems to his predecessor in trying to govern the republic. The new president was unable to rebuild the war-ravaged country and was unable to prevent a number of warlords taking effective control. Chechnya collapsed economically and quickly descended into political anarchy even

---

[16] Vance Phillips, Staff Writer, USIA, May 1996.
[17] 'Interview with Michel Camdessus', *Foreign Policy*, October 2000, p. 41 (thanks to Lee Marsden for giving me this source); *Keesing's Record of World Events*, 1995, p. 40513.

worse than that experienced during the Dudaev administration. Over a two-year period more than a thousand died as a result of terrorism in Chechnya, with kidnapping an important source of revenue for the warlords.[18] During this period, Chechnya enjoyed *de facto* independence and yet, in the words of one Russian critic, it had 'ended in a total and unspeakable breakdown of all civilizational norms'.[19] As the politics in Chechnya continued to polarize, Maskhadov closed down parliament and introduced aspects of Sharia law in March 1999. This may have been an attempt to court the favour of the Islamists; if so, it failed, as the radicals Shamil Basaev and Omar ibn Khattab continued to act to undermine the Maskhadov government. In April 1998, this radical group publicly declared its long-term aim to be the creation of a union of Chechnya and Dagestan under Islamic rule and the expulsion of Russia from the entire Caucasus region.[20] In an attempt to speed up this process, a number of militants, led by the ethnic Chechen Basaev and the Saudi-born Khattab, crossed into the neighbouring Russian republic of Dagestan and called on all Muslims to 'take up arms against Russia in a holy war'.[21]

Russian and local Dagestani soldiers repelled the intervention, but only after 1,500 (including 270 Russians) had been killed.[22] This was a major military operation, which is generally underplayed or ignored in Western coverage of the Chechen crisis. Yet the action by the Islamic militants was clearly highly provocative and intended to export the Islamic revolution further into the Russian Federation. The lack of support for the Chechen militants can be used as evidence of Moscow consistently exaggerating the possibility of instability spreading further into the Caucasus but, on the other hand, leaders in the region feared the destabilizing effects of the Chechen Islamists and welcomed the Russian intervention.[23] After the rebels had finally been driven back from Dagestan, there were a series of terrorist bombings across Russia. An estimated 300 civilians were killed in Moscow, Buinansk and Volgodonsk in September 1999. Plans were already in place for Russian forces to return to Chechnya, but the attack on Dagestan and the subsequent terrorist atrocities legitimized the subsequent military action in the eyes of the Russian public.

What is interesting about the Western coverage of this period was the scant attention paid to the Chechen intervention in Dagestan, and the

[18] Anatol Lieven, 'Nightmare in the Caucasus', *Washington Quarterly*, Vol. 23, No. 1, fulltext.asp?resultSetId = R00000000&hitNum = 31&booleanTerm = chechnya&fuzzyTerm: 1–11: p. 3.

[19] Sergei Roy, 'Dubrovka Wasn't Enough', *Moscow News*, 4–10 December 2002, p. 3.

[20] Lieven, 'Nightmare in the Caucasus', *op cit*, p. 9.

[21] BBC News, 'Regions and Territories: Chechnya', 3 February 2004: news.bbc.co.uk/1/hi/world/europe/country_profiles/2565049.stm, pp. 1–7: p. 2.

[22] Anonymous, *Chechnya: The White Paper* (Moscow, Novosti Press, 2000), p. 53; and Anatol Lieven, 'Through a Distorted Lens', *op cit*, p. 326.

[23] Lieven, 'Nightmare in the Caucasus', *op cit*, 2000, p. 10.

contrasting emphasis placed on theories that suggested that the September bombs had been placed by FSB operatives to justify the war and to promote their former boss, Putin, as the future president of Russia.[24] Of course, it was valid to state that there was some suspicion over the discovery of devices left in a Ryazan apartment block, which were similar to those used in Moscow, and appeared to have links with the Russian secret services.[25] However, the more general inference drawn from this, that all the September bombings were carried out by the Russian authorities, was uncorroborated by evidence. It also ignored the history of Chechen terrorism and the more recent public threats by various Chechen rebels following their military defeat in Dagestan, which included Khattab telling a Czech newspaper only days before the bombings in Moscow that 'Russian women and children will pay for the crimes of Russian generals'.[26]

The Second War, 1999–2000

Because of the lawlessness in Chechnya, the rebel attack on Dagestan in August and the terrorist atrocities against civilian targets the following month, the second war appeared more justified than the first. This perception was also backed up by a shift in Russian public opinion, which now strongly supported the use of military action against the Chechen militants.[27] A large part of the Western media, however, preferred to view the military action as a pretext for Putin to push himself as the successor to Yeltsin as Russian President,[28] and this time, the rhetoric from official Western circles also sounded rather less supportive. While the official position hardly changed at all in practice, there was a greater willingness among Western leaders to criticize the war in public. The West still acknowledged the Russian right to defend its territorial integrity, but it was more open in its concern over proportionality. The UN Human Rights Commission passed a resolution in April 2000 in favour of an EU motion criticizing Russia 'for disproportionate and indiscriminate use of military force, particularly against civilians'.[29] At the same time, the Council of Europe's Parliamentary Assembly (PACE)

---

[24] Just one example of this was BBC 3, 'Conflicts: Chechnya', 30 April 2004: www.bbc.co.uk/bbcthree/tv/conflicts.shtml.

[25] For balanced coverage of this issue, see Bennett, *op cit*, pp. 546–7. The conspiracy theory has always been rejected, of course, by the Russian authorities, see for example, the view of Vladimir Putin, *First Person* (London, Hutchinson, 2000), p. 143.

[26] *Afterposten Interaktiv*, 7 September 1999 (thanks to Oystein Brekke for pointing this source out to me). For some of the comments by radical Islamists, see *Keesings Record of World Events* (Bristol, Keesings Publications, 1999), p. 43120.

[27] 67% in a poll in December 1999 favoured continuing the war against Chechnya, according to the VCIOM polling organization: russiavotes.org. The percentage had fallen to 22% by January 2004.

[28] 'How Strongmen of Grozny Turned into a Rebel Target', *Guardian*, 10 May 2004, p. 13; see also Laure Mandeville, *Le Figaro*, 10 May 2004 (quoted in *Guardian*, 11 May 2004, p. 24).

[29] BBC, 25 April 2000: bbc.co.uk/l/hi/world/europe/726214stm.

suspended Russia's voting rights for its part in the Chechen conflict, although its membership was restored in January 2001 after Russia declared the war formally over. In a speech to the State Duma in June 2000, President Clinton said he recognized Russia's right to protect its territorial integrity, but disagreed 'as a friend' with its war in Chechnya 'because it had caused large numbers of civilian casualties whilst lacking a clear path towards a political solution'.[30] The US State Department spokesman, James Rubin, backed this up when he said that Russia's tactics were not in keeping with the Geneva Convention and its commitments to the OSCE, most notably in respect to deliberate attacks on civilian populations.[31]

Despite severe restrictions on reporting the war in Chechnya, there was sufficient evidence to suggest that the Russians were again committing war crimes in the struggle to 'waste the Chechen terrorists on the bog', as Putin indelicately put it.[32] There was evidence of Russia targeting civilians, firing on retreating convoys flying the white flag, and using banned weapons in Chechnya, including vacuum bombs.[33] There was also evidence that violations of human rights were being perpetrated by the Russians against Chechen civilians. Filtration centres, set up during the first war, were again used to interrogate suspected terrorists, but the *zachistki* (sweeps) were perceived by the majority of Chechens to be arbitrary, with virtually all ethnic Chechen males at risk of being picked up. Furthermore, torture was routinely employed against suspects, and a number taken into custody never returned to their homes. The number of 'disappeared' rose to three per week in 2003, and the uncovering of mass graves in the republic revealed the extent of Russian brutality.[34] Russia did accept that human rights violations had taken place, but few Russian soldiers ever faced trial as a result.[35]

International Islamism

Although Western governments had always been more sympathetic than much of the media to the idea that militant Islam posed a threat to Moscow,

---

[30] BBC: 'Clinton Seeks to Ease Russian Fears', 5 June 2000: news. bbc.co.uk/1/hi/world/europe/777420.stm: pp. 1–4; p. 3.
[31] BBC News: 'US Warns Russia Over Chechnya', 8 November 1999: news.bbc.co.uk/1/hi/world/europe/510193.stm; pp. 1–4; p. 1.
[32] Boris Yeltsin, *Midnight Diaries* (London, Weidenfeld and Nicholson, 2000), p. 338.
[33] See for example, *Amnesty*, No. 16, November–December 2002, p. 8.
[34] Human Rights Watch, 'On the Human Rights Situation in Chechnya', *Human Rights Watch Briefing Paper to the 59th Session of the UN Commission on Human Rights*, 7 April 2003, pp. 1–11, p. 2; and Yelena Shishkounova, 'Chechens Display Burnt Bodies to Prove Russian Cruelty', www.gazeta.ru/2002/03/14/ChechensDisp.shtml, pp. 1–3.
[35] See Scott Peterson, ''Lawless' Russian Actions Reflect Mounting Frustration', *Christian Science Monitor*, 13 July 2001 (www.csmonitor.com/atcsmonitor/specials/chechnya/ch1.html); Nick Paton-Walsh, 'Russian Colonel Jailed for Murder', *Guardian*, 26 July 2003, p. 14; and Ian Traynor, 'A War That Doesn't Exist', *Guardian*, 10 May 2004, p. 16.

they initially tended to be more critical of Moscow's methods in dealing with the terrorist threat second time around. For example, the US Secretary of State, Madeleine Albright, on a trip to Moscow in 2000, described Russia's war in Chechnya as 'an incredible act of misery. In order to deal with what is clearly a problem of terrorism,' she went on, 'there has been excessive force used and civilians have been, I think, indiscriminately targeted in a way that has broadened and widened the problem'.[36] The rhetoric shifted post-9/11, even if nothing much changed in terms of practical policy. At the Okinawa G8 summit in July 2000, Putin emphasized that Chechnya was a part of the war on international terrorism: 'an Islamic axis of terrorism', he said is stretching 'from the Philippines through Africa to the Caucasus'.[37] It was not coincidental that Putin was the first political leader on the phone to President Bush after the 9/11 atrocities. He pledged support for the Americans in the war against terrorism, and was as good as his word.[38] Against the wishes of some of his hardliners, Putin opened up Russian airspace for the Americans in their war against Afghanistan, and shared intelligence with Washington on the Taliban and al-Qaeda. He also facilitated the US's construction of military bases in the former Soviet Central Asia, which were important in America's military campaign in Afghanistan.

President Bush accepted the link between al-Qaeda and Chechnya, and told the rebels there to sever all links with terrorism. Gerhard Schroeder, Chancellor of Germany, also called for a 'new evaluation' of Russia's war with Chechnya in the wake of 9/11.[39] This represented more of a shift of policy, since Germany and the EU had previously been far more critical of Russia's conduct in Chechnya than the US or Britain. Since the defeat of al-Qaeda in Afghanistan, the CIA has reported that the terrorist organization has shifted some of its bases into Chechnya,[40] and its director, George Tenet, said that Chechnya is 'breeding a new generation of terrorists who threaten the west'.[41] In June 2003 Tony Blair explained some of the problems facing the British and Americans in postwar Iraq, arguing that 'some of the people offering resistance were extremists from Chechnya'.[42]

Most Western commentators, however, have tended to be far more sceptical of Putin's claim that the conflict in Chechnya could be the result of

---

[36] BBC, 'US Warns Russia Over Chechnya', http://news.bbc.co.uk/1/hi/world/europe/625189.stm, 31 January 2000, pp. 1–4, pp. 1–2.

[37] Bridget Kendall, 'Russia's Place in the World', *World Today*, Vol. 58, No. 5, May 2002, p. 20.

[38] 'Statement by President Putin of Russia on the Terrorist Acts in the US', Moscow, 12 September 2001, Ministry of Foreign Affairs of the Russian Federation, Information and Press Department, p. 1.

[39] *Guardian Unlimited*, John Hooper and Kevin O'Flynn, 'Russia Exploits the War Dividend', Wednesday 26 September 2001, pp. 1–3: p. 1.

[40] *Observer*, 18 May 2003, p. 15.

[41] 'Chechen Peace Amid Gunfire', CNN.com.world, 21 December 2002: pp. 1–3; p. 1.

[42] *www.publications.parliament.uk/pa/cm200203/cmhansard*, 23 June 2003.

militant Islamism. Ian Traynor in the *Guardian*, for example, talked about the link between Chechnya and international terrorism as being 'specious'. Russia, he wrote, is fighting 'a homegrown war in its own backyard', and 'one of the last battles of Russian colonialism'.[43] Jason Burke, who has written extensively on al-Qaeda, agreed: the groups in Chechnya, he wrote are 'well-established' with 'no real connection to bin Laden'.[44] It is certainly true that the rebellion in 1991 began largely as an indigenous secessionist struggle, although it was always a power struggle between local leaders as well. At that stage, Islam was an aspect of Chechen identity that helped differentiate the Chechens from their Russian 'oppressor', but radical Islamism was a marginal influence in political terms. Even the leaders of the independence movement, such as Dudaev and Maskhadov, were scarcely committed Muslims.[45] It is also true, as Thomas de Waal states, that the actions of the Russians, most notably in launching a war against the breakaway republic in 1994 and their brutal behaviour since, have been the crucial factor in radicalizing the Chechen people.[46] Nevertheless, it is also clear that radicalization acquired an increasingly Islamist tinge throughout the 1990s. At the very least, the growing influence of the Islamists made a settlement more difficult to find. For militant Islamists are not simply nationalists – they favour the formation of an Islamic union across the Caucasus and the complete withdrawal of Russian troops from the entire region. Such an aim is not only unacceptable to Moscow, but also to the leaders and the majority of people in the Caucasus itself.

The presence of Islamists in Chechnya cannot be denied. More controversial, however, is the extent of specifically foreign influence in Chechnya, and particularly the influence of al-Qaeda. As Jason Burke wrote in the *Observer*, al-Qaeda is a very loose multinational organization in which locals initiate actions which are then financed and organised by al-Qaeda.[47] This makes it difficult to prove al-Qaeda influence in terrorist actions, especially as it rarely accepts responsibility for its terrorist attacks. Nevertheless, there is evidence of al-Qaeda activity in Chechnya. How much and how significant that activity is remains the only question. The number of foreign Islamists has remained relatively small, although the lack of a unitary authority in the republic has made it ideal for penetration by militants, especially since 9/11. Yandarbiev, who briefly succeeded Dudaev as President after his death in 1996, was central in initiating the relationship with al-Qaeda and got the Taliban to recognize Chechnya's independence. Leading militants like Basaev, Khattab and Walid have all trained in al-Qaeda camps in Afghanistan or Pakistan along with

[43] Ian Traynor, 'A War That Doesn't Exist', *Guardian*, 10 May 2004, p. 16; see also Manfred Quiring, *Die Welt*, 10 May 2004, quoted in *Guardian*, 11 May 2004, p. 24.
[44] *Observer*, 18 May 2003, p. 17.
[45] On Dudaev, see Bennett, *op cit*, p. 244; on Maskhadov, see Lieven, *op cit*, p 3.
[46] See Thomas de Waal, 'Reinventing the Caucasus', *World Policy Journal*, Vol. XIX, No 1, Spring 2002, p. 58.
[47] *Observer* 18 May 2003, p. 17.

several hundred other Chechens.[48] According to Rohan Gunaratna, an expert on al-Qaeda, Basaev, Khattab and Walid have all had close relations with Osama bin Laden,[49] and they have, in turn, set up terrorist camps in Chechnya.[50] There is also evidence of significant funding from al-Qaeda and other groups overseas.[51] Yandarbiev was a leading fundraiser in Qatar before his murder in 2004, and Gunaratna has found that the intelligence agencies of Saudi Arabia, Lebanon and Iran 'directly and indirectly supported the Chechen guerillas'.[52] Increasingly, Chechen terrorists have adopted al-Qaeda strategies, including the use of female suicide bombers since Walid became leader of the foreign Islamists after Khattab's death in March 2002.

The Normalization Process

From the year 2000, under pressure from the West, Putin made efforts to 'normalize' the situation in Chechnya. A referendum was held in March 2003 that overwhelmingly ratified a new constitution, granting Chechnya 'wide autonomy' but as an 'integral part of the Russian Federation'.[53] The high turnout of 80 per cent and the majority of 96 per cent in favour of the constitution led to suspicions over the result, but Tony Blair, at the celebration of St Petersburg's 300th anniversary in May 2003, described the referendum as 'a good step forward'.[54] The *Economist*, however, expressed the more common view outside government circles when it described the referendum as 'a sham', and went on to observe that 'the referendum was meant as an exercise not in democracy but in political control'.[55] The subsequent October presidential election, won by pro-Kremlin Akhmed – again with an overwhelming majority – was just as controversial. Critics, like Lord Judd of the Council of Europe, argued that the war-like conditions in Chechnya meant no democratic election was possible. In what appeared to be something of a dry run for Putin's own presidential election a few months later, credible opponents to Kadyrov were left off the ballot paper, while the media gave disproportionate coverage to the pro-Kremlin candidate. Given the circumstances, the turnout and Kadyrov's majority were suspiciously high.[56]

As the democratic deficit became obvious, the West became more critical of Putin's normalization process. A few weeks after Kadyrov's victory, the American ambassador to Moscow, Alexander Vershbow, described the

---

[48] Rohan Gunaratna, *Inside al-Qaeda: Global Network of Terror* (London, Hurst, 2002), p. 135.
[49] *Ibid*, p. 134.
[50] *Ibid*, p. 5; MI5 evidence to the *Observer*, 10 March 2002, p. 3.
[51] *Moscow News*, 15, 21–27 April 2004, p. 3.
[52] Gunaratna, *op cit*, p. 135.
[53] *Moscow News*, 26 March–1 April 2003, p. 3.
[54] Nick Paton-Walsh, 'Blair Lauds Putin's Handling of Chechen Rebellion', *Observer*, 1 June 2003, p. 23.
[55] *The Economist*, 'Russia and Chechnya: Far From Normal', 22 March 2003, p. 44; and *The Economist*, 'Chechnya's Referendum: The Vote of Dead Souls', 29 March 2003, p. 44.
[56] *Sunday Times*, 5 October 2003, p. 27.

election as 'a missed opportunity'. The flawed nature of the elections undoubtedly undermined the claim of legitimacy, which was important if Moscow really wanted to marginalize the radicals and unite the centre around a compromise settlement. Although Vershbow expressed concern over 'the continuing stalemate on the ground', he saw no alternative to 'the political process'.[57] For this to succeed, Vershbow said there was a need to invest in the economy, to isolate the terrorists and to rebuild trust amongst the people of Chechnya. This, he suggested, required holding to account the security services and military responsible for human rights violations.

However, Akhmed Kadyrov did not use his election victory to seek compromise. On the contrary, he pursued an even tougher policy to eliminate the militant Islamic opposition altogether. Since he had been prominent in fighting against Russia in the first war, this U-turn was perceived by his enemies as a particularly painful betrayal of the Chechen nation – significantly, Maskhadov called him 'enemy number one'.[58] Before Kadyrov's dramatic assassination on 9 May 2004, however, it appeared his uncompromising strategy might be having some success. Leading militants had been killed, including Khattab (in 2002), Walid and Yandarbiev (in 2004), and there were also persistent reports that Maskhadov was willing to negotiate as many of his supporters switched sides. Kadyrov's murder, however temporarily, stilled such hopes. Whilst Putin declared 'retribution' and called Kadyrov 'a real hero',[59] the EU Commission described the explosion as a 'heinous attack' and a spokesman for President Bush said Washington 'resolutely rejected all acts of terrorism'.[60] Yet the Western media was noticeably less sympathetic.[61] The view of much of the Western media was summed up by Akhmed Zakaev, a spokesman for Maskhadov, who said, 'Kadyrov cannot be considered a civilian: he was one of those waging war in Chechnya and a marionette in the hands of the Kremlin'.[62]

Relations between Russia and the West

Putin might have had great hopes for a transformed relationship with the West after lending his support in the war against terrorism. If so, he was left somewhat disappointed. Moscow was able to re-emphasize its continuing

[57] *Moscow News*, No. 46, 10–16 December 2003, p. 4.
[58] BBC, 'Nine Lives of Moscow's Man in Chechnya', 6 November 2000 (bbc.co.uk/hi/english/world/monitoring/media_reports/newsid_1…/1009533.st).
[59] *Guardian*, 10 May 2004, p. 2.
[60] *Moscow News*, No. 17, 12–18 May 2004, p. 3.
[61] See, for example, Nick Paton-Walsh, 'How Strongman of Grozny Turned into a Rebel Target', *Guardian*, 10 May 2004, p. 13; Ian Traynor, 'A War that Doesn't Exist', *Guardian*, 10 May 2004, p. 16; Obituary, *Guardian*, 10 May 2004, p. 19; Editorial, *Guardian*, 11 May 2004, p. 23.
[62] Quoted in Nick Paton-Walsh, 'Chechen President Dies in Stadium Blast', *Guardian*, 10 May 2004, p. 2.

strategic importance during the war in Afghanistan, but Bush has not shifted policy on a number of important areas for Moscow. As expected, Bush abrogated the ABM Treaty in 2002, NATO expanded in May 2004 to include the three former Soviet Baltic republics, and the US retained its military presence in Central Asia and Georgia. Perhaps in an attempt to reassert Russian authority, Putin opposed the US- and UK-sponsored war in Iraq in 2003. Given Russian interests in Iraq, including an estimated debt to Moscow of $8 billion,[63] Putin may have been unwilling to join the coalition against Saddam Hussein, although his defection was, no doubt, made easier by the French and German opposition to the war.

On the particular issue of Chechnya, the Western position has remained largely unchanged. President Bush, while sounding positive towards Putin, has also continued to emphasize the importance of differentiating more carefully between 'combatants and civilians'.[64] It is true that the words have never been accompanied by any effective measures, but since the end of the Iraq War, both the US and Britain have strengthened the rhetoric against Moscow by expressing open concern about the supposed threat to democracy in Putin's Russia. Secretary of State Colin Powell expressed this concern in an article in *Izvestiya* in January 2004,[65] and shortly afterwards the British FCO Minister, Bill Rammell, said: 'We have growing concerns about the Russian commitment to pluralism and a free media. Both are essential to a democracy'.[66] For Western critics of Russia, the abuse of human rights taking place Chechnya is not an aberration dependent on specific circumstances in the rebel republic, but symptomatic of Russia's decline into dictatorship.

Conclusion

For Western governments, Chechnya has always been a low priority. Despite a willingness publicly to condemn war crimes and human rights violations, the West has been unwilling to take effective action. In an interview with Russian journalists, Ambassador Vershbow was compelled to deny that the West's condemnation was merely ritualistic.[67] Leverage on this issue may well be less effective now in the light of human rights violations committed by the American and British troops in Iraq.[68] A further

---

[63] *Moscow News*, 48, 24–29 December 2003, p. 1.
[64] Radio Free Europe/Radio Liberty, 'Bush Urges Respect For Human Rights in Chechnya', 24 May 2002: www.rferl.org/nca/features/2002/05/24052002104227.asp, p. 1.
[65] Reported in *Moscow News*, No. 3, 28 January–3 February 2004, p. 3.
[66] Patrick Wintour, 'Britain to Voice Doubts on Putin', *Guardian*, 5 April 2004, p. 5.
[67] *Moscow News*, No. 46, 10–16 December 2003, p. 4.
[68] Hypocrisy and double-standards are charges frequently used against Western policy and Western media coverage of the conflict in Chechnya. See, for example, Igor Ivanov's comments on the BBC: 'US Warns Russia Over Chechnya', news.bbc.co.uk/1/hi/world/europe/510193.stm, pp. 1–2. The journalist Sergei Roy has also noted the West's 'concern over the human rights of terrorists rather than the victims of terrorism': see Roy, 'Fighting Russia', *Moscow News*, 30 October–5 November 2002, p. 3.

complication arises from the fact that the West believe its interests lie in supporting Moscow. Tony Blair has acknowledged that national interests must play a part in determining foreign policy towards Russia, but he has justified British policy by arguing that it is better to negotiate with Russia rather than isolate it. To this end, he has also called for the greater involvement of international organizations in Chechnya, an idea which Putin has so far rejected.[69] Indeed, Moscow insisted the OSCE withdraw from Chechnya in 2003 after its criticism of the normalization process.

The media has demanded that more pressure be placed on the Kremlin to moderate its policies in Chechnya and to seek more actively a political solution. What that pressure should consist of is unclear, and how successful it would be remains a matter of debate. Chechnya is a complex issue, and there are no easy solutions. Moscow is reluctant to make compromises on an issue it perceives to be a major threat to its own security. The immediacy of the threat is something many Russians feel is overlooked by the West. Nevertheless, a case can be made for international organizations to help with mediation, and there might be a time when international peacekeepers have a role to play in Chechnya, although this will always be an extremely sensitive issue for Russia. Military threats against Moscow are out of the question, while economic sanctions of any kind are likely to be counter-productive. So, continued diplomacy appears to be the best way forward, and Western governments duty-bound to highlight the issue of human rights violations in the republic. The effects of such pressure will be slow to bear fruit, but the alternatives appear worse. This kind of conclusion will hardly excite the media, but there are occasions when the West's morally uncomfortable position might best serve the interests of the majority inside and outside Chechnya.

---

[69] Prime Minister's Internet Broadcast, 13 April 2000: 'Relations with Russia': www.number-10. gov.uk/output/page325.asp. Putin has rejected the idea of international peacekeepers on numerous occasions, but see for example, Putin, *First Person*, p. 175.

12

A War by Any Other Name: Chechnya, 11 September and the War Against Terrorism

John Russell

Following a sequence of terrorism-related incidents, most notably the 9/11 attacks on New York and Washington, the Putin administration in Russia portrayed its entire conflict with Chechnya (1994–6 and from 1999 onwards) successfully to the outside world as part of the global war against terrorism. Internationally, the need to maintain the US-led coalition against Islamic fundamentalism persuaded foreign leaders to downplay other crucial elements in this complex and multi-layered confrontation. In Russia, the demonization of all shades of Chechen resistance, intensified since the apartment bombs of Autumn 1999 and reinforced by the sieges of Dubrovka and Beslan, helped maintain support for Putin's hard line and uncompromising policy in Chechnya.

A War Like No Other

A curious feature of the Russo-Chechen conflict is the lengths that successive Russian administrations have gone to avoid depicting the confrontation as a 'war',[1] while throughout Russia, Chechnya and the rest of the world it is routinely referred to as the 'Russo-Chechen war' or the 'war in Chechnya'.[2]

[1] The expert evidence brought on behalf of the Russian Government in the 2003 extradition case in London against Akhmed Zakaev, placed great emphasis on the fact that the conflict between Russia and Chechnya was not a war, an argument ultimately rejected by the British judge. See David Hearst, 'Judge Refuses to Extradite Chechen', *Guardian*, 14 November 2003.
[2] Marshal Viktor Kulikov, speaking in the debate in July 2002 on changing the law 'On Veterans', with a view to extending the law to include those who had fought in Chechnya, said: 'You can say what you like, but it is undoubtedly a war', *http://milprob.narod.ru/17.05.02gazeta86.htm*.

Whereas President Yeltsin's campaign (1994–6) for the 'restoration of constitutional order' was generally perceived, both in Russia and abroad, to be little more than a fig leaf for a war aimed at preventing Chechnya's secession, President Putin's equally euphemistic 'counter-terrorism operation' (1999 to date), has not been subjected to the same disparagement. Indeed, Putin has managed, albeit not entirely successfully, to have the entire Russo-Chechen conflict retrospectively viewed as part of the global war against terrorism. This has enabled him not only to conflate notions of 'just war' (*jus ad bellum*) with those of 'a justly fought war' (*jus in bello*),[3] but also to eradicate memories of Yeltsin's 'bad' war, by presenting the entire confrontation with the Chechens as, if not a 'good', then certainly a 'necessary' war.

This apparent paradox stems from the contradiction inherent in the concept of a war against terrorism, which, along with 'wars' against crime or poverty, is radically different from a war against a given country.[4] Because of the acknowledged special conditions pertaining in war, acts that otherwise fulfil the criteria for being classified 'terrorist' (such as the bombing of Hiroshima, the activities of the French resistance in World War II, assassinations of enemy leaders, and so on) are exempt. Indeed, one definition of an act of terrorism is 'the peacetime equivalent of a war crime',[5] implying that terror and war are incompatible. There is some utility to the Russians, therefore, in presenting the conflict as part of the war against terrorism (in which, by definition, only the other side can be accused of employing terror) rather than a war against Chechnya (in which the rules of war would apply to both sides).

Of course, this argument has only gained broad support outside Russia since the 9/11 attacks and the subsequent declaration of the war against global terrorism. Prior to that, the conflict in Chechnya was a cause for embarrassment, if not complaint, amongst Russia's Western partners and the target of considerable criticism from human rights organizations in both Russia and the West. Although these organizations, with the support of brave and outspoken public figures, have continued this criticism throughout the second war, the Russian public at large was converted to the new perception of the conflict two years earlier when the war in Chechnya

[3] For a detailed examination of these concepts in the Chechen context, see Richard Sakwa, 'Chechnya: A Just War Fought Unjustly?' in Bruno Coppieters and Richard Sakwa, *Contextualising Secession: Normative Studies in Comparative Perspective* (Oxford, Oxford University Press, 2003), pp. 156–86.

[4] This point is made well by Grenville Byford, who writes that 'Wars have typically been fought against proper nouns (Germany, say) for the good reason that proper nouns can surrender and promise not to do it again. Wars against common nouns (poverty, crime, drugs) have been less successful. Such opponents never give up. The war on terrorism, unfortunately, falls in to the second category'. 'The Wrong War', *Foreign Affairs*, Vol. 81, No. 4, July/August 2002, p. 34.

[5] Short legal definition proposed by A. P. Schmid to United Nations Crime Branch (1992), see *http://www.unodc.org/unodc/terrorism_definitions.html*.

(i.e. Russians fighting on Chechen soil) became conflated with the war against terrorism (i.e. Chechens bringing the war to Russia). Russians, therefore, suffer no psychological discomfort from the apparent contradiction that the country is engaged in one war on terrorism (which they support) and, simultaneously, another against the Chechen people (which they do not).[6]

Apart from a couple of major hostage-taking incidents, the concept of a war against terror was largely absent in the first confrontation, which was perceived as a war in the traditional sense.[7] The most successful feature film made of the conflict so far by a Russian director is called simply *War*.[8] The fact that a peace treaty was signed at the end of the first conflict, that internationally recognized elections were held in a *de facto* independent Chechnya-Ichkeria, that most combatants on both sides (except for those Chechens accused of leading the hostage-taking incidents) were offered an amnesty and that Russian soldiers who had fought in Chechnya have been accorded the status of war veterans, would all seem to emphasize the perception of the struggle as a war. The intensity of the fighting and the scale of casualties – as many as 100,000 deaths, according to some estimates – would appear to confirm this.[9]

The problem at the end of the first war was not just that none of the outstanding issues in the long-running confrontation between Russia and Chechnya had been resolved satisfactorily, but also that it had spawned new elements that were to shape the second conflict. Thus, the centuries old clash of cultures between the mountain tribes of Chechnya and the 'civilizing' ambitions of the conquering Russians remained unresolved, and both the Chechen quest for self-determination and the Russian imperative of territorial integrity unfulfilled. Moreover, the lawlessness, the arbitrary brutality and the unaccountability of those engaged in it, was exacerbated by the Chechen victory in the first war.[10] The new elements to emerge from the first

[6] Thus, an opinion poll in July 2003 indicated that at the same time as 61% of Russians polled favoured flushing out the Chechen fighters by means of *zachistki* (sweeps), 67% acknowledged that a partisan war was going on in Chechnya. *http://www.vciom-a.ru/press/2003081100.html*.

[7] During the first war, the leader of the Chechen armed resistance, Aslan Maskhadov, repeatedly asserted that 'Never will we descend to terrorism. We are warriors, not assassins', see, for example, *Transition*, 19 April 1996, p. 2. Even at the start of the second war, there were those Russian observers who refused to accept that Shamil Basaev, leader of the raid on Budennovsk, was a terrorist: 'call him what you will, a bandit, a romantic or a murderer, only not a terrorist', *Novoe vremya*, 1999, No. 38, p. 10.

[8] *Voina* (*War*) by Aleksei Balabanov (2002) CTB Film Company. For a full review of what the critic labels 'this piece of nationalist, warmongering propaganda', see Andrew James Horton, 'War, what is it good for?' *http://www.kinoeye.org/02/18/horton18_no3.php*.

[9] This is the figure quoted by Russian human rights' activist, Sergei Kovalev, in his 'Russia after Chechnya', *New York Review of Books*, 17 July 1997, p. 27; John Dunlop suggests a figure of 46,500 in his 'The Forgotten War' *Hoover Digest*, 2002, No.1, *http://www.hoover.stanford.edu/publications/digest/021/dunlop.html*.

[10] I have previously identified these components in John Russell, 'On the Side of Might', *The World Today*, Vol. 56, No. 12, December 2002, pp. 17–18.

conflict were Islamic fundamentalist terror; part of what Mary Kaldor has termed 'regressive globalisation', (the exploitation of aspects of globalization for narrow ideological, economic and political interests)[11] and a new understanding of the importance of 'information warfare'.[12]

When, in the wake of the apartment bombings in Moscow, Buinaksk and Volgodonsk in September 1999, Putin launched the second war, it certainly contained elements of a 'counter-terrorist operation'.[13] However, once the generals were given the go-ahead to flatten Grozny again and occupy the entire territory of Chechnya, Russia entered the same impasse of guerrilla fighting in the mountains and an *intifada* in the foothills and on the plains, with casualties on a scale similar to those of the first war.[14] As a result the nomenclature became every bit as inappropriate as that employed by Yeltsin, and public support for the war, predictably, began to wane.[15] It was events elsewhere in the world that came to Putin's rescue.

First, there was the outbreak of the al-Aqsa *intifada* in September 2000, characterized by a terrifying new wave of suicide bombing.[16] The extremely tough and uncompromising stance taken against this form of insurgency by the Israelis met with support and understanding in Russia, whose population had been similarly traumatized by the terrorist attacks a year earlier. The concept arose of 'traumatized' democracies, in which ordinary citizens felt their security to be so threatened as to demand, whatever the cost to personal freedoms and without reference to the norms of international law, action that was rapid, resolute and immediately effective.[17] The harder the leaders

---

[11] Mary Kaldor, 'Terrorism as Regressive Globalisation', Open Democracy website, 25 September 2003, *http://www.opendemocracy.net/debates/article-3-77-1501.jsp*.

[12] Strictly speaking, the 'propaganda war' might be characterised as a fifth conflict within the Russo-Chechen war. However, I take the view that it is the vehicle by which the Putin administration has highlighted the war on terror and downplayed the other conflicts. For details of the 'information war', see T. L. Thomas, 'Manipulating the Mass Consciousness: Russian & Chechen 'Information War' Tactics in the Second Chechen-Russian Conflict', in A. C. Aldis (ed.), 'The Second Chechen War', *Conflict Studies Research Centre, Report P31*, June 2000, pp. 112–29.

[13] One would anticipate that Ministry of Interior (MVD) and Federal Security Service (FSB) troops, rather than those of the Russian Ministry of Defence, should be employed in such an operation, see Dr J. S. Main, "Counter-terrorist Operation' in Chechnya: on the Legality of the Current Conflict', in Aldis (ed.), 'The Second Chechen War', pp. 19–37.

[14] Reliable casualty figures for the conflict are extremely hard to find, there being some agreement that the second war has been just as bloody as the first, see Dunlop, 'The Forgotten War', op. cit.

[15] Eventually, in August 2003, the All-Russian Centre for the Study of Public Opinion (VTsIOM) was taken over by the state after it had published a poll showing that only 28% of those Russians polled supported the war, with 57% advocating peace talks with the rebels. *http://www.vciom-a.ru/press/2003081100.html*.

[16] A considerable literature has been built up on this phenomenon, one of the most informative works being that by Scott Atran, 'The Genesis and Future of Suicide Terrorism', *http://www.interdisciplines.org/terrorism/papers/1/22/*.

[17] In the Israeli context, a former Lieutenant-Colonel in the IDF has written; 'Israelis' misunderstanding of the new Palestinian way of war may come back to haunt them. Their

cracked down on terrorism in these societies, the higher their popularity rose; the short-term application of 'might' proving far more popular in electoral terms than any notions of 'right' or 'rational' political solutions.[18]

The appearance of 'traumatized' democracies coincided with the spread of what I term 'complexity fatigue',[19] a growing reluctance on the part of the public throughout the world to negotiate the extremely complex and undoubtedly difficult factors underlying such seemingly intractable conflicts as those in Northern Ireland, the Middle East, Kashmir, Kosovo or, of course, Chechnya. Simplistic, short-term 'fixes' based on force were clearly not without attraction either to those citizens who, apparently, preferred escapist entertainment to engagement with complex issues.[20]

Finally, after the events of 9/11, the world's only military superpower joined the ranks of 'traumatized' democracies and the population of the USA was quick to call for the same rapid, resolute and effective reaction demanded by the peoples of Russia and Israel. Almost overnight, Russia had become a key ally of the USA and Israel in a common struggle – the global war on terrorism – and against a common foe, Islamic fundamentalism.[21] For Putin's Russia, this presented another golden opportunity. Since 9/11, the Bali bomb of October 2002, together with a succession of domestic terrorist-related incidents – organized with or without the collusion of the Russian authorities – in Russia (especially the sieges at a Moscow theatre later that month and at a school in Beslan in September 2004) and Chechnya (where the appearance of female suicide bombers has paralleled developments in the

perception of their enemy's weakness is likely to embolden them and encourage more broad punitive operations in response to future attacks. But Israel's military responses will eventually exhaust themselves, whereas the Palestinians will still have legions of willing 'martyrs'. In fact, despite defiant Israeli rhetoric insisting that there will be no surrender to terrorism, one can already see the opposite happening. Israelis are willing to pay an increasingly high economic and diplomatic price for increasingly short periods of calm. As a result, more and more people support panaceas such as unilateral separation – the building of walls, fences, and buffer zones to protect Israel's population centers from Palestinian wrath'. Gal Luft, 'The Palestinian H-Bomb' in *Foreign Affairs*, Vol. 81, No. 4, July/August 2002, pp. 6–7.

[18] The Russian rationale for this is given concisely in Yurii Fedorov, 'A Global Web of Terror', *International Affairs* (Moscow), Vol.49, No. 2, 2003, pp. 93–101.

[19] Derived from the concept in politics of 'compassion fatigue', see Susan D. Mieller, *Compassion Fatigue: How the Media Sells Disease, Famine, War and Death* (New York, Routledge, 1999).

[20] By way of a graphic example, the film director, Paul Mitchell, told me that his acclaimed documentary 'Greetings from Grozny' was denied a screening on British terrestrial TV, not because of any censorship, but that it had been explained to him that the British public did not want to come home from work and be confronted with the tragedy and complexity of Chechnya when they could watch 'Big Brother' or 'Pop Idol'. From a conversation held at the 'Chechnya Today' conference, School of Oriental and African Studies, London, 22 November 2002.

[21] For the impact of 9/11 on the 'Islamic factor' in the war in Chechnya, see John Russell, 'Exploitation of the 'Islamic factor' in the Russo-Chechen conflict before and after 11 September 2001', in *European Security*, Vol. 11, No. 4, Winter 2002, pp. 96–109.

Middle East) has not only kept anti-Chechen sentiments high among Russians, but has done enough to persuade Western leaders that Chechnya is Russia's frontline in the war on terrorism.

Traditional Versus Modernising Societies

While it would be incorrect and patronizing to describe Chechen society in the twenty-first century as anything other than 'modernizing', there are aspects of traditional Chechen culture that have yet to be accommodated adequately within either the form of modernization that the Soviet Union/ Russia has attempted to impose, or the blueprint for globalization emanating from the USA in the post-Cold War era. Foremost amongst these are the lack of a resolution of the precise relationship between the Chechens and the Russians, and the failure to date of Chechen society to establish a viable, normative state, capable of operating successfully within the global community. Manifestations of these traditional aspects of Chechen society, particularly the gruesome practice of ritually severing the heads or otherwise mutilating hostages held in primitive *zindans* (dungeons),[22] can and have been used by the Russians to consolidate a negative image of all Chechen opponents as savage bandits and thus to facilitate the depiction of rebel leaders as terrorists. Since 9/11, of course, such traditional practices, perceived by the modern world as medieval, barbaric and evil, have made it much easier for Putin to characterize his opponents in Chechnya as being on the 'other side' in both the global war against terrorism and the 'clash of civilizations'.

Elsewhere, I have drawn parallels between the Chechens' struggle to maintain their distinctive way of life against foreign oppressors, bent upon bringing them to submission, with that of the Scottish highlanders against the British redcoats.[23] The difference was that, once the perceived threat from the Jacobites had been removed, not only were Scottish 'modernizers' given an opportunity to compete on more or less equal terms with their English counterparts, but also, commencing with the romantic novels of Walter Scott and culminating in the reign of Queen Victoria, there appeared a positive, albeit highly stylized and sanitized, cult of the symbols of highland life (bagpipes, clan tartans, dirks, Highland Games, deer hunting).[24]

---

[22] Videos of these atrocities are widely available on the Internet, being used by the Chechen side for raising funds and morale, by the Russians (and then by CNN), to demonise their enemy. The film *Voina* (see note 8) opens with a scene in which a Chechen commander, using the traditional *kinzhal* (dagger), severs the head of a Russian officer, for whom he has paid a substantial sum in order to 'redeem' a blood vendetta.

[23] See John Russell, 'Mujahedeen, Mafia, Madmen: Russian Perceptions of Chechens During the Wars in Chechnya, 1994–96 and 1999–2001' in *Communist Studies and Transition Politics*, Vol. 18, No. 1, March 2002, pp. 73–96.

[24] An account of the early years of this transition may be found in Robert Clyde, *From Rebel to Hero: the Image of the Highlander, 1745–1830* (East Linton, Tuckwell Press, 1998).

Moreover, Scottish regiments became the pride of the British army. Taken together, these measures went a long way to offset the traumatic folk memory of the Highland clearances and the ruthless suppression of the Gaelic language and traditional way of life. In other words, the transition from traditional to modern society was achieved partly by defining a new relationship between the English and the Scots from which both benefited. Unsurprisingly, it is with the Scottish highlanders before their defeat by the English that the Chechen fighters themselves like to identify.[25]

Elements paralleling these processes may be detected in the Russo-Chechen relationship, from the romantic descriptions of Chechen *dzigits* (mounted warriors) by Lermontov and Tolstoi to Soviet successes in codifying the Chechen language and establishing a modern system of education. However, the mainstream cultural narrative[26] of the Chechen people is based firmly on brave resistance, led by charismatic leaders (from the theocratic Imam Shamil to the 'international terrorist' Shamil Basaev) against any attempt by the Russians, or any other nation, to extinguish their desire to live as they choose. Moreover, the abiding folk memory for all Chechens remains the tragedies of the diaspora after the First Caucasian War, the forceful suppression of their indigenous code of customs (*adaat*), and the deportation of the entire Chechen nation by Stalin during the Second World War.[27]

In this respect, the Chechen case resembles more that of the American Indians than the Scottish highlanders,[28] and begs the question: why the Chechens and not, for example, the Dagestanis, Cherkess or even Ingush?[29] One Western academic has concluded that, even amongst the Caucasian mountain people, the Chechens are feared and renowned for their ferocity, brigandage and aggression, and, as such, must shoulder much of the blame

---

[25] An American mercenary fighting on the Chechen side notes that *Braveheart*, Hollywood's romanticized portrayal of the highlanders, was the favourite video amongst the Chechen fighters with whom he was hospitalised: 'we watched it at least once every couple of days', Matt Bivens, 'An American Fighter's War in Chechnya', *http://www.themoscowtimes.com/stories/2003/07/21.*

[26] For the importance of cultural narrative in the Armenian case, see Khachig Tololyan, 'Cultural Narrative and the Motivation of the Terrorist', *The Journal of Strategic Studies*, Special Issue: Inside Terrorist Organizations, edited by David C. Rapoport, Vol. 10, No. 4, December 1987, pp. 218–33.

[27] See the report on Chechnya in 1992 of the International Alert fact-finding commission, *http://www.international-alert.org/simple/projects/fsu/chechen2.htm* p. 3.

[28] The language employed in the first tentative attempts by Russia to bring the Chechens under their control tends to reinforce this view. In an agreement signed by Chechen elders in 1806 with General Khudovich, setting out the terms upon which the Chechen people might become subjects of the Russian Empire, one clause states: 'Finally, if the Chechens do not refrain from carrying out raids, they must expect to be completely exterminated and destroyed', in Ivan Rybkin, *Consent in Chechnya, Consent in Russia* (London, Lytten Trading, 1998), p. 157.

[29] Charles King poses this question in his 'Crisis in the Caucasus: a New Look at Russia's Chechen Impasse', *Foreign Affairs*, Vol. 82, No. 2, March/April 2003, pp. [PAGE NUMBERS].

for their current condition.[30] The Chechen 'Eurasianist' Khozh-Akhmed Nukhaev has even suggested that the mountainous area of Chechnya, home of 'the staunchest bearers of the pre-modern national traditions, refuting any form of statehood whatsoever...' be turned into a kind of tribal reservation separated from Russia by a 'modern' Chechnya on the plains.[31]

On the other hand, the Russian obsession with the eradication of the spirit of freedom amongst the Chechens has been long identified, but never satisfactorily explained.[32] One might suggest that it is the specific *siloviki*[33] mindset of Russia's political elites, including the quintessentially Russian concepts of *derzhavnost'* (belief in Russia as a power) and *gosudarstvennost'* (belief in the power of the state), demanding conformity and submission, while suppressing dissidence or anarchy in any form.[34] The Russian sociologist, Olga Kryshtanovskaya, estimated recently that there are currently 4.5 million *siloviki* in Russia.[35] Such people can hardly be expected to comprehend, let alone value, the cultural importance to Chechens of what they call

---

[30] Robert Bruce Ware has long been virtually a lone voice in the West on this issue. As far back as 2000 he co-authored, with Ira Straus, an article in the *Christian Science Monitor* drawing attention to Western media bias *against* the Russians over Chechnya, stating 'We in the West are naive to think that the choice in the Caucasus is between the massive human rights abuses committed by Russians in Chechnya and no human rights abuses. The real choice is between the current Russian abuses and the massive abuses previously committed by Chechen groups in Dagestan and other areas near the Chechen border'. *http://search.csmonitor.com/durable/2000/03/15/f-p11s2.shtml*. For a recent, balanced account of this see his interview, published on 18 December 2003, with Peter Lavelle, United Press International's Moscow–based analyst, *http://www.untimely-thoughts.com/?art=268*.

[31] From 'Eurasia Insight', 14 September 2001, *www.reliefweb.int/w/R*; the leading Russian ethnologist, Sergei Arutyunov, also advocates such a division of Chechnya, see his 'Chechenskaya voina mozhet prodlit'sya do 2020 goda', *http://zakaev.ru/turnover/comment/15042.html*.

[32] For an American viewpoint, see David Remnick, *Resurrection: the struggle for a new Russia* (New York, Random House, 1997), p. 266; a recent Russian explanation maintains that 'the impression has been created that our authorities have a sort of drug addiction to everything connected with Chechnya. And sometimes they react irrationally to it', see Nairi Hovsepyan and Lyubov Tsukanova, 'Chechnya and Russia: War and Peace', in *New Times*, December 2003, *http://www.newtimes.ru/eng/detail.asp?art_id=535*. For an earlier Russian view, see Sergei Kovalev, 'After Chechnya', *New York Review of Books*, 17 July 1997.

[33] The *siloviki* refer to elite leaders in the Russian ministries of law and order (FSB, MVD, MOD, SVR etc.). A feature of the administration of Putin (himself, of course, a former head of the FSB) is the extremely high proportion of former security chiefs in key positions. See Gregory Feifer, 'Russia: President boosts Power of Security Services', *Centre for Defense Information Weekly*, No. 248, *http://www.cdi.org/russia/248-16.cfm*.

[34] In his first state of the federation address as president in July 2000 Putin claimed that authority 'should rely on the law and a single, vertical line of executive power', leader in the *Guardian*, 12 July 2000.

[35] Interview with Andrei Uglanov, 'Pobeda vlasti; zhertva prinyata, *Argumenty i fakty*, No. 50, 10 December 2003. Ivan Rybkin estimated in 2002 that 26% of Putin's administration are drawn from the security services, compared to 3.6% of Gorbachev's, see 'Towards Peace in Chechnya', Carnegie Endowment for International Peace, Russian & Eurasian Program, 23 October 2002, *http://www.ceip.org/files/events/events.asp?pr=2&EventID=525*.

'freedom'. On the other hand, those 'modernist' Chechen leaders who had succeeded in Soviet/ Russian society (such as Aslan Maskhadov, Ruslan Khasbulatov or Akhmed Zakaev), and who might be expected more easily to see the conflict from both sides, represent precisely the kind of mediator that was excluded from the political process in Chechnya, in effect after 9/11 and particularly after the Dubrovka theatre (staging the 'Nord-Ost' show) hostage-taking drama in October 2002.

In terms of state formation, Chechnya, in its two brief periods of *de facto* self-government (1991–4 and 1996–9), appeared incapable of establishing the foundations of a viable system on its own. In this it was not helped by the obstructive policies of Russia.[36] Since 9/11, there has been genuine concern in the West that an independent Chechnya would become a 'failed' state like Afghanistan and Lebanon when they, too, were run by a collection of feuding warlords; the Bush administration has made quite explicit the linkage between such states and terrorism.[37] During these two periods of autonomy, the absence of Russian forces, a common enemy against which Chechens could unify, local warlords were quite capable of undermining attempts to establish effective national institutions, norms and hierarchies for their own parochial interests.[38] Although its role in Chechen society undoubtedly has been exaggerated,[39] the traditional *teip* (clan), as a social institution did facilitate the emergence of such military and/ or criminal warlords.[40]

Having twice failed to establish its own viable institutions, and in the absence of any prospect of an East Timor type of solution involving substantial outside aid and an interim administration under the auspices of the

---

[36] Anatol Lieven , 'Nightmare in the Caucasus', *The Washington Quarterly*, Winter, 2000, p. 149.

[37] The connection between 'failed' states and the rise of terrorism, although not specifically directed at Chechnya, is forcefully argued in Robert I. Rotberg, 'Failed States in a World of Terror', *Foreign Affairs*, Vol. 81, No. 4, July/August 2002, pp. 127–40.

[38] See Richard Sakwa, 'Chechnya: the Pre-Politics of Partition', London Centre of International Relations, *Ethics and Transnational Politics Working Paper*, No. 4, 2001. Igor Porshnev, correspondent of *Interfax-Vremya*, wrote in July 1999: 'the 'mountain generals' do not want Maskhadov's contacts with Moscow to succeed, as this would strengthen the positions of the Chechen leader. Analysts believe that the field commanders need to maintain the status quo under which Maskhadov controls no more than 20% of the republican territory and armed formations. Each field commander wants to be the king of his province – Arbi Baraev in Urus-Martan, Shamil Basaev in Vedeno, etc… If field commanders pooled forces, they would have easily got rid of Maskhadov, but they have no such plans so far', Federation of American Scientists, *The Chechen Chronicles 1999*, *http://www.fas.org/man/dod101/ops/war/2000/01/chechen/185.htm*.

[39] Both James Hughes, 'Chechnya: the Causes of a Protracted Post-Soviet Conflict', in *Civil Wars*, Vol. 4, No. 4, Winter 2001, pp. [PAGE NUMBERS] and Ruslan Khasbulatov, *Nezavisimaya gazeta*, 14 December 2000, have warned against overemphasising 'ethnic' components in the Russo-Chechen conflict. However, they clearly remain a factor in the unresolved confrontation.

[40] For an analysis of 'warlordism' (*caudillismo*), see Georgi Derlugian, 'The Structures of Chechnya's Quagmire', *PONARS Policy Memo 309*, November 2003, pp. 3–4.

United Nations, it would appear that the Chechens are faced with state institutions being imposed from without, by either the Islamic fundamentalist *wahhabis* or the Russians. Although neither meets the understandable aspirations of the majority of the Chechen people for a normal, prosperous and secure way of life, one can understand why a younger generation, raised with first-hand experience of Russian brutality and Western indifference, might be more tempted, both financially and ideologically, by the allure of a *jihad*, than by the alternatives offered by either Russia or US-led globalization. This, in turn, will lead the coalition against terror to identify even closer the Chechen with the Palestinian cause – with all too predictable results.

Self-Determination Versus Territorial Integrity

Due to the countervailing right of territorial integrity for all existing states, Chechens are by no means the only group to have missed out on the self-determination that is enshrined in international law as the right of all peoples. In Western Europe, separatist and irredentist groups that have taken up the armed struggle for their cause are routinely labelled 'terrorist' (the Provisional IRA, ETA, the FLNC in Corsica, and so on), on the basis that peaceful alternatives to violence (via the ballot box) exist. Further afield, things are more ambiguous. If it is accepted that the Kurds and the Kosovars have equal rights to self-determination, it is hardly consistent to label the PKK a terrorist enemy and the KLA an ally in the struggle for freedom. Similarly, on what criteria, other than self-interest, did the West support *Falintil*, the armed rebel group in East Timor, but not the Chechens, the Tamils or the Uighurs?

The last wave of new independent states appeared with the more or less simultaneous collapse of the three federations of the former socialist bloc in Central and Eastern Europe (the USSR, Yugoslavia and Czechoslovakia). Even so, some peoples failed to achieve self-determination (for example, the Abkhaz in Georgia, the Albanians in Macedonia and the Ruthenians in Slovakia and Ukraine). In the only remaining federation in the region, Russia moved to prevent a repeat of the disintegration of the USSR by insisting on territorial integrity. Whether this was to preserve the integrity of a new democratically inclined multinational Russian state made up of a federation of willing constituent peoples, or to shore up by force the remnants of a Russian empire, is a moot point. Certainly, the 'Putin' constitution for Chechnya, ostensibly adopted by an overwhelming majority of Chechnya's voters in March 2003,[41] contains provisions that smack of imperialist *diktat*,

---

[41] Officially, the turnout was 89.48%, with 95.97% approving the Constitution. For a sceptical account of the vote, see International Helsinki Federation for Human Rights report, 'The Constitutional referendum in Chechnya was neither free nor fair', *http://www.osce-ngo. net/030328.pdf.*

including the effective banning of political parties advocating Chechen independence.[42]

In the event, only Tatarstan and Chechnya stood firm, the former eventually coming to an accommodation with Moscow (see Chapter 3) and the latter fighting a seemingly successful war of secession. However, the failure of the international community to recognize the independence of Chechnya-Ichkeria lent legitimacy to Russia's claim, on reinvading Chechnya in 1999, that the rebellious republic remained part of the Russian Federation.

Whereas the cause of the Tatars was weakened by their wide diaspora across Russia, and the fact that Tatarstan is surrounded by Russian territory, the Chechens could argue that they met all conditions set by Stalin, on the basis of which the right of secession had been granted to the 15 former Union Republics: (a) that they had a population of a million or more; b) that the titular nation comprised the majority; and c) that they shared a border with a foreign state (in Chechnya's case, Georgia). The central dilemma should be, therefore, which right takes precedence, that of self-determination or that of territorial integrity?[43] In the case of Tatarstan, the agreement reached indicated that the latter held sway, whereas in Chechnya's case, the Chechens attempted to impose the former, the Russians responding by applying even greater force in order to achieve the latter.

It was the disproportionate and indiscriminate application of force by the Russians, not Dudaev's pre-emptive push for independence (characterized by Alexander Lebed as a 'mafia squabble at state level'),[44] that caused the overwhelming majority of Chechens to perceive this conflict as the defence of their right to self-determination[45] – a partisan war that is recognized as such by even the Russian public.[46] This is not necessarily the same thing as a classical war of liberation (decolonization) akin to that fought by the Algerians against the French in the 1950s and 1960s.

Moreover, Putin has had some success in splitting the Chechen opposition between those who can and those who cannot tolerate the influence of the Wahhabis. In so far as Maskhadov proved incapable of reining in the

---

[42] Article 8, point 4, forbids the creation and functioning of social organisations that aim to violate the territory integrity of the Russian Federation. The Russian President is also given the right to remove the elected President of Chechnya (Article 72d). See *http://www.chechnya. gov.ru/republic/const/*.

[43] A useful Russian perspective on this dilemma is provided by Zinaida Sikevich, 'Process of National Self-Determination', a special for the Rosbalt News Agency on 18 February 2003, translated by Robin Jones, *http://www.rosbaltnews.com/2003/02/19/61421.html*.

[44] Ravil Zaripov, 'Interview with General Aleksandr Lebed', *Komsomol'skaya pravda*, 19 March 1996.

[45] This was recognized in *The Russia Journal* even before the second war started when in March 1999 it claimed: 'The point is that those who fight against invaders, even the worst criminals, are defenders, and this status justifies the use of any means, including terrorism', 22–28 March 1999.

[46] See note 6 above.

excesses of Basaev and his allies, and has been obliged at times to move towards public reconciliation with them, the prospect diminishes of the Russians accepting him as a participant in any political solution.[47]

Putin's insistence that the entire Chechen war should be viewed in the context of the global war on terrorism has not been harmed by our natural propensity to reinterpret history retrospectively in the light of subsequent events. With the end of the Cold War and after the attacks of 9/11, it no longer seemed unreasonable to claim that the real enemy of first the Soviet Union and then Russia was not the USA or NATO, but Islamic fundamentalism, with which, it turned out, the successors to the Red Army had been fighting in Afghanistan, Tajikistan and Chechnya since 1979. Similarly, Putin's reference to the threat of Islamic-based terrorism contained in his interview with *Paris Match* on 6 July 2000, 'We are witnessing today the formation of a fundamentalist international, a sort of arc of instability extending from the Philippines to Kosovo', not only sounded far more convincing after 9/11, but also reminded the West how foolish it had been to ignore these early warnings. This message was underlined by the fact that links were ultimately discovered between Chechen militants and some of the suicide attackers of 9/11, as well as with their alleged co-conspirator, Zacarias Moussaoui.[48]

The Russian *casus belli* for the 'counter-terrorist operation' launched in September 1999 was the incursion of Wahhabite militants into Dagestan. This action, led by Basaev and Khattab, is the subject of numerous 'conspiracy theories' of Kremlin involvement.[49] However, even this assault on Russia's southern border would not have sufficiently mobilized Russian public opinion for an invasion of Chechnya, which the then interior minister Sergei Stepashin had been pushing for since March 1999.[50] Stepashin claimed that 'Russia has reached the limit of its tolerance for Chechnya's orgy of crime. In line with international practice, the bases and strongholds of these terrorists will be

---

[47] The video of Maskhadov's meeting in July 2002 with Basaev and Khattab's successor as leader of the 'international Wahhabites, Abu Walid, before a Chechen flag, upon which Arabic script and swords had replaced the traditional Chechen wolf, was used to great effect by the Russian authorities to discredit the Chechen leader. See, 'Maskhadov pokazal arabskim zhurnalistam zhivogo Basaeva', *Lenta.Ru*, 22 July 2002, *http://www.46info.ru/html/lenta/2002-6/22/a317.html* Maskhadov, one can only speculate, made this video and the subsequent one in September 2002 (after the shooting down in August of the Mi-26 military helicopter with 121 Russian casualties) in order to secure much-needed funding from Islamic supporters abroad. See Pavel Felgenhauer, 'Bloody Chechen Deadlock', *Moscow Times*, 26 September 2002.

[48] *http://www.terrorismanswers.com/groups/chechens.html.*

[49] For example, the BBC's Malcolm Haslett's analysis 'Jihad or Russian conspiracy?', 11 August 1999, *http://news.bbc.co.uk/1/hi/world/europe/417797.stm.*

[50] Sergei Stepashin had called for this on NTV's *Itogi* programme on 7 March 1999 after the abduction by Chechen rebels at Grozny airport of MVD General Gennady Shpigun. See his interview on NTV's *Geroi dnya* (Hero of the Day), 5 October 1999, in which he also said: 'A full-scale military operation is out of the question now, as it would lead to huge losses'. *http://www.yabloko.ru/Engl/TV/step-ntvr-geroy-1.html.*

eliminated'.[51] Although overridden by then prime minister, Yevgeny Primakov, it does appear that a contingency plan for the invasion of Chechnya had been in place at least by July 1999,[52] US officials having been warned by Russian military sources of an impending attack as early as April of that year.[53] Stepashin replaced Primakov as prime minister in May 1999 and became head of the Federal Anti-Terrorist Commission the following month, with Vladimir Putin, head of the FSB, and the interior minister Vladimir Rushailo as his deputies.[54] In August, during the crisis in Dagestan, Putin replaced Stepashin in both posts and the push towards war accelerated.

The threat to Russia's territorial integrity posed by an independent Chechnya-Ichkeria seemed to have persuaded the new Kremlin leadership that resolute action must be taken, and that the Russian public be made fully aware of the threat facing it.[55] Moreover, there was genuine concern that the USA was ready to exploit any power vacuum on Russia's southern flank.[56] In any event, the bombing of apartment blocks in Buinaksk, Moscow and Volgodonsk in September 1999 came either at an extremely fortuitous juncture, or with a helping hand from the Russian security services;[57] unanswered questions about the 'bomb' discovered in Ryazan on 22 September adding fuel to the fire of conspiracy theorists.[58] Certainly, both Maskhadov and Basaev denied any involvement in these bombings, whereas Basaev readily owned up to the attacks on both Dubrovka in 2002 and Beslan in 2004.[59] None of those tried and imprisoned for the bombings

---

[51] Quoted in 'Chechnya: Impotent Fury', *The Russia Journal*, 22–28 March 1999.

[52] Report of Vladimir Rushailo, who had replaced Stepashin as interior minister in May 1999, to the Federation Council on 3 July 1999. See Yelena Loria in *Novye izvestiya*, 7 July 1999, calling for the application of Russia's counter-terrorism laws to deal with Chechen banditry.

[53] Svante E. Cornell, 'The War Against Terrorism and the Conflict in Chechnya; a Case for Distinction', in *The Fletcher Forum of World Affairs*, Vol. 27, No. 2, Summer/Fall 2002, p. 171.

[54] Mark A Smith, 'Russian Perspectives on Terrorism', *Conflict Studies Research Centre Report C110*, Defence Academy of the United Kingdom, January 2004, p. 3.

[55] Smith, 'Russian Perspectives on Terrorism', pp. 3–4.

[56] This aspect of the conflict has tended to be overlooked by Western observers, although is implicit in Putin's warning about the 'arc of instability extending from the Philippines to Kosovo', see interview with *Paris Match*, 6 July 2000. See also, Aleksei Malashenko and Dmitrii Trenin, *Vremya yuga: Rossiya v Chechne, Chechnya v Rossii* (Moscow, Gendal'f, 2002), pp. 186–8.

[57] The sources pointing to a 'conspiracy' are far too numerous to list, the most widely reviewed being Yuri Felshtinsky and Alexander Litvinenko, *Blowing Up Russia* (New York, Liberty, 2002), and David Satter, *Darkness at Dawn; the Rise of the Russian Criminal State* (New Haven, CT, Yale University Press, 2003), as well as the documentary film *Assassination of Russia*, Charles Gazelle Transparences Productions, France, 2002, financed by Boris Berezovsky.

[58] See Channel 4 *Dispatches* programme 'Dying for the President', screened on 9 March 2000.

[59] For Basaev's denial of the apartment bombs in Moscow, see 'Chechen Warlord Denies Connection to Moscow Explosion', report by Associated Press on 12 September 1999, posted on the Chechen website, *http://www.amina.com/news/99/99.9.12.html*; for his admission that he masterminded 'Nord-Ost', see 'Chechen Warlord Claims Theatre Attack', on the BBC website, 1 November 2002, *http://news.bbc.co.uk/1/hi/world/europe/2388857.stm*; for Beslan, see *http://www.daymohk.info/cgi-bin/orsi3/index.cgi?id=8428;idt=17200409;section=1*.

have turned out to be Chechens, the perpetrators appearing to be Karachai and Dagestani militants allegedly acting under the orders of the Saudi-born Khattab and the Egyptian Abu Ammar, who were both killed in the second conflict and led the small Arab presence amongst the Chechen fighters.[60] However, the very presence of these 'international jihadists' on Chechen soil was enough to establish a link, however tenuous, between the rebels and al-Qaeda.

Moreover, Putin's intemperate threat to 'wipe out the terrorists even in the outhouse' captured the mood of the traumatized and enraged Russian population.[61] It seems probable, therefore, that the Moscow bombings were the key link in a chain of events that not only led to the second Chechen war, but that also replaced an unpopular and ailing president with one of the *siloviki*'s own – a career Chekist (intelligence officer) who could be relied upon not to rein in his generals. [62] Once Putin had allowed Russian forces to raze Grozny to the ground and attack the heartlands of Chechen resistance in the mountains, the war became a humanitarian disaster – not just for the civilians of Chechnya, who suffered from the disproportional and indiscriminate force employed against them, but also for the million and a half federal troops that have fought so far in this conflict, for whom the arbitrary brutality and sense of virtual impunity became part of their everyday life in Chechnya.[63]

Tight control over the media and access to Chechnya were the most effective means by which Putin could hide from the public actions that, by any objective criteria, deserve investigation as war crimes. Early examples of these were the declaration issued by the Russian military on 6 December 1999 that 'Those who remain in Grozny after December 11 will be viewed as terrorists and bandits and will be destroyed by artillery and aviation';[64] the atrocities at Katyr Yurt in February 2000;[65] and the violations routinely

---

[60] See Anatoly Medetsky, 'Two Get Life in Prison for '99 Bombings', *Moscow Times*, 13 January 2004; estimates of the number of Arab mercenaries fighting in Chechnya do not exceed 300, see *http://www.rferl.org/features/2002/05/02052002092430.asp*. Even Russian military sources concur with this figure, claiming that one-fifth of Chechen fighters are Arabs, see Bronwen Maddox, 'An Unwinnable War, but Russia Cannot Quit', *The Times*, 13 May 2003, but assessing the total strength of the opposition at only 1,500 men, as reported by the pro-Moscow *chechnyafree.ru* website, on 22 January 2004.

[61] *Nezavisimaya gazeta*, 25 September 1999.

[62] State Duma Security Committee Chairman, Viktor Ilyukhin, complained in November 1999 that President Yeltsin was totally unpredictable and claimed that a 'fifth column' of Yavlinsky, Kirienko and Borovoi was acting to terminate the counter-terrorist operation', *The Russia Journal*, 1–7 November 1999.

[63] Chechen political scientist, Zaindi Choltaev made this estimate in December 2003, see Hovsepyan and Tsukanova, 'Chechnya and Russia: War and Peace'.

[64] 'The Russian Ultimatum to Chechnya: a Humanitarian Outrage', *Relief International*, 7 December 1999.

[65] John Sweeney, 'Revealed: Russia's Worst War Crime in Chechnya', *Observer*, 5 March 2000.

occurring at the notorious Chernokozovo filtration camp.[66] However, 67 per cent of the Russian public supported the campaign to expel the Chechen fighters from Grozny,[67] during which three leading Chechen rebels were killed and Shamil Basaev badly wounded.[68]

Western governments clearly did not want the Chechen separatists to win again, but restricted their criticism of Russia's conduct in the war to diplomatic attempts to persuade the new Russian president to seek a political solution.[69] With the Russian electorate sick and tired of the war in Chechnya, the key mistake Putin made – having won a huge mandate in the presidential election of March 2000 and the battle for Grozny – was to fail to engage with the secessionist leaders of Chechnya, thereby isolating the Islamic fundamentalists. Instead, from June 2000, he announced that the only Chechen with whom he would negotiate would be Akhmad Kadyrov, a former resistance fighter and religious leader that Putin had made his Chief of Administration in Chechnya.

This move in effect defined all Chechen nationalists as terrorists and isolated the Chechen resistance fighters, leaving them with little alternative to abject surrender or sabotage and terrorism. A long-drawn out guerrilla war continued out of the gaze of an indifferent Russian public and the largely excluded Western media. The Russian forces continued to alienate the Chechen population and international human rights agencies, through use of illegal fuel-air and cluster bombs in their air attacks and *zachistki* (sweeps) in their ground operations, in which victims were much more likely to be civilians, rather than Chechen fighters, let alone 'terrorists'.[70] For both internal and external consumption, Putin and his team continued to use every opportunity to press home that 'the actions of Russia are against extremism…they are directed entirely against international extremism and terrorism'.[71] Western leaders and the Russian public chose to ignore what was, certainly until 11 September 2001, a grossly distorted representation of the war in Chechnya.

---

[66]'The Chernokozovo Detention Center', Human Rights Watch Report, "Welcome to Hell': Arbitrary Detention, Torture and Extortion in Chechnya', see *http://hrw.org/reports/2000/russia_chechnya4/*.

[67] C. W. Blandy, 'Chechnya: Dynamics of War, Brutality & Stress', *Conflict Studies Research Centre, Report P35*, July 2001, p. 10.

[68] See *http://www.cdi.org/issues/Europe/feb2000.html*.

[69] President Clinton's Secretary of State, Madeleine Albright, was an outspoken critic of the war, calling it 'an incredible act of misery', see *http://www.cbsnews.com/stories/2000/01/31/world/main155042.shtml*.

[70] See Pavel Felgenhauer, 'The Russian Army in Chechnya', Crimes of War Project, 18 April 2003, *http://crimesofwar.org/print/chechnya/chech-felgenhauer-print.html*.

[71] Reuters report in *Russia Today*, 18 April 2000. On 2 March 2000, Agence France Presse quoted Presidential advisor, Sergei Yastrzhembsky, as saying: 'The West does not understand the circumstances of terrorism in Russia. No country in the world has confronted terrorism on such a grand scale'.

The War Against Terrorism

The events of 9/11 did not give Putin a free hand in Chechnya, but retrospectively confirmed that, as far as the international community was concerned, he could act as he wished. At the Camp David meeting with the Russian President in the aftermath of 9/11 President Bush's endorsement of Putin's vision for Russia 'as a country at peace within its borders, with its neighbors, a country in which democracy and freedom and rule of law thrive', seemed to say: 'Stand by my side and proclaim yourself an ally in the war on terror, and all else may be forgiven'.[72] To exert pressure on the Chechens, Bush insisted that Maskhadov choose between the Islamic militants and Putin, no real choice given the situation.[73] Declarations from other Western leaders followed, epitomised by NATO Secretary General George Robertson's comment that 'we have come to see the scourge of terrorism in Chechnya with different eyes'.[74] On receiving President Putin at Chequers in December 2001,Tony Blair drew parallels between the September 1999 bombings and the attacks on 9/11.[75]

With such international and domestic support, and with control over the mass media, by 17 April 2002 Putin was able to declare in his state of the federation address that the military phase of the conflict was over, even though attacks on his forces were continuing as he spoke.[76] Within a month, on 'Victory Day' (9 May 2002), a bomb planted at a military parade in the Dagestani town of Kaspiisk killed 42 soldiers and family members. Although Dagestani rather than Chechen militants were blamed, an enraged Russian public was not minded to draw so fine a distinction.[77]

The Chechen resistance was again put in a difficult position. Whatever the rectitude of their cause, they were seen primarily by the US Administration to be backing the wrong side and were made to pay the price. This allowed Putin to cut off the exploratory peace talks in Moscow with Maskhadov's envoy, Akhmed Zakaev, and to adopt new, tougher military measures in Chechnya. In an interview with *Reuters* on 9 September 2002, Zakaev accused the Russian authorities of 'trying to thrust our movement into the context of international terrorism, in particular after the tragic events in the United States…but the Russo-Chechen conflict started long before these events, when people did not know of the existence of such terrorism and they did not understand what it meant'. In the wake of the Dubrovka theatre siege, extradition charges were laid

---

[72] Fred Hiatt, 'Democracy on Hold', *Washington Post*, 6 October 2001.

[73] *Novaya gazeta* 15 October 2001.

[74] *Guardian*, 29 November 2001.

[75] *Guardian*, 22 December 2001.

[76] *http://news.bbc.co.uk/1/hi/world/europe/1936998.stm.*

[77] *http://www.grani.ru/blast.*

retrospectively against Zakaev, generally considered to be the most moderate of all Chechen leaders,[78] for acts of terrorism carried out in the first Chechen war.

Speaking after the Moscow theatre siege in October 2002, Dominique de Villepin, the French Foreign Minister, expressed what the Western diplomatic community must have known but appeared reluctant to articulate in public, with the comment: 'one must distinguish between terrorism, which is reprehensible in all its forms and wherever it might be, and crises which genuinely call for the search of a political solution. This is clearly the case in Chechnya, as we've said for years'.[79]

The Dubrovka siege, occurring in the wake of the Bali terrorist bombing, came at an extremely fortuitous juncture for Putin. Genuine progress was being made throughout the summer of 2002 by Chechen, Russian and Western mediators to elaborate a peace plan for Chechnya. Akhmed Zakaev attended a major conference in Liechtenstein in August 2002, alongside high-profile members of the Chechen diaspora such as Ruslan Khasbulatov, the former Speaker of Russia's parliament; Aslanbek Aslakhanov, Duma deputy for Chechnya; prominent Russians such as Ivan Rybkin, another former Speaker of the State Duma and National Security Advisor; and Yury Shchekochikin, a deputy from the Russian parliament; as well as highly-respected American public figures, such as former National Security Advisor to President Carter, Zbigniew Brzezinski; Alexander Haig, former Secretary of State under President Reagan; and Max Kampelman, Chair of the American Academy of Diplomacy. A compromise peace plan was hammered out which would grant Chechnya autonomy within the Russian territorial space. This represented the best peace plan yet tabled for a peaceful resolution of the Chechen conflict and would have satisfied the preferences of the Russian public as expressed in opinion polls. As a result of internal and international pressure Putin had, for the first time, been obliged on 24 June 2002 to draw a clear distinction between the Chechen 'terrorists' and the Chechen people, promising to stop demonizing the latter as 'terrorists'.[80]

The murky circumstances surrounding the October 2002 siege have attracted as much speculation as had the Moscow bombings of 1999, with key questions about the Russian administration's handling of the whole

---

[78] Lord Frank Judd, rapporteur for Chechnya and a member of the Parliamentary Assembly of the Council of Europe (PACE) said of Zakaev: 'of those associated with the Chechen fighters with whom I have met and spoken, it is with him that I have been able to have some of the most intelligent discussions about the global realities as they affect the people of the Chechen Republic and about the need for a political settlement. His removal at this stage from even tentative steps towards engagement in a political settlement does not seem to me self-evidently to help', *Chechnya Weekly*, Vol. 4, Issue 3, 6 February 2003.

[79] In a radio interview on 26 October 2002 to Europe One, reported in the *Irish Examiner*, 28 October 2002.

[80] *RFE/RL Newsline*, 25 June 2002.

operation still as yet unanswered.[81] What the Chechens, other than the extremist elements led by the mastermind of the operation, Basaev, had to gain from this act other than the highly improbable obtaining of their sole demand, to end the war in Chechnya, is unclear. The prominence of the 'black widow' female hostage takers, dressed in their black *hijabs*, made it easy to draw parallels between Palestinian and Chechen tactics.[82]

What is indisputable is that Putin won back the support of public opinion in Russia for his war, received further backing from the Bush administration, which arranged for Basaev's three fighting units to be added to the list of proscribed terrorist organizations;[83] it also allowed him to scupper both the Liechtenstein peace process and the World Chechen Congress, which opened in Copenhagen within days of the hostage drama in Moscow. Even before the siege the US Ambassador to Russia had voiced his 'increasing scepticism' towards President Maskhadov as a credible participant in a political solution for Chechnya.[84]

Putin seized the moment to outline a proposed new constitution for Chechnya and announce a referendum on this and the election of a president of Chechnya within Russia. But as the seasoned Russian political commentator Otto Latsis wrote:

> [T]he authorities are pursuing one very transparent aim with their idea of a referendum and new presidential elections for Chechnya. They want an argument against those who say they should negotiate with Aslan Maskhadov, the man who was elected Chechen President with Moscow's approval in 1997. The Kremlin doesn't want to talk to Maskhadov, something that is only confirmed by Moscow's insistent campaign to have Akhmed Zakaev, Maskhadov's representative at negotiations, extradited to Russia. The Kremlin's new plan is clear and could be carried out. The idea is to hold a managed referendum followed by a managed election that would elect a new president with whom

---

[81] In an important recent article, John Dunlop analyses Kremlin involvement in the Dubrovka drama in his 'The October 2002 Moscow Hostage-Taking Incident', *RFE/RL Organized Crime and Terrorism Watch*, 18 December 2003 and 8 and 15 January 2004.

[82] The first female Chechen suicide bomber would appear to be Khaba Baraeva, sister of the notorious warlord, Arbi Baraev and aunt of the leader of the Dubrovka hostage-takers, Movsar. On 6 June 2000, she and a woman associate drove a truck bomb into a military building in Chechnya, killing themselves and two OMON soldiers. See Vadim Dubnov, 'Lyudi-bomby' (Human bombs), *Novoe vremya*, No. 25, 2003, p.15.

[83] The three banned groups are the Islamic International Brigade, the Special Purpose Islamic Regiment and the Riyadus-Salikhin Reconnaissance and Sabotage Battalion of Chechen Martyrs, see *http://news.bbc.co.uk/1/hi/world/europe/2810153.stm*.

[84] Agence France Presse, 9 September 2002; Ambassador Vershbow had been more circumspect when, in March 2002, he had claimed: 'the issue of Chechnya is certainly a difficult item in our relations. International terrorism is part of the Chechen problem. Some Chechen separatists, indeed, have participated in terrorist acts.' *http://www.wps.ru/chitalka/terror/en/archives.php3?d=20&m=3*.

Moscow would then negotiate. The problem is that the only real way to end any war is to make peace with your adversary and, in the case of the guerrilla war underway in Chechnya, the adversary is the Chechen people, which will only accept negotiations and deals with its own representative – Maskhadov – as legitimate. To ignore this is to let the war continue.[85]

Following the debacle of the Dubrovka affair, even moderate Chechens such as Zakaev became fugitives from Russian law,[86] while those intent on carrying on the fight switched their tactics to suicide bombing. After trucks driven by suicide bombers had destroyed the government headquarters in Grozny in December 2002 with a death toll of 80, and killed a further 59 in Znamenskoe in May 2003, female suicide bombers struck in Moscow in July and December 2003, in southern Russia in June, August and December and in Chechnya in May. With over 300 dead, these attacks proved just as bloody as the series of apartment blasts in 1999.[87]

In 1999, 2001 and 2002, Putin skilfully exploited perceived 'terrorist acts' to convince the public that Russia was on the front line against Islamic extremist terror. Typical of this are his comments on the struggle against Islamic fundamentalism in Chechnya in his interview in *The New York Times* on 6 October 2003:

> It is not right to regard members of al-Qaeda who are fighting in Chechnya as supporters of independence and democratic development of Chechnya, and to regard those same representatives of al-Qaeda who are fighting in Afghanistan and Iraq as criminals. Such a policy will not lead to effective results in joint work on the battle against terrorism.

In the first war, the arbitrary brutality of the federal forces was kept in the public consciousness in Russia and abroad, and the Russian authorities admitted that it had 'lost' the battle for the hearts and minds.[88] Even before the commencement of the second war, Putin's administration was successfully manipulating both the domestic and international mass media coverage. By drawing on lessons learned from NATO's information war in

---

[85] *The Russia Journal*, 31 January 2003.

[86] The prospects for any alleged or convicted Chechen 'terrorist' surviving long in Russian jails are grim if one studies the fate of Turpal-Ali Atgeriev and Salman Raduev, both of whom were arrested, tried and convicted in Dagestan. Both died in mysterious circumstances in Russian jails, allegedly the former of a heart attack and the latter through internal bleeding.

[87] http://news.bbc.co.uk/1/low/world/europe/3020231.stm. The Beslan school siege of September 2004, also with over 300 dead, provides a similar example of the continuing scale of violence.

[88] 'The Chechen campaign of 1994–6 was the first 'televised war' in the history of Russia. The "picture" presented of this war played an enormous role in changes for the worse in attitudes to the Russian military machine'. Malashenko and Trenin, *Vremya yuga*, p. 173.

Kosovo, elite 'liberal' opposition was marginalized and discounted while popular support was maintained.[89] As a result, the second war only made the headlines, both domestically and internationally, when the Chechens launched a 'terrorist spectacular' along the lines of the Moscow theatre siege of 2002, the suicide bombings of 2003, and the Beslan school siege of 2004, hardening convictions at home and abroad, particularly in the wake of 9/11, that the conflict was, indeed, part of the global struggle against terrorism.

The role of the 'information war' is therefore seen as crucial in preventing both Russian and world opinion from perceiving the renewed conflict for what in essence it was: a series of overlapping conflicts which included the fight against terrorism, but which also involved a continuation of the battle for Russian territorial integrity, an attempt to control the black hole of lawlessness that independent Chechnya-Ichkeria had become and, insofar as the generals were itching for revenge for their humiliating defeat in the first war, a clash of culture in which the 'civilized' Russians could tame the 'savage' Chechens. The impact of this media manipulation was not lost on more observant Russian commentators:

> In contrast to the previous war in Chechnya, this one has failed to evoke indignation among Russians. The public seldom hears the bad news from Chechnya, Russian losses aren't regularly disclosed and major media report only the deadliest attacks. The government makes it virtually impossible for journalists to work in Chechnya except in close coordination with the military. The media are banned from reporting interviews with the rebels.[90]

One can only speculate what influence might have been exerted on Russian public opinion by the publication of the true figures of Russian losses during the war; in August 2003, the Mothers of Russian Soldiers Committee estimated that the death toll stood at 12,000 dead since 1999.[91] A detailed opinion poll, run by VTsIOM for the Program On New Approaches to Russian Security (PONARS) just after 9/11 demonstrated how effective Putin's efforts had been in presenting the war as a struggle against terrorism: fully 93 per cent thought this important in framing their attitude to the war. At the same time only 48 per cent thought human rights issues were important and 9 per cent thought the views of the international community on the war very

---

[89] Stephen Badsey, 'Media Interaction in the Kosovo Conflict, March–June 1999', paper at the Political Studies Association conference, London, 2000, *http://www.psa.ac.uk/cps/2000/Badsey%20Stephen.pdf*.

[90] 'No End in Sight to the War in Chechnya', *The Russia Journal*, 16 September 2002.

[91] Agence France Presse, 11 August 2003. By May 2004, Valentina Melnikova, of the Russian Soldiers' Mothers Committee, claimed that this figure had risen to 25,000. See Charles Gurin, 'Group Claims 25,000 Russian Soldiers Have Died in Chechnya', The Jamestown Foundation, *Eurasia Daily Monitor*, vol. 1, Issue 3, 5 May 2004.

important.[92] The complexity of Russian views on Chechnya are illustrated by another VTsIOM poll, published in March 2003, which asked Russians to rate Putin's performance over three years as President. This poll indicated that, in the immediate aftermath of the Dubrovka theatre siege, a mere 18 per cent thought he had been successful in defeating the fighters in Chechnya, and just 16 per cent thought his efforts to achieve a political solution there had worked. Nearly three-quarters (74 per cent and 73 per cent respectively) thought he had been unsuccessful in these two areas. At the same time 71 per cent (against 22 per cent) thought that he had consolidated Russia's position in the world.[93] As late as January 2004, 80 per cent declared that they intended to vote for him in the forthcoming presidential elections, and in the event in March Putin easily won a second term with 71 per cent of the vote.[94]

From this it might be deduced that the Russian people wanted better results – and thus a higher level of security – than those achieved by Putin's policies (particularly in light of the Dubrovka theatre siege), but appeared to favour either an intensification of the military effort to finally defeat the 'terrorists' or, if that could not provide security, then a negotiated political settlement that could. Putin, however, is not being held personally to blame for the failure of his policy in Chechnya, even though, to the outsider, he either feels beholden to his generals to continue the war[95] or is aware that the Russian public is more prepared to tolerate his policies in times of crisis. Thus, although during and immediately after the hostage drama, Russian public opinion temporarily favoured military action in Chechnya over the opening of peace talks, by the beginning of 2003 the approximate 60-30 split in favour of talks had been regained; this would appear to reflect more accurately the attitude of ordinary Russians to the war.[96]

Chechnya – A Black Hole of Lawlessness

In the context of this war the problem of lawlessness highlights how prolonging the armed struggle benefits the few to the detriment of the many.

---

[92] Theodore P. Gerber and Sarah E Mendelson, 'The Disconnect in How Russians Think About Human Rights and Chechnya: A Consequence of Media Manipulation', *PONARS Policy Memo*, No. 244, January, 2002.

[93] 'Tri goda Prezidentstva', *http://www.vciom-a.ru/press/2003032601.html*.

[94] *http://www.vciom-a.ru/press/2004012800.html*. Putin's approval rating dropped to 66% in the wake of the beslan school siege in September 2004, rising to 69% by November of that year, *http://www.levada.ru/prezident.html*.

[95] Ruslan Khasbulatov claims that Vladimir Putin is personally against the war, but is effectively a 'hostage' to those Russian military leaders, who are growing wealthy from their illicit economic activities in Chechnya'. Interview in *Le Monde*, 4 November 2002, reported in *Johnson's Russia List* (*JRL*), No. 6536, 6 November 2002.

[96] *http://www.vciom-a.ru/press/2003032601.html*; by the end of 2003, this had hardened to 67% in favour of peace negotiations and only 20% for continuing the war, *http://vciom-a.ru/press/2003121301.html*, but, by November 2004 (after Beslan) stabilised at 59-27, *http://www.levada.ru/press/2004120202.html*.

That this applies to both sides in the conflict is scant consolation to the long suffering civilian population of Chechnya or indeed to the much abused, traumatized Russian troops that have served in this horrendous conflict. Stories of corruption, of Russian army generals and Chechen field commanders working hand in glove, of arbitrary brutality and impunity from prosecution of those carrying it out, of illegal drug trafficking, extortion, hostage taking and kidnapping for ransom, of large-scale criminal fraud, are all so common as to give the impression that there remains no semblance of a law-governed state in Chechnya.[97] All this, of course, takes place against a background of the disproportionate and indiscriminate use of military force against the civilian population.

A war that started in 1994 as a squabble between corrupt elites has descended into one of the dirtiest conflicts that the European continent has witnessed, comparable only to the horrific civil wars in the former Yugoslavia for sheer human degradation and the violation of basic human rights.[98] Neither the United Nations, through its High Commission for Refugees, nor the European Union, through the Council of Europe,[99] has been able to persuade governments to act on its recommendations regarding Chechnya. Russia has protested robustly whenever representatives of these international organizations have attempted to mediate in the conflict.[100] Even President Putin appears to be easily provoked on this subject, as demonstrated by his bizarre outburst in Brussels on 12 November 2002, when he invited a French journalist asking probing questions about Chechnya to Moscow to get circumcised.[101]

[97] The sources on this topic are too numerous to list here. For an excellent article by a Chechen still living in the war zone, that covers many of the wide range of abuses committed in Chechnya, see Imran Ismailov, 'Paradoxes of the war in Chechnya', *Prague Watchdog*, 31 October 2002, *http://watchdog.cz/index.php?show=000000-000005-000001-000119&lang=1*; Among good articles by Russians to appear on this topic are Pavel Felgenhauer, 'The Russian Army in Chechnya', *op.cit*; Anna Politkovsaya, 'S kem vesti peregovory v Chechnye', *Novaya gazeta*, 1 October 2001; for hostage taking by the Chechen side, see Valerii Zhuravel' and Viktor Velichkovskii, 'Pokhishcheniya prodolzhayutsya', *Nezavisimoe voennoe obozrenie*, 23 August 2002, *http://nvo.ng.ru/printed/wars/2002-08-23/2_help.html*; for Western viewpoints, see Jeremy Putley, 'Crime Without Punishment: Russian Policy in Chechnya', 28 July 2003, *http://www.opendemocracy.net/debates/article-2-95-1388.jsp* and Anne Nivat, 'Chechnya: Brutality and Indifference', Crimes of War project, 6 January 2003, *http://www.crimesofwar.org/print/onnews/chechnya-print.html*.
[98] Of the many reports compiled by human rights organizations on war crimes committed in Chechnya, one of the most detailed is that produced by the Physicians for Human Rights in May 2001, 'Endless Brutality: War Crimes in Chechnya', see *http://www.phrusa.org/research/pdf/chech_report_final.pdf*.
[99] In April 2003, the Council of Europe threatened to set up an international war crimes tribunal on Chechnya, if the situation did not improve, Agence France Presse, 2 April 2003; see also the report of the Council of Europe's Committee for the Prevention of Torture and Inhuman or Degrading treatment or Punishment, concerning the Chechen Republic of the Russian Federation, 10 July 2003, *http://www.cpt.coe.int/documents/rus/2003-33-inf-eng.htm*.
[100] For example when UN war crimes prosecutor Carla del Ponte met Akhmed Zakaev in March 2002, see Agence France Presse, 11 March 2002.
[101] See Robert Wielaard, 'Chechnya Query Incenses Putin', *Washington Post*, 13 November 2002.

Those engaged in the war on both sides have suffered terribly; the Chechens from psychological, mental and physical traumas and the Russians from the dreaded 'Chechen' syndrome, the post-traumatic stress condition that affects a high proportion of the million and a half Russian troops that have served in Chechnya, and which has created thousands of human 'time bombs' in towns and villages across the Russian Federation.[102] Since the Dubrovka hostage drama of October 2002, Putin's only political solution appears to be a 'Chechenization' of the conflict, transferring responsibility for countering the Chechen secessionists to pro-Moscow Chechens under president Akhmad Kadyrov,[103] whom the award-winning *Novaya gazeta* journalist, Anna Politkovskaya, has called 'Putin's Chechen clone'.[104] The particularly brutal strong-arm tactics employed by Kadyrov's feared Chechen police force[105] indicate not only that his legitimacy rests solely on Kremlin support, but also that strong traditional taboos have been eroded by the current conflict, such as Chechen-against-Chechen conflict and Chechen women sacrificing themselves as suicide bombers. Yet, as *The Economist* commented on Kadyrov: '...a weak leader in a lawless republic is likely to use any means he can to keep control. So Chechnya will carry on much as before: a corrupt, unstable mess of competing armed bands, fighting over oil, selling arms and terrorising the population.'[106] Kadyrov's assassination in May 2004 did not put an end to the attempt to Chechenize the conflict, and in August Alu Alkhanov was elected as the new pro-Moscow president of the republic.

From the Chechen warlord' point of view, the situation is reminiscent of Afghanistan, where, according to a Human Rights Watch report of December 2002:

> Warlords now represent the primary threat to peace and stability in the country... The power of the warlords has made it impossible for (the government) to establish its authority much beyond Kabul. The enduring system of 'fiefdoms'... reinforced by the policies of the

---

[102] For aspects of the 'Chechen syndrome', see Yuri Zarakhovich, 'Chechnya's Walking Wounded', *Time Europe*, 28 September 2003, *http://www.time.com/time/europe/html/031006/syndrome.html*.

[103] For a good account of Kadyrov's position, see Ilya Milshtein, 'Simply Kadyrov', *http://www.newtimes.ru/eng/detail.asp?art_id=865*.

[104] Interview with 'Ekho' radio, published in *Komsomol'skaya pravda*, 19 January 2004, *http://www.kp.ru/online/news/8202/*.

[105] A recent translation of an article published in *Die Welt* alleged that Kadyrov's son, Ramzan, has a prison in his house for torturing captured Chechens, who were beginning to fear his so-called 'death battalions', even more than the Russian forces. *http://www.inopressa. ru/print/welt/2004/01/23/11:20:42/Chechnia*. For more allegations of Ramzan Kadyrov's brutality against fellow Chechens as well as the description of his father being 'reviled by Chechens as a traitor', see Nick Paton Walsh, 'Russia's Man in Reign of Terror in Chechnya', *Guardian*, 13 January 2004.

[106] *The Economist*, 11–17 October 2003.

US…is simply not conducive to long-term stability or to the protection of human rights.[107]

The critical difference is that, in Afghanistan, the outside forces may be reluctant to intervene, but at least they are not as arbitrary, brutal or corrupt as are the Russian occupation forces in Chechnya. The resulting consequences of the conflict for Chechnya, Russia and the world may not be so different from the fall-out from the Afghanistan conflict predicted by the US Council for Foreign Relations and the Asia Society in summer 2003:

> Unless the situation improves, Afghanistan risks sliding back into the anarchy and warlordism that prevailed in the 1990s and helped give rise to the Taliban. Such a reversion would have disastrous consequences for Afghanistan and would be a profound setback for the US war on terrorism.[108]

Conclusion

Given the traumatic circumstances of the 9/11 terror attacks on New York and Washington, and their obvious potential for repetition elsewhere once President Bush had declared that, in the global war against terrorism, 'you are either with us or against us', every conflict in the world now tends to be viewed in the context of this war. Although contrary to international law, such concepts as 'pre-emptive defence' and 'illegal combatants' have been legitimized. For Putin's Russia, embroiled in a stalemate in Chechnya, this came as a blessing. In a world in which media-fuelled stereotypes exert unprecedented power on public perceptions, the complex Chechen cocktail of medieval tradition, nineteenth-century theocratic autonomy and belated twentieth century nationalism could all too easily be simplified, for both the Russian public and the international community, as anti-Western Islamic terrorism – the so-called scourge of the 21st century.

Through skilful manipulation and control of the Russian mass media and by constantly reminding the world of Russia's membership of the global alliance against terror,[109] Putin's administration has effectively taken all other issues of the Chechen war off the political agenda at home and abroad. The Chechen rebels are caught between a rock and a hard place. Even if one allows that Maskhadov, Zakaev, Gelaev (killed early in 2004) and other leaders of the secessionist movement have presented their struggle as one of

---

[107] Ahmed Rashid, 'The Mess in Afghanistan', _New York Review of Books_, 12 February 2004, p. 26.

[108] Rashid, 'The Mess in Afghanistan', p. 27.

[109] See, for example, Aleksei Meshkov, '2003: Crucial year for Fighting Terrorism', _International Affairs_, (Moscow), Vol. 49, No. 2, 2003, pp. 6–10.

national liberation, any return to normalcy that guaranteed an end to arbitrary violence from either side would be likely to meet with the approval of the Chechens, no matter how far short of independence it fell, given the negative memories of the period of *de facto* independence in 1996–9 and the general war-weariness of the Chechen population.[110] Although throughout the second war there appeared to be a division of opinion over strategy between the 'nationalist partisans', from Gelaev, who wished to restrict the fight to Chechnya and its surroundings, to 'religious fundamentalists' such as Basaev, who wished to take the battle to Russia, they shared a common cause as long as Russian troops remained in Chechnya.[111] Maskhadov appeared to fluctuate in his support between the two sides, but as he, Gelaev and Basaev were all heroes of the first war, especially the recapture of Grozny in August 1996, the issues that bound them together probably held more weight than those that divided them. There is no place in the post-9/11 world for such ambiguity.

As long as no compromise is allowed in the war against terrorism, there is little room for moderation in a conflict that one side perceives to be about self-determination and the other about countering terrorism. The rational compromise programme, advanced by Russians, Chechens and Westerners engaged in the peace process that was interrupted and eventually broken off by the Moscow theatre siege of October 2002, would have granted Chechnya a degree of autonomy within Russia, with security guaranteed by international bodies. This would have allowed Chechens to reintroduce aspects of traditional custom (*adaat*) into their socio-political structure, reducing their dependence on *sharia* law.[112] Although designed to marginalize extremists on both sides and bring a halt to the fighting, at best this plan would only have produced weak and untried institutions, and would probably have required decades rather than years to heal the ecological, economic and humanitarian wounds that have accumulated in the ten years of war.[113] The experience of postwar reconstruction in Kosovo, Afghanistan and Iraq does not make one optimistic about a secure and prosperous future anytime soon for the people of Chechnya.

---

[110] Chechnya received the lowest rating of 7 for both level of political rights and civil liberties in the Freedom House country ratings for 2003, see *http://www.freedomhouse.org/ratings/index.htm.*

[111] See Umalt Dudaev, 'Chechnya: the Fighting Goes On', in *Caucasus Reporting Service*, No. 214, 15 January 2004.

[112] Islam represents the easiest way for Chechens to distinguish themselves from the Russians, an important requirement in a civil war. Were they able to live, as they would prefer, according to their own customs (i.e. *adaat*), they would not require imported elements of Islam (i.e. *sharia*) to make this distinction.

[113] To his credit, the former Speaker of the Russian Parliament, Ruslan Khasbulatov, has persisted in advocating this peace plan, despite no encouragement whatsoever from the Putin administration. For a round-table discussion of this plan, see Hovsepyan and Tsukanova, 'Chechnya and Russia: War and Peace'.

As for Russia, it is hard to disagree with Zbigniew Brzezinski, who stated in February 2002 that 'the war in Chechnya certainly is not helping the evolution of democracy. It is strengthening the worst remnants of the Soviet system – the apparatus of suppression, the apparatus of coercion. It's not contributing to a healthy political evolution'.[114] The price could be high for the Russian people. Putin's blueprint for Russia as a 'controlled' or 'managed' democracy could just as easily be leading to authoritarianism as to democracy.[115]

[114] *http://www.rferl.org/nca/features/2002/02/01022002102012.asp.*
[115]Vitalii Tret'yakov drew attention to this phenomenon in his article 'Diagnoz: upravlyayemaya demokratiya', *Nezavisimaya gazeta,* 13 January 2000.

13

The Peace Process in Chechnya

James Hughes

When asked in early 2004 by a journalist about the road to peace in Chechnya, president Putin retorted combatively: 'Russia does not negotiate with terrorists, we destroy them'.[1] Putin's public eschewing of negotiations with Chechen insurgents is reminiscent of the assertions by past leaders of imperial regimes, and of contemporary democratic Western leaders, most recently in Iraq. The Russian-Chechen war is undoubtedly one of the most protracted, most bitter and bloodiest of the post-Soviet conflicts, involving terrorist acts such as those by Chechen extremists at the Budennovsk hospital, the Dubrovka theatre, and the Beslan school, and by the Russian military's terror-bombing of Grozny and massacre at Samashki. It is also a conflict, however, that involves a complex peace process which has engaged the main protagonists in periodic attempts to reach a settlement through dialogue and negotiations. The peace process in the conflict in Chechnya is littered by a 'truce', a 'treaty' and several 'agreements', though a final peace 'settlement' to the conflict remains elusive. While the key issue at the centre of the conflict is sovereignty for an independent Chechnya , the dynamics of the conflict have developed through several different phases, alternating between military conflict and negotiations. By examining these dynamics we can track how the mutual interaction of the military conflict and the peace process has shaped the parameters of a potential agreement. What might have been the basis for compromise and a settlement at one stage of the conflict may over time become redundant as new issues and new protagonists emerge, and new events transform the nature of the conflict and negotiation. What is evident in the case of Chechnya is that there has been a radicalization – and therefore a polarization – on both sides, which is diluting a shared understanding of the issues at stake and reinforcing divisive issues such as racism and sectarianism that are associated with the most intractable conflicts.

---

[1] Press conference at the Kremlin, 6 February 2004. *http://www.kremlin.ru/appears/2004/02/06/1949_type63380_60388.shtml.*

Conflicts are multi-dimensional and dynamic phenomena, whose most noteworthy causes, actors, strategies, issues and idioms change over time. Similarly, most conflicts tend to have ongoing peace processes of dialogue, negotiation and mediation, though the focal points of any conflict may alternate between the political, military and diplomatic arenas. As a result, peace processes, as with military conflict, go through periods of heightened activity and dormancy. Conflicts that involve insurgency and terrorism are generally framed by the protagonists' use of political idioms of the most derogatory nature. This uncompromising rhetoric can blind even detached observers from the undercurrents of pragmatism in the pursuit of a peace process, often simultaneously with conflict, as actors manoeuvre for positional advantage and compromise in a continuing search for an acceptable exit strategy.

The undercurrents of pragmatism in such conflicts can be illustrated by the historical irony in which anti-colonial insurgencies have generally been proclaimed as 'terrorism' by the leaderships of imperial powers, yet the insurgent leaders have subsequently been feted as the statesmen of independent states by the very same leaderships. In recent times Western leaders such as president Reagan, prime minister Thatcher, prime minister Rabin, and prime minister Blair vigorously asserted that they would 'never negotiate' with 'terrorists'. Reagan's 'Irangate', Thatcher's 'back channel' negotiations with the IRA, Rabin's peace process with the PLO, and Blair's face-to-face negotiations with IRA leaders in Sinn Fein are, however, classic demonstrations of how political pragmatism can trump ideological repulsion in negotiations with insurgents and 'terrorists'. Harsh and seemingly intransigent rhetoric from actors about non-negotiation tends to be a political by-product of any conflict, even while the very same actors are secretly in active negotiating mode. Furthermore, assertions about non-negotiation are often a deliberate strategy in the pre-negotiation phase, as protagonists entrench and harden their positions in advance of bargaining and compromise. These methods are particularly significant in the context of the current war in Chechnya.

Conceptualizing Peace in Chechnya

Many conflicts are intractable because the protagonists contest the very basis of what the conflict is about. The contested idioms, perhaps best encapsulated by the old adage bequeathed by decades of colonial insurgencies that 'one person's terrorist is another's freedom fighter', are critical not only for how conflicts are framed by the protagonists, but also for how each side shapes public and international perceptions. Whether an insurgency is 'criminalised' as a 'terrorist' problem by one party, will clearly have a formative effect on that actor's strategies, and in particular its military strategy. Comparative experience shows that media management is an important instrument in this battle of idioms and perceptions.

The Russian political elite generally offers a structural, ethnic, and ideological rationale for the roots of the conflict in Chechnya. First, the structural causes are seen as deriving from social problems in the region such as poverty and backwardness. Second, the ethnic roots of the conflict are attributed to the oft-cited 'historical enmity', an interpretation equally favoured by Western journalists. In Russia and Chechnya historicist views tend to reflect racist stereotypes; the Russian view of the Chechens, for example, stresses their supposed violence and criminality. Third, the ideological factor in the conflict has received increasing attention from Russians as the conflict has evolved and presently borders on a paranoid fear that Chechens are Islamic radicals. Consequently, the conflict is frequently interpreted in Russia as one of the fault lines in Huntington's cultural war between 'Western civilization' and 'Islam'. In fact, if we compare the Chechen war with comparable conflicts it is evident that this kind of threefold rationale, stressing backwardness, race and religion, is not particular to Chechnya but is common to colonialist elites engaged in counter-insurgency.

As noted earlier, idiomatic and ideological barriers are not insurmountable. However, greater complexity and difficulties arise when a conflict involves disputed shared territory, or when some divisions are reinforcing, for example religious, ethnic and territorial cleavages. In these cases the differing views of 'what the conflict is about' compound the cost-benefit calculations made with regard to any exit from the conflict through negotiation and compromise, and thereby greatly reduce the possibilities of any potential settlement. Similarly, the definition of what constitutes a 'solution' may radically differ across the parties to a conflict to such an extent that negotiation becomes almost impossible. A sensible compromise for some may be a 'sell-out' to others, and a 'just peace' may be derided as a 'capitulation to terrorists'. Where there is what Horowitz has termed a 'meta-conflict' over the very conceptualisation of the issues at stake, the potential for agreement is more difficult to achieve.[2]

There is no 'meta-conflict' in Chechnya. While many of the accounts of the conflict tend towards historicist and conspiracy theory interpretations of the causes of the conflict, there is a broad agreement among the parties that the core issue is secession (generally referred to as 'separatism' by successive Russian presidents and governments).[3] This common view of the conflict should however be distinguished from difference within and between the parties involved in the conflict. The use of the terms 'Russians' and 'Chechens' to describe the protagonists, for example, is a misleading oversimplification. The 'Russian' side of the conflict is best

[2] See Donald L. Horowitz, *A Democratic South Africa?: Constitutional Engineering in a Divided Society* (Berkeley, University of California Press, 1991), p. 2.
[3] For a critical analysis of the literature on the causes of the conflict see James Hughes, 'Chechnya: The Causes of a Protracted Post-Soviet Conflict', *Civil Wars*, Vol. 4, No. 4, Winter 2001, pp. 11–48.

categorized by dividing it into pro-interventionist and anti-interventionist, or pro-militarist and anti-militarist positions. These positions cut across Russian politics, as support for either is drawn from the elites to the right and left of the political spectrum. On the 'Chechen' side, the differences among the elites are both regional and sociological. The lowland steppe regions of Nadterechny and Grozny were historically the most integrated into the Soviet regime, and the elites of the former in particular continue to have closer, more collaborative relations with Russia. The less modernized highland regions of the south of Chechnya are historically bastions of anti-Russian sentiment, and it is these regions that form the heartland of support for the insurgency.[4] Furthermore, we can distinguish between the two periods of military conflict (1994–6 and 1999–present) each of which is characterized by issues and differences.

The common view of the conflict as a straightforward war of secession has been increasingly eroded by a dual radicalization of the protagonists as the conflict has become more protracted.[5] In particular, the intra-elite competition for power that has fragmented the Chechen insurgents after Chechnya's independence was recognised de facto by Russia in 1996, has led to a further 'meta-cleavage' on the Chechen side, along a religious fault line. The second period of military conflict from late 1999 has shown this to be the most significant bone of contention between Chechen insurgents. The independence movement composed of largely secular and traditional Sufi Islamicist factions, broadly led by Aslan Maskhadov, has increasingly been challenged and sidestepped by a growing faction of foreign Wahhabi-influenced and Al-Qaeda-linked Islamic fundamentalists under Shamil Basaev, who aspire not only to achieve an independent Chechnya but also seek a jihad to create a Caliphate across the whole of the North Caucasus. This rift is exaggerated by tactical divisions. Maskhadov's forces have conducted a military campaign of guerrilla operations against the Russian military within Chechnya; Basaev, while doing the same, has also tended to organize spectacular, headline-grabbing terrorist acts against civilians in the Russian Federation proper.

This religious and tactical schism was evident as far back as the Budennovsk hospital siege in June 1995, when women and children were targeted in an operation led by Basaev, but it has become the defining cleavage in the Chechnya conflict since the renewal of war in the Autumn of 1999. The competition among Chechen leaders to control the insurgency led some traditionalists such as Mufti Akhmad Kadyrov, who feared the growing power of the Islamic fundamentalists, to abandon the armed struggle altogether and to collaborate with Russia's 'Chechenization' policy under Putin. The proselytising, militant version of Islam that informs the Basaev group makes this new schism a significant added complication for

---

[4] Hughes, 'Chechnya', pp. 18–24.
[5] Hughes, 'Chechnya', pp. 34–6.

the peace process, both from the perspective of the main insurgent forces under Maskhadov, and for Putin and the Russian government. Nevertheless, the main issue at the core of the conflict that must be addressed by the peace process is the issue of secession.

Secession: The Core Issue

For the Chechen secessionists, their right to self-determination and independence from the colonial power – the former USSR and its successor state the Russian Federation – is paramount and legitimate. For the Russian interventionists, the secession of Chechnya is a threat to Russian statehood, as it undermines the territorial integrity and sovereignty of Russia: it must be prevented at all costs. To understand why the secession of Chechnya is such a problematic issue, it is important to locate it within the international norms that govern the recognition of new states. In general, the right to self-determination has been highly circumscribed in international practice and law; it has been geographically confined and temporally constrained.[6] The UN Charter of 1948, which enshrined the right to self-determination of 'peoples', contains an inherent obstacle to the exercise of this 'right', in that 'peoples' is not a defined category. Exceptionally, disputed territories have been given an indeterminate status, but the charter has been invoked conservatively to reinforce the status quo. The acceptance of new states by the international system has been governed by the experience of decolonization, which embedded the doctrine of *uti possidetis juris* as part of customary international law. This is a conservative doctrine, which holds that new states may be formed on the basis of the highest administrative units and within the established administrative borders of the colonial era, and discourages the unilateral redrawing of boundaries by secession or territorial seizure.[7]

The collapse of communism gave rise to a host of secessionist claims, concentrated in the federal states of the USSR and Yugoslavia, some of which have been recognized by the international system and many of which have not. Broadly, in the case of the USSR the international system followed the colonial–era doctrine of *uti possidetis*. Thus, the fifteen 'Union Republics' were recognized as independent new states, while assertions of

---

[6] For a discussion of the issues of secession and international relations in the post-Soviet context see James Hughes and Gwendolyn Sasse, 'Comparing Regional and Ethnic Conflicts in Post-Soviet Transition States', in James Hughes and Gwendolyn Sasse (eds), *Ethnicity and Territory in the Former Soviet Union: Regions in Conflict* (London, Frank Cass, 2002), pp. 12–20. For the issue of secession in the case of Chechnya, see Richard Sakwa, 'A Just War Fought Unjustly', in Bruno Coppeters and Richard Sakwa (eds), *Contextualizing Secession: Normative Studies in Comparative Perspective* (Oxford, Oxford University Press, 2003), pp. 156–86.

[7] For further analysis of *uti possidetis* and the international legal aspects of secession see Malcolm Shaw, *International Law*, 5th edition (Cambridge, Cambridge University, 2004), pp. 46–51, and chapters 8 and 9 passim.

secession by other administrative entities, such as those by autonomous republics, have not been recognized. This situation has led to a number of 'frozen' conflicts, in which entities have de facto independence but exist with an indeterminate status in the international system. The international system was less consistent in its practice with regard to Yugoslavia. For example, the Badinter Commission of the European Community (EC) advised in November 1991 that the secessions from Yugoslavia should be recognized because the state was 'in a process of dissolution'.[8] This radical, if tautological, position was an attempt to reconcile EC political interests and international customary law on secession. The conservatism of the international system towards secession was however reasserted after the Kosovo war of 1999, when the rule of the territory was turned over to a UN administration while nominally remaining under Federal Republic of Yugoslavia (FRY) sovereignty.

The greatest test for international norms on secession arises in cases where there is no agreement between the parties and where the entity aspiring to self-determination falls outside the administrative category recognised under *uti possidetis*. Both of these factors apply in the case of the conflict in Chechnya. Much, then, hinges on whether the inclusion or incorporation of Chechnya into the new post-Soviet state, the Russian Federation, in January 1992 was legal or illegal or of dubious legality. Indeed, we should distinguish between the material, moral and legal aspects of the right of Chechnya to self-determination. I will now examine these issues in reverse order.

Material

The notion that economic self-sufficiency is an essential attribute of a state is spurious. Historically, not only have many of the states that have been accorded the right to self-determination not been self-sufficient, they have remained heavily dependent economically on their former colonial rulers. Many states in the UN are wholly impoverished and dependent on external assistance. Moreover, in an increasingly interdependent world, few states are truly economically self-sufficient. While Chechnya holds minor oil deposits and was an important oil-refining base in the Soviet era, the destruction of its economic infrastructure by almost a decade of war makes the issue of its economic attributes redundant in the medium term. The questions of the moral and legal aspects of self-determination for Chechnya are more complex.

Moral

The morality of secession or self-determination for a 'people' is generally determined by the strength of association between 'people' and territory,

---

[8] See Roland Rich, 'Recognition of States: The Collapse of Yugoslavia and the Soviet Union', *European Journal of International Law*, Vol. 4, 1993, pp. 36–65.

whether this is an uncontested association (i.e., are there other groups residing on the territory with an equal claim?), and whether the demand is legitimated by an articulation of popular opinion, for example by elections or referenda. The morality of Chechnya's claim is contestable in two respects. First, about one-quarter of the population of Chechnya were non-indigenous, mainly Russophone Slavs, in 1991.[9] The bulk of this substantial minority were in effect forcibly expelled between 1991 and 1993 by inter-ethnic harassment and violence that was tolerated by the secessionist government in Chechnya. A strong case could be made for the secessionists in Chechnya attempting to strengthen their claim to self-determination by engaging in 'ethnic cleansing' and that, consequently, it would be wrong of the international system to legitimize secession consolidated by such means. Second, the idea that the current territory of Chechnya corresponds to an historical Chechen homeland is contestable because two regions of northern Chechnya bordering Russia, the regions of Naursky and Shelkovsky, were transferred from Russian jurisdiction to Chechnya under Khrushchev in 1957. Consequently, the use of a referendum by the Dudaev regime in November 1992 to assert the moral legitimacy of its claim to secession must be qualified by the above factors.

Legal

The legal dimension of Chechnya's secession is best understood by analysing it within the context of the collapse of the USSR. It is widely assumed that the recognition of post-Soviet states by the international system was founded on the right of Union Republics to secede under Soviet law, on the basis that they were constituent 'members' of the USSR, and were thus the only administrative tier that met the condition of *uti possidetis*. This ignores three crucial legal landmarks passed by the USSR Congress of People's Deputies during Gorbachev's *perestroika* that radically transformed the constitutional architecture of Soviet federalism: the law of 3 April 1990 'On the Procedure for Deciding Questions Concerning the Withdrawal of a Union Republic from the USSR'; the law of 10 April 1990 'On Principles of Economic Relations of the USSR, the Union and Autonomous Republics'; and the law of 26 April 1990 'On the Delimitation of Powers Between the USSR and the Subjects of Federation'. These laws eradicated core features of the constitutional distinction between Union Republics and Autonomous Republics; both were now given equal status as 'subjects of the federation'. At a time when some Union Republics – including Russia under Yeltsin – were claiming 'sovereignty' and demanding independence, and Gorbachev was desperately attempting to shore up the crumbling political order of the

---

[9] According to the 1989 USSR census the population of areas now in Chechnya comprised just over one million persons, around 715,000 of whom declared themselves as Chechens, 269,000 as Russians, and about 25,000 as Ingush.

USSR, this law created a constitutional potential for a domino effect of secessionism, as Article One of the law of 26 April gave all subjects of the federation the right to 'free self-determination'. The combined effect of the laws was to make any secessionist Union Republic exercising its right to 'sovereignty' under the 1977 Soviet Constitution liable to a challenge of similar secessionist demands from its own Autonomous Republic(s). This was not a threat to the Baltic states, which had no autonomous areas, but it was a serious potential danger for Russia, the Union Republic which contained most Autonomous Republics.[10] This kind of political manoeuvre is not unusual in state break-ups, as the centre attempts to constrain secessionism by arguing that peripheries within the secessionist unit should also have the right of secession.

The Capacity for Secession

The constitutional changes legitimized a whole new political discourse in the USSR, characterized by the language of 'delimiting powers', 'power-sharing', 'sovereignty', 'secession' and 'separatism'. In the summer of 1990,Yeltsin himself further legitimated the discourse of declaring 'sovereignty' within Russia. The secessionist movement in Chechnya that began to assert itself under Dudaev's leadership in late 1991 held that the USSR laws cited above established the right of an Autonomous Republic to decide its own fate: to sign up voluntarily to Gorbachev's draft 'Union Treaty' of May 1991, or to leave the USSR. The latter option seemed the most appropriate in conditions when the USSR appeared to be in the process of disintegration, as was the case after the August 1991 coup. While the Zavgaev leadership of the Checheno-Ingush Republic was one of the least separatist and among the most conservative in the USSR, and its contribution to the 'parade of sovereignties' by a 'Declaration on State Sovereignty' of 27 November 1990 was one of the last in the USSR, the republic remained arguably de jure – and certainly de facto – sovereign outside the USSR within the terms of Soviet Constitutional law, in the absence of a constitutional ratification of the new Union Treaty (pre-empted by the August coup).

While most of Russia's autonomous republics declared their sovereignty with the proviso that they remained 'within the RSFSR' (Russian Soviet Federal Socialist Republic), there were two exceptions that saw themselves as fully independent states: Checheno-Ingushetia and Tatarstan. Both of these republics persisted with their sovereignty claims after the breakup of the Soviet Union in December 1991. When the Russian Federation reconstitutionalized itself in a Federal Treaty of March 1992, neither Checheno-Ingushetia nor Tatarstan participated.[11] Both republics refused to recognize

---

[10] The law has also been employed as a justification for secessions of other autonomous regions, such as the Autonomous Area of Nagorno-Karabakh from Azerbaijan.
[11] Subsequently in July 1992, Ingushetia and Chechnya separated by mutual agreement and Ingushetia signed the Federal Treaty.

the authority of the Russian president or parliament. Neither republic participated in the Russian parliament or other governing bodies, nor did they hold elections to the new Duma or conduct the referendum to ratify a new constitution in December 1993. In political and constitutional spheres, these republics acted as if they were independent states outside the jurisdiction of Russia, akin to the other newly independent states that had been union republics of the USSR. On the other hand, both republics continued to operate within Russia's fiscal federal system by accepting subventions from the Russian budget – in order to pay government salaries and pensions, for example – though without transferring tax and other federal revenues to Moscow. However, unlike Tatarstan, which is located in the heart of European Russia, Chechnya's geographic position on the Caucasus frontier – bordering Georgia and at one remove Azerbaijan, newly independent states that were also keen to distance themselves from Russia – was a key factor in its capacity to assert its secession and in Russia's inability to constrain it effectively.

If geography enhanced Chechnya's capacity to assert its independence, it was the militarization of the secessionist movement, partly through Russian support, that provided the means for Chechnya to defend its newly won freedom. Soviet military hardware in Chechnya was transferred or abandoned by Russian military forces in late 1991 and early 1992, and *matériel* was also seized or purchased from the Russian military by the secessionists. Moreover, once Russian governmental authority was removed from the republic, the secessionist government of Dudaev became closely involved in Russian military corruption and arms trading.[12] As former Soviet military officers, Dudaev and his chief lieutenant Aslan Maskhadov were acutely aware of the need to militarize Chechnya in order to resist any attempt by the Yeltsin government to force it back into the Russian Federation.

The Yeltsin administration that consolidated its power after the August coup was more concerned initially with reinforcing its authority internally over the Russian regions, and subsequently with economic reform, than with reasserting Russian sovereignty over secessionist republics such as Chechnya and Tatarstan. Russia's historic involvement and perceptions of its immediate strategic security and economic interests in the North and South Caucasus region made interference in Chechnya inevitable. Dudaev won the presidential and parliamentary elections in October 1991, and viewed them as a referendum on, and mandate to declare, independence. He formally declared independence in his first decree as president on 1 November 1991. In response Yeltsin declared a state of emergency (though this was unenforceable given the withdrawal of Russian forces from Chechnya), and a standoff ensued that could only be settled by force or

---

[12] See Robert Seely, *Russo-Chechen Conflict, 1800–2000: A Deadly Embrace* (London, Frank Cass, 2001), pp. 212–15.

negotiation. The refusal of the international system to recognize Chechnya's secession meant ignoring the changes in the Soviet constitutional order in the late Gorbachev era. In practice, the collapse of the USSR was treated as a case of decolonisation the outcome of which was to be determined by the innate conservatism of the principle of *uti possidetis*. Western interests in shoring up the Yeltsin regime, and fears of instability in Russia strengthened the trend for policy caution in Europe and the USA. The potential for international leverage to influence the negotiation of a peaceful resolution to the Chechnya question by pressurising Russia was sacrificed to Western interests which stressed support for the 'reformers' under Yeltsin.

Fluctuations in the Peace Process

The peace process in Chechnya has broadly involved fluctuation between, on the one hand, military coercion and negotiation, and between favouring internal and external solutions in the peace process on the other (see Appendices). These fluctuations are partly driven by changes in the balance of military power in the course of the conflict, and partly by changes in how the conflict has been instrumentalized by political leaders in pursuit of other goals un-connected with the conflict per se. In particular, the dynamic between conflict and peace process has been strongly shaped by power struggles within both Russian and Chechen camps. Both positions have alternated between a search for a power-sharing treaty that would keep Chechnya under Russian sovereignty but with a special autonomy status and a large degree of self-rule, or an agreement that would provide recognition of Chechnya's de facto or de jure secession. These fluctuations have also been reflected in two key policy dimensions that have characterized the peace process: Chechenization and internationalization.

Policy Fluctuations in the Peace Process

Internal Solution	*External Solution*
Power-sharing Treaty	Treaty of Recognition
Chechenization	Internationalization

Political Uses of Conflict and Peace

In Russia the Chechnya issue has been exploited in different ways by competing political forces from the outset, and three main types of exploitation can be identified. First, in the period 1991–3 the issue was employed by both sides in the president versus parliament conflict as both Ruslan Khasbulatov (the speaker of the Russian parliament) and Yeltsin competed to reach a deal either with Dudaev or with other groups in Chechnya as a means to enhance their standing in the eyes of the Russian public. Yeltsin's decision to go to war in December 1994 was partly an attempt to outflank Khasbulatov's efforts to rebuild his authority by mediating a peace deal with Dudaev; it was a decision taken under the illusion that a 'short victorious war' would be the outcome and would serve to boost Yeltsin's political authority in Russia. Second, the push for a peace agreement intensified in the run-up to the presidential election of 1996. By this time the Russia military was bogged down in a classic counter-insurgency involving guerrilla war, terror and counter-terror. The economic and political costs for Yeltsin appeared to be unsustainable, given the mounting military and civilian casualties and the reporting of the conflict's horrors by non-state controlled media such as NTV.

Yeltsin's unconvincing performance in the first round of the June 1996 presidential election considerably weakened his authority, as did the subsequent decision to coopt Alexander Lebed into his administration as head of the Security Council in order to secure victory in the second round. The late summer of 1996 presented a small window of opportunity to push through a peace settlement, when Lebed's authority was sufficiently strong within the presidential administration and government.

The third type of exploitation of the Chechnya issue in Russian politics occurred during August-September 1999, when Putin – by then Yeltsin's designated presidential heir-apparent – seized upon the opportunity presented by Basaev's and Khattab's incursion into Dagestan and the apartment bombings in Moscow and other cities to launch a new war against Chechnya. As in December 1994, the war policy was driven by an illusion within the Russian governing elite that such a war would be short and victorious, thereby allowing Putin to ride a wave of patriotism to claim the presidency in a 'khaki election' in March 2000. Events have demonstrated, however, that Putin has been incapable of developing his Chechen policy beyond the war aims of 1999–2000. While the overwhelming use of Russian military power secured an early ousting of Maskhadov's government, as well as the dispersal of Chechen forces and considerable further destruction of the social and economic infrastructure of Chechnya, the conflict soon returned to the pattern of insurgency and counter-insurgency, terrorism and counter-terrorism, that bogged down Russian forces in 1995–6.

Within the Chechen secessionist movement, questions of conflict and peace have been seized upon by two broad groups in establishing their authority. These are the largely secular forces of Dudaev and his successor Maskhadov; and the radicalized Wahhabist inspired groups led by Basaev. When Dudaev seized power in 1991 he saw himself as the leader of a secular anti-colonial nationalist movement. The Chechen constitution of March 1992 reflected his nationalist and secular ideals. The speedy militarization of his nationalist forces after the August coup, with Russian assistance, was one of the factors that helped Dudaev to take and consolidate power in Chechnya, but we should also not underestimate the popular appeal of his radical nationalist vision of an independent Chechnya. Dudaev is often described as lacking in political skills, yet his hardline stance against any internal settlement within the Russian Federation allowed him successfully to outflank potential rivals, both those old *nomenklatura* collaborationist elites that aspired to reintegrate with Russia, and more moderate opponents within the Chechen nationalist movement. Similarly, Dudaev's successor Maskhadov skilfully turned military victory against Russia in summer 1996 into political victory, by winning the presidential election in Chechnya in January 1997 and by securing a peace treaty with Russia in May 1997 that brought de facto recognition of independence. Maskhadov failed, however, to transform these successes into a legitimating device for consolidating his power in Chechnya because of the refusal of a radicalized minority under Basaev to accept the peace agreement with Russia. The nature of the 1994–6 war had opened up Chechen military formations to the influence of the radicalized Wahhabist Islam that had previously inspired, armed and financed Afghan resistance to Soviet occupation forces in 1980–8 war. By 1998 Basaev's radical forces were similarly influenced by Arab Islamic internationalists led by Khattab, who advocated an Islamic jihad against Russia. The radical Islamicists challenged and undermined the authority of Maskhadov's government, which was seen as insufficiently 'Islamic' despite the appointment of Basaev as prime minister and the introduction of a Sharia law code in February 1999. Seeking to radicalize the political environment in Chechnya, Basaev led an incursion by his fighters into Dagestan in summer 1999. The attack may well have been intended to precipitate an all-out Russian military invasion of Chechnya, not only to initiate the jihad across the North Caucasus, but also to pre-empt any further consolidation by Maskhadov's government.

This fundamental division within the Chechen secessionist movement between radicalised Islamicists and largely secular forces has had a major impact on the peace process. On the one hand, the spectacular terrorist attacks on Russian Federation targets that have been organized, funded or inspired by the Basaev group allows Russia to label all Chechen secessionist forces as 'terrorists' and are used by Putin to justify his non-negotiation policy. Furthermore, international support for Maskhadov, which was hesitant even in 1997–9, has been further marginalized since due to several developments: evidence of direct links between Basaev's group and Al-Qaeda; the increasingly cautious policy towards support for insurgents suspected of 'terrorism' internationally in light of the 'War on Terror'; and a trend towards a pro-Putin policy in the USA and the most powerful EU states such as the UK, Germany, France and Italy. In the aftermath of the Beslan massacre, the divisions within the Chechen secessionist movement have polarized the two main groups, with Maskhadov undertaking to put Basaev on trial for murder.

So, while there is an essential continuity in the conflict over time in that the core issue that is at stake remains secession – or put another way, the right of Chechnya to self-determination – there are important discontinuities that have critically affected the peace process. The protracted nature of the conflict, the increasing radicalization of the protagonists, the changed international environment after 9/11 – all these issues have brought to a halt the fluctuation between war and negotiation that was evident under Yeltsin. Putin's policy has been more rigidly oriented toward finding a military solution and, consequently, the prospects for a renewed peace process have diminished significantly since his election as Russian president in March 2000.

The Search for a Power-Sharing Treaty

In the period between the coup of August 1991 and the Russian military invasion in December 1994, there were three principal attempts by the Russian government to secure an internal settlement in Chechnya. The first was Ruslan Khasbulatov's trip to northern Chechnya in October 1992, which was approved by the Russian parliament as an attempt to outflank Yeltsin. Khasbulatov's self styled 'peace mission' was essentially an attempt to sow internal divisions within Chechnya by offering inducements to the residual old Soviet Nadterechny *nomenklatura* elite actively to oppose Dudaev. Though Khasbulatov's visit was a failure, Yeltsin recognized the political need to have a peace process in tandem with his then policy of aggressive blockade. Negotiators sent by Yeltsin in 1993 initially included Russian experts, such as Galina Starovoitova and Valery Tishkov, who were sensitive to the political complexity of nationality issues, but they were unable to bridge the gap between the Russian and Chechen positions.

To manage the separatism in Chechnya and Tatarstan the Yeltsin administration employed a special constitutional device, the power-sharing treaty. Such treaties were provided for though only vaguely defined by, the constitution of 1993. They were highly controversial because the Russian political elite, in particular the regional elites, were opposed to any special 'privileging' of Russia's titular ethnic republics, especially with regard to economic powers and any symbolic 'sovereign' status. This kind of 'asymmetric federalism' was viewed widely within the Russian political elite as undermining Russia's 'single' constitutional space, encouraging separatism, destabilizing the political situation and threatening Russia's territorial integrity.[13] Most of the special powers that had been allocated to the republics by the Federal Treaty had been eliminated by the new constitution. Consequently, Yeltsin was compelled to bypass the Russian parliament and negotiate the new power-sharing treaties directly with Tatarstan and other key republics as a kind of presidential federal arrangement.

---

[13] For asymmetric federalism in Russia see James Hughes, 'Managing Secession Potential in the Russian Federation' in Hughes and Sasse (eds), *Ethnicity and Territory in the Former Soviet Union*, pp. 36–68.

The treaty with Tatarstan, signed in February 1994, gave the republic a special status of 'association' with Russia, and involved the devolution of extensive powers of political, economic and cultural self-rule (see Chapter 3). As the negotiations with Tatarstan reached a conclusion in late 1993 and early 1994 Yeltsin and his key constitutional adviser Shakhrai focussed on securing a similar power-sharing treaty with Dudaev.

The negotiations over a power-sharing treaty faced two major obstacles. The first was how to reconcile the Chechen demand for independence with Russia's demand for Chechnya to remain under Russian sovereignty. The use of what has recently been termed 'constructive ambiguity' has often played a significant role in providing the necessary terminological fudges to assist with the conclusion of peace agreements. Whether such a device, which is after all a ruse, can provide a lasting basis for peace in a situation where a core principle such as sovereignty must be negotiated is questionable, though it can provide an interim solution.[14] In the case of the treaty with Tatarstan, both Russia and Tatarstan had accepted a 'constructive ambiguity' over the sovereignty question by employing the term 'association' to describe Tatarstan's connection with the Russian Federation, and by the Yeltsin administration's toleration of language in the Tatarstan constitution that declared the republic to be a 'sovereign state'.[15] Such a fudge was not possible in Chechnya because Dudaev insisted on clarity rather than ambiguity over the question of independence. The negotiations were also hampered by the fact that Dudaev was a very different leader to Shaimiev, the president of Tatarstan. Shamiev and most of his ruling cadre were former Soviet communist party *apparatchiks* and as such were thoroughly sovietized, far from being avowed nationalists – and were suitably deferential to Yeltsin when it mattered. Not only were their values, behaviour and thinking were closely aligned with their counterparts in the Yeltsin team, but they were more interested in securing concessions over economic control of assets within the republic, especially oil processing and manufacturing industries, than in defending the principle of independence per se. All of this made for a much more comfortable negotiating environment and wider parameters for compromise.

Many accounts of the failure of the power-sharing treaty process in the case of Chechnya have stressed personality issues in the clash between Yeltsin and Dudaev and primordial ethnic rivalries. Since neither leader ever met face-to-face, any personal animus that existed was at one remove. The fundamental obstacle to a treaty was an irreconcilable difference of opinion regarding the acceptability of the principle of an internal solution.

---

[14] The term originated in the discussion that led to the Oslo Accords of 1993 between Israel and the PLO. The concept was taken up by negotiators in other conflicts, most notably by Irish and British civil servants in the long build up to the Belfast Agreement of 1998. This agreement has, however, broken down because of the lack of clarity on key issues.
[15] See Hughes, 'Managing Secession Potential'.

Certainly, the negotiating environment was in marked contrast to that concerning Tatarstan. As a former soviet air force general, Dudaev was an outsider to the old Soviet party *nomenklatura* networks and their operating codes. Moreover, he was a convert to nationalism and was antipathetic to any concession that would dilute Chechnya's independence and allow Russia to maintain its 'colonial' rule. It was Dudaev's charismatic speech to the June 1991 meeting of the National Congress of the Chechen People (NCCP), in which he rejected 'colonial freedom' or any 'hybrid' version of sovereignty, that established him as the leader of the nationalist movement in Chechnya. Unlike Shaimiev, who exploited the issue of separatism for other ends, Dudaev was a convinced secessionist who believed in the morality, legality and necessity of independence for Chechnya; he made these values abundantly clear in his public speeches and interviews, and in his private meetings with representatives of Yeltsin. Whether from a principled stance, a lack of political nous or because of a military-instilled decisiveness, Dudaev's refusal to compromise on the core issue of secession created an impasse to an internal settlement. This factor above all others impelled the policy of the Yeltsin administration down the route to a military solution and led to the invasion of December 1994.

Treaty of Recognition

The context for the next major landmark in the peace process was the defeat and encirclement of Russian military forces in Chechnya in summer 1996. To avoid a catastrophic military and political defeat for Russia and for his presidency, Yeltsin was forced to make major concessions to Chechnya in its independence struggle. Yeltsin craftily remained personally aloof from the negotiations, sending the head of the Security Council, Alexander Lebed, with a supposed *carte blanche* to extricate Russia from the cataclysm. Truce negotiations were held with a Chechen delegation led by Maskhadov (Dudaev having been assassinated by Russia in April 1996) at the village of Khasavyurt in neighbouring Dagestan in August 1996. For the first time in the peace process the key negotiators were like-minded, connected in both career training and character – both were products of the Soviet officer corps. The mutual respect between Lebed and Maskhadov was conducive to the negotiations. Moreover, the Chechens now had a Russian negotiating partner who was prepared to compromise on the issue of sovereignty and self-rule, and who at that time appeared to have the necessary political collateral to ensure its implementation by the Russian side. The negotiations were attended by the head of the OSCE-Assistance Group in Chechnya, Tim Guldimann, whose presence was acknowledged by both sides to be a significant factor in striking an agreement.

The agreement at Khasavyurt (see Appendix 1) reflected a shift from previous Russian policy towards the peace process, moving away from the search for an internalized solution that would retain Russian sovereignty of

Chechnya in a power-sharing treaty akin to the Tatarstan 'model', towards de facto recognition of independence. The direct negotiation with Chechen military leaders, and the agreement of a military truce to be monitored by joint military patrols was a recognition by Russia of the Chechen forces' legitimacy. The text of the Joint Statement stressed that both parties aimed to resolve the conflict through international norms, and specifically cited international law on self-determination, minority protection, the Universal Declaration of Human Rights of 1949 and the International Covenant on Civil and Political Rights of 1966. This form of 'internationalization' was reiterated in the 'Principles' for determining the future relations between Russia and Chechnya that were appended to the Joint Statement. The Principles also established a Joint Commission to decide on the Russian military withdrawal, measures to combat crime terrorism and ethnic violence (aimed at protecting Russians still living in Chechnya), future economic relations, reconstruction and emergency aid.

The Chechens could claim to have won recognition and the internationalization of the conflict, while equally the Russians could claim to have averted de jure recognition of independence. Nevertheless, the agreement was a de facto recognition of Chechnya's independence and was widely understood as such. However, the core issue of the secession struggle, legal sovereignty, was postponed for future negotiation. The agreement stipulated that the negotiations over the nature of the relations between Russia and Chechnya should be decided before 31 December 2001 (i.e., a period of five years and four months), but that they should be governed by the 'generally accepted principles and norms of international law'. The formulation was an example of 'constructive ambiguity' to move the peace process forward and appears to have been influenced by Guldimann.[16] The formulation derived from Guldimann's advocacy of the benefits of international intervention in ethnic conflicts, and in particular of the use of international leverage on states to ensure compliance with the 'internationally accepted standards and rules' of the 'international community'.[17] In the case of the conflict in Chechnya, however, Guldimann's belief in international leverage on Russia was misplaced.

Maskhadov's decisive victory (polling 65 per cent of the vote) over Basaev in the January 1997 presidential elections held in Chechnya, which were declared 'democratic and free' by international monitors, established the legitimacy of his government not only internally within Chechnya and

---

[16] See Ivan Rybkin, *Consent in Russia, Consent in Chechnya* ([no place of publication], Lytten Trading and Investment Ltd, Abacus Trust and Management Services Ltd, 1998), pp. 229–30. The moratorium on the status issue had a precedent in a similar arrangement in the Chechen-Ingush agreement on partition of July 1991.

[17] For Guldimann's views on international intervention see *Tim Guldimann*, 'International Intervention: Improved Conditions – Deficient Implementation – a Learning Process', Center for Development Research (ZEF Bonn): Facing Ethnic Conflicts (14–16 December 2000), pp. 1–6. *http://www.zef.de/download/ethnic_conflict/guldimann.pdf.*

in Russia, but also internationally. Full recognition of the sovereign status of Chechnya, however, required an agreement with Russia. A formal peace treaty between Russia and the 'Chechen Republic of Ichkeria' (see Appendix 2) was signed at a televised ceremony in the Kremlin on 12 May 1997, though it was highly unusual in form, and unlike any of the power-sharing treaties that Yeltsin had signed with Tatarstan and other republics of the Russian Federation. In theory, the May 1997 treaty was significant because it locked the Yeltsin leadership into the peace process – the Khasavyurt agreement had been made with Lebed, who had been sacked by Yeltsin in October 1996. The treaty also had a symbolic importance in that Maskhadov, previously denounced as a 'bandit' and 'terrorist' by the Yeltsin leadership, was now recognized as a legitimate president of Chechnya. It was, however, short and sparse on substance, lacking, for example, the detailed agreements on policy issues that accompanied the power-sharing treaty with Tatarstan. The treaty did little more than restate the basic principle of internationalization that was agreed at Khasavyurt, with both sides accepting that their mutual relations were to be regulated by 'standards of international law', and renouncing 'forever' the 'use or the threat of force in the resolution of any disputes between them'. Two further agreements on the integration of Chechnya into Russia's economic space and a common currency were signed at the same time.

The agreement of 1996 and treaty of 1997 have played a prominent role in determining Putin's post-2000 policy framework for managing the conflict in Chechnya, as Putin argues that the de facto recognition conceded by Russia at that time led to further chaos and the growth of 'terrorism'. In fact, despite the formal agreements and the Russian military withdrawal from Chechnya, there was no serious attempt from either side to negotiate on the core issue of sovereignty, or indeed to implement the subsidiary agreements. Russia failed to deliver the promised economic and reconstruction aid, and returned to its pre-invasion policy of blockade and subversion in Chechnya, and of attempting to secure its international isolation. Meanwhile, Maskhadov's government failed to deliver on the combating of crime, terrorism and ethnic violence.

Chechnya was consigned to a limbo in the international order. Western governments, especially the Clinton administration, were anxious to support the Yeltsin presidency at all costs, having set the tone of US policy by comparing Yeltsin's struggle with Chechen secessionists with Lincoln's epic struggle against the South.[18] With the exceptions of Estonia and the Taliban

---

[18] In April 1996 Clinton, referring to Russia's war in Chechnya at a summit with Yeltsin in the Kremlin, stated: 'I would remind you that we once had a civil war in our country... over the proposition that Abraham Lincoln gave his life for, that no state had a right to withdrawal from our union', *The Washington Post*, 23 April 1996. He barely mentions Chechnya in his memoirs, referring briefly twice to his complaints to Russia about 'excessive' use of force.

regime of Afghanistan, no foreign state normalized relations with Chechnya. When Maskhadov and his key deputies travelled abroad, they were not formally and publicly received by foreign governments.[19] Isolated and blockaded, Maskhadov's government lacked the capacity to manage a devastated society that had been brutalized, militarized and radicalized by two and half years of occupation by poorly disciplined and demoralized Russian troops. Without external support, furthermore, his government was unable to counter the proactive destabilization by the radical Islamicists, led by Basaev, who were opposed to the peace process. Consequently, a failure fully to implement the commitments undertaken in 1996–7 created conditions that allowed Chechnya to become, according to the 1998 and 1999 annual reports of the Assistance Group of the OSCE, a 'hotbed of crime and terror'.[20]

Putin's War and Peace

A preference for coercion rather than negotiation has been the dominant characteristic of Putin's policy towards Chechnya since his launching of a second war in September 1999 to boost his popularity with Russian voters as a 'strong' presidential successor to Yeltsin. Putin's training and experience as a KGB officer may have instilled in him an inclination to the use of violence as a policy instrument. A reticence to negotiate is also rational when coercion appears to be working, as it did in late 1999–early 2000. Moreover, even if Putin had wished to enter negotiations (and there is no evidence that he did) his room for compromise was severely constrained by nationalist sentiment in the Russian military high command. In November 1999 several leading Russian generals threatened to resign if Putin started negotiations before they had completed their military campaign. Subsequently, Putin brushed aside attempts to mediate by president Ruslan Aushev of Ingushetia and president Mintimer Shaimiev of Tatarstan.[21]

Despite his non-negotiation rhetoric, Putin has in fact kept the prospect of negotiations just above alive, but has set impossible preconditions (such as the complete disarmament of Chechen forces, the surrender of 'terrorists' such as Basaev, and the abandonment of the bid for independence) that have effectively stalled the peace process. Putin set this uncompromising agenda after the 9/11 attacks, and it formed the basis for the subsequent talks held near Sheremetevo airport between Russian presidential envoy for

[19] For example, Maskhadov visited the UK in March 1998 and met with government officials 'informally'; his Foreign Minister Ilyas Akhmadov met with a State Department official in January 2000.
[20] Organization for Security and Co-operation in Europe, Annual Reports 1998 and 1999: *http://www.osce.org/docs.*
[21] See *Moskovsky komsomolets,* 5 November 1999; *Nezavisimaya gazeta,* 12 April 2000.

the Southern Russia Federal District, General Viktor Kazantsev, and Maskhadov's envoy Akhmed Zakaev on 18 November 2001. The tenacity with which Russia pursued even the moderate insurgent leaders living abroad in 2001–3, seeking the extradition of Zakaev from the UK and Akhmadov from the USA, indicates just how remote an idea negotiations were for Putin.

The pursuit of a policy of coercion and non-negotiation has become less rational as it has become increasingly evident that this policy has demonstrably failed to deliver peace and security to either Chechnya or Russia. To some extent Putin's militarism and stubborn adherence to coercion over negotiations is a mirror image of the ideologically intransigent position of Basaev. This 'dual radicalization' has fuelled the intensity of the second war, which has developed into a spiral of terror and counter-terror alongside a more conventional insurgency. Putin's intransigence over negotiations with Maskhadov, however, has not simply been based on an ideologically driven and unsuccessful policy of coercion, but since 2002 has also been founded on a second platform that, he hoped, would make a critical contribution to the stabilization of Chechnya: the policy of Chechenization.

Chechenization

Proxy rule by a collaborationist indigenous elite to manage rebellious territories is an essential instrument in the imperialist's toolkit and, since 1991, Russia has periodically attempted to achieve this by implementing a policy of Chechenization. Under Yeltsin the policy relied on the promotion of several ex-communist party *nomenklatura* figures as a 'legal' and 'moderate' alternative leadership to the nationalists: Khajiev in February 1995 and Zavgaev in June 1996. Although Zavgaev had a regional base of support in Nadterechny, his credibility within Chechnya was irreparably damaged by his decision to back the August coup plotters and thereafter by his 'collaboration' with Russia. The Russian wager on Zavgaev was finally lost by the Russian military defeat in August 1996 and the democratic legitimization achieved by Maskhadov in the election of January 1997.

Russia's involvement in Chechnya is driven by the aim of retaining Chechnya under Russian sovereignty, and its policies towards the conflict are determined by that fundamental position. Equally, the introduction of a policy of proxy rule is inevitable at some point in a conflict's trajectory if long-term military occupation and direct rule is to be avoided. Proxy rule is an attractive option when the conflict induces war weariness and the increasing political costs of conflict are magnified by occupation and direct rule, especially where this does not succeed in limiting attacks by insurgents on targets in the occupier's homeland. It was rational for Putin to seek to return to the policy of Chechenization as a substitute for a real peace process once the immediate war aims of removing Maskhadov from power had been attained.

The major problem for Putin was to find a credible partner, a 'civilized' leader as he put it, on the Chechen side. In late 1999 he released from prison Beslan Gantemirov, a notorious former mayor of Grozny and Dudaev loyalist, in an unsuccessful attempt to form a pro-Moscow Chechen leadership. The policy of Chechenization was made viable only when Kadyrov, a leading figure in the resistance movement, decided to abandon the insurgency and help Putin in 1999. Kadyrov may have been motivated partly by personal ambition and partly by a concern with the desperate condition of the Chechen population, which was again subjected to arbitrary military occupation. He was also driven, however, by a fear of the growing sectarian Wahhabi influence on the insurgency.[22]

As under Yeltsin, the policy of Chechenization ended in failure for Putin, albeit for different reasons. There was an inherent contradiction in Putin's use of this policy, in that its success depended on a level of mutual trust between Russia and the collaborationist administration that could not in fact be realized. Attempts by Russia to build Kadyrov's authority barely moved beyond the rhetorical level, as Chechnya remained under de facto Russian military occupation and emergency rule. Moreover, the poor discipline of Russian forces and the exigencies of counter-terror operations, which involved systematic murder, torture and mass human rights abuses, could not but underline the puppet nature of the collaborationist administration and prevent it from accumulating credibility. As in the case of Zavgaev in 1996, Russia resorted to electoral fraud to secure a victory for Kadyrov in the referendum on a new 'constitution' held in March 2003, which affirmed Russian sovereignty over Chechnya, and the presidential election of October 2003. In the same way that Yeltsin did, Putin desperately sought a power-sharing treaty that would stabilize Chechnya. He offered to give Chechnya under Kadyrov's leadership 'autonomy in the broadest sense of the word' within the Russian constitution.[23] Putin's Chechenization policy was finally given the coup de grace by the assassination of Kadyrov in May 2004, which demonstrated the fragility of a policy that was founded on one Chechen leader.

The 'War on Terror'

Putin's justification for his policy of coercion in Chechnya has stressed not the principle of secession but the fact that the de facto independent

[22] Kadyrov's increasingly vocal criticism of Wahhabi influence on the insurgency led Maskhadov to remove him as Mufti in August 1999. Shortly after this, Kadyrov declared that he was ready to support Russia in Chechnya. He proclaimed the city of Gudermes as well as the Gudermes and Kurchaloi districts 'a Wahhabite-free territory' in October 1999, and was instrumental in their peaceful surrender to Russian forces. He was appointed by Putin to head the puppet Chechen civil administration on 12 June 2000.
[23] 'Remarks at Meeting with Head of the Administration of Chechnya Akhmed Kadyrov', 27 March 2003, President of Russia Official Web Portal.

Chechnya of 1996–9 was a failed state whose instability threatened Russia. Implicit in this is the suggestion that an independent Chechnya that was stable and non-threatening to Russia might be acceptable. As Putin explained in an interview shortly after 9/11, 'it is not an issue of Chechnya's membership, or non-membership, of the Russian Federation'; rather, it is the fact that Chechnya was an 'irresponsible quasi-state' that became 'a gangster enclave while the ideological vacuum was quickly filled by fundamentalist organisations'.[24] Putin has refined his position, however, to exploit opportunistically the new international climate brought about by the USA's 'war on terror'.

The systemic human rights abuses and atrocities perpetrated by Russian forces during the second Chechen war initially generated severe international criticism from Western governments and international organizations.[25] The criticism levelled by Western governments tended to speak diplomatically of Russia's 'excessive' use of force and to call for a negotiated settlement. This period of criticism peaked with the rare joint declaration by the United Nations, the OSCE and the Council of Europe on 8 December 1999 urging Russia to respect human rights in Chechnya. The Bush administration adopted a pragmatic approach to the issue of Chechnya. The natural Russia-bashing tendency of the Republican neocons was constrained by Bush after the Slovenia summit in June 2001, as the US prioritized securing concessions from Russia over the Anti-Ballistic Missile Treaty. The 9/11 attacks led to moral revulsion against anything remotely connected with 'terrorism'. Putin's imposition of stringent controls on media reports on the war greatly enhanced the Russian government's ability to shape the new idiom of the conflict. The tenuous associations between the Chechen radicals under Basaev and Al-Qaeda were emphasized, while Putin frequently – and with great irritation – brushed aside questioning by Western journalists. Putin has been consistent in branding the insurgency in Chechnya as a case of 'terrorism' and has made Russia a key actor in the international 'anti-terrorist coalition'.[26] By this means Russia has largely succeeded in portraying the whole Chechen insurgency an offshoot of 'international terrorism', and legitimizing its policy of coercion under the umbrella of the 'war on terror'. The international pressure on Putin over Chechnya eased in conjunction with the emergence of Kadyrov as the standard-bearer for the Chechenization policy. The combined effect of this was to give Putin no incentive to negotiate with Maskhadov, a position that

[24] Cited from an interview in *Focus*, 21 September 2001.
[25] For the human rights abuses see Anna Politkovskaya, *A Dirty War: A Russian Reporter in Chechnya* (London, Harvill, 2001).
[26] Examples of Putin's idiom on the conflict include declaring Chechnya 'a platform for the expansion of terrorism into Russia', 'hotbeds of terrorism', 'an outpost of international terrorism', a 'bandit enclave' for foreign-funded 'Islamic fundamentalists', a 'Medieval world'. See, for example, Putin, *Annual Address to the Federal Assembly*, 16 May 2003 and *Annual Address to the Federal Assembly*, 26 May 2004.

has been further entrenched by the international and domestic revulsion to the Beslan massacre.

Conclusion

Comparative experience of conflicts suggests that a common conceptualization of the conflict among the main protagonists is of fundamental importance for a peace process. This factor is present in Chechnya as the protagonists agree that the core issue is secession. Will Chechnya be a sovereign independent state or will it have broad autonomy through a power-sharing treaty with Russia? The peace process in Chechnya highlights the serious obstacles to a negotiated settlement over such a profoundly divisive issue. In April 2002 Putin declared that the 'military stage of the conflict can be considered to be completed'.[27] As the second war enters its sixth year, the prospects for either a military solution or a negotiated settlement seem more remote than ever. The basic conditions for a negotiated peace such as trust; propitious timing; conducive domestic and international climates; and the presence of skilful mediation are not currently evident in the case of Chechnya. In many conflict negotiations the most problematic issue is often pushed to the back of the agenda so that the peace process can be progressed, and 'constructive ambiguity' in wordplay plays a critical role in generating acceptable compromises. The negotiated settlement at Khasavyurt in 1996 and treaty of 1997 followed this pattern by their judicious use of ambiguity and postponement of a decision on secession. Postponing the most difficult issue has however not advanced peace and stability in Chechnya. The ambiguities of peacemaking left the de facto independent government of Maskhadov in limbo: neither Russia or the international community was locked into a process of reconstruction and state-building which would have helped to stabilize Chechnya. The lesson of the successful 1996–7 peace process is that in the absence of external support for an independent Chechnya and external pressure on Russia to comply with agreements, the entity was and would be easy prey for subversion by Islamic radicals.

The current lack of impetus for the Chechnya peace process is unprecedented. Mediation is unlikely, as the domestic mediators of the past have either retired (Aushev) or are being threatened by Putin's institutional reforms (Shaimiev); meanwhile, international actors are distracted by a largely illusory 'war on terror'. Putin retains a 'back channel' to Maskhadov, as was demonstrated by the Russian government's request to Maskhadov for assistance over Beslan (channelled through Zakaev in London). Putin may have placed a bounty on the heads of Basaev and Maskhadov, but this is illustrative of the harsh idiom of saying 'no to

---

[27] Putin, *Annual Address to the Federal Assembly*, 18 April 2002.

negotiation with terrorists', while engaging some of them, however remotely, behind the scenes. The fluctuation between war and peacemaking in Chechnya has diminished over time as the cycle of terror and counter-terror, together with a steely acceptance of the costs of a war of attrition, have hardened the militarist approach on both sides. Putin's policy instruments for managing the Chechnya conflict today are reduced to a 'one club' approach – to keep hammering the Chechen insurgency into submission, while the Chechen insurgents are increasingly taking the conflict to Russia itself through spectacular acts of terror. In the absence of negotiations, more of the same patterns of violence, or perhaps even worse, can be expected. In a Utopian setting, as Yeats said, 'peace comes dropping slow'; how much more demanding peace is to achieve in a protracted conflict like Chechnya.

Afterword

Lord Frank Judd

It was April 2000. Together with several colleagues I stood in the middle of Grozny. This was the second of nine visits I was to make to the Chechen Republic in the years 2000–3; the first had been in January, when the fighting made access to the capital impossible. Our group fell totally silent. In all directions the devastation of the city was terrible and total. Of those buildings still standing most would have to be demolished before effective reconstruction could begin. The streets through the rubble were deserted except for the Russian military and a handful of courageous citizens, mainly women, struggling to survive in the ruins of their homes. And this was at the beginning of the new millennium in a member state of the Council of Europe with all its commitment to peace, human rights and accountable democratic government. It would have been easy to despair.

By contrast, four years later, in July 2004, I was at Covent Garden in London. The stage of the Linbury Studio Theatre had been taken by storm by a group of incredible youth dancers from Grozny, who had travelled across Europe by bus. The audience was gripped. Their skill, style, vigour, vitality and enthusiasm were exhilarating. Not for the first or last time, I reflected on the extraordinary resilience and spirit of the oppressed. Back at home their conditions were still grim. The humanitarian situation remained bad and the economy was in tatters. The human rights abuses, unlawful killing, torture, harassment, checkpoints and heartbreaking disappearances continued. But it was an inspiring performance.

As the troubles have spilled over into neighbouring Ingushetia, North Ossetia and the adjacent region, the thousands of homeless, displaced people have once more been faced with another dismal winter. Talk of normalization has rung hollow. Just weeks before their arrival in London, these same dancers had narrowly escaped death when the stadium in Grozny in which they were about to perform was blown apart by a huge explosion in which the president was assassinated. Yet here they were, in amazing form, undefeated and apparently full of cheerful determination. It was impossible to leave Covent Garden that evening without a sense both of humility and of hope coupled with a renewed commitment to work for a lasting settlement. The young – but not only the young – more than deserve that. The Chechen people have suffered too long and bitterly, as indeed have many Russians. It is therefore sobering that, less than two months later, in September, the atrocities at Beslan took place. Peace is not an easy challenge.

This timely book contributes scholarship and experience to an analysis of Chechen history and politics. For me there are several inescapable observations. First, terrorism against the innocent can never be justified. It is wrong and it betrays any legitimate cause in whose name it is carried out. It is morally self-corrupting, but it is also politically counter-productive. It provokes extremism, intransigence and polarization, and must be unequivocally condemned. However, this applies every bit as much to state terrorism, whether overt or covert, as it does to any other form of terrorism. Indeed, state terrorism by those who formally proclaim their commitment to freedom, human rights, the rule of law and democracy is especially to be condemned. It cynically negates those very principles.

This is why so much of the Russian action in the Chechen Republic is inexcusable. It is wrong, but it is also disastrously counter-productive. It drives the young and able-bodied into the arms of the more extreme among the fighting rebels. To compound this, the Russian refusal to countenance negotiation with the more moderate fighters undermines the potential authority of those moderates and strengthens the influence of the extremists. It is frequently argued that it is impossible to find authoritative negotiating parties amongst the fighters, but Russian intransigence has become dangerously self-fulfilling in this respect.

Here the analogy of 'motes and beams' is, of course, relevant. Inexcusability and counter-productivity are not the exclusive monopoly of Russia in the Chechen Republic, but to a greater or lesser extent characterize the conduct of coalition partners in Iraq, not least in the deaths of thousands of innocent civilians; the behaviour of Israel in the Middle East; the way the 'war' against global terrorism is pursued at Guantánamo Bay; or indeed by the UK's derogation from the European Convention on Human Rights. Significantly, recent UK policy in Northern Ireland has been an impressive example of how to overcome such counter-productivity. It is an imaginative model that should be more consistently followed. In personal terms, after fifty years in politics and public life, I find that it is counter-productivity in human affairs with which I become most exasperated.

To fulfil its potential to ensure stability and security, the Rule of Law must be transparent, even-handed and consistent. The perpetrators of Beslan and other similar terrorist atrocities must be brought to justice – but so must the perpetrators of unacceptable action by the regular or irregular security forces of the Russian federal government and the Chechen authorities. The huge disparity between the high number of registered, convincing complaints about such unacceptable action, and the small number of cases convincingly pursued, investigated and brought to a conclusion with the guilty identified and punished, could not be better calculated to generate bitterness and alienation among the Chechen people. The climate of impunity is obvious at every level, as is the exploitative corruption. Until this is convincingly addressed there will be little prospect of abiding peace.

The depth and scale of the Chechen people's prolonged suffering have never been fully recognized in the West. Apart from the security and human rights issues, the state of basic amenities like water, sanitation and housing is still a nightmare. Imagine struggling to keep going in an unheated block of flats where everyone, including the frail, elderly and sick, has to descend on foot and walk to collect water or to use the latrines and then has to climb back up the stairs carrying water to reach home again. Nevertheless, the displaced wish to return despite the hardships, but the promised funds to help them rehabilitate their homes and lives seldom materialize, often intercepted by corrupt officials. Health and educational facilities in Chechnya make the concerns of Western countries about the adequacy of their public health services and educational institutions look insignificant by comparison. Food supplies are limited and public transport is primitive. Yet all too few humanitarian agencies are operative in the Chechen Republic. Too often one hears the refrain that it is 'too dangerous and impossible a place in which to work'. Dangerous and difficult it unquestionably is, but surely, if humanitarian commitment means anything, places like the Chechen Republic should constantly be at the top of the 'how can we find ways to work there?' agenda rather than slipping into the 'hopeless' file. The dedication that took NGOs into Central America in the bad years of the 1980s, into Mozambique during the civil war, and into Cambodia surely challenges them to seek to follow that example in the Caucasus. Similarly, in this age of European institution-building, the European Union, the Council of Europe and the OSCE should – if European solidarity and values mean anything – be constantly striving to mobilize resources for desperately needed large-scale and infrastructural economic and social regeneration in Chechnya.

Most importantly of all, there has to be an inclusive political process. Enduring peace will only be built on meaningful stakeholding and 'owner-ship' among the widest possible cross section of Chechen people. More intransigent people, not just the more amenable, will have to be involved. Winning hearts and minds is not a wet liberal option; it is pragmatic and essential. Undoubtedly some decent, learned and well-intentioned people worked with the Russian authorities in drafting the new constitution. While in less significant respects some will argue it reads quite well, it neverthe-less adamantly closes the door on the future status of the republic. However, the fatal flaw is that it was not the product of a tough, forging, representative process – sound foundations for its implementation and success were just not there. Rather than reflecting a substantial consensus, everything about it was a top-down affair; the referendum in March 2003, held to approve it, continued this 'take it or leave it' approach. This process has been in total contrast to what has happened in Northern Ireland or South Africa. It has been a deplorably naïve or cynical exercise – or both – and the cost will inevitably be high. The referendum took place in the absence of any context of debate, free evaluation or pluralist media coverage. The registering of voters was fundamentally flawed, while the polling arrangements did not begin to provide a meaningful atmosphere of freedom. If all this was in effect a political fraud, where did it leave the election of October 2003 that was organized in its wake? It is hardly surprising that the overall situation remains perilously unstable.

To be successful, any solution must be one that is shared in by as many Russians and Chechens as possible. Blueprints imposed from outside will not help. Where the wider world can assist is in tirelessly re-emphasizing to all sides that there can be no military solution; that it is necessary to lay down arms and that a satisfactory outcome can only be reached through dialogue. It is also important to be equally candid with both the federal authorities and their friends, and with the fighters. Sanity demands that short-sighted policies which aggravate widespread alienation and security, thereby jeopardizing still further the viability of oil supplies, must be resisted.

We should be telling the Russians that they must engage in dialogue with the fighters who are prepared to commit themselves to a political agenda. However much analogies with Northern Ireland and the Middle East may be resented by the Russians, it is vital to insist on the relevant messages. A peace process in Northern Ireland – whatever its ups and downs – became possible only when British governments were prepared to talk to the political representatives of the IRA on condition that, for their part, they were prepared to demonstrate their commitment to finding a political solution. In the Middle East, sadly, the net has never yet been thrown wide enough to include all those who have to be won back into a political process. When President Putin says that, in the Chechen Republic, Russia is in the front line of the confrontation with militant Islam, he is right. However, the brutal paradox of the Kremlin's policy in the Chechen republic is not only that it drives ambivalent, disempowered Islamic people into the arms of the extremists but that it also sends a powerful message – as does the West's condoning of it – to the Islamic world as a whole. That message reads that there is no room for compromise; self-respecting tough moderates have no place in the way forward.

While the sad history of the Chechen Republic and its global significance are important in themselves, they are also clearly symptomatic of what is wrong within the Russian Federation itself. The cynical manipulation of politics, the erosion of human rights, the disciplining and control of the media, a tame, compliant judicial system and all-pervasive corruption are characteristic of the wider situation. We are told that Russians favour a strong centre, but one lesson of history is that a strong centre without effective accountability is corrupted, or corrupts itself. To be concerned about events in the Chechen Republic without being aware of and concerned by the condition of the Russian Federation would be naive.

So what do we do? There is a desperate need to speak openly and firmly to all sides. The Russians must take seriously the self-respect, dignity, aspiration for representative self-governance, and culture of the Chechen people. The Chechens must take seriously the legitimate anxieties of the Russian Federation about its survival and the security of its southern flank. Every opportunity should be taken by the EU, OSCE, the Council of Europe, academic institutions and NGOs to provide a variety of opportunities that enable wider circles of Chechens and Russians to get to know each other, to start talking, and to begin to edge towards a shared desire to find a peaceful solution. Meanwhile, leaders in the West must more forthrightly urge Russia to change its policies, which aggravate the threat of global terrorism. Hopefully those same leaders will, at the same time, examine their own positions in this respect.

If a new spirit of openness can be created around the politicians of Moscow and the Chechen Republic, who repeatedly box themselves into a hopeless corner, it could provide an opportunity for them to become more imaginative about the road to peace. At the very least it may possibly encourage them to question the wisdom of their longstanding intransigence.

At the time of the first Camp David summit on the Middle East, initiated by President Carter, I was Minister of State at the Foreign and Commonwealth Office. I recall some officials remarking to me that I did not look altogether thrilled. I confirmed their observation. I said that, in the midst of it all, there remained the real Palestinian dimension rather than an unrepresentative and highly selective Palestinian dimension. I believed that the ownership of what was being proposed was just not sufficiently wide and inclusive.

If I have come to one firm conclusion in life it is that lasting peace and security cannot be imposed. They are not achievable through a paternalistic management approach. They have to be built and owned by ordinary people from the foundations upwards. The responsibility of leadership is to provide an enlightened context. Peace has to belong to everybody, or it is no peace at all.

Appendix 1

The Khasavyurt Peace Agreement

The Khasavyurt Russian-Chechen Agreement
31 August 1996

JOINT STATEMENT

We the undersigned,

Taking into consideration the progress achieved in the realisation of the Agreement on the cessation of military actions;

Making efforts to achieve mutually acceptable preconditions for a political settlement of the armed conflict;

Acknowledging that the use or threat of armed force to settle disputes is unacceptable; Based on the generally accepted principles of the right of peoples to self-determination, the principles of equal rights, voluntariness and freedom of choice, the strengthening of national agreement and the security of peoples;

Expressing the intent unconditionally to defend the human rights and freedoms of citizens, regardless of national origin, religious denomination, place of residence or other differences, an end to acts of violence between political opponents, in accordance with the Universal Declaration of Human Rights of 1949 and the international covenant on Civil and Political Rights of 1966,

We have worked out principles* for the determination of basis of relations between the Russian Federation and the Chechen Republic, on the basis of which further negotiation will take place.

Signed by

A. Lebed
A. Maskhadov
S. Kharlamov,
S. Abumuslimov

In the presence of the Head of the OSCE Assistance Cooperation in the Chechen Republic, signed by T. Guldiman

* Principles for the determination of relations between the Russian Federation and the Chechen Republic.

a. Agreement on the terms for relations between the Russian Federation and the Chechen Republic, to be decided in accordance with generally accepted principles and norms of international law, must be reached before 31 December 2001.
b. No later than 1 October 1996 a Joint commission will be formed from the representatives of State organs of the Russian Federation and the Chechen Republic, whose tasks will consist of:

   1. control of the implementation of Decree No. 985 of the president of the Russian Federation of 25 June 1996 and preparation of proposals for the complete withdrawal of armed forces;
   2. preparation of agreed upon measures to combat crime, terrorism and manifestations of national and religious conflict and control of their implementation;
   3. preparation of proposals for monetary and budgetary relations;
   4. preparation and creation by the government of the Russian Federation of a programme of rehabilitation of the economic infrastructure of the Chechen Republic;
   5. control of the activities of organs of state power and other organisations in the supplying of food and medicine to the population.

c. The laws of the Chechen Republic will be based on respect for human rights and rights of citizens, the right of peoples to self-determination, the principles of equality of peoples, the protection of peace, international harmony and security of civilians living in the territory of the Chechen Republic, regardless of their national origin, religious denomination or other differences.
d. The joint commission will undertake its work in accordance with mutual agreement.

Source: *Nezavisimaya gazeta*, 3 September 1996, p. 3.

Appendix 2

Treaty on Peace and the Principles of Mutual Relations between the Russian Federation and the Chechen Republic of Ichkeria

The esteemed parties to the agreement, desiring to end their centuries-long antagonism and striving to establish firm, equal and mutually beneficial relations, hereby agree:

1. To reject forever the use of force or threat of force in resolving all matters of dispute.
2. To develop their relations on generally recognised principles and norms of international law. In doing so, the sides shall interact on the basis of specific concrete agreements.
3. This treaty shall serve as the basis for concluding further agreements and accords on the full range of relations.
4. This treaty is written on two copies and both have equal legal power.
5. This treaty is effective from the day of signing.

Moscow, 12 May 1997.

B. Yeltsin
President of the Russian Federation

Aslan Maskhadov
President of the Chechen Republic of Ichkeria

Source: Reproduced in Otto Latsis, 'Dogovor s Chechnei: kto pobedil, kto proigral?', *Izvestiya*, 14 May 1997.

Further Reading

Baddeley, J. F., *The Russian Conquest of the Caucasus*, foreword by Moshe Gammer (London, RoutledgeCurzon).

Baev, Pavel, 'The Russian Army and Chechnya: Victory Instead of Reform?', in Stephen J. Cimbala (ed.), *The Russian Military into the Twenty-First Century* (London, Frank Cass, 2001), pp. 75–94.

Baiev, Khassam with Ruth and Nicholas Daniloff, *The Oath: A Surgeon Under Fire* (New York, Walker and Company, 2003).

Bowker, Michael, 'Conflict in Chechnya', in Cameron Ross (ed.), *Russian Politics under Putin* (Manchester, MUP, 2004), pp. 225–68.

Broxup, Marie Bennigsen and Moshe Gammer, *The Chechen Struggle for Independence* (London, Hurst, 1997).

Cornell, Svante E., 'International Reactions to Massive Human Rights Violations: The Case of Chechnya', *Europe-Asia Studies*, Vol. 51, No. 1, 1999, pp. 85–100.

Dunlop, John, *Russia Confronts Chechnya: Roots of a Separatist Conflict* (Cambridge University Press, 1998).

Elkner, Julie, 'Rethinking Yermolov's Legacy: New Patriotic Narratives of Russia's Engagement with Chechnya', in Stephen G. Wheatcroft (ed.), *Challenging Traditional Views of Russian History* (Basingstoke, Palgrave Macmillan, 2002), pp. 203–16.

Elshtain, Jean Bethke, *Just War against Terror* (New York, Basic Books, 2003).

Evangelista, Matthew, *The Chechen Wars: Will Russia go the Way of the Soviet Union?* (Washington, DC, Brookings institution Press, 2003).

Fowkes, Ben (ed.), *Russia and Chechnia: The Permanent Crisis. Essays on Russo-Chechen Relations* (Basingstoke, Macmillan, 1998).

Gall, Carlotta and Thomas de Waal, *Chechnya: Calamity in the Caucasus* (New York, New York University Press, 1998).

Gerber, Theodore P. and Sarah E. Mendelson, 'Russian Public Opinion on Human Rights and the War in Chechnya', *Post-Soviet Affairs*, Vol. 18, No. 4, 2002, pp. 271–305.

German, Tracey C., *Russia's Chechen War* (London, Routledge, 2003).

Goldenberg, Suzanne, *Pride of Small Nations: The Caucasus and Post-Soviet Disorder* (London, Zed Books, 1994).

Goltz, Thomas, *Chechnya Diary: A war Correspondent's Story of Surviving the War in Chechnya* (New York, St Martin's Press, 2003).

Hughes, James, 'Chechnya: The Causes of a Protracted Post-Soviet Conflict', *Civil Wars*, Vol. 4, No. 4, Winter 2001, pp. 11–48.

Greene, Stanley, *Open Wound: Chechnya, 1994–2003* (Stanley Greene/Agence Vu).

Jaimoukha, Amjad, *The Chechens: A Handbook*, Peoples of the Caucasus Handbooks (London, RoutledgeCurzon, 2004).

Jonson, Lena and Murad Esenov (eds), *Chechnya: The International Community and Strategies for Peace and Stability* (Stockholm, The Swedish Institute for International Affairs, 2000).

Khlebnikov, Pavel, *Razgovor s varvarom: Besedy s chechenskim polevym komandirom Khozh-Akhmedom Nukhaevym o banditizme i islame* (Moscow, Detektivpress, 2003).

Lapidus, Gail, 'Putin's War on Terrorism: Lessons from Chechnya', *Post-Soviet Affairs*, Vol. 18, No. 1, January–March 2002, pp. 41–48.

Lieven, Anatol, *Chechnya: Tombstone of Russian Power* (New Haven, CT, Yale University Press, 1998).

Meier, Andrew, *Chechnya: To the Heart of a Conflict* (New York, W. W. Norton, 2004).

Nivat, Anne, *Chienne de Guerre: A Women Reporter Behind the Lines of the War in Chechnya* (New York, Public Affairs, 2000).

Nivat, Anne, *La guerre qui n'aura pas eu lieu* (Paris, Editions Fayard, 2004).

Politkovskaya, Anna, *A Dirty War: A Russian Reporter in Chechnya*, Introduction by Thomas de Waal, translated by John Crowfoot (London, The Harvill Press, 2001).

Politkovskaya, Anna, *A Small Corner of Hell*, translated by Alexander Burry and Tatiana Tulchinsky (Chicago, University of Chicago Press Pounds, 2003).

Politkovskaya, Anna, *Putin's Russia* (London, Harvill, 2004).

Popova, Tatyana, *Nord-Ost glazami zalozhnitsy* (Moscow, Vagrius, 2002).

Sakwa, Richard, 'Chechnya: A Just War Fought Unjustly?', in Bruno Coppieters and Richard Sakwa (eds), *Contextualizing Secession: Normative Studies in Comparative Perspective* (Oxford, Oxford University Press, 2003), pp. 156–86.

Seely, Robert, *Russo-Chechen Relations, 1800–2000: A Deadly Embrace* (London, Frank Cass, 2000).

Smith, Sebastian, *Allah's Mountains: Politics and War in the Russian Caucasus* (London, I. B. Tauris, 1998).

Tishkov, Valery, *Life in a War-Torn Society* (Berkeley, University of California Press, 2004).

Trenin, Dmitri and Aleksei Malashenko, with Anatol Lieven, *Russia's Restless Frontier: The Chechnya Factor in Post-Soviet Russia* (Washington DC, Carnegie Endowment for International Peace, 2004).

Umalatov, Umalat, *Chechnya glazami chechentsa* (Moscow, Edinstvo, 2001).

Ware, Robert Bruce, Enver F. Kisriev, Werner J. Patzelt, and Ute Roericht, 'Dagestani Perspectives on Russia and Chechnya', *Post-Soviet Affairs*, Vol. 18, No. 4, 2002, pp. 306–31.

Wilhellmsen, Julie, 'Between a Rock and a hard Place: The Islamisation of the Chechen Separatist Movement', *Europe-Asia Studies*, Vol. 57, No. 1, January 2005, pp. 35–59.